D1591160

DUMBARTON OAKS
MEDIEVAL LIBRARY

Daniel Donoghue, General Editor

FORTUNE AND MISFORTUNE AT SAINT GALL

EKKEHARD IV

DOML 68

Fortune and Misfortune at Saint Gall

Casus sancti Galli

Ekkehard IV

Translated by

EMILY ALBU

and

NATALIA LOZOVSKY

DUMBARTON OAKS
MEDIEVAL LIBRARY

HARVARD UNIVERSITY PRESS
CAMBRIDGE, MASSACHUSETTS
LONDON, ENGLAND
2021

Printed in the United States of America

First Printing

Library of Congress Cataloging-in-Publication Data available from the Library of Congress

ISBN 978-0-674-25146-5 (cloth : alk. paper)

Contents

Introduction

Ekkehard IV: Life and Works

The stories recounted by Ekkehard IV in his *Fortune and Misfortune at Saint Gall (Casus sancti Galli)* have given shape and color to much of what we know about medieval monks and the wider world beyond their monastery. The outlines of his biography are nonetheless uncertain, reconstructed mostly from his own scant notes. Ekkehard, the fourth monk of Saint Gall who bore that name, probably came from a distinguished family that lived near Saint Gall, which would explain the interest he showed in the local lineages of the Notkers and Ekkehards. He was born sometime before 1000, since he witnessed the events that followed the death of Henry, a young scion of the Welf noble family (chapter 21) and was able to talk to monks who had lived through the great fire that destroyed Saint Gall in 937 (chapter 67).[1] He most probably came to the abbey as a child oblate, where he studied under Notker the German, a prolific scholar and translator. Around 1022, after Notker and Abbot Burhard II had died, Ekkehard moved to Mainz, then ruled by Archbishop Aribo (1021–1031). If we accept that Ekkehard was writing about himself when he described an unnamed monk being rewarded by Emperor Conrad II (chapter 66), he must have been in charge of the cathedral school in Mainz in 1030. Ekkehard probably left Mainz after the death of Aribo and arrived at Saint Gall before or during the abbacy of Norbert (1034–1072), whom he mentions in the preface. Ekkehard was still alive in the summer of 1057 because in a gloss in a Saint Gall manuscript he noted the recent death of Pope Victor II.[2] According to the Saint Gall necrology, Ekkehard died on October 21, sometime between 1060 and 1080.[3]

While living at Saint Gall, Ekkehard wrote a continuation of the house chronicle (his *Casus* printed here) and numerous compositions in verse that included blessings and inscriptions for wall paintings. He probably produced liturgical music, and he actively worked in the monastic library, correcting manuscripts and commenting on a variety of texts. Ekkehard's hand has been detected in as many as sixty-two codices, in which Latin and German glosses testify to his broad interests and meticulous scholarly approach.[4] The texts that he glossed include his own poetic compositions, works of Augustine and Boethius, and histories by Orosius and Hegesippus (the Latin Josephus). Ekkehard's extensive readings informed and shaped his monastic chronicle.

The World of the *Casus*

As a monk of Saint Gall, Ekkehard belonged to a distinguished and influential community. According to tradition, the abbey was founded in 612 by Gallus (Gall), a monk who arrived from Ireland as one of the followers of Columbanus. After long travels, Gall settled as a hermit on the river Steinach in what is now Switzerland and was soon joined by his disciples. Later, in 720, Otmar established there a community of monks.

In the early decades of its existence, the abbey fought off the attacks of local magnates and struggled for independence from the bishops of Constance. The abbey's annals and chronicles carefully preserved the memory of those events, which Ekkehard's *Casus* also dutifully recorded. The monastery grew and accumulated material wealth through gifts and purchases, acquiring estates well beyond its immediate vicinity in Thurgau, as far as the upper Rhine valley and, later, northern Italy.[5] Saint Gall's location on the main transalpine land routes, known since Roman times but increasingly used from the ninth century on, turned it into a major way station connecting economic and cultural centers of the wider world, from Italy and the Mediterranean to northern Europe.[6] Its political importance also increased, especially when it was ruled by abbots who had connections to the court. Under Carolingian rulers, Saint Gall developed into a large royal abbey. In 818 Emperor Louis the Pious granted the abbey immunity, which freed the abbey from supervision by royal or imperial officials. In 833, Louis the German confirmed this privilege and granted the monks the right of freely electing their abbot. In 854, the abbey was freed of the obligation to pay tribute to the bishop of Constance. Ottonian rulers also favored the abbey and confirmed its privileges.[7]

The rule of Abbot Gozbert (816–837) marked the beginning of what is often called the abbey's golden age, which lasted through the tenth century. During this time, Saint Gall emerged as an influential center of religious and intellectual life. The monks enriched and developed the traditions of liturgy and sacred music. Hymns and sequences composed by Notker Balbulus (Notker the Stammerer) were especially influential; some of them survive in hundreds of manuscripts throughout Europe.[8] Ekkehard proudly recorded the names of Notker and other monks who excelled in music and other arts, relating their stories and listing their compositions.

At that time, the abbey's school and its masters such as Notker Balbulus and Notker the German, Ekkehard's teacher, boasted graduates who went on to occupy top ecclesiastical positions throughout the realm. From an initially modest handful of books, the library expanded and developed between the ninth and eleventh century into an excellent collection that included religious and secular texts, from the Bible to history, geography, and mathematics. The monastic scriptorium actively produced manuscripts: around one hundred scribal hands have been identified for the period of Abbot Gozbert's rule alone. The core of the medieval collection of books and charters still survives, preserved at the Stiftsbibliothek and Stiftsarchiv Sankt Gallen.[9]

Royal favor that supported the monks also meant that the abbey often became the focus of royal attention. While it gained independence from local bishops and magnates, Saint Gall became directly responsible to the kings and stayed in contact with the court. Carolingian and Ottonian rulers visited the abbey on several occasions, and some of its monks, who came from local nobility, served the kings and emperors as teachers and advisors.[10] The abbey also participated in the affairs of the world when managing estates and dependents who owed it obligations, from peasants who worked the land to the *milites* (fighting men) who defended the monks. Saint Gall had to balance between attending to its political and economic business in the world outside and fulfilling its main purpose as a place of retreat where monks served God and prayed on behalf of the world. The boundaries between the cloister and the world had to be constantly negotiated, with tensions arising as the monks protected their traditions and way of life from outside interventions. Throughout the *Casus,* we can see problems and conflicts that resulted when monks perceived outsiders as threatening Saint Gall, from their initial distrust of Salomo III, the bishop of Constance and later abbot of Saint Gall who was close to the royal court, to their hostility toward Sandrat, a reformer sent by Emperor Otto I to correct Saint Gall monks.[11]

Within the cloister, the life of the Saint Gall monastic community was governed by strict rules. In the beginning the monks may have lived under a mixed Rule, but in 747, during the abbacy of Otmar, Saint Gall started following the Rule of Benedict.[12] Later, under Louis the Pious, the Rule of Benedict became standard for monastic communities of the Carolingian empire, and it remained so under the Ottonians. The Rule provided general guidelines, such as the obligation for the monks to stay within the monastery and obey their abbot. It also gave detailed prescriptions on most aspects of the monks' lives, from the number and character of daily services to clothes, food, and drink.[13]

Although strict, the Benedictine Rule still left sufficient room for interpretation, and its understanding and implementation differed from one monastery to another. By the tenth century, the life of monastic houses such as Saint Gall was regulated not only by the Rule but also by a set of *consuetudines* (customs) that guided the monastery's interactions with the outside world, from the administration of its properties to its relations with local lords and a royal or imperial court. These and other factors, different in each case, shaped the ideas and practice of monastic renewal in the tenth and eleventh centuries in different parts of Europe. In 933, a movement for a stricter observance of the Rule began at the Lotharingian abbey of Gorze. In the next year, changes came to Saint Maximin at Trier and then spread to Lotharingia and Alemannia.[14] Saint Gall was one of the places where the reformers' insistence on a more severe discipline and changes in customs met with opposition. The process continued in Ekkehard's time, and the *Casus* reflected his reaction to the upheavals that deeply influenced the monks.[15]

The *Casus*: Goals and Main Themes

When Ekkehard started working on his *Casus,* he had a solid foundation to build on. The monks of Saint Gall were very diligent in documenting their abbey's past and present. They preserved charters, practiced commemoration in liturgy, and recorded their history in saints' lives and in a house chronicle. Ratpert wrote the first part of the chronicle around 884, covering the period from the foundation of Saint Gall to the visit of Emperor Charles III the Fat in 883. Ekkehard began where Ratpert left off, in the 880s, and brought his account to 972 when another emperor, Otto II, visited the monastery. Several more installments followed, all in Latin except the last German one, which brought the account into the fourteenth century.[16]

Earlier scholars and editors, especially those working in the nineteenth and early twentieth centuries, acknowledged Ekkehard's talent as a storyteller but severely criticized him for what they considered his uncertain grasp of facts, lack of structure, and bad Latin.[17] A shift began when in a series of articles Hans Haefele demonstrated the skillful composition of Ekkehard's *Casus,* discussing its leading themes, organizing principles, and fine sense of language. Building on Haefele's work, scholars have turned their attention to the ways in which Ekkehard's *Casus* reflected the controversies of his time, monastic life, and medieval culture.[18]

Continuing Ratpert's account, Ekkehard inherited its title and some of its main themes. In the earliest surviving manuscript, Ratpert's chronicle is called *Textus de origine et diversis casibus monasterii sancti Galli* (Book about the origin and various changing fortunes at the monastery of Saint Gall). Ekkehard abbreviated it in his preface (*De casibus,* "On changing fortunes") and in the beginning of chapter 1 (*Libri de casibus monasterii,* "Books on changing fortunes at the monastery"). The same title, with minor variations, appears in the codices containing later installments. *Casus* can be translated as "downfalls," "misfortunes," "sudden occurrences," or "legal cases," and all these meanings play an important role in the Saint Gall chronicle. At the same time, Hans Haefele and other scholars have argued that *casus* can best be interpreted as "reversals of fortune," "vicissitudes," or "ups and downs," and that changing fortunes became a leading theme of Ekkehard's account.[19] After long and enjoyable discussions with members of the Dumbarton Oaks Medieval Latin editorial board, we finally agreed on an English title that captures one sense of the multivalent Latin *Casus.*

In his preface, Ekkehard states that he will record "fortunate and unfortunate events that happened at the monastery of Saint Gall and Saint Otmar," repeating the words *fortunia et infortunia* three times in the same introductory passage. Ekkehard's interest in the workings of Fortuna was inspired by Boethius's *Consolation of Philosophy,* a work he alludes to in his *Casus.*[20] Glosses left by Ekkehard in the texts that he read in the library of Saint Gall show the same interest. In the manuscript of Orosius's *Seven Books of History Against the Pagans,* Ekkehard consistently noted the instances in which fortune or misfortune played a role in the rise and the decline of kingdoms and empires.[21]

In the preface, Ekkehard also warns his audience that tracing the changing fortunes of his monastery will be a difficult task because that will touch on the controversial subject of monastic discipline. Here Ekkehard introduces a theme that he and his fellow monks found vitally important because of the issues lying at the heart of monastic reform. From the very beginning, Ekkehard expresses his disapproval of the reform movement by alluding to Cicero's exclamation "O tempora! O mores!" (Oh the times! Oh the customs!) and quoting the biblical passage concerning "those who walk in levity" (Tobit 3:17). Further, in the list of the abbots who ruled Saint Gall, Ekkehard accompanies the name of Norbert with a telling aside: "under whose rule we live now not as he and we, as they say, wish, but as we can." Ekkehard's fellow monks would have understood his veiled criticism. They knew that Abbot Norbert, a student and protégé of Poppo of Stavelot (978–1048), an active proponent of the reform, had been appointed by Emperor Conrad II in violation of the right of free election.[22] In chapter 87, Ekkehard goes even further and condemns, again without naming the culprits, the "novel behavior" of monks who "perform the many unspeakable acts, which, in the name of piety, they practice in accordance with some schismatic superstition."

In the *Casus* Ekkehard only hints at contemporary debates and figures, but he was more outspoken when adding notes in the margins of manuscripts. In the codex of Eugippius's excerpts from Augustine, for example, Ekkehard named one of the champions of the reform, Poppo of Stavelot, whose "schisms" inflicted a grievous wound upon the community of Saint Gall. In a gloss to Notker's Psalter, Ekkehard called Poppo and his patron Richard, abbot of Saint-Vanne in Verdun (ca. 970–1046), heretics.[23] For Ekkehard, the major issue at stake was the understanding of monastic discipline as dictated by the Rule of Benedict, and in broader terms, the nature and meaning of monastic life in its relationship to the world outside.[24]

These interwoven themes, developed in a roughly chronological order, structure Ekkehard's account. He demonstrates how good fortune favored his community when the monks observed the discipline of the Rule and what misfortunes befell them when it broke down. Contemplating the nature and meaning of monastic discipline, he insists that the monks of Saint Gall possessed deep knowledge of the Rule, interpreted it correctly, and obeyed its precepts. Some practices approved by the abbey's customs deviated from the Rule, as was the case with the monks' private storage spaces (chapters 102–3). The bishops and abbots sent to inspect Saint Gall should have been opposed to individual storage of food and concerned by the resulting reliance of some monks on their own families. Ekkehard, however, has the visitors accept the monks' explanation that nothing was done without the abbot's permission. He also has two of the bishops praise the strict observance of discipline at Saint Gall and proclaim that no better rule or communal life could be found anywhere in the kingdom. To further reinforce his point, Ekkehard immediately introduces a scene in which a Saint Gall monk rebukes one of the visitors who was holding a book of the Rule: "Are you bringing this book forward against me, this book that I know better closed than you do open? Close it!" In response to the rigid disciplinarians of the reform movement, Ekkehard showed how the fundamental principles of Christian faith and life, grounded in *caritas* (Christian charity and love), allowed for a more flexible understanding of discipline.[25]

Ekkehard's Art of Storytelling

In his choice of models, material, and style Ekkehard did not directly follow Ratpert, although he consulted both Ratpert's *Casus* and the same sources that his predecessor had used, namely the lives of the house saints and documents from the Saint Gall archive. The text that Ekkehard's *Casus* most closely resembles is the *Gesta Caroli Magni,* written in approximately 885 by Notker Balbulus, a monk of Saint Gall (d. 912). Notker's book was a collection of anecdotes about Charlemagne and a broad assortment of characters, including bishops, monks, nobles, and peasants. In his vivid and entertaining tales, Notker also raised serious questions about ecclesiastical and secular governance, virtues and sins, and the monastic way of life.[26]

Like Notker, Ekkehard used stories to convey his view

of the past and relied on the oral tradition of his monastic community, declaring in the preface that he will faithfully record what he had learned from "the fathers," or senior monks. Some of the stories were told by eyewitnesses, still alive in Ekkehard's day, such as the story of the great fire of 937. Some were transmitted through several generations, such as the anecdotes about famous monks. Some were based on Ekkehard's own recollections. As happens with memories, Ekkehard's version of events often directly contradicts what we find in other sources. For instance, Ekkehard compresses chronology in his account of Salomo and his rivalry with the three friends, Notker, Ratpert, and Tuotilo, making them all contemporaries and fellow students taught by Iso.[27] He also relays bits of information that find no support in archeological research or contemporary sources. For instance, he writes that Hatto, archbishop of Mainz, ordered that city "to be moved from its ancient location and placed closer to the Rhine" (chapter 11). Ekkehard appears to be the only source for this puzzling statement, which may be a distorted echo of oral or written reports about the construction of the Mainz city walls in the ninth century.[28]

Ekkehard depicts a wide variety of characters in such vivid detail, often unique to the *Casus,* that it is tempting to take his portraits at face value. While some details may have come to him through the oral tradition, which he embellished in the process, his characters essentially represent certain ideal types: good and bad monks, formidable rulers, virtuous and sinful women.[29] In the cycle of stories about the three inseparable friends, Notker is introduced as a scholar and teacher, timid in everyday life but brave when fighting demons. Tuotilo, accustomed to facing the challenges of the outside world, nonetheless always behaves in a manner that distinguishes him as a Saint Gall monk. Ratpert is deeply religious but quick in making decisions and taking action. Even Salomo, who appears in the opening chapters as a schemer and a trickster, eventually becomes a model of religious devotion and a great benefactor of Saint Gall. The way to salvation could vary from one person to another, as Ekkehard suggests in the words of Bishop Arnulf of Toul (chapter 100): "It is not by a single path or rule that we climb our way to heaven and to the kingdom of God. Because it is within us, it is granted to some to ascend by one way but to others by another."

Ekkehard also shows a variety of negative types. Unlike most of the monks of Saint Gall who were superior in every aspect, from their religious observance to their learning to their music and poetry, the proponents of reform appear in the *Casus* as bad monks and thoroughly unpleasant figures. Ruodmann, who secretly entered the cloister at night, is an "accuser of brethren," a spy, and a coward. Sandrat, sent to the monks by the emperor to teach them the correct ways of the Rule, is unmasked as a hypocrite who indulged in unrestrained anger and excessive drinking.

Ekkehard wrote for the audience of his fellow monks about the history of a male community, so it is not surprising that male characters take center stage. But even though the *Casus* does not fully reflect the real-life roles and influence of women in the history of the abbey, female characters have significant parts to play in Ekkehard's story.[30] Ekkehard presents a variety of portraits that combine ideal features and lively individual details. Wiborada appears as a model of female sanctity and as a mother figure and spiritual teacher to both women and men. Under her stern guidance, the aristocratic widow Wendilgart, first introduced in the *Casus* as a faithful wife, eventually rejects the sinful temptations of luxury to become a nun. The formidable duchess Hadwig, a beautiful and educated woman, uses the male title *dux* (duke) and exercises judicial and economic power that directly influenced the affairs of the abbey.[31]

Although he repeatedly claims that he is only faithfully recording what he had heard, Ekkehard carefully selected and constructed his stories. He followed the rules of rhetoric to instruct and entertain his audience, and he used his learning and literary skills to convey tragedy and humor.[32] Frequent references to a number of texts not only illustrate his points but also add emphasis and depth. Among these, the Bible and the Rule of Benedict occupy the most important place, while Terence and Virgil are the most often quoted secular writers. Ekkehard creatively uses his sources, sometimes casually appropriating a turn of phrase, sometimes deliberately weaving a quotation or paraphrase into the texture of his narrative. Thus in chapter 7 he borrows an expression from Acts 8:13 to describe "the *signs and miracles* of Saint Gall" and has a visitor express his admiration in a paraphrase of 1 Kings (3 Kings) 10:7: "The grace accorded this site *surpasses the report I have heard.*" Classical and biblical quotations allow Ekkehard to condemn the reform movement while avoiding direct personal attacks. In his preface, Ekkehard achieves this goal by turning to Cicero and the Bible, and he sharpens his critique in chapter 87 by paraphrasing Psalms 106(105):29: "The novel behavior of monks who nowadays often *provoke God to anger* with their newfangled ways *so that more and more disasters befall them.*" Ekkehard skillfully introduces a Virgilian allusion in a scene where Ekkehard II is tutoring Duchess Hadwig and reading the *Aeneid* with her (chapter 95). He uses the familiar quotation, "I fear the Greeks even when they bear gifts," to introduce suspicions against a hostile abbot of nearby Reichenau, then further dramatizes the circumstances with a subtle Virgilian reference alluding to the Greeks' assault on Troy, a complex recollection of the abbot's slipping into Saint Gall.

Ekkehard knew Roman literature and history well, and he relies on its technical vocabulary as a shorthand conveying the sense of events to those learned enough to understand it. In chapter 6, in the scene depicting a discussion between the abbot and senior monks, Ekkehard refers to the senior members of the monastic community as "the senate of our republic." He also has the "senators" quote Virgil and employ Roman imagery in their arguments. These references showcase the learning ascribed to Ekkehard's characters and assume an equally learned audience who knew that only adult Roman citizens were entitled to wear a toga and that boys wore a *toga praetexta.* The Roman references reminded his readers that their monastic *res publica* was once independent and ruled by "the senators." These terms also sound intentionally ironic, and Ekkehard adds to the comic effect in the next chapter, when he calls Salomo "our *praetextatus,*" one more Roman term that effectively conveys the meaning of a "would-be" or "wannabe monk."

Ekkehard's treatment of the Hungarians and their invasion of 926 combines erudition, humor, and high drama. Ekkehard the meticulous scholar was keen to define the place of the Hungarians in the learned geo-ethnographical taxonomy of the time. In chapter 82 of the *Casus* and in his glosses to Orosius's history, he criticizes his fellow monks who confused the Hungarians and the Muslims.[33] Ekkehard the storyteller gives his audience a colorful yarn of terrible danger and survival, of heroes and villains, full of vivid details. He depicts the fire-red sky that announced the approach of the Hungarians to Saint Gall, the bristling weapons of the enemy, their drunken celebration and cruel games. He introduces the simpleminded yet steadfast Brother Heribald who stayed behind when everyone else fled. Contrary to expectations, the frightening Hungarians spared this monk after sharing a good laugh at his expense.[34] Ekkehard's entertaining stories also deliver a moral message: virtue triumphs in the end, and the villains receive their just punishment, as did the two Hungarians who fell from the roof to their deaths when attempting to desecrate the image that they believed to be Saint Gall.

With a keen appreciation for the power of words, Ekkehard describes situations arising from the coexistence of different languages spoken at Saint Gall. The monastic community included native speakers of Romance and Germanic dialects; the *nutriti,* the monks who had been raised in the monastery, were fluent in Latin. In chapter 36, Ekkehard relates how the three friends, Notker, Ratpert, and Tuotilo, used their Latin to thwart Sindolf, a monk who did not understand the language. In this story, the humorous situation highlights the difference between the three highly literate friends who belonged to the monastic elite, and Sindolf, a "good-for-nothing" upstart, meddler, and spy. Ekkehard also derives humor from misunderstandings that arose between monks who spoke different languages. In chapter 88, he plays on different meanings of the word *cald,* "cold" in German and "hot" in Rhaetian, and he uses Latin to explain the joke to his readers.[35]

Influence, Editions, Translations

Ekkehard's *Casus* was intended primarily for an audience of his fellow monks, and it had no circulation beyond Saint Gall. The continuators were familiar with it, even citing it on occasions, but its direct influence was limited to the *Vita Notkeri Balbuli (Life of Notker the Stammerer).* Written in the early thirteenth century by a monk of Saint Gall, this text included all the information from Ekkehard's *Casus,* copying his account verbatim in places.[36]

The *Casus* was edited for the first time by Melchior Goldast in 1606. Its next edition, by Ildefons von Arx, appeared in MGH SS 2 in 1829. Gerold Meyer von Knonau published his edition and German translation, both accompanied by extensive notes, in 1879 and 1891, respectively. Hans Haefele published his edition, lacking a critical apparatus but accompanied by a German translation, in 1980. He accomplished fundamental research on the *Casus* in preparation for a new critical edition but died before finishing it. In 2020 Haefele's work was brought to completion by Ernst Tremp and Franzisca Schnoor.

Ekkehard's *Casus* has been translated into German three times. There also exist a Polish and an Italian translation. Only excerpts have appeared in English so far.[37] This translation is based on Haefele, Tremp, and Schnoor's MGH edition. Where possible, names of people and places have been given in their modern equivalents or spelled according to current scholarly usage (Charles for Carolus, Liutfrid for Luitfridus). Biblical references are to the Revised Standard Version (RSV), with the alternative Douai-Reims titles and/or numeration included in parentheses, for instance, Nehemiah 8:4 (2 Esdras 8:4). Translations of biblical passages mostly follow the RSV, using the Douai-Reims text for the books not included in the RSV (such as Wisdom) and occasionally modifying both when necessary. Translations of other quotations are our own. In the Latin text and the corresponding English translation we have italicized quotations and close paraphrases of classical and medieval works.

We aimed at keeping close to the Latin to make the most of the en-face bilingual format while attempting to preserve the character of Ekkehard's writing. His language and tone present a particular challenge for the translator. He often used rare words, and he delighted in double entendres and wordplay, which are nearly always impossible to capture in translation. Works that focus on Ekkehard's language have been especially helpful. Among them are *A Study of the Lexicography of the "Casus sancti Galli"* by Helen Edna Loth and articles by Hans Haefele.

We owe a great debt to earlier scholars and editors, including Gerold Meyer von Knonau, Hans F. Haefele, and Peter Erhart, whose learned comments have provided material for our notes. DOML has been blessed in its dealings with the *Monumenta Germaniae Historica* in Munich. We are extremely grateful to Dr. Horst Zimmerhackl, Geschäftsführer there, for his cooperation and to Professor Ernst Tremp for sharing his then-forthcoming MGH edition of the *Casus* with us. We were able to use his text as a point of departure for our own, which necessarily needed to be normalized to DOML orthographic standards. For detailed treatment of various questions and a comprehensive bibliography, the reader should consult those works.

We owe a special debt of gratitude to Julia Barrow for

her invaluable support of this project from the very beginning. David Traill read early drafts and answered our continuing questions with inimitable erudition and grace. We are grateful to Joan Cadden, Ralph Hexter, Sally McKee, and David Traill, who discussed Ekkehard with us during translation workshops at the University of California at Davis. For their help with various questions, we thank Mayke de Jong, Wojtek Jezierski, Lori Kruckenberg, and Marcia Kupfer. The editorial board and staff of Dumbarton Oaks Medieval Library provided an ideal environment. Danuta Shanzer and Jan Ziolkowski gave important feedback. Julia Barrow and Thomas Noble carefully read our complete translation and contributed numerous corrections and insights. DOML editors (Raquel Begleiter and Nicole Eddy) and interns (George Hu, Ned Sanger, Hannelore Segers, and Diana Myers) assisted in many practical matters. We are also grateful to colleagues who answered our call for help as the pandemic continues to close our libraries: Sarah Hamilton, Walter Herke, Ludger Koerntgen, and Yin Liu; and again to Nicole Eddy, who hunted down many references for us in these challenging circumstances.

This volume is dedicated to Leo Beigelman and Alan Taylor and our families.

Notes

1 Hans Haefele, "Ekkehard IV. von St. Gallen," *Die deutsche Literatur des Mittelalters. Verfasserslexikon* (Berlin, 1880), vol. 2, cols. 455–56; Tremp, *Casus,* 1–8. For the local noble families in that period, see Bernar Zeller, "Lokale Eliten im thurgauischen Umfeld des Klosters St. Gallen (8.–11. Jahr-

hundert): 'Ekkeharte' und 'Notkere,'" in Kössinger, Krotz, and Müller, *Ekkehart IV,* 231–43. For aristocracy in a larger context, see Timothy Reuter, ed., *The Medieval Nobility: Studies on the Ruling Classes of France and Germany from the Sixth to the Twelfth Century* (Amsterdam, New York, and Oxford, 1979); Timothy Reuter, *Medieval Polities and Modern Mentalities,* ed. Janet Nelson (Cambridge, 2006), especially 111–26 and 300–324; Marios Costambeys, Matthew Innes, and Simon MacLean, *The Carolingian World* (Cambridge, 2011), especially 271–323; Isabelle Rosé, "Interactions between Monks and the Lay Nobility (from the Carolingian Era through the Eleventh Century)," trans. Matthew Mattingly, in *The Cambridge History of Medieval Monasticism in the Latin West,* ed. Alison I. Beach and Isabelle Cochlin (Cambridge, 2020), 579–98.

2 Saint Gall, Stiftsbibliothek MS 621, p. 279 B, digital reproduction available at CESG.

3 MGH Necr. vol. 1, p. 483; Dümmler, "Ekkehart IV," 1–2.

4 See, most recently, Heidi Eisenhut, "Handschriften mit Spuren Ekkeharts IV. von St. Gallen," in Kössinger, Krotz, and Müller, *Ekkehart IV,* 133–52, and other essays in that volume.

5 Werner Vogler, "Historical Sketch of the Abbey of St. Gall," in King and Vogler, *Culture,* 10–12.

6 Michael McCormick, *Origins of the European Economy: Communications and Commerce AD 300–900* (Cambridge, 2001), 79.

7 Vogler, "Historical Sketch," 13–15; see also notes to 6.3, 16.1, 25.1, 96.2, 128.4.

8 Notker himself appears in the *Casus* on many occasions, often as a major character; for references, see Index of Names. For Notker's and other monks' contributions, see Ivo Auf der Maur, "St. Gall's Contribution to the Liturgy," in King and Vogler, *Culture,* 44; Johannes Duft, "The Contributions of the Abbey of St. Gall to Sacred Music," in King and Vogler, *Culture,* 59; Calvin M. Bower, ed., *The Liber Ymnorum of Notker Balbulus,* 2 vols. (Woodbridge, 2016).

9 For the books and their production at Saint Gall, see the essays by Walter Berschin, Christoph Eggenberger, Johannes Duft, and Rosamond McKitterick in King and Vogler, *Culture.* Digital reproductions of Saint Gall manuscripts are available at CESG.

10 Vogler, "Historical Sketch," 14–15.

11 For a discussion of the interactions between monasteries and the world, see Richard E. Sullivan, "What Was Carolingian Monasticism? The Plan of St. Gall and the History of Monasticism," in *After Rome's Fall: Narrators and Sources of Early Medieval History*, ed. Alexander Callander Murray (Toronto, 1998), 251–87; de Jong, "Internal Cloisters," 209–21; Sarah Hamilton, *Church and People in the Medieval West, 900–1200* (Harlow, 2013), especially 119–60. For monastic conflicts in a larger context, see Steffen Patzold, *Konflikte im Kloster: Studien zur Auseinandersetzungen in monastischen Gemeinschaften des ottonisch-salischen Reichs* (Husum, 2000).

12 Vogler, "Historical Sketch," 9; Clark, *The Abbey of St. Gall,* 3–4 and 23–24.

13 Venarde, *The Rule of Saint Benedict.*

14 Earlier scholars presented monastic reform as a systematic process; see for instance Kassius Hallinger, *Gorze-Kluny: Studien zu den monastischen Lebensformen und Gegensätzen im Hochmittelalter,* 2 vols. (Rome, 1950–1951). Current works, however, have emphasized multiple factors and agents that influenced monastic change. For a reevaluation of the concept of monastic reform, see Joachim Wollasch, "Monasticism: The First Wave of Reform," in *New Cambridge Medieval History,* vol. 3, *c. 900–c.1024,* ed. Timothy Reuter (Cambridge, 1999), 163–85; John Nightingale, *Monasteries and Patrons in the Gorze Reform: Lotharingia c. 850–1000* (Oxford, 2001); Julia Barrow, "Ideas and Applications of Reform," in *Early Medieval Christianities, c. 600–c. 1100,* ed. Thomas F. X. Noble, Julia M. H. Smith, and Roberta A. Baranowski, The Cambridge History of Christianity 3 (Cambridge, 2008), 345–62; Steven Vanderputten, *Imagining Religious Leadership in the Middle Ages: Richard of Saint-Vanne and the Politics of Reform* (Ithaca, N.Y., 2015).

15 For the influence of reforms on Petershausen, a monastic community in southwestern Germany, compare Alison I. Beach, *The Trauma of Monastic Reform* (Cambridge, 2017).

16 For a brief summary, see Walter Berschin, "Latin Literature from St. Gall," in King and Vogler, *Culture,* 152–54. For the Latin parts of the *Casus* and further references, see the edition and Italian translation by Alesio, Erhart, and Crivello.

17 See, for instance, numerous critical comments made by Meyer von Knonau in his edition, *Ekkeharti Casus,* and his translation, *Ekkeharts "Casus sancti Galli";* Clark, *Abbey,* 254–55.

18 Haefele, "Untersuchungen," part 1, pp. 145–90, and part 2, pp. 120–70;

Hans Haefele, "Zum Aufbau der Casus Sancti Galli Ekkehards IV," in *Typologia Litterarum: Festschrift für Max Wehrli,* ed. Stefan Sonderegger, Alois M. Haas, and Harald Burger (Zurich, 1969), 155–66; Hellgardt, "Die *Casus sancti Galli* Ekkeharts IV," 27–50; de Jong, "Internal Cloisters"; Lori Kruckenberg, "Singing History: Chant in Ekkehard IV's *Casus sancti Galli,*" in *Medieval Cantors and Their Craft: Music, Liturgy and the Shaping of History, 800–1500,* ed. Katie Ann-Marie Bugyis, A. B. Kraebel, and Margot E. Fassler (Woodbridge, Suffolk, 2017), 59–88.

19 The editors of the chronicle, beginning with Ildefons von Arx, have adopted the title *Casus sancti Galli.* For the meaning of *casus,* see Hannes Steiner, ed. and trans., *St. Galler Klostergeschichten: Casus sancti Galli,* MGH SRG 75 (Hanover 2002), 14–16; Haefele, "Zum Aufbau," especially 158–60; Nelson, "Feasts," 269; Christina Pössel, "The Consolation of Community: Innovation and Ideas of History in Ratpert's *Casus sancti Galli,*" *Journal of Ecclesiastical History* 65 (2014): 8 and 18–19.

20 Haefele, "Zum Aufbau," especially 160; see the critique in Hellgardt, "*Casus sancti Galli* Ekkeharts IV," 34.

21 Natalia Lozovsky, "The Uses of Classical History and Geography in Medieval St Gall," in *Mapping Medieval Geographies: Geographical Encounters in the Latin West and Beyond, 300–1600,* ed. Keith L. Lilley (Cambridge, 2013), 81.

22 Hellgardt, "*Casus sancti Galli* Ekkeharts IV," 29–30; Tremp, "Ekkehart IV von St. Gallen," especially 84–85.

23 Dümmler, "Ekkehart IV," 6–8; Hellgardt, "*Casus sancti Galli* Ekkeharts IV," 31–32; Vanderputten, *Imagining Religious Leadership.*

24 De Jong, "Internal Cloisters," 209–10; Steffen Patzold, "Nachtrag," in *St. Galler Klostergeschichten,* trans. Hans Haefele, 4th ed., Ausgewählte Quellen zur deutschen Geschichte des Mittelalters 10 (Darmstadt, 2003), especially 300–301.

25 De Jong, "Internal Cloisters"; Patzold, "Nachtrag."

26 De Jong, "Internal Cloisters," 209; David Ganz, "Humour as History in Notker's Gesta Karoli Magni," in *Monks, Nuns, and Friars in Mediaeval Society,* ed. Edward B King, Jacqueline T, Schaefer, William B. Wadley (Sewanee, Tenn., 1989), 171–183.

27 See chapters 1, 3, 33 and detailed notes in editions and translations by Gerold Meyer von Knonau, Peter Erhart, and Ernst Tremp.

28 See Karl Heinz Esser, "Grabungsergebnisse zur rheinseitigen Stadtmauer," *Führer zu vor- und frühgeschichtlichen Denkmälern* 11 (1969): 132–40; L. Falck, "Geschichte von Mainz," *Führer zu vor- und frühgeschichtlichen Denkmälern* 11 (1969): 94; Mechthild Schulze-Dörrlamm, "Mainz im 9. und frühen 10. Jahrhundert," in *Glanz der späten Karolinger. Hatto I. Erzbischof von Mainz (891–913): Von der Reichenau in den Mäuseturm,* ed. Winfried Wilhelmi (Regensburg, 2013), 103–5.

29 For Ekkehard's typology of monastic attitudes, see de Jong, "Internal Cloisters," 217–18.

30 For a concise introduction to the theme, see Theres Flury and others, *Frauen im Galluskloster: Katalog zur Ausstellung in der Stiftsbibliothek St. Gallen (20. März–12. November 2006)* (Saint Gall, 2006).

31 Jürgen Dendorfer, "Herzogin Hadwig auf dem Hohentwiel—Landesgeschichtliche Perspektiven für das Früh- und Hochmittelalter," *Zeitschrift für die Geschichte des Oberrheins* 161 (2013): 11–42 (available online at https://freidok.uni-freiburg.de/data/10225.

32 Haefele, "Untersuchungen," part 2, pp. 162–70.

33 Saint Gall MS 621, p. 315 A; Lozovsky, "Uses of Classical History," 71–72.

34 Ernst Tremp, "Eine Randfigur im Rampenlicht: Heribald von St. Gallen und die Ungarn," in *Scripturus vitam: Lateinische Biographie von der Antike bis in die Gegenwart,* ed. Dorothea Waltz (Heidelberg, 2002), 435–41.

35 Grotans, *Reading,* especially 121–31.

36 Elmar Lechner, *Vita Notkeri Balbuli. Geistesgeschichtlicher Standort und historische Kritik* (Saint Gall, 1972).

37 Coulton, *Life in the Middle Ages,* 50–84.

FORTUNE AND MISFORTUNE AT SAINT GALL

Praeloquium Ekkehardi Iunioris: De casibus

Moniti a loci nostri fratribus id operae pretium putantibus, quaedam coenobii sanctorum Galli et Othmari cum infortuniis tradere fortunia, rem arduam aggressi sumus. Enimvero obloquiis patere non dubitamus, quoniam, ut nunc morum et temporum est, si quicquam asperum, et maxime quod disciplinae sit, tetigeris, si malorum libertates et impunitates non laudare videberis, velut impostor et calumniator apud eos, *qui in levitate ambulant,* habeberis. At vero quoniam rerum loco nostro gestarum etiam alii veritati nihil parcentes fortunia et infortunia, quomodolibet erant, edixerant, temptantes quidem et nos ea, quae a patribus audivimus, ea aviditate qua illi, quam verissime datum est, stilo et atramento veritatem perstringere, fortunia et infortunia loci nostri veritati nihil parcentes edisserere.

2 De Salomone etenim abbate nostro, post episcopo, ingressi sumus. Quem per ordinem secuti rebus nostris potiti sunt Hartmannus, Engilpertus, Thieto, Cralo, cui interstitium regiminis frater suus fecerat Anno. Sequuntur

Preface by Ekkehard the Younger: Concerning Fortunate and Unfortunate Events

At the suggestion of the brothers of my community, who thought it would be worthwhile to record some of the fortunate and unfortunate events that happened at the monastery of Saint Gall and Saint Otmar, I have embarked on this difficult task. However, I do not doubt that I am exposing myself to opprobrium, for such are the ways of our times that if you touch upon a thorny subject, especially something concerning discipline, and if you seem not to praise the freedoms and lack of restraint of the wicked, you will be held to be a fraud and a slanderer by those *who walk in levity.* Nevertheless, since other people have related with unsparing truthfulness what took place at our monastery, events of whatever kind—fortunate or unfortunate—I will try, with the same zeal as they have shown in adhering to the truth to the fullest extent possible for pen and ink, to set out with an unsparing regard for the truth what I have heard from the fathers about the fortunate and unfortunate events that occurred at our monastery.

I start with Salomo, our abbot and later bishop. He was 2
followed in order of succession by those who subsequently took over as abbots of our house: Hartmann, Engilbert, Thieto, and Craloh, whose brother Anno took his place for a

Purchardus, Notkerus, Ymmo, Vodalricus, Kerhardus, Purchardus alter, Thiepaldus, Norpertus, cuius hodie sub regimine quidem *non prout ipse et nos, ut inquiunt, volumus, sed prout possumus,* vivimus. Scripserat ante nos Radpertus, homo doctissimus, et ipse codicellum similis materiae a sancto Gallo et Othmaro usque ad se ipsum, a quo nos incepisse videmur, Salomonem episcopum. Cuius nominis tamen aequivocatiae sit, ut bene cerneret, praemonemus. Nam tres eius nominis cum Constantiae praefuerint, secundum Rathpertus censum a loco nostro exegisse scripsit. De tertio nos, prout Deo dante potuimus, sic incipiemus.

time. Then followed Burchard, Notker, Immo, Ulrich, Gerhard, Burchard the second, Thiepald, and Norbert under whose rule we live now *not as he and we, as they say, wish, but as we can.* Ratpert, a highly learned man, wrote a short book covering similar ground before us, from the time of Saint Gall and Saint Otmar up to the very man with whom I have decided to begin, Bishop Salomo. I warn you right away, however, to keep in mind how confusing that name is. For there were three bishops of Constance bearing this name; Ratpert wrote that the second had demanded a tribute from our monastery. It is with the third Salomo that I will begin, God willing, to the best of my ability.

INCIPIUNT LIBRI DE
CASIBUS MONASTERII.

Salomonis tertii parentes cum essent clari et illustres, ipsum Isoni sancti Galli monacho, tunc temporis doctori nominatissimo, tradunt erudiendum et clericatui initiandum. Quem adprime, ut aiunt, ipse erudierat; sed et Notkeri, Tuotilonis, Ratperti, Harthmanni commonachorum statui praetulerat et delicatius quasi canonicum educaverat. Creverant tamen inde clandestine inter summae indolis condiscipulos invidiae; et cum conliberales genere essent et ingenio, ut ea aetas solet, aequanimiter non ferebant alienum sibi, qui fratres essent, praeferri, et qui natalibus quidem essent pares, doctrinarum provectibus ab illo praeiri.

2 Defunguntur Salomonis adhuc pueri parentes, tandem autem et frater, et ipse rerum heres effectus ad maximas res animum intenderat. Scholisque ablatus, Grimaldo abbate nostro, archicapellano eius, iuvante, capellanus fit Ludowici regis, cuius singulari gratia in brevi potitus Elewangis adhuc canonicus primo praeficitur; post etiam Campidonensibus variis suimet et loci damnis illum detrectantibus praeponitur. In processu autem Hattone archiepiscopo Magontino, sibi propter animi acutissimam sollertiam amicissimo, opitulante plurimis locis praeficitur, tandem et nobis. Postremo

HERE BEGIN THE BOOKS ON THE FORTUNATE AND UNFORTUNATE EVENTS AT OUR MONASTERY.

Since the parents of Salomo III were noble and highly regarded, they handed him over to Iso, a monk of Saint Gall and the most distinguished teacher at that time, to be educated and initiated into the clerical life. Iso gave him an excellent education, they say, but also ranked him above his fellow monks Notker, Tuotilo, Ratpert, and Hartmann and instructed him more indulgently, like a canon. As a result jealousies grew in secret among his highly talented fellow students; and because they were equally noble in birth and intelligence, they could not, as is typical for young men of that age, bear with equanimity that an outsider was preferred to themselves, who were brothers of the monastery, and that he was surpassing them, though they were surely his equals in birth, in the progress of his studies.

Salomo's parents passed away when he was still a boy, and 2
later his brother died too, and after he had become heir to the property himself, Salomo turned his attention to grand affairs. He left school and became chaplain to King Louis with the help of our abbot Grimald, who was then his archchaplain. Soon he gained the king's special favor and while still a canon, obtained Ellwangen; later he was put in charge of Kempten, whose inmates disparaged him for various damages to themselves and their community. Nevertheless in due course, with the help of Hatto, archbishop of Mainz, who was very friendly with him because of his very keen intelligence, Salomo was put in charge of many monasteries

vero et Constantiae pastor et episcopus efficitur. His partim per transgressum praelibatis ad ordinem incepti operis revertamur.

2. Grimaldi temporibus canonici abbatis, Hartmuoto eius quasi proabbate, Marcus quidam Scotigena episcopus Gallum tamquam compatriotam suum Roma rediens visitat. Comitatur eum sororis filius Moengal, postea a nostris Marcellus diminutive a Marco avunculo sic nominatus. Hic erat in divinis et humanis eruditissimus. Rogatur episcopus loco nostro aliquamdiu stare allecto nepote. Diu secum deliberantes vix tandem consenserant. Dieque condicto partitur Marcellus nummos avunculi sui multos per fenestram, *timens, ne discerperetur ab eis. Fremebant enim in illum,* quasi ipsius suasu episcopus restaret. Equos autem et mulos, quibus ipse voluit, nominatim episcopus tradidit. Libros vero, aurum et pallia sibi et sancto Gallo retinuit. Stola tandem indutus abeuntes benedixit. Multis autem lacrimis utrimque discessum est.

2 Remanserat episcopus cum nepote et paucis suae linguae apparitoribus. Traduntur post tempus Marcello scholae claustri cum Notkero, postea cognomine Balbulo, et ceteris monachici habitus pueris; exteriores autem, id est canonicae, Ysoni cum Salomone et eius comparibus. Iucundum est memorari, quantum cella sancti Galli his auspiciis crescere

and finally ours. Ultimately, he was also made pastor and bishop of Constance. Now that I have given a partial foretaste of these events by skipping over segments, let me go back to an orderly account of the story I had begun.

2. When Canon Grimald was abbot and Hartmut was acting as his deputy, a certain Marcus, a bishop of Irish stock, was returning from Rome and visited Gall as his compatriot. Marcus was accompanied by his sister's son Moengal, later called by our brothers Marcellus, a diminutive form of his uncle Marcus's name. Marcellus was most learned in the divine and human disciplines. The bishop was invited to stay for a while at our monastery with his nephew who had already been admitted. After protracted deliberations with one another, with difficulty they finally reached agreement. On the day agreed upon Marcellus distributed many of his uncle's coins—through a window, *out of fear that that he would be torn to pieces by their entourage. In fact, they were railing at him,* as if it was at Marcellus's suggestion that the bishop was staying. The bishop also handed over his horses and mules to people he wished, by name. The books, gold, and precious cloths, however, he kept for himself and for Saint Gall. Finally, wearing his stole, he blessed them as they were leaving. With much crying on both sides, the company departed.

The bishop stayed with his nephew and a few attendants 2
who spoke his language. After a while the claustral school that included Notker (later called the Stammerer) and other boys in monastic habits, was entrusted to Marcellus, while the external school, that is the school for canons, which included Salomo and others like him, was entrusted to Iso. It is pleasant to recall how much the cell of Saint Gall began to

ceperit tandemque floruerit Hartmuoto eam, Crimaldi quidem vicario tandemque abbate, omnimodis augmentante.

3. Petiit tandem Salomon iam adolescens bene educatus, ut frater conscriptus nobis fieri mereretur. Quod Crimaldo iubente et Hartmoto iuvante a patribus est consecutus. Tradidit autem de praediis, quibus abundaverat, sancto Gallo locum, qui Colda dicitur, concambium sibi faciens, ut annonam monachi et locum hospitis in refectorio haberet, dum viveret, et collem quendam, qui ultra Iram amoenior sibi videbatur, cum pratis sibi et agellis adiacentibus possideret, ut *mansione* ibi *parata* crebro velut frater adveniens abbati non esset onerosus neque familiae incommodus.

2 Talibus homini velut iam tum cum Fortuna ludenti ad votum cedentibus, aulam regis Luodowici, ut diximus, adiit; capellanus factus eius fit intimus et praelibatis abbatiis proclive est praelatus. Locum autem nostrum sibi prae omnibus habitum subinde adiit. Claustrumque ille, quia potens erat, absque duce et, quod magnae confusionis tunc erat et est, lineus diatim introiit. Surgunt inde ab aemulis illius murmuria ipso ignaro; comitantur, ut assolent, in absentem obloquia. Plurima fratribus velut dives opum commoda fecit. Quorum cum uni reverendo quidem, ut erant tunc

grow under their auspices and how it eventually flourished when Hartmut, first as deputy for Grimald and ultimately as abbot, expanded it in every way.

3. After a while Salomo, by now a well-educated young man, sought the privilege of becoming an enrolled brother among us. This he obtained from the fathers, by Grimald's order and with Hartmut's help. From his estates, which he had in abundance, he handed over to Saint Gall a place called Goldach, in exchange for a monk's rations and a place as a guest in the refectory for as long as he lived. He also asked for a certain hill beyond the Ira that seemed rather pleasant to him, together with adjacent meadows and small fields, so that once *a dwelling place* had been *prepared* for him there he would not be frequently burdening the abbot or inconveniencing the monastic household like a visiting brother.

As these things were happening as he prayed they would, 2
as if even then he were playing a game with Fortune, he moved to the court of King Louis, as I said earlier. Once appointed chaplain, he became close to the king and was quickly entrusted with authority over the abbeys mentioned above. He frequently came to our monastery, which he preferred to all the others. Because he was powerful, he daily entered our cloister without a guide, and, moreover, dressed in linen, a practice which was a cause of considerable embarrassment then as it is still today. Then without his knowledge, mutterings arose among his rivals; they were accompanied by abusive remarks in his absence, as is usually the case. As a rich man, he conferred many benefits on the brothers. When he gave a fur cloak to one brother who was particularly venerable, as many of them were in those days, and

plurimi, pellicium traderet et sui eum apud Deum memorem fore rogaret: "Pellicium," ait ille, "tuum, si volueris, tibi optime repretiabor. Nam duas cucullas ab abbate habeo, quarum unam tibi, ut claustrum decentius nobiscum in ea introeas, induendam contrado." Et ille: "Eia," inquit, "haec utique Tuotilo et Ratpert vel alii invidi mei *in ore tuo posuerant.* Nonne, quaeso, et abbas vester lineus claustrum tot annis ingreditur?" "Claustra," ait ille, "tuorum, qui te eius habitus abbatem susceperant aut pro peccatis aut aliquo Dei nutu, et tu quidem, etsi non licenter, intras tamen potenter. Sed nos in fraternitatem interdum et laicos recipimus, quibus tamen in laico habitu nequaquam," inquit, "in claustro abutimur."

4. Recessit homo artificiosus ratione simplicis quasi devictus. Ibat autem secum reputans hominem tanti meriti non nisi in spiritu Dei sibi talia prolocutum. Abstinuit tandem absque aliquo patrum, ut moris est, praeduce claustrum introire. Saepius tamen, ut diximus, loco sancti Galli, quantum a regibus et coenobiis suis licuit, immoratus, fratribus, quae potuit, hilariter dedit, maxime Ysoni magistro. Caute etiam Crimaldus iam senescens et Hartmotus cum illo egerant, ne animum et per se divitis et in regno potentis in aliquo laederent. Incipit igitur tandem in colle concambii sui ecclesiam in honorem et modum sanctae crucis aedificare, in quam ad unguem perductam sancti Magni

asked the man to remember him to God, the man said, "I will pay you back handsomely for your fur cloak if you want. For I have two cowls from the abbot, and I will give you one of them to put on so you may enter the cloister with us in a more decent fashion." And Salomo said, "Come on now, surely Tuotilo and Ratpert or some other people envious of me *put these words in your mouth.* Tell me, hasn't your abbot also been entering the cloister dressed in linen all these years?" "The monasteries that house your monks," the brother said, "accepted you, dressed in this habit, as an abbot either for their sins or at some sign from God, and you enter them thanks to your power, though you do so illicitly. We do admit laymen into our confraternity now and then, but they never show us disrespect by wearing lay habits in the cloister."

4. The crafty man withdrew, as if defeated by the artless man's arguments. Salomo went on his way thinking to himself that a man of such merit had not told him these things without being prompted by God's Holy Spirit. He finally stopped entering the cloister without being accompanied by one of the fathers, as was customary. However, as I have said, he quite often stayed at the monastery of Saint Gall, when he could get away from kings and his abbeys, and he happily gave what he could to the brothers, especially to his teacher Iso. Grimald, by that time an old man, and also Hartmut were cautious in dealing with him, for fear that they somehow offend a man who was both independently rich and powerful in the kingdom. Finally he began building a church in honor of and in the shape of the Holy Cross, on the hill he had received in his exchange transaction. When every last detail of the church was complete, he brought

bracchium, Adalberone episcopo dante et prosequente, de Faucibus sumptum magnis hinc inde velut triumphi tripudiis intulit, et in honore eam sanctae crucis et eiusdem privati patroni nostri dedicavit et praediis suis, id est Tegerinowa, Bernhardicella, Sitiruntorf, Coldaham etiam, quam, ut diximus, concambians iam loco tradiderat, et aliis quibusdam eam dotaverat. Hartmuoti, tunc quidem abbatis, concessione, ut in die sancti ipsius fratres convivarent, constituerat; se etiam, si Deo placeret, ibi sepeliri velle aiebat.

5. Accidit autem post aliquantum temporis, ut a palatio veniens quadragesimam loco nostro ei tempori aptissimo viso agere eligeret. Ingrediturque clam penetralia claustri nostri bonus *fur noctibus,* nudipes, cappa quidem, uti fratrum unus putaretur, indutus. Senserat illum Notker, Ratpreth, Tuotilo, et aliquamdiu sanctam fraudem texerant. Nimis tamen, ut iam diximus, insolens semper erat et est praeter monachici nostri habitus quemquam introire intima nostra, maxime noctibus. Initur consilium, ut, quoniam moris est duos nobis fratres claustri vigilias agere, intranti illi ipsi vigiles cum lumine, quia solis loqui licuit, occurrerent et, quis esset, silentio quaererent. Verebantur enim hominem palatinum, qui iam quasdam abbatias canonicus habebat, ne aliquid irregulare, ut forte fit, videns sibi viam apud regem occasione hac etiam ad nostram aperire temptaret, quibus

into it an arm of Saint Magnus taken from Füssen, with great celebration from there to here as in a triumph, with Bishop Adalbero both granting and accompanying the relic. Salomo dedicated the church in honor of the Holy Cross and to our special patron and endowed it with his estates, namely Degenau, Bernhardzell, Sitterdorf, and also Goldach (which, as I have said, he had already handed over to the monastery in his transaction) and some others. With the permission of Hartmut, who was still abbot at that time, Salomo instituted a feast for the brothers on the saint's day; he also said that he wanted to be buried there, if it pleased God.

5. However, it so happened that somewhat later, returning from the palace, Salomo chose to spend Lent in our monastery, because he found it the most suitable place for passing that season. The good *thief in the night* secretly entered the innermost parts of our cloister, barefoot and covered by a cowl so that he might pass for one of the brothers. Notker, Ratpert, and Tuotilo noticed him, but for a while covered up the pious deception. However, as I have already said, it was very unusual and is very much against the practice of our monastery for anyone but monks of our order to enter our inner space, especially at night. Because two of our brothers customarily keep a watch over the cloister, a plan was made: when Salomo entered, the guards with the lantern, who alone were allowed to speak, would stop him and quietly ask him who he was. For they feared that the man of the court, who as a canon already had several abbeys, would see some violation of the Rule, as can happen, and that he would try to use this occasion before the king as a way to get ours as well, though by that time, after canon-

nunc post canonicos abbates monachus pater domesticus praeerat Hartmuotus, homo amantissimus.

2 *Ingreditur* iterum *ut heri et nudius tertius* fur ille vitabundus; Ratpert et Tuotilo sunt vigiles: unus illorum circumibat, alter ad introitum clandestini illius servabat. Progreditur interea *praeventor maturitatis* ad sepulchra coemeterii oraturus pater, eius temporis nostrorum apud Deum potentissimus, Ruodkerus. Cuius gravitatem reveriti vigiles loco paulisper cedunt. Senserat ille pater post modicum pedetemptivum nesciens quem. Signo vocis et strepitu pedum notat quasi furem. Vigiles cum lumine confestim approperant. Agnitus est. Atque ilico pater ille: "Per sancti Galli," inquid, "meritum"—sic enim patres iurabant—"hunc in claustro eius his horis non patimur habitum." Vigiles illi pro tempore siluerunt, qui tantum interpretem rupto habuere silentio. Tremefactus autem ille ab non ignari hominis verbis tali tempore sibi inusitatis: "Patere me," ait, "pater reverende, vel oratorium sancti Petri, quod proximum est, ingredi! Ibi postquam oravero, numquam isto habitu nisi ductu alicuius primorum, ut lex loci habet, claustrum intrabo. Te autem iuvante et fratribus ad hoc idoneis, cras abbatem precari est animo, ut monachico habitu mihi liceat claustrum ingredi, vobiscum in eo versari ut monachum et egredi; deforis autem coram militibus meis et ceteris canonico, ut soleo, vestimento versari." "Immo," ait ille, "sanctus Gallus tibi in

abbots, we were ruled by Hartmut, a monk and a father of our own house, a much beloved man.

That elusive thief *went in* again *as yesterday and the day be-* 2
fore. Ratpert and Tuotilo stood on guard: one walked around while the other stood watch for the entrance of that furtive person. Meanwhile father Ruodker, *he who rises before dawn,* at that time the mightiest before God among our monks, proceeded to the graves in the cemetery in order to pray. Out of reverence for this dignified man, the monks on guard stepped back a little. Soon the father noticed that someone was moving cautiously, but he did not know who it was. Raising his voice and stamping his feet, Ruodker branded him as a thief. The watchmen with the lantern immediately hurried up. Salomo was recognized. On the spot the father said, "By the merit of Saint Gall," for this is the way the fathers used to swear, "we don't allow such dress at this hour in his cloister." The guards kept quiet for a while, because with the silence now broken they had such a distinguished spokesman. Salomo was frightened by language he was not used to hearing at such a time from a man who was not unknown. "At least allow me, reverend father," he said, "to enter the chapel of Saint Peter, which is very close by. After praying there, I will never again enter the cloister in this habit unless accompanied by one of the elders, as the rule of the monastery requires. With the help of yourself and appropriate brothers, tomorrow I intend to ask the abbot's permission to enter the cloister in monastic habit, intermingle with you in that habit as a monk, and then leave, but to remain dressed as a canon outside the monastery before my fighting men and others, as I usually do." Ruodker answered, "Rather, may Saint Gall put it into your heart that if you

cor mittat, ut, si semel eo induaris, numquam, quoad vixeris, nisi solito monachis tempore exuaris!"

6. Panditur abbati animus hominis et petitio Ruodkero astipulante et ceteris aliquibus, enimvero non omnibus. Erat senatus rei publicae nostrae tunc quidem sanctissimus. Consuluntur Hartmannus *consilio magnus,* ille quidem qui *Humili prece* melodiam fecerat, Notkerus qui sequentias, Ratpert qui *Ardua spes mundi,* Tuotilo qui *Hodie cantandus est,* et pleraque alia dictaverant. Qui denique, ut diximus, in condiscipulatu animum eius didicerant et in rebus, quas vellet, patrandis artificia.

2 Loquique iussi sunt: "Regula nostra," Hartmannus ait, "non similitudinem monachi, sed monachum ipsum quaerit." Notker: "Mihi praetexta haec, qua superindui," inquit, "desiderat, si togam praetenderet, non utique displiceret." Ratpert: "*Aut haec in nostros fabricata est machina muros, aut aliquis latet hic error,*" ait. Tuotilo: "Fraternitatem illi," inquit, "integre ante concessimus. Hanc ei, quantum in me est, abba mi, ego non denego. Si autem lupum ovino vellere quaerit induere, per alius quam mei consensum perficiat."

3 Audiens abbas, quod suspicarentur in homine, videlicet ne hoc schemate indutus proximior esset dominatui abbatiae, cuius per ipsum tunc tertio quidem recepimus privilegium: "Scio," inquit, "fratres et filii, quid ab illo vereamini; sed hoc et mihi quoque quiddam subolet. Existimo tamen melius nobiscum actum fore, si sic apud nos initiatus

once put on the monk's habit, you should never take it off as long as you live except at the customary hour for monks to do so!"

6. Salomo's intentions and his request were made known to the abbot, with the agreement of Ruodker and some but to be sure not all of the others. Indeed, the senate of our republic was then at its holiest. The following were consulted: Hartmann, *great in counsel,* who composed the melody for *With a Humble Prayer* and Notker, the author of sequences, and Ratpert, who composed *The Lofty Hope of the World* and Tuotilo, who wrote *Today We Must Sing*—they had also composed many other works. In short, as I said, as fellow students they had come to know Salomo's character and his schemes for getting what he wanted.

They were asked to speak. "Our rule," Hartmann said, 2
"looks for the monk himself, not the imitation of a monk." Notker said: "I wouldn't object to this boy's toga that he wishes to wear if his goal were the man's toga." Ratpert said: "*Either this device has been built to use against our walls, or some other trick is hidden here.*" Tuotilo said: "We have already granted him full brotherhood. As far as I am concerned, my abbot, I will not deny him it. But if he seeks to dress a wolf in a sheep's clothing, let him do it with someone else's approval, not mine."

When the abbot heard their suspicions about Salomo, 3
namely, that dressed in this fashion, he would get closer to ruling the abbey (for which we in fact received a privilege for the third time through Hartmut himself), he said: "I understand, brothers and sons, what you fear from Salomo; indeed, a whiff of something like that occurs to me too. However, I think that it would be better for us if Salomo were

monachum se aliquando nostrum faciat, ne iterum canonico subdamur ut antea. Placet igitur, ut agamus cum illo, quo re vera habitum sumat a sancto Gallo, ut, si arte sua acciderit, quod veremur, noster tamen sit frater et monachus."

4 Mittitur ad illum Ruotkerus cum aliis quibusdam rem suasurus. In processu temporis Deo dante pollicetur facere, quod petitur; tantum interim propter claustri reverentiam talis habitus sibimet, rogat, sit licitus. Variis fratrum hinc inde tractatibus vix tandem conceditur. Designaturque ei locus, quem hodie quadris lapidibus notatum videmus, quibus intrans habitum indueret, exiens exueret. Ingrediturque claustrum noster praemonachus nocte et die, de talis consortii permisso laetissimus. Parat autem pro hoc beneficio insignem crucem sancto Gallo, quam argento partim deaurato vestitam analogio nocturnali superposuit. Hanc nostris temporibus Norpertus noster columnae deargentatae infixam confessionis superposuit altario.

7. Convivia fratribus duodecim diebus in anno, id est in Kalendis, praetextatus noster, quamdiu saeculariter vixit, hilariter facere suevit. In quibus et ipse, si aderat, minister procedebat. Solebant id ipsum autem etiam quidam alii fratres conscripti nostratibus caritatis signum exhibere: prae omnibus quidem Karolus rex ipse, qui sancti Otmari

admitted into our community and at some point became one of our monks, so that we are not made subject to a canon again, as happened before. Therefore I think that we should cooperate with him so that he actually takes the monastic habit of Saint Gall: so that if what we fear comes to pass through his craftiness, at least he will be our brother and monk."

Ruodker was sent to Salomo, along with certain others, 4
to convince him of the matter. He promised to do what was asked, in the fullness of time, God willing, only in the meantime, out of deep respect for the cloister, he asked for permission to wear the habit. After a variety of discussions back and forth with the brothers, finally they just barely agreed to his request. A place was assigned to him, which we see today marked by squared stones, where he could put on the habit when he entered and take it off when he left. Now our future monk entered the cloister night and day, extremely pleased at receiving permission to join our community in such a way. And in return for this privilege he gave to Saint Gall a splendid cross covered with silver that was gilded in places, which he put over the nighttime lectern. In our own day our Norbert fixed this cross on a silver-plated column and set it on the high altar.

7. Twelve days a year, on the first of every month, for as long as he lived in the world our would-be monk was accustomed cheerfully to provide feasts for the brothers. If he was present, he himself would also show up as a server at these meals. But some other enrolled brothers also offered this very same sign of affection to our own brothers: preeminent among all of them was King Charles himself, who acted as steward and butler, providing food from the village

hebdomada ipse propositor et pincerna per triduum de vico
Stamhem servivit volatiliaque nos edere fecit; sed et Adalbero, qui supra, Augustensis multo tempore antistes. Qui
signa et virtutes sancti Galli a plurimis audiens, locum in die
sancti Galli orandi gratia adiit et praesens plura conspiciens:
"*Maior est*," inquit, "gratia loci huius *quam rumor, quem au-*
2 *divi*." Devovit autem benedictione fratribus data, anno altero vita comite se rediturum et uti tunc quidem nequaquam venire nudimanum. Domum rediit. Interrogatusque
inter cetera aliquando a suis, essetne nobiscum, ut fama vul-
gavit, religio cum doctrina, severitas cum disciplina: "Quid
ceteri," inquit, "sentiant, nescio; quod mihi animo est, pro-
nuntio. Unum egomet sanctum et hunc defunctum quaesivi;
vivos autem sanctissimos, ut vere fatear, fratres inveni. Doctrinam autem illorum et disciplinam in virtutum eorum
operibus videre est. Delectat enim me talium memorari,
quos quidem ut iterum videam, vix exspecto. Oportet autem, ut omnibus meis me iuvantibus me praeparem, quatenus, uti me et meos decet, ad proximum sancti Galli diem
viros Dei visitem, frater illorum conscriptus fiam et, quantum mihi copiae est, caritatem illorum regratier." Venerat
Dei electus die dicto, ut spoponderat. Quantus autem venerit et qualis in donis sancto Gallo, fratribus et familiae
fuerit, capitulum, quod in memoriam eius regulae nostrae
codici ascriptum est, plenius pandit.

of Stammheim for our feasts for three days in the week of
Saint Otmar, and he had us eat fowl; also the aforementioned Adalbero, who was for a long time bishop of Augsburg, did the same. After hearing from many people about
the *signs and miracles* of Saint Gall, he came to the monastery
to pray on Saint Gall's feast day, and after witnessing many
of these personally, said, "The grace accorded this site *surpasses the report I have heard.*" After he gave the brothers his 2
farewell blessing, he vowed that he would return the next
year if he was still living and that at that time he would certainly not come empty-handed. He went back home. When
asked by his own people, among other things, whether we
possessed, as rumor had it, religious devotion combined
with erudition, and severity together with discipline, he
said, "What others may think I do not know, but I will tell
you what I believe. I went looking for a saint and a dead one
at that, but, to speak truly, I found the most saintly of men
alive among the brothers. One can see the erudition and discipline in their holy works. It is a pleasure to recall such remarkable men the like of whom I can scarcely expect ever to
see again. I need to make preparations, with the help of all
my men, for how I am to visit the men of God, as it befits
me and my men, on the next Saint Gall's day and to become
a brother enrolled along with them, and insofar as it lies
within my power, to repay their love." God's chosen one
came on the appointed day, as he had promised. A chapter
which was added in his memory to the codex containing our
monastic Rule more fully discloses how splendidly he came
and how richly endowed he was with gifts to Saint Gall, to
the brothers and their dependents.

8. Post non multum quoque temporis forte accidit Pe-
trum etiam Veronensem episcopum a palatio redeuntem
simili loci gratia inopinatum venire. Fratres autem susci-
pientes illum, quod melius quidem habebant, evangelium ei
offerebant. Ille autem arbitratus se despici, quoniam famam
loci magnam audiverat, de vilitate libri secum fluctuabat. Ad
missas argenti calix etiam, qui melior habetur, proponitur.
Quibus peractis etiam de calice sinistrum quiddam secum
trutinat. Prandium ei exhibetur sumptuosum. Surgens a
mensa fratrum postulat alloquium. Quibus collectis—nam
abbas loco deerat—"Bene," ait, "mecum, domini mei, abbate vestro absente egistis; sed pro evangelio et calice vilio-
ribus mihi propositis aliquid subolet. Quamvis enim ipse
sim vilis et indignus, non tamen vilis loci nominor episco-
2 pus." Quibus constanter meliora non esse sancto Gallo pro-
testantibus, spiritus hominis paulisper quieverat. Sumens-
que tandem quosdam fratrum in partem, secreto eis locutus:
"Mittite," inquit, "post me Veronam sex, quos habetis, fidis-
simos viatores. Quique bini et bini per tres vias, quae hinc
illo ducunt, mihi adveniant et peregrinos se habitu et verbis
simulent; singillatim tamen se mihi bini et bini ostendant
et pollice sic in manum recurvo eleemosynam petant.
Quos ego, ut alios soleo, in penetral meum quoddam solus
solos coram meis inducam et vestiam. Aurum autem, cuius
equipondium nunc vobis do, cruribus eorum fasciolis

8. Not long after this, it happened by chance that Peter, bishop of Verona, on his way back from the palace, also arrived unexpectedly, drawn by a similar favor for the place. When welcoming him, the brothers presented him with the best Gospel they had. But thinking he was being insulted because he had heard of the great reputation of the place, he kept fretting over the trifling value of the book. A silver chalice, which was also considered the best, was set out for Mass. And when the Mass ended, he thought to himself that there was something wrong with the chalice. He was offered a lavish meal. When he rose from the table, he demanded to speak with the brothers. After they had been assembled (for the abbot was not at the monastery) he said, "You have treated me well, my lords, even though your abbot was away. But regarding the Gospel and chalice, the lowly items set before me, something does not smell quite right. Though I am lowly and unworthy, still I am not known as the bishop
of a lowly place." When they kept protesting that better 2
things did not exist at Saint Gall, the man's temper soon calmed down. Finally he took some brothers aside and spoke to them privately. "Send to Verona after me the six most trusty messengers you have. Have them approach me in pairs on the three roads that lead there from here and pretend to be pilgrims in their dress and talk. Have each pair present themselves to me three times two by two and ask for alms, with the thumb bent back into the hand like this. Before the eyes of my attendants I will take them, as I usually do with others, into an inner room of mine, where I alone in front of my people will drape and clothe them alone. With bandages on their legs I will bind gold, equivalent in weight to what I am giving you now, and send them

circumligabo et dimittam eos, ut ad vos eodem, quo venerant, fortuna comite artificio redeant." Factum est, ut largitor acutus docuit. Allatum est sancto Gallo grave pondus auri Veronensis. Concordat pondus equipondio. Fit de auro Petri cavea evangelii, fit calix, fit capsa. Quae omnia Salomon, primo frater conscriptus noster, ut praemisimus, deinde et monachus, tandem abbas, gemmis et arte Gallo paravit.

9. Hartmotus autem pro Crimaldo, ut et Rapertus scribit, rem publicam nostram strenue gubernans, per semet ipsum quoque non mediocriter amplificans, iamque senescens Berinhardo monacho nostro abbatiam suam fratrum conmuni electione per regem Karolum tradit. Ipse autem Herginisowam cum Waltchincha et Puera Minore sibi et posteris abbatibus a potestate forte cedentibus imperiali auctoritate ipsius Karoli retinuit. Obiens autem post multas, quas per se statuit et per Berinhardum obtinuit fratribus et familiae, benivolentiae constitutiones, circa Landaloum episcopum, in titulo apostolorum conditum, cognatum et amicum suum, extra parietem tamen, sepeliri se petiit.

2 De quo ipso Landaloho, sancto Darviensi quidem archiepiscopo, pauca scribere necessarium puto. Suevus hic et nobilis erat, apud sanctum Gallum quidem educatus et doctus, cuius Windinissa cum multis aliis hereditas erat. Igitur episcopus factus Romam pergere solebat; per Iovis itaque montem transiens ibat, per Septimum autem rediens Gallum et Hartmotum suum salutabat. Devoverat etiam sancto Gallo Lolingam villam dare; sed cognatis renitentibus

off to return to you—if good luck travels with them—in the same guise in which they came." It happened just as the clever benefactor instructed. A heavy weight of Veronese gold was brought to Saint Gall. The weight exactly equals the counterweight. Peter's gold was used to make a case for the Gospel, a chalice, and a reliquary. Salomo, who was first our enrolled brother, as I said earlier, then also our fellow monk, and finally our abbot, furnished all these with gems and fine craftsmanship for Gall.

9. In the place of Grimald, as Ratpert also writes, Hartmut governed our commonwealth vigorously, enlarging it considerably by his own efforts as well. And when he grew old, he handed over his abbacy through King Charles to our monk Bernhard by the common choice of the brothers. On the imperial authority of Charles himself he kept Herisau along with Waldkirch and Minderbüren for himself and for subsequent abbots who might chance to retire. After many arrangements set up by himself or obtained through Bernhard to benefit the brothers and the dependents, he asked when he was dying that he be buried near Bishop Landaloh, his relative and friend, who was laid to rest in the church of the Apostles though it was outside the walls.

About this very Landaloh, holy archbishop of Treviso, I 2
consider it essential to write a few words. He was a Swabian nobleman reared and educated at Saint Gall. His hereditary estate was Windisch along with many other properties. When he became bishop he regularly traveled to Rome. He went there taking the pass by the mountain of Jupiter but came back over the Septimer and paid his respects to his friends Gall and Hartmut. He had even made a vow to give the village of Lolingen to Saint Gall, but since his relatives

conquisitionis suae loca quaedam cuidam Uodalrico comiti, ut Gallo Ahadorf cum eisdem locis disponeret, concanbiens tradidit. Rediit autem tandem aliquando Roma, et ad Gallum suum tendens, Italici aeris vitio febre correptus, vix ad Rorscanchin pervenire praevalens Hartmuoto cum fratribus ad se advocato nobiliter diem obiit. Disposuit igitur adhuc vivens ad titulum sancti Petri, cui iam ibat, qui est in coemeterio sancti Galli, capellam, qua itinerans utebatur, cum reliquiis et libris et omnibus utensilibus sacris; in quo et corpus illius cum omni honore humatum est. Phreneticus, ut aiunt, in septimo eius super illius corruens tumbam sanus surrexit. Tradunt et alias infirmitates saepe illic meritis eius curatas.

10. Sed ut ad ea, unde digressi sumus, redeamus: Salomon praemonachus noster idem semper loco nostro et fratribus *apud Deum et homines* permanebat. Ruodkerum autem semper prae oculis habebat, quem sibi in his, quae ad Deum fuerant, ducem et custodem elegerat. A quo dum quadam die ab aula veniens psalmo benedictionis susciperetur, surgens ad osculum patris gloriebatur inter cetera de muneribus regis Arnoldi, quae se sancto Gallo daturum ait. Nam, ut id genus hominum est, laudis avidissimus per quaedam erat; de quo in periculum, uti post liquebit, aliquando venit. Erat munus illud capsa solide aurea, gemmis regaliter inclita, reliquiis summis referta, in formam capellae creata, cui simile quidem nihil umquam vidimus. Superscriptio eius est:

opposed that, he exchanged some pieces of his own property with a certain Count Ulrich so that he could bequeath Aadorf and these same places to Saint Gall. At long last on one occasion he returned from Rome, and as he was heading for his friend Gall he was afflicted with a fever caused by the pernicious Italian air. Scarcely able to reach Rorschach, he summoned Hartmut along with the brothers and died nobly. While he was still living, he bequeathed the portable equipment for the chapel that he used when he traveled, together with relics and books and sacred vessels, to the church of Saint Peter in the cemetery of Saint Gall, to which he was headed. There too his body was interred with full honors. A madman, so they say, falling down on this tomb on the seventh day after his death, rose up healed. They also claim that through his merits other ailments too have often been cured at that spot.

10. But let us return to the point from which we digressed. Our future monk Salomo remained unwaveringly the same with regard to our monastery and our brothers *before God and men.* Yet he always held Ruodker before his eyes, whom he had chosen as his guide and guardian in those matters that pertained to God. One day when he came from court and was received with the psalm of blessing by Ruodker, as Salomo rose up for the father's kiss, he boasted among other things about the gifts of King Arnulf, which he said he was going to give to Saint Gall. Like other men of this sort, he was very eager in certain respects to be praised. This sometimes got him into trouble, as will later become clear. The gift was a reliquary of solid gold, regally adorned with jewels and filled with precious relics. It was fashioned in the shape of a chapel, and the likes of it we had never seen. Its inscription reads:

En crucis atque piae cum sanctis capsa Mariae.
Hanc Karolus summam delegit habere capellam.

2 Suadet Ruodkerus homini non aurum, sed se ipsum, ut saepe pollicitus est, Gallo suo offerre et monachum se eius verum iam tandem perficere. Factum est, ut *magni consilii angelus* hortatus est. Regi tandem datori suo postquam votum suum aperuit, capsam ille ipsam quadam die suspendens collo, tunica monachi et cuculla indutus aram sancti Galli Berhardo annuente nudipes adiit, peccata deflevit saeculoque abrenuntians sancti Galli fit monachus. Abbas illum tamquam de palatio monachum delicatius tractavit et omnibus, qui sub se militabant, praehabuit.

3 Post non multum vero temporis, consiliis hominis carere non posse re publica tota personante, abbatis sui permisso rex eum iterum in aulam assumpsit et priorum honorum statibus restituit, tandem quoque et adauxit. Nam Augense ei tunc coenobium tradidit. Aiunt autem hominem fortunatum tandem duodecim abbatias rexisse.

11. Berhardo itaque abbate, ut alias relatum est, deposito, per Hattonem archiepiscopum nobis oblatus et nostrum locum suscepit regendum. Quem prae omnibus postea, quae gubernavit, locis apud Deum et homines amplificare curavit. Cum autem annum et dimidium nobis praeesset, Constantiae tandem praelatus Dei factus est pastor et episcopus. Sic quoque ipse et Hatto ille Magontinus archiepiscopus

Behold, a reliquary of the cross and merciful Mary with the saints.
Charles has chosen this for his leading chapel to hold.

Ruodker urged Salomo to offer his beloved Saint Gall not gold but himself, as he had often promised to do, and finally make himself a real monk. It came to pass just as *the angel of great counsel* urged. At length after he disclosed his vow to his patron the king, one day, wearing the monk's tunic and cowl and with that very reliquary hanging from his neck, he approached, with Abbot Bernhard's approval, the altar of Saint Gall barefoot. He wept for his sins and, renouncing the world, became a monk of Saint Gall. The abbot treated him quite gently, as a monk from the court, and preferred him above all others who served under him. 2

Not much later, however, the entire commonwealth cried out that it could not do without Salomo's counsel, and with his abbot's permission the king brought him back to court, restoring him to his former honors, even eventually increasing them, for he handed over the monastery of Reichenau to him. In the end, they say, the fortunate man ruled twelve abbeys. 3

11. After Abbot Bernhard was deposed, as related elsewhere, Salomo was presented to us by Archbishop Hatto and assumed the responsibility for our monastery. Afterward he saw to enhancing its importance in the eyes of God and men, ahead of all the other monasteries that he governed. After presiding over us for a year and a half, he was finally made God's prelate in Constance, its pastor and bishop. And thus he held power, second only to the king, together with that Hatto, the archbishop of Mainz, who had

sibi semper amicissimus, quem "cor regis" nominabant, cum et ipse, ut aiunt, duodecim abbatiis praefuerit, post regem imperium tenuerant. Fultensis enim et ille erat monachus et abbas. Qui Magontiam ipsam a loco suo antiquo motam propius Rheno statuerat, et in hoc et in aliis multis animi sui magnitudinem ostenderat.

2 Nondum adhuc illo tempore Suevia in ducatum erat redacta; sed fisco regio peculialiter parebat, sicut hodie et Francia. Procurabant ambas camerae, quos sic vocabant, nuntii: Franciam Adalpert cum Werinhere, Sueviam autem Pertolt et Erchinger fratres. Quorum utrorumque multa dicioni subtracta sunt per munificentias regias in utrosque episcopos. Surgunt inde invidiae et odia utrorumque in ambos. Praeter scelera, quae in reges ipsos machinati sunt, Hattonem Franci illi saepe perdere moliti sunt. Sed astutia hominis in falsam regis gratiam suasi, qualiter Adalpert, fraude eius de urbe Pabinberch detractus, capite sit plexus—alter enim morbo obierat—quoniam vulgo concinnatur et canitur, scribere supersedeo. Ad Salamonem redeo.

12. Huic, sicut diximus, cum aliquae Potamum, camerae nuntiorum iuris oppidum, pertinentia a regibus darentur, sicut Werinhere et Ruodhart domnum Otmarum, sic ipsi insequi conati sunt et ipsum. Sed episcopio et abbatiis ille multiplex variorumque militum manu fortior casu aliquando viris occursaverat, pacem salutando prior, si forte resalutare

always been very friendly with Salomo. Hatto was called "the heart of the king" because he too is said to have presided over twelve abbeys. Now Hatto was also a monk and abbot of Fulda. He ordered Mainz to be moved from its ancient location and placed closer to the Rhine. In this, as in many other things, he showed the greatness of his spirit.

At that time Swabia had not yet been turned into a duchy 2
but was the property of the royal fisc, just like Franconia today. So-called agents of the treasury managed both territories, Adalbert with Werinher in Franconia and two brothers, Berthold and Erchinger, in Swabia. Their power was much diminished because of the king's generosity toward both bishops. As a result, jealousies and grudges arose in both sets of agents against the two bishops. Besides the criminal activity they contrived against the kings themselves, the Franconian agents often attempted to destroy Hatto. But I will refrain from writing about how through Hatto's cunning, they were falsely persuaded that the king favored them and how Adalbert was inveigled by him out of the city of Babenberg and beheaded (for the other agent had died of a disease), because this has all been widely celebrated in tales and songs. I return to Salomo.

12. Since, as I have said, certain properties belonging to Bodman, a town under the jurisdiction of agents of the treasury, were given to him by the kings, so those agents tried to proceed against him just as Werinher and Ruodhard had against Lord Otmar. But Salomo was wealthy through his bishopric and abbacies and more powerful with his band of different sorts of soldiers. One time he met Berthold and Erchinger by chance and, by greeting them first, waited to make peace if they were willing to return his greeting, but in

velint, incassum exspectat; nuntiis post eos missis, qui rem
2 agerent, pacificari nolebant. Ille autem cum prae omnibus sancti Galli claustro semper maneret, quadam nocte praemonitus vim sibi ab illis, nisi fugeret, inferendam, secessit securus in silvam Vallis Turbatae, ea tempestate quidem vastissimam. At illi sancto Gallo invaso episcopum capere volebant, si adesset. Ille vero, capellula in ea solitudine in nomine sancti Galli fabricata, plurimis suorum, ubi esset, ad
3 tempus ignaris, ad aulam nuntiis directis, latuit. Iubentur a rege, tunc quidem Arnoldo, episcopus et ipsi sub banno pacis ad aulam Magontiae venire. Ubi causa publice peracta, rei maiestatis lege pronuntiati ipsi illi in Ingilinheim truduntur, usque dum exilio aut morte punirentur. Egit tandem Salomon cum Hattone episcopo, anxius, ne caedis illorum ipse quidem causa foret, ut eos liberaret. Adeunt supplices ambo secreto imperium. Cor regis molliunt, hostes illos in gratiam reducunt; coram omnibus Salamoni supplices facti pacificantur, potestati pristinae ipso iuvante restituuntur. Redeunt tandem domum tamquam amicissimi iuramento coram rege dato, ne umquam episcopum laederent, numquam episcopum in rebus fiscalibus sibi dono traditis se esse laesuros.

13. Invitantur post haec viri ab episcopo Constantiam ad convivium et munera. Sedetur ad mensam. Et, ut fit, inter

vain. He sent envoys after them to settle the matter, but
they were unwilling to be reconciled. One night Salomo, 2
who always stayed in the monastery of Saint Gall rather
than in all other places, was warned that unless he fled, force
would be brought against him by those men, and he retreated safely into the forest at Turbental, which at that
time was immense. But the royal agents invaded Saint Gall,
intending to capture the bishop if he was there. Salomo, for
his part, erected a small chapel dedicated to Saint Gall in
this wilderness, sent messengers to the court, and remained
in hiding, while for the time being most of his associates did
not know where he was. The bishop and the agents were or- 3
dered by the king, at that point Arnulf, to come to the court
at Mainz under the proclamation of peace. There the case
was judged in public, the royal agents were pronounced
guilty of treason and escorted to Ingelheim to await punishment by exile or death. In the end Salomo, who was anxious
not to become the cause of their execution, took action together with Bishop Hatto to free them. Both bishops came
in secret to plead before the throne. They softened the
king's heart and restored those enemies to royal favor. Before all, they became suppliants and were reconciled with
Salomo, and were restored to their former power with his
help. Finally they returned home acting in the most friendly
fashion, having sworn an oath before the king that they
would never harm the bishop and would never damage the
bishop in the estates of the fisc that had been granted to
him as a gift.

13. After these events the bishop invited the two men to Constance for gifts and a feast. They sat down at the table. As often happens, the guests, while enjoying their drinks,

delicias potationum cum mirarentur artificia vasorum auri argentique, maxime autem vitreorum, episcopus laudis quidem quiddam, ut diximus, avidior, quaedam inter ceteras divitias, quas a regibus haberet, extollens, hospitibus arte tacitis laudis verba etiam de sancti Galli rebus magnis, quibus animos dudum vulneratos offenderat, intulit. Quae ta-
2 men, cum essent levia, mala conflabant gravia. Dixerat enim illis ipse utique indiscrete ludens, habere se apud sanctum Gallum clibanum, qui uno calore ambobus illis panes coqueret in annum; nam mille coqui posse aiunt. Simile etiam quiddam de lebete aeneo grandi et de tarra avenis centum maltrarum commoda cum proiectasset, pastores gregum se habere adiunxit, quibus etiam ipsi, si viros viderent, pilleis capitibus inclinarent detractis. Patienter tulerunt homines fraudulenti episcopi gloriam usque ad capitum pastoribus inclinationes; id enim numquam fieri posse refellentes loquuntur.

3 Afferuntur tamen viris animosis cara munera tandem recessuris. Inter quae erant vascula duo vitrea nimis insignia, quae ipsi pridem in convivio prae ceteris mirabantur. Quae illi in manus sumentes, consilio latenti uterque suum decidere sinens, frustata ridebant. Ceteris omnibus, milia gratiarum episcopo remittentes, callide abstinebant. Missione tandem data cum eos praesul osculo peteret: "Vestra," inquit, "erant; ideo vos tanti pretii pocula confringere non piguit. Sed multa animabus vestris, si ea pro nummis dantes

admired some vessels, skillfully made of gold, silver, and especially glass. The bishop, who, as I have said, was all too eager for a certain amount of praise, after extolling some pieces, among other riches that he had received from kings, went on, since they remained tactfully silent, to praise the fine treasures of Saint Gall, thereby offending their already wounded spirits. Salomo's words, though spoken in a light
vein, kindled serious trouble. For instance, he told them, 2
undoubtedly with thoughtless mockery, that at Saint Gall he had an oven which could at one firing bake enough bread to last the two of them for a year, for it is said that it could bake a thousand loaves. In the same vein, he also threw out a remark about a large bronze cauldron and an oat kiln that could easily hold four hundred pecks of oats. He added that he had shepherds before whom, if his guests only saw them, they would pull their hats off and bow down. The guests patiently listened to the bishop's tall tales up to the bowing before the shepherds; for that, they said in rebuttal, could never happen.

Finally, when the two angry men were about to leave, ex- 3
pensive gifts were brought to them. Among the gifts there were two very remarkable glass vessels, which the men had admired more than the rest earlier during the feast. They took the vessels in their hands, and by unspoken agreement each let his vessel fall to the ground and laughed at the broken fragments. They craftily refrained from damaging any other objects, thanking the bishop profusely. Finally, when they had taken their leave and the bishop was leaning in to kiss them, he said: "Those precious drinking vessels were yours; so I was not annoyed that you broke them. But if you had given them to the poor in place of money, you could

pauperibus dedissetis, remedia facere poteratis." "Vitrei," inquiunt, "amici vitro sunt donandi; sed nos, qui vitrei esse nolumus, vitrum confregimus." Amoreque, ut moris est, osculato et epoto laetabundi discedunt.

14. Non multo post tempore Chuonradus tunc rex natale Domini Constantiae egit. Ipsa die post mensam cum episcopus ei processiones vespertinas tridui illius apud sanctum Gallum laudaret: "Rex," inquit, "o utinam ibi essemus!" "Et quare illuc, anime mi, matutini non ibimus?" Parantur continuo naves. Quibus mane conscensis cum episcopis et cetero comitatu rex litus nostrum meridianus attigit et sancto Gallo cum tripudiis appropians novis laudibus dictatis in loco gloriose susceptus est. Tribusque noctibus in omni hilaritate loco immoratus, quarto die Arbonam tandem nocturnus venit.

2 Longum est dicere, quibus iocunditatibus dies exegerit et noctes, maxime in processione infantum. Quibus poma in medio ecclesiae pavimento antesterni iubens, cum nec unum parvissimorum moveri nec ad ea attendere vidisset, miratus est disciplinam. Refectorium quoque fratrum hora mensae cum duobus episcopis cum intrasset in infantum die, plura sibi assurgentibus laeta locutus: "Nobiscum," ait, "velitis nolitis, partiri habebitis." Decanum autem, qui

have done your souls much good." They answered, "Glass friends should be given glass, but we don't want to be glass friends; so we broke the glass." After they had lovingly kissed, as is customary, and had finished their drinks, they departed full of joy.

14. Shortly after this, Conrad, who was then king, spent Christmas at Constance. On Christmas Day itself after the meal the bishop began singing the praises of the evening processions that took place at Saint Gall over three nights. He said: "Oh, my king, if only we could be there!" "Then," said the king, "why don't we go there tomorrow morning, my dear friend?" Ships were made ready immediately. In the morning the king, along with the bishops and the rest of his retinue went on board, and by noon they reached our shore. After approaching Saint Gall to the accompaniment of great rejoicing, he received a glorious welcome at the monastery with new hymns of praise. For three nights he stayed there among all joyful celebrations; finally in the evening of the fourth day he arrived at Arbon.

It would take too long to tell you how delightfully the 2
king spent those days and nights at Saint Gall, particularly at the children's procession. The king ordered that apples be scattered in front of the children in the middle of the paved floor of the church, and when he saw that not even the smallest child was excited by or paid any attention to the apples, he was amazed at their discipline. Also, on the Feast of the Innocents, the king entered the refectory with two bishops when the brothers were having their meal and spoke long and cheerfully to the brothers, who rose to greet him. He said: "You will have to share with us, willy-nilly." He

mensa abbatis sui causa cedere parabat, amplexatum retinens assedit. Et ei apposita ad se sumens, omnes circumspectans et arridens: "His interim," inquit, "participemur."

3 Misit autem quantocius ad Salamonem, ne sibi superveniret, sed uterque pro altero mensas teneret. Praeposito dein cum nihil sibi, nisi quod fratribus paratum esset, iuberet apponi: "O rex," inquit, "nostra infortunia, quod superventurum diem non exspectabas! Cras enim panem et fabas nudas forsitan habebimus, sed hodie non sic." "Enimvero," ait ille, "et cras vobis Deus misereri poterit." Infantulis deinde per ordinem lectitantibus et analogio descendentibus aureos in ora ad se elevatis misit. Quorum unus pusillior cum clamitans aurum exspueret: "*Iste,*" inquit, "*si vixerit,* bonus quandoque monachus *erit.*" Surgens tandem a mensa, hilariter fratribus multa locutus, optime spei esse monebat, quoniam, si adviveret, tales convivas laetificaret. Rediit igitur ad suos, Salamoni et omnibus numquam se laetius convivatum gloriatus.

15. Inter haec autem Perhtoldum et Erchingerum tristes invenit et exasperatos. Causam quaesivit hilariter. Quae quidem haec erat. Magistri pastorum duo, *homines* utique *silvestres,* hirsuti et prolixis barbis, ut id genus multum videri solet, quasi venerandi, cum tales pridie pro ferina iuberentur die nocteque laborare, ursum de lustro unus, alter

restrained the dean who was about to leave the abbot's table to make room for him, embraced him, and sat down beside him. And taking up what was placed before him, the king looked around the table at everyone, laughed, and said: "In the meantime let's share this!"

He sent a message with all speed to Salomo, telling him 3
not to come, but saying that each of them should hold a feast on behalf of the other. He then ordered the provost to serve him only the food that had been prepared for the brothers. "Oh my king," the provost said, "it is our misfortune that you did not wait a day to arrive. Tomorrow, you see, we may have bread and plain beans, which we do not have today." The king answered, "Tomorrow, too, God can have mercy on you." Then as little children performed readings and came down from the pulpit one by one, the king had them lifted up to him, and he placed golden coins in their mouths. When one rather small child cried out and spat out the coin, the king said: "*This one will make* a good monk someday, *if he lives.*" Finally, getting up from the table, the king spoke of many things jovially with the brothers and encouraged them to be of good cheer, because if he lived with them, he would rejoice in such table companions. He returned home, boasting to Salomo and everyone else that he had never had a merrier feast.

15. Meanwhile, the king found Berthold and Erchinger sad and embittered. He cheerfully asked them the reason, and it was this: Two chief herdsmen, veritable *men of the woods,* shaggy haired and with flowing beards, looking almost venerable, as their kind often does, had been ordered the day before to hunt for game day and night. One of them had brought back from the woods a bear and the other a

cervum recens occisos attulerat. Quod Salamoni cum ministri super mensam silentio intimarent, iubet homines feras
fratribus illis, qui per se quidem tunc mensa utebantur ut
2 primates, oblatione propria offerre. Fingebantur autem
vicini esse et liberi. Quibus talibus aspectis assurgunt germani, pilleis detractis regratiant venatores reverenter inclinati. Quod videns episcopus ante dictorum memor secum
gaudebat. At illi scioli quidem facti feras coram episcopo
poni fecerant a dicentibus: "Sint tua tibi; nobis satis est
haberi derisui." Timore tamen imperii animum prementes
iram fregerant.

3 Quod rex sapiens prudenti leniit consilio: "Quoniam ad gaudia quidem convenimus, mei iuris est," inquit, "omnia nullius periculi ludicra defendere et, si in rixas venerint, imperiali decreto annullare. Quapropter sedato animo, iudices mei, ambos vos esse volo et in gratiam redire cum episcopo." Reconciliantur enim umbratili pace tunc secundo.

16. At rex vesperum et noctem cum egisset hilariter, diluculo conventum fratrum petens, omnium votis faventibus fit frater conscriptus. Tribuit cuique fratrum argenti libram, ut habeat ad vestitum. Puerolis edixit tres dies ad ludendum, et tunc quidem et in posterum. Ingressusque sancti Galli basilicam palliis vestivit altaria. Immunitatem etiam loci a Crimaldo inceptam, sed adhuc non firmam, episcopo admittente ipse manu sua et sigillo solidam fecit et perpetuam.

deer that they had just killed. When servants silently informed Salomo of this during a meal, he ordered the two men to offer the animals as their own gifts to the brothers who, being of noble birth, had a table to themselves at that
time. The shepherds were falsely presented as neighbors 2
and free men. Perceiving them as such, the brothers stood up, pulled off their hats, and gave thanks to the hunters, bowing respectfully. Seeing this, the bishop, mindful of what had been said earlier, was secretly amused. Now, when the brothers realized their folly, they had the animals placed before the bishop with the following message: "What is yours should be restored to you; for us it is enough to have been mocked." Fear of the king, however, forced them to suppress their anger.

The wise king defused the tension with good advice: 3
"Since we have gathered here to rejoice," he said, "it is within my authority to protect all forms of amusements that are not dangerous, and if any should descend into squabbling, to annul them by royal decree. Because of this, I want both of you, my judges, to calm down and go back to being on good terms with the bishop." For a second time they were then reconciled in a tenuous peace.

16. After spending the evening and night happily, the king came early in the morning to the brothers' assembly and by a unanimous vote became an enrolled brother. He gave each brother a pound of silver for buying clothes. For the little children he instituted three days of play, both on that occasion and in perpetuity. He entered the basilica of Saint Gall and decorated the altars with fine altar cloths. With his own hand and seal and with the bishop's approval, the king also made firm and permanent the monastery's immunity granted during Grimald's time but not yet confirmed.

2 Ingreditur tandem oratorium beati Otmari auctoritate Romana in sanctum levati—nam parentes eius erant, qui eum vexaverant—seque reum, quasi ipse interfuerit factis, ad eius aram reddidit; palliis quoque, auro et argento sanctum placavit. Sed et circa Stamhem villam sancto Otmaro a Karolo datam quaedam loca regii iuris adhuc erant. Ille vero, quicquid inibi regii fisci erat, totum in manum advocati super aram eius tradiderat et sigillo suo roboraverat. Et conversus ad Salamonem: "Eo," inquit, "pacto, ut fratres nostri conscripti pro convivio nostro hesterno habundantius a Karolo statutam hebdomadam natalis domini mei huius etiam in memoriam mei debeant convivari." Et subridens: "Nam et ego hodie frater conscriptus volo prandere cum fratribus et fabas nostras de meo piperare."

3 Aguntur celeres regi missae a fratribus super id ipsum altare. Praematuratur prandium; impletur refectorium; vix unum lector recitaverat periodum. *Caritas,* quae *non agit perperam,* licenter sprevit disciplinam. Nemo ait hoc aut illud esse insolitum, quamvis ante numquam sit visum vel auditum. Numquam ea domo saporatum monachum odorem ferinae hauriunt et carnium. Saltant satirici; psallunt symphoniaci. Numquam tale per se tripudium Galli habuit refectorium. Graviores fratrum rex spectat inter strepitum, ridet quorundam vultus contractos propter rerum talium insolentiam.

Finally, the king entered the oratory of the blessed Otmar, who had been elevated to sainthood by the authority of Rome, and he acknowledged his own guilt before the altar, as if he had taken part in those acts himself, though it was the king's ancestors who had persecuted the saint; he also placated the saint by the gifts of precious cloths, gold, and silver. Near the village of Stammheim, which Charles had given to Saint Otmar, there were also some places that were still under the king's jurisdiction. Whatever belonged therein to the royal fisc the king transferred into the hand of the advocate upon the altar of Otmar and confirmed this with his seal. Turning to Salomo, the king said: "With the understanding that, in recognition of our shared feast yesterday, our enrolled brothers will be obliged to feast more lavishly during the week celebrating this lord of mine, instituted by Charles, and also in memory of me." And smiling, he added: "As an enrolled brother, I also want to eat with my brothers today, and I want to add pepper from my bounty to our beans." 2

The brothers promptly celebrated Mass for the king on that very altar. The meal started early; the refectory filled with monks; the lector had barely recited one sentence. *Love that does no wrong* freely disregarded discipline. No one said that this or that was unusual, even though it had never been seen or heard before. Never had the monks sniffed the savory smell of game and meat in their house. Actors danced; musicians played their instruments. Never had the refectory of Saint Gall had such rejoicing for its own sake. The king looked at the more severe of the brothers in the midst of the din and laughed at how some of them frowned at the unaccustomed nature of such matters. 3

4 Carpuntur iterum cordibus fratres illi saepe dicti pro damno regii fisci. Nam castellum quoddam super Stamhem iamdudum struxerant, quod conquisitionis suae proprietate coram rege sibi vindicabant. Quibus rex: “Castellum,” inquit, “sine oppidanorum damno habere nequibitis; quibus si iniuriosi quidem fueritis, mei gratia carebitis.” Discedit rex vespertinus fratrum suorum laudibus lacrimosis prosecutus. Quibus, si vivere liceret, non semel benefacturum promiserat.

17. Invadit loca lege Almannica cum advocato episcopus, tribus diebus, uti ius erat, homines fisci iuramentis sancto Otmaro vindicantes. Quibus custodes castelli, nisi sibi pareant, male habituros minantur minasque factis exsequuntur. Nam victimas et cetera, quae libebat, sponte nolentibus dare fiscalibus, vi quidem auferebant. Quod cum advocatus tum per se tum verbis Salamonis fratribus illis non semel quereretur, aut ficta verba aut iniuriosa passus recessit. Cumque hoc per annum paene pateretur, quadam die ipse viris obvius iniurias queritur episcopus. Et cum indigne quidem ipsius verba tulissent, episcopus subintulit: “Enimvero,” ait, “cum mei causa in eis aliquando angustiis coram rege Arnolfo fueritis, unde aegerrime ego ipse vos eripui, iam eius articuli semper liceat recordari.”

2 Ilico Luitfridus, sororis amborum filius, iuvenis pertinacissimus: “Gloriaturne,” inquit, “monachorum sceleratissimus iniuriarum pro se vobis inlatarum, o avunculi, et *vivere*

The oft-mentioned brothers were once again pained in 4
their hearts on account of the damage to the royal fisc. Much earlier, you see, they had built a castle above Stammheim, and in the king's presence they claimed it as theirs by right of conquest. The king said to them: "You will not be able to hold the castle without harm to the townsfolk, and if you injure them, you will lose my favor." The king left in the evening, to the accompaniment of tearful praise from his brothers. He promised to confer benefits on them repeatedly, if he were allowed to live.

17. In accordance with Alemannic law the bishop, accompanied by the advocate boldly made his way to the place and for three days, as the law allowed, they sought to avenge the men of the fisc in fulfillment of their oaths to Saint Otmar. The wardens of the castle threatened that they would suffer badly if they did not do as they said, and followed up their threats with action. When the men of the fisc refused to willingly give animals to be slaughtered and other items the wardens wanted, they took them by force. But when the advocate repeatedly complained to the brothers, not only on his own account but also in the words of Salomo, he was met with either lies or insults and left. After enduring this for almost a year, one day the bishop himself encountered the brothers and complained to them about their wrongdoing. When they bristled at his words, the bishop added: "When you were in the narrowest of straits with King Arnulf back then on my account and I myself just barely rescued you—may you always keep that episode in mind."

At that very moment Liutfrid, the son of the sister of 2
both of them and a really obstinate young man, said, "Is this most nefarious of monks boasting of the wrongs he has committed against you, my uncles, and *you are letting* him

eum *patimini?*" Extractoque gladio, nisi ab ambobus premeretur, episcopum occidisset. Ipse autem, ut iugulum declinaret, cum citius equo diverteret, a fratribus ambobus freno tentus comprehensus est. Quidam autem suorum cum gladium educentem iuvenem illum ipse econtra gladio stricto incurrere vellet, lanceis circumvallantium transfixus interiit.

3 Ducitur episcopus in diverticulum quoddam propinquum, ubi descendere iussus sedit, usque dum illi in partem cedentes, quid de eo facturi sint, tractent. Ipse autem confisus in Domino suum dominum Gallum incessanter inclamitat.

18. Suadet Luifridus, ut ei aut oculos eruant aut dexteram abscidant. Militum autem pars sanior, ne quid *amplius in* christum Domini *insanirent,* omnimodis flagitat; sed et incolumem relinqui optimum fore aiebant. Stat tandem fratribus consilium, ut in Thietpoldispurch, ubi Perhta, uxor Erchingeri, tunc agebat, duceretur. Ipsam enim, cum esset quidem alias strenua, ad dolos acutissimam aiebant, et, quoniam ei amore mariti saepe ante male optabat, incunctanter eum quoquo modo apud illam periturum.

2 Sternitur viro Dei vilior interea equus. Porcarii autem cum viderent turbam, ad spectandum accurrunt. Quibus visis Perhtolt: "Inclinare coram istis," inquit, "Dei maledicte, et, ut tibi veniam precentur, pedes eis lambe!" Ille vero, quoniam vim sciebat, quod iussus est, fecerat. Commissus

live?" He drew his sword and would have killed the bishop if both his uncles had not restrained him. When Salomo quickly turned away on his horse to avoid having his throat slashed, the two brothers grabbed his reins and seized him. As Liutfrid was in the act of unsheathing his sword, one of Salomo's men responded by charging with drawn sword but was impaled by the lances of the surrounding men and killed.

The bishop was taken to a nearby hideout, where, or- 3
dered to dismount, he took a seat while the men went off to the side and discussed what they were going to do about him. He trusted in the Lord and kept calling on his lord, Saint Gall, to aid him.

18. Liutfrid argued that they should either rip out his eyes or cut off his right hand. But the more reasonable group of fighting men urged them by no means *to act with any further madness against* the Lord's anointed. They said it would be best if he were left completely unharmed. Finally the brothers agreed on a plan for him to be taken to Thietpoldsburg, where Erchinger's wife, Bertha, was staying at that time. Though no sluggard in other respects, she was, they maintained, especially sharp-witted at trickery, and since out of love for her husband she had often wished the bishop ill in the past, they thought that in her hands he would promptly perish one way or other.

Meanwhile they saddled up a cheaper horse for the man 2
of God. Swineherds saw the crowd and ran up to have a look. When Berthold saw them, he said, "Bow before them, you cursed by God, and to get them to beg for mercy on your behalf, lick their feet!" Seeing where the power lay, he did as he was ordered. Finally, he was handed over to guards

tandem satellitibus, qui eum ducerent, Perthae qui factum panderet, celer praemittitur. At mulier facinore audito percutiens pectus ingemuit et: "Haec," inquit, "est dies, quae honoribus nostris apud Deum et homines finem datura est." Parat ilico basilicam et aram. Parat tapetiis et pallio dorsuali caminatam. Evangelio episcopum aliquos, qui aderant, pres-
3 byteros recipere iubet. Progreditur adventanti ipsa obviam ad portam. In manum illum sumens, si se dignetur osculari, lacrimans rogat. At milites dolo haec fieri sibimet silenter aiebant. Paratur citissime lavacrum, ut pulvere et lassitudinis tergeretur sudore. Verebatur et ipse, quamvis fortunatus, infortunia. Clauditur caminata super episcopum et duos solos, qui aderant, presbyteros. Nam, ut ipsum dixisse aiunt, quietam noctem agere poterat, nisi quod *tubarum clangores* et vigilum aegre passus est clamores. Ingreditur ad hospitem tantum illa cum una sola pedisequa. Salutem homini et maturum ad suos pollicetur reditum. Reficit cum reficiente. Per puellam sibi, per presbyteros apponitur episcopo.

19. Postquam episcopum viri illi a se, ut dictum est, dimiserant, Duellium montem, victualia convehentes, nocte die nituntur munire; ipsi interim cum suis, quos haberent, fidissimis clandestini agere, in silvis pascuosis noctibus delitescere. Intimantur tertia tanti facinoris nocte Sigefrido, episcopi patrui filio. Qui ilico propinquis et episcopi

to take him away, and a courier was sent ahead to tell Bertha
what had happened. But when the woman heard about the
evil deed, she beat her breast, groaned, and said, "This is the
day that will bring an end to our honorable standing before
God and men." Straightaway she prepared the church and
altar. She prepared a chamber with tapestries and drapery
for his back, and she ordered some priests who were in attendance to receive the bishop with a Gospel book. As he 3
approached, she herself went out to meet him at the gate.
Taking him by the hand, she asked him tearfully if he would
deign to kiss her. The soldiers, meanwhile, were whispering
to one another that she was doing this as a trick. A bath was
quickly prepared to wash away the dust and sweat from his
exhausting ordeal. Salomo himself, though blessed with
good fortune, was afraid that bad fortune was in store. The
chamber door was shut tight behind the bishop and two
lone priests who were attending him. As they say he himself
said, he was able to spend the night undisturbed, if he did
not mind the *blasts of trumpets* and the watchmen's cries.
Bertha went in to see her guest with just a single maidservant. She promised him safekeeping and a speedy return to
his people. She shared a meal with him, served to her by the
girl and to the bishop by the priests.

19. After the men sent the bishop off, as reported above, they gathered provisions and worked day and night to secure the fortress at Mount Hohentwiel. They themselves meanwhile remained secretly active with the most loyal men they had and at night were hiding in woodland pastures. On the third night after their terrible crime, Siegfried, the son of the bishop's uncle, got wind of it. At once he rounded up as many of the bishop's kin and fighting men as

militibus, quantis *hora concluso* licuit, collectis in silva quadam matutinus eos aggreditur dormientes. Experrecti vero pauci contra turmas loricis et galeis tutas arma rapiunt inutilia. Ipsos tres viros, quamvis animose repugnantes, armis exuunt, *vivos comprehendunt,* vinctos abducunt.

2 Currunt ilico celeres, qui Perthae et urbanis suis dicerent, nisi christum Domini citissime solverent, dominos suos machinis pensilibus impositos tribus partibus urbis in faciem sibi ad solem torrendos. Quo audito custodes falli se primo aestimantes, certiores facti omnes urbe viris vacuefacta dilapsi sunt. Relinquitur episcopus liber cum presbyteris et Pertha *flens et eiulans* cum pedisequis. Quam tamen ipse pro tempore consolatus, manu tenens urbis portas obviam suis egreditur. Nam nocte proxima cum eo de furtiva dimissione per quoddam latens ostiolum condixit, quoniam sibi per nuntium viri sui innotuit nocte alia illum aut Duellium aut, quod magis timebat, ad perdendum esse transportandum.

3 Fuga urbanorum comperta equis potentiores praevolant curraces. Episcopo pro portis conspecto, clamativo illum cantu salutant: "*Heil herro! Heil liebo!*" et cetera. Urbem tamen intrare praeter nominatos propter mulieris res servandas episcopus noluit. Nam in itinere armatorum se suis adiungentium et prosequentium turba erat innumerabilis. Tum virum alloqui mulieri desideranti solus ad horam

he could *on short notice,* and at dawn he attacked the sleepers in a wood. Awakened, a few men grabbed weapons, but these were of no avail against troops protected by helmets and coats of mail. Although the three resisted valiantly, the attackers stripped them of their weapons, *captured them alive,* tied them up, and led them away.

At once couriers raced to tell Bertha and her garrison that 2
if they did not release the Lord's anointed very quickly, their own lords would be put in suspended cages at three sides of the castle to burn in the sun before their very eyes. When they heard this, the guards at first thought they were being tricked, but as they became more convinced, they all slipped away, leaving the castle emptied of men. The bishop was set free with the priests, while Bertha was *weeping and wailing* with her attendants. He consoled her for a while, and then took her by the hand and went out of the fortress gates to meet his men. On the previous night she had discussed with him a secret escape through a little hidden doorway since she had learned through a message from her husband that on the next night his captors intended to convey him either to Hohentwiel or—what she feared even more—to certain death.

When they learned that the garrison had fled, the more 3
powerful men dashed forth on their horses at a gallop. When they caught sight of the bishop before the gates, they greeted him with a clamorous chant: "Hail, lord! Hail, beloved!" and so on. But to protect the woman's property, the bishop refused to let anyone enter the fortress except those named by him, because the throng of armed men that had joined his retinue on the march and was following along was countless. Just at that moment Erchinger was brought alone

adducitur. Quem complexa, cum prae fletu naribus cruor proflueret, vix ab ipso quoque plorante avellitur. Movebat et inimicos tam repentina *rerum mutatio.* Episcopo autem cum vinctus procidens sibi remitti supplicaret: "Quantum in me est," inquit, "remitto," et a custodibus iratis amotum benedictione prosequitur.

4 Egit tamen cum nepote et militibus, ut mulier ad suos cum honore et rebus suis duceretur tutatis. Et cum ibi pernoctassent, ipse eius omnia bona fidelibus suis commendans ordinavit avehenda. Dimittens autem illam invitavit ad se, rebus in melius vergentibus, Constantiam, ut, si fidei memor sit, in laetiori experiretur fortunio. Rediit cum comitatu famoso Petrus alter ereptus ab Herodibus Constantiam, tali omnium circumquaque convenientium quidem tripudio, quali nec, si ipse quondam Romae *tertius de caelo ceciderit,* receptus sit *Cato.*

20. Traduntur damnosi tres illi in Duellium ad cognitionem publicam reservandi, plurimis suorum iam, si forte ad ereptionem illorum in via occasio daretur, in arma collectis. Quod milites abbatiarum et episcopii cum cognatis christi Domini circumvallando providebant. *Innotuit res* Chuonrado, in Francia tunc posito. Nam *veredarii,* et episcopo capto et recepto, dies et noctes *celeres* ibant. Aiebant autem

to his wife, who wanted to speak to her husband. She embraced him, and crying so hard that blood flowed from her nose, she could scarcely be torn from him as he wept, too. Such a sudden *change of fortune* moved even their enemies. However, when the bound man fell down before the bishop and begged his forgiveness, he said, "Insofar as it lies with me, *I* forgive you," and he dispatched him with a blessing as the enraged guards took him away.

However, Salomo saw to it with his cousin and the 4
knights that the wife should be returned to her people with her dignity and property intact. And after they had spent the night there, he personally arranged for all her property to be taken safely away, entrusting it to his loyal men. As he sent her off, he invited her to visit him in Constance once conditions started to improve, so that she could see under happier circumstances if he kept his word. A second Peter rescued from his Herods, he returned to Constance with his storied retinue amid such demonstrations of joy from crowds gathered from all around as not even *a third Cato* would have received if one had ever *fallen from the sky* at Rome.

20. While those three troublemakers were being conveyed to Hohentwiel to be held there for an official hearing, large numbers of their people in arms had already gathered just in case an opportunity arose for rescuing the three on the way. The fighting men from the abbeys and the bishopric, along with the relatives of Christ's anointed, foresaw this possibility and forestalled it by surrounding the prisoners on all sides. *News of the affair reached* Conrad in Franconia, where he was staying at that moment. *Couriers* were *racing* day and night to report on the bishop's capture

illum mane evigilantem, fama a prioribus audita, lecto exilisse et patientiam regiam nullo modo tenere potuisse; a sequentibus autem corde sibi reddito parumper quievisse. *In se* vero *reversus* de valitudine capti et recepti cum quaesisset: "Constat," inquiunt, "O rex, dure tractatum adhuc male valere; et si, quia mox venturus sit, nosset, per nos vobis profecto mandasset." Quo audito seorsum cedens *flevit; erumpebant* enim *lacrimae* et non poterant se *continere.*

2 Consilio dehinc habito, primo colloquium publicum Magontiae, postea generale edixit concilium. Ubi tribus illis lege abiuratis et proscriptis praediisque eorum in fiscum redactis, maiestatis reis capita damnata sunt. Ceteris omnibus, qui tanto facinori intererant, tamquam rei publicae hostibus prosequi iussis, Sueviae principum assensu statuitur Alemannis dux primus Purchardus, gentis illius nobilissimus et virtutum dote probatissimus. Cui et praedia damnatorum confiscata in beneficium sunt tradita, exceptis dotibus Perhtae, sibimet edicto, quoniam viro non assenserat, stabilitis. Episcopo autem apud ducem indutias damnatis rogante, ut, si fieri posset, exilium eis a rege intercederet, aliquot eos dies dux in custodia tenuit. Rex autem crebro ab eo fatigatus tandem eos iugulari praecepit. Quibus tamen episcopus multum eorum nece tristatus, indulgentia, quantum

and subsequent release. They said that when the king awoke in the morning and heard the tale from those first to arrive, he sprang from his bed and could by no means maintain his royal patience. But he took heart at the news brought by the next couriers and calmed down a bit. When, *having regained his composure,* he asked about the condition of the man who had been captured and released, they told him, "It is evident, O king, that he was roughly treated and is still in bad shape, and if he knew he would be able to come here soon, he would certainly have sent word to you through us." When the king heard this, he went away and *wept, for the tears poured out* and they could not *be held back.*

Then after taking counsel, he first announced a public as- 2
sembly at Mainz, to be followed by a general synod. There the three were legally repudiated and outlawed with their estates returned to the fisc, and condemned to death for high treason. As for all the rest who were involved in this terrible crime, they were to be pursued as enemies of the state. With the consent of the leading men of Swabia, Burchard, the noblest of that family and the one most richly endowed with virtues, was proclaimed duke of Alemannia. The estates confiscated from the condemned were also assigned to him as a benefice, except for Bertha's dowry, ensured for her by an edict, because she did not side with her husband. When the bishop asked the duke for a stay of execution, so that he could intercede with the king and if possible obtain for them the punishment of exile, the duke held them in custody for a few days. But the king, wearied by the bishop's incessant importuning on their behalf, finally had them executed. Their deaths deeply saddened the bishop. While they were still alive he absolved them, as much as it

in se erat, etiam vivis data, sepulturam concessit ad ecclesiam.

21. Rex vero castellum illud odiosum sancto Otmaro, *causam mali tanti,* tradidit diruendum. Omnique anno ille, dum vixit, censum capitis sui in cera ad sepulchrum eius, uti filius carnificum illorum, pro reatu in eum quasi proprio misit. Quod et Ruodolfus postea, Welfhardi comitis pater, cum eiusdem quidem prosapiae fuerit, in censu calibum de metallo Faucium Iuliarum fecit. Sed id ipsum Welfhardus et Henricus, filii eius, aliquot annis dum facerent, motus rubore Henricus, quasi homo sit censarius, fratre invito censum supersedit. Accidit autem, ut in vigiliarum sancti Otmari die fratres ambo capreum venantes, in cacumen quoddam rupis artissimae ducti, lassi cum consedissent, repente petra, super quam Henricus sedit, collapsa, adolescens ille magnae indolis, pro dolor, in profundissimas valles rueret et periret. Vix spiritum habere poterat mater orbata. Scripturi nunc sumus, quod vidimus. Necdum luctu finito, cum filio et filia unicis ad pedes sancti cum muneribus et calibe supersesso venit; quod in censu non soluto peccatum est, tres pro se et defuncto paenituerunt.

2 Salamon autem videns fortunam, ut solet, ludicra rotae reciprocare, immo *Deum in se* non occultis indiciis *potentiam suam ostendere,* apud imperium severus *accusator sui,* permisso dato Romam petiit flens et eiulans atque dicens: "*Merito haec*

lay in his power to do so, and he allowed them a church burial.

21. The king gave that hateful castle, *the cause of such great misery,* to Saint Otmar to be destroyed. And every year for the rest of his life the king, as a descendant of those murderers, sent a tribute in wax to the saint's tomb, in compensation for the crime against the saint as if it had been his own. Rudolf, the father of Count Welfhard, later did the same, since he also came from that stock, and paid his tribute in iron from the mine of Füssen. His sons, Welfhard and Henry, also did the same for a while, until Henry against his brother's wishes stopped doing so out of shame, because it made him look like a tribute payer. Then it so happened that on the eve of Saint Otmar's Day, when the two brothers were hunting a goat, they chased it up to the top of a very narrow crag and sat down exhausted, the rock on which Henry had sat suddenly gave way and alas, this young man of great talents tumbled down into the valley far below and was killed. The bereaved mother could barely keep her will to live. Now I will write down what I saw myself. While still in mourning, the mother with her only remaining son and her only daughter kneeled at the feet of the saint, bearing gifts and the iron that had been withheld; for the sin of the unpaid tribute, those three did penance for themselves and for the deceased.

As for Salomo, when he saw that Fortune, playing her 2
usual game, was turning her wheel around, or rather that *God was demonstrating his might to him* with no uncertain signs, the bishop appeared before the king as an unforgiving *accuser of himself.* Given permission, he went to Rome, weeping and lamenting in this vein: "*I have deserved to suffer these*

passus sum, quia peccavi coram Deo in caelum. Veniam petere habeo ab ipso, miserante me Petro." A papa vero benigne susceptus, cum ibi supplicans aliquamdiu moraretur, indulgentiam sibi ab eo plorans petiit—maxime autem, quod sui causa tres illi quidem decapitati sint—paenitentiae quem vellet modum sibi, rogavit, imponeret. Tandem autem ab apostolico indulgentiam adeptus, domum redire laetanter aggreditur. Reliquiisque sanctorum donatus quam plurimis, maxime animo toto reditu suo contenderat, quomodo illas, quam decentissime posset, domum veniens honorificaret: prae ceteris autem corpus Pelagii martyris, in cuius die inimicis suis subactis ipse liberatus est a vinculis. Qui cum multorum miraculorum virtutibus insignis esset, cottidie rumor eius non solum proximas sed et exteras Constantiam fecit orandi causa turmatim confluere regiones.

Opinabile autem erat, in quantum se post reditum suum in virtutibus christus Dei exercuerit: quam assiduus nocte dieque in precibus, quam largus in dando, maxime autem pauperibus, quam promptus et assiduus in pacificationibus.

22. Accidit autem, ut, eo quidem domum reverso, Hatto archiepiscopus, sodes utique, ut sibimet dicebant, suus, Italiam ius regium exacturus tendens, Constantiam deveniret. Aiebant autem illum Magontinis suis minus confisum totum, quod in thesauris haberet, sodali suo, dum rediret, commissurum secum tulisse. Erat autem sodalitatis illorum, quoniam ambo acutissimi erant, ius mirabile. Nam uterque illorum, in quo alterum in verbis et in rebus per astutiam

things, because I have sinned before God against heaven. With Peter's mercy, I will beg him to forgive me." Salomo was graciously received by the pope; after kneeling there in supplication for some time, he tearfully begged the pope to absolve his sins (especially because those three men had certainly been beheaded on his account), and he asked the pope to impose on him whatever kind of penance he wished. Having finally obtained absolution from the pope, Salomo happily set out to return home. He had received a great number of saints' relics as gifts, and all the way back he was thinking how to honor them in the most appropriate way possible once he reached home; above all, Salomo cherished the body of Pelagius the martyr, on whose day Salomo's enemies had been defeated and he had been set free from his bonds. He was famous for the power shown by his many miracles, and his fame caused large crowds, not only from the regions nearby but also from a distance, to flock to Constance daily to pray.

It is also worth noting how eager the Lord's anointed was in his practice of virtues after his return: how assiduous in praying day and night, how liberal in giving, especially to the poor, how prompt and assiduous in peacemaking.

22. After Salomo had returned home, it happened that Archbishop Hatto, his best friend as they called each other, came to Constance on his way to Italy, where he was headed in order to demand the king's justice. They used to say that Hatto had little trust in his Mainz subjects and brought all his valuables with him so that he might entrust them to his friend until his return. Now since both were very cunning, their friendship had an amazing quality. Each man usually did his best to deploy his cunning in words or deeds to de-

decipere posset, agere solebat. Ut in cantharo quodam, quo Salomon utebatur, gemmato gravissimi ponderis aureo. Quo cum uterque, ut solebant, coram convivis ieiuni aquam quasi vinum potarent, Salamon autem in conclavi vase quodam aeneo mire figurato ad aquam inferendam uteretur, Hatto abiturus inter cetera viro ait: "Vas illud aquae," inquit, "quo in conclavi tuo uteris, mihi, sodes, tribue!" Quo hilariter annuente Hatto pincernae ait latenter: "Coppam auream domini tui, quoniam sic ego et sodes meus," inquit, "condiximus, pincernae meo confestim offerto!" Quod mox, uti ille iussus est, fecerat. Ablata est coppa, fraude amica interim tecta. At Salamon mensa sequenti dum eam exegisset, deceptum se sentiens: "Enimvero si vixero," ait, "idem illi modius remetietur."

2 Thesaurosque suos postea, uti praemisimus, sodali suo sodes eo pacto, ut, si defunctum audiret, pro animabus amborum, quibus vellet, eos dilapidaret, abiens consignaverat. Vix mensis, ut aiunt, abiit, et mercatores ab Italia redeuntes defunctum Salomon diffamare per nuntios praemonuit. Doloreque ad horam simulato, scriniis reclusis multos denarios distribuit pauperibus. Fabrorum quoque copia contracta, cantharum quondam suum primo dispertiens, sarcophagum illud magnificum, quod hodie miramur, sancto Pelagio ex

ceive the other, as happened, for instance, with regard to a certain drinking bowl that Salomo used, which was made of gold, studded with precious stones, and very heavy. In front of their table companions, both men when fasting drank water out of it as if it was wine, while in his chamber Salomo used a wonderfully molded bronze vessel for water. When Hatto was about to leave, he said to Salomo among other things: "My friend, why don't you give me that vessel for water that you use in your chamber?" When Salomo cheerfully agreed, Hatto quietly told Salomo's wine servant: "Quickly, bring your master's golden drinking bowl to my wine servant, because my friend and I have agreed on this." The man promptly did as he was told. The bowl was carried off, and the friend's deception was not noticed right away. But when at the next meal Salomo asked for the bowl, he realized that he had been tricked and said: "If I live, I'll make sure he is paid back in the same coin."

After the incident mentioned earlier, as Hatto was leav- 2
ing, he entrusted his treasure to Salomo, friend to friend, with the following proviso: if Salomo were to hear that Hatto had died, he should give everything away with reckless abandon to whomever he wished for the sake of both their souls. Scarcely a month had passed, they say, when Salomo advised merchants who were coming back from Italy to spread the word that Hatto was dead. For a short time Salomo, pretending that he was grieving, opened the chests and distributed a large amount of money among the poor. He also hired a great many goldsmiths and first had them take apart the drinking bowl that had once belonged to him. Then he used Hatto's gold and choice gems to put together the magnificent reliquary for Saint Pelagius that we admire

auro viri et gemmis electis compegit; martyris ossa solemniter intulit. Crucem etiam illam honorandam sanctae Mariae, Tuotilone nostro anaglyphas parante, ex eodem auro et gemmis mirificavit. Altare vero sanctae Mariae et analogium evangelicum, eiusdem fratris nostri artificio in locis congruis deaurata, Hattonis sui de scriniis vestivit argento et dyptivit, ut videre est, ex auro electo.

3 Sancto Gallo etiam, in nullis fortuniis immemor eius, duas tabulas eburneas de eisdem scriniis attulit, quibus alias magnitudine equipares rarissime videre est: quasi sic dentatus elephans aliorum fuerit gigas. Erant autem tabulae quondam quidem ad scribendum ceratae, quas latere lectuli soporantem ponere solitum in vita sua scriptor eius Karolum dixit. Quarum una cum sculptura esset et sit insignissima, altera planitiae politissima, Tuotiloni nostro politam tradidit sculpendam. Quibus longioris et latioris moduli Sintrammum nostrum scribere iussit evangelium, ut, quod tabulis habundaret, auro et gemmis Hattonis ornaret. Hoc hodie est evangelium et scriptura, cui nulla, ut opinamur, par erit ultra; quia, cum omnis orbis cisalpinus Sintrammi digitos miretur, in hoc uno, ut celebre est, triumphat. Mirari autem est hominem unum tanta scripsisse, quia in nominatissimis locis plerisque harum regni partium Sintrammi characteris

today and solemnly placed the martyr's bones inside. Using the same gold and gems, he also fashioned the wonderful cross in honor of Saint Mary, which our brother Tuotilo decorated with carvings in relief. Salomo also adorned the altar of Saint Mary, as well as the lectern used for reading the Gospel lesson, both of which were gilded in suitable places by the same brother; he covered them with the silver he took from the chests of his friend Hatto, and, as can be seen, he set them off with choice gold.

He also gave two ivory tablets coming from the same chests to Saint Gall, whom he never forgot in any circumstances, fortunate or otherwise. You very rarely see other ivories of equal size; it is almost as if the elephant endowed with such tusks was a giant among his kind. These tablets were once covered with wax for writing on; the biographer of Charles said in his biography that he used to put them near his bed when he went to sleep. One of the tablets, decorated with carvings, was and is very remarkable, while the other had a very smoothly polished surface. Salomo gave the polished tablet to our brother Tuotilo, to be decorated with carvings. He ordered our brother Sintram to write a copy of the Gospels on pages of longer and broader dimensions, so that he might decorate with Hatto's gold and gems a book already rich with ivory covers. This Gospel book with its handwritten text exists today, and in my opinion nothing will ever match it; because while the entire world this side of the Alps admires Sintram's handiwork, it is common knowledge that in this particular case he reached his triumph. And it is amazing that one man wrote so much, for books in Sintram's hand, the hostages of Saint Gall as it were, are found in many of the most renowned places in these parts of the

libri, sancti Galli obsides, habentur. Sed et hoc in homine mirabile erat et singulare, quod, cum delicata eius scriptura iucunde sit directa, raro in pagina vel unius verbi mendacium invenias rasum.

23. Rediit dives ille ab Italia ditissimus, neque iam damnum istud sentire habebat. Nam prius abiens cum Pelagii eum miracula terrerent aspecta magnisque eum laudibus prosecutus honorare eum disponeret, cum rediret; dispendium tamen gazae cum Chumo propians audiret, sodalem suum omnium *hominum* submurmurat *versutissimum.* Multaque in illum cum *spiritu infremeret,* tristius agebat. Curiaeque sibi cum multis occursantem cum alloqui nollet, ita conventus est a suis: "Hoc vos ludicrum, pater, si semper decuit, si per hanc aleam semper alter alterum decepistis et tabulam, patere et te nunc deceptum, sicut et ille multotiens, ut bene scimus, deceptus est." Salamone autem iuratores ei praeponente, non aliter se, quam ut condixerant, egisse, vix tandem alloquio eius frui valuit. Comperto autem, quod maior pars adhuc sibi supererat, cum quietior iam aliquid esset, Salamon ait: "Fidei violatae innoxium vel in hoc, 'sodes,' certus esse poteris, quod cantharum meum, quem mihi iure assumere possem, pro anima tua carissima primo partitus sum. Sed et amplius pace tua, sodes amande, loqui liceat. Bene enim et optime tecum actum noveris, velim. Eleemosynae enim, quae obitum praecedunt, certiores et Deo sunt, quam

kingdom. But what was also amazing and unique about the man is that although his elegant writing is so delightfully simple, you hardly ever find the erased mistake of even a single word on a page.

23. The rich Hatto came back from Italy extremely rich, and he was not yet aware of these losses. Earlier on, when he left, Hatto was filled with awe by the miracles of Pelagius that he witnessed; he held the saint in high esteem and determined to honor him upon his return. When on his approach to Como, however, he heard about the loss of his treasures, Hatto murmured under his breath that his friend was *the craftiest of men.* And as he *worked up a spirited rage* against Salomo, he became gloomier. When Hatto did not want to talk to Salomo, who came out with a large retinue to meet him at Chur, Hatto's men encouraged him as follows: "Father, if this game playing has always suited you and if you two have always tricked each other with this dice and gaming board, accept that now you too have been tricked, just as he was tricked many times before, as we well know." Only when Salomo brought before Hatto sworn witnesses confirming that he had not acted differently from their agreement did he finally manage with difficulty to engage Hatto in conversation. When Hatto found out that the greater part of his treasure still remained to him and he at last calmed down a bit, Salomo said: "You can be sure that I am not guilty of betraying your trust at least in this instance, my friend, because first of all, on behalf of your very dear soul, I took apart my drinking bowl, which I could have taken back by right. But with your permission, my beloved friend, let me tell you more. I would like you to know that it turned out well, very well indeed, for you, for the alms that precede

quae sequuntur, cariores. Modo quidem si etiam ad tuos vivus perveneris, quod nescis, casuque, qui ignotus est, obieris, paucissima de scriniis tuis post te quidem daturi sunt tibi." Tandem in pristinam redeunt condicto mutuo sodalitatem, ut ultra neuter alterum nec serio deciperet nec ioco.

2 Veniens Hatto Constantiam festiveque receptus sarcophago Pelagium precaturus appropiat. Miratur opus tantum tam brevi peractum. Miratur et crucem lapidibus crystallinis circumclusam. Amplexatus sodalem, ut de tanto thesauro suo vel illam sit asportandi sibi permissio, osculis rogat. Et ille: "Si civium," inquit, "seditionem non vererer, permittere poteram." Dictoque citius ab audientibus urbs undique concluditur. Quaerenti, quid id utique esset: sua pretia, inquiunt cives, in cruce esse quam maxima, nolleque nec episcopo suo iubente sanctae Mariae oblata dimittere. Et ille: "Quod meum est," inquit, "mihi liceat abducere." Illis autem non ad votum sibi respondentibus, Salamon illi silentio: "Sine illos!" inquit; "quia aptiori tempore, si ab *incepto* non *desistis,* cavea inclusam, quocumque mihi dixeris, nave terrave eam tibi mittam." Sedato tandem animo turbam ille dimisit. Dein Constantia relicta abiit in sua. Parvo autem post tempore confectus Italica febre, cruce non exacta, diem obiit. Sicque in verba Salamonis tamquam prophetica devenit. Egit tamen ille pro anima eius precibus et opibus,

death are more certain and more pleasing to God than those that follow. Even if you reach your own people alive, which you don't know, and die due to an accident yet unknown, they will assign to you very little indeed from your treasure chests after you die." Finally their former friendship was restored, with mutual agreement that from then on neither of them would trick the other as a joke or in earnest.

When Hatto came to Constance, after a festive reception 2
he approached the tomb of Saint Pelagius to pray to the saint. He admired this work completed in such a short time. He also admired the cross edged with inset stones of rock crystal. Hatto embraced his friend, kissed him and asked if he could be permitted at least to take away the cross out of all his great treasure. Salomo replied: "If I did not fear the townsfolk's unrest, I would be able to allow it." No sooner had he said this than those who heard him closed all the city gates. When Salomo asked what on earth was going on, the townspeople said that the cross was their most valuable possession and that they did not want to give away an object dedicated to Saint Mary even on their bishop's orders. Then Hatto said: "I should be allowed to carry away what's mine." But when the people did not respond as he wished, Salomo quietly said to him: "Let them be! If you have not *abandoned the claim you have raised,* I will, at a more suitable time, put the cross in a case and send it to you wherever you tell me, by land or ship." Finally, Salomo calmed Hatto down and sent the crowd away. Then he left Constance and went home. A short time after that, however, he contracted Italian fever and died, the cross never claimed. In this way things turned out in accordance with Salomo's words, as if they were prophetic. However, Salomo did for Hatto's soul

quantumcumque potuit. Scrinia eius palatio addicta sibi *non prodērant.* Sapientia autem equivoci sui antiqua Salomon noster amici sui animam, ut diximus, auro suo, vellet nollet, forte redemerat. Et ut vellet, artifex acutus tandem effecerat.

24. Patravit quoque multa Salomon studiis suis in honorem sanctae Mariae nec non et Galli unici sui, id est libros, vasa, vestes varias; scribere iubens in aliquibus aevo longiore duraturis:

Tertius haec hagiae Salomon dat dona Mariae.
Tertius haec almo Salomon dat munera Gallo.

Nec hoc quidem praetereundum, quod aliquando pridie pal-
marum, id est sabbato, quo papa vacat et eleemosynam dat,
cum primo sole ipse per se omnibus urbis sive regionis
dispersisset pauperibus, fatigatus his, ut solebat, in ecclesia
orationi prostratus iacebat. Inter orandum autem vigiliis
longis soporatus cum obdormiret essetque iam circa horam
quidem tertiam, expergefactus conclave festinus intraverat.
Antiphonamque *Pater iuste* secum silentio cantitans: "O,"
inquit, "quali studio et vocibus futuram diem fratres mei
apud sanctum Gallum sunt acturi! Sternatur utique," ait,
"ambulatrix mea quantocius, quia istam ipse vespere levatu-
2 rus sum antiphonam." Ascendensque equitem illam velo-
cissimam quaesitus, quos secum vellet: "Utinam," inquit,

as much as he could, with his prayers and wealth. Hatto's chests were claimed by the court, and he never *benefitted* from them. But maybe with the wisdom of his ancient namesake, our Solomon redeemed his friend's soul with Hatto's own gold, as we have related, whether Hatto was willing or not, and the clever schemer had ultimately succeeded in ensuring that he was willing.

24. By his own efforts, Salomo also obtained many objects for the honor of Saint Mary and no less for his one and only Saint Gall, including books, vessels, and various vestments. He had the following verses inscribed on some objects that would be longer lasting:

> Salomo the Third gives these gifts to Hagia Maria.
> Salomo the Third gives these presents to the gracious Gall.

We should not omit to mention that once, on the day before
Palm Sunday, that is on the Saturday, when the pope is free
and gives alms, Salomo got up at dawn and personally distributed alms among all the poor in the city and the surrounding territory. Wearied by this effort, he lay down prostrate in the church for prayer as usual. However, exhausted
by his long vigils, he fell asleep in the middle of his prayers.
When he woke up, it was already around the third hour, and
he hurried to his chamber. Quietly singing the antiphon *Just*
Father over and over again, Salomo said: "Ah, the great zeal
and loud voices, with which my brothers at Saint Gall are
about to greet the new day! Saddle up my ambling mare
right away! For," he said, "I will sing this antiphon myself at
Vespers." As he was mounting his fastest mare, they asked 2
him whom he wished to take with him. "I wish I could take

"omnes!" Suis autem procuratoribus, ut *necessaria victui,* quaeque possent, post se transmitterent, edixit. Sicque urbanorum populus plurimus pedibus, navibus, equis post illum nocte dieque cucurrerant. At ille spiritu Dei vectus circa nonam aderat coenobio antiphonamque praeoptatam ipse in evangelium levavit et clare percantavit. Cenam fratribus caritativam hilariter exhibuit. Quod reliquum diei erat, mandato et pauperibus impendebat. Crastinam autem processionem ad mansionariam suam sanctae crucis disponens ecclesiam, in proximo prato stationari iussit. Ibi de *gradibus ligneis* Esdras Domini populum legem novam edocuit. Et quod Esdrae veteri non licuit, indulgentiam dedit. Gradibus descendens omnem plebem, quae aderat, missis persolutis in pratum ipsum ad panis rogaverat confractionem. Quid dies illa consumpserit, Dominus solus novit, qui *hospes* verus in prandium illo *collectus* est et cibatus. Ibant refecti singuli in sua gaudentes et laudes dantes Deo, grates sancti Galli coenobio.

25. At vir Domini videns se aetate iam gravescere, post pascha proximum adiit palatium et omnia loca, quae Constantiam sive ad alia monasteria studio proprio vel regum conquisivit munificentia, cartis et sigillis tunc regis Chuonradi fecit roborari. Erant autem, quae sancto Gallo conquisierat. Abbatia Favariensis longum dictu, qualibus per illum sancto Gallo quaesita et stabilita sit artibus. Cuius quidem

everyone!" he said. Then he ordered those responsible to send there all the *necessary provisions* they could after his departure. So it was that a great many townspeople followed him day and night, on foot, by ships, and on horseback. Borne on by God's Holy Spirit, he arrived at the monastery by the ninth hour, and he himself began intoning the Gospel antiphon he had chosen earlier and sang it to the end in a loud voice. He gave a merry love feast for the brothers and devoted the rest of the day to washing feet and giving alms to the poor. On the following day he arranged a procession to his private church of the Holy Cross, and ordered them to make a stop at the nearest meadow. There, from *wooden steps,* like Esdras, he taught the new law to God's people. He absolved the people of their sins, which the Esdras of old had not been allowed to do. Salomo stepped down from the steps and invited all the people who were there to break bread after the Mass in the same meadow. Only the Lord knows how much was consumed on that day, for he was a true *guest* at that feast, *invited* and fed. Refreshed and happy, people went home one by one, giving praises to God and thanks to the monastery of Saint Gall.

25. But since the man of God now began to feel the burden of old age he went to the court after the following Easter and got Conrad, who was king at that time, to confirm with charters and seals all the places that he had acquired for Constance and for monasteries too through his own effort or the generosity of kings. There were also some properties that he had acquired for Saint Gall. As for Pfäfers Abbey, it would take too long to tell you by what devices he sought and secured it for Saint Gall. The charters for almost

fere omnium locorum cartae, quae tunc ad illam pertinebant, in sancti Galli adhuc hodie servantur armario. Qualiter autem sancto Gallo ablata sit, loco suo dicere habebimus. Sunt et alia multa, quae sancto Gallo conquisierat loca, quae, quia senes interrogati in armario quaeri oportere tam plurima dicerent, intacta reliquimus, hoc verissime asserentes, quia prae omnibus, quae rexit, monasteriis Gallo suo semper conquisivit. Tradidit autem Arnoldus quidem rex ei quandam villam in Ararispago, Chollinchoven dictam, sibi in possessionem. Quam rogatus ut Constantiae daret, Gallo suo daturum pollicitus obiens peregit. Multa sunt etiam, quae per concambium ei adquisivit, quae item in chartis armarii, qui scire voluerit, legere poterit.

Tantis pro donis sit pax animae Salamonis.

2 Qui et de abbatiis aliquando Augensi et Sanctigallensi requisitus, si neutram haberet, utram mallet: "Augensis quidem est latior et ditior; sancti Galli autem commodior et satulatior est. Commoditas talentum," inquit, "valet. *Hanc* quia *exquisivi a iuventute mea et amator factus sum formae illius,* semper praehabui." Hunc ergo tantum virum *dilectum sibi et hominibus* cum ad se recipere vellet Dominus, nativitatem quidem suam nobiscum ut sanus ageret et laetissimus, sancto Gallo concessit.

26. Cumque quattuor singulis diebus verbo Domini, quo semper abundaverat, prae omnibus diebus suis abundantius

all places that then belonged to Pfäfers are preserved to this day in the archive of Saint Gall. I will tell you in its proper place how Pfäfers was taken away from Saint Gall. There are also many other places he acquired for Saint Gall that I have not mentioned because when I asked our elders, they said there would be too many documents to search through in the archive; this we can most truthfully assert, because Salomo always provided for his beloved Saint Gall more generously than all other monasteries in his charge. So for instance king Arnulf gave him an estate in Aargau, called Köllikon, for his personal possession. When Salomo was asked to donate it to Constance, he promised to give it to his beloved Saint Gall, and this he did on his deathbed. There are also many properties that he acquired for Saint Gall through exchange, and anyone who would like to know can read about them as well in the charters in the archive.

May Salomo's soul be at peace in return for so many gifts.

When once asked which of the two abbeys, Reichenau or 2
Saint Gall, he would rather have if he had neither, he said, "While Reichenau is more spacious and wealthy, Saint Gall is more comfortable and pleasant. Comfort is worth the same as riches. For *I have sought it out from the time of my youth, and I became a lover of its beauty,* and I have always preferred it." When the Lord wished to take back to himself this great man, *beloved by him and men,* he allowed Saint Gall the kindness that Salomo should at least spend Christmas with us, in good health and great happiness.

26. After Salomo nourished his people on four separate days with the word of the Lord (which was ever to be found in him in abundance but now in even greater abundance

populum pasceret, mane post Innocentum diem Constantiam pergere cum disponeret, fratribus valedictis scholas praeteriit. Erat autem hic dies scholarium. Hostium quoque, ut, quomodo se haberent, perspiceret, aperuit et intravit. Erat utique ius illorum, sicut adhuc hodie quidem est, quoniam exleges quidem sunt, ut hospites intrantes capiant, captos, usque dum se redimant, teneant. Ille vero uti dominus loci securus in medium illorum progressus cum staret: "Episcopum," inquiunt inter se, "non domnum abbatem capiamus!" Ille vero libentissime hoc perpessus, quomodolibet se tractare vellent, consensit. Capientes vero illum in magistri posuerunt, vellet nollet, solium. Et ille: "Si in magistri," inquit, "solio sedeo, iure eius uti habeo. Omnes exuimini!" At illi incunctanter id agentes, liceret sibi, tandem rogant, ab ipso se, sicut a magistro soliti sint, redimere. Cum ille subiunxisset: "Quomodo?" parvuli Latine pro nosse, medii rhythmice, ceteri vero metrice, quasi pro rostris rhetorice etiam illum affantur. Quorum duorum, quoniam a patribus verba recepimus, unus:

"Quid," inquit, "tibi fecimus tale,
  ut nobis facias male?
Appellamus regem,
  quia nostram fecimus legem."

At alter versificator inquit:

than in all the days before), in the morning after the Feast of the Innocents he decided to go on to Constance and after the brothers bid him farewell, he passed by the school. It was Students' Day at Saint Gall. He opened the door and went in to see what they were up to. Since they were exempt from the rules, students then had a special custom, which they still have today, to seize visitors who enter and hold them captive until they pay ransom. When Salomo confidently walked up to them like the lord of the place and stood there in their midst, they said to one another, "Let's seize the bishop rather than our lord abbot!" Very good-naturedly he went along with this and agreed to however they wanted to treat him. They seized him and put him in the master's chair, willy-nilly. He said, "If I sit in the master's chair, I have to have his authority! Everybody, take off your outer clothes!" They did so at once and then asked him if they should pay ransom to him in the same way as they usually would to their master. When he added, "In what way?" the youngest pupils addressed him in Latin to the best of their ability, those who were a bit older in rhythmic verse, and the rest in quantitative verse, as if they were addressing him like rhetoricians from the rostrum. I have heard from the fathers what two of them said; one said:

"What have we done to you
  that you treat us so badly?
We will appeal to the king,
  because we made our own law."

And the other versifier said:

"Non nobis, pie, spes fuerat, cum sis novus hospes,
ut vetus in peius transvertere tute velis ius."

2 Et ille, cum studiis loco sancti Galli semper inolitis iucundaretur suis temporibus adhuc solide stantibus, omnes ita, ut erant in lineis, exsurgens amplexatus et osculatus: "Induite!" inquit. "Enimvero si vixero," ait, "me redimam et talem indolem remunerabo." Collectisque quantocius ante ianuam scholarum fratrum primis, statuit pueris illis et eorum perpetuo posteris pro testamento: singulis annis ludi sui tribus ab imperio statutis diebus in eisdem scholarum aedibus carnibus vesci et de abbatis curte singulos tribus donari escis cottidie et potibus. Quod cum ipse quidem annuatim praesens solvi iuberet, postea ita solutum est usque ad Ungrorum, de quibus loco suo dicturi sumus, invasiones. Abiit tandem, quo disposuit, benedictis nostratibus et ultime, pro dolor, valefactis.

27. Peractis ergo missis Constantiae in octava nativitatis Domini die secretario residens capitis dolorem querebatur. Pauperibus ergo, ut solebat, ante prandium suum hilariter consolatis, mensam cum fratribus et civibus tenens largissimam, dolorem continenter tulit sicque diem ipsam in

"Never did we expect, O pious one, that being a 'new guest,'
you would want safely to change an old law for the worse."

Since Salomo was happy to see that scholarship, always 2
firmly established at the monastery of Saint Gall, still remained solid in his day, he rose from his seat, embraced and kissed all the students, just as they were, in their linen tunics, and said, "Put your clothes on! As I live, I will pay my ransom and reward such talents." After gathering the most eminent of the brothers in front of the school doors as quickly as possible, he established the following as a bequest for these boys and their successors in perpetuity: every year during the three days of play established by imperial rule they were to eat meat in the very schoolrooms and three times every day each student was to be given food and drink from the abbot's estate. Every year when Salomo himself would be present he ordered that these instructions be carried out. Afterward they were carried out in the same way until the invasion of the Hungarians, about which I will tell you in its proper place. Finally Salomo went off to where he planned to go, after blessing our brothers and saying, alas, his final farewells.

27. On the eighth day after the Nativity of the Lord, after finishing the Mass in Constance, he was sitting in the sacristy, when he complained of a headache. Before his meal he cheerfully spoke words of comfort to the poor as usual, but, in the course of an abundant feast he had with the brothers and townsfolk, he endured continuous pain with composure

gaudiis peregit. Sole autem sequente cum languor ingravesceret, missis circumquaque apparitoribus presbyteros, monachos et canonicos collegit, quo citius potuit, praecipue autem nostrates. In octava igitur sancti Iohannis missas sustentatus agens, ab omnibus indulgentiam publice confessus petiit et dedit. Postea vero loca quaedam nondum data sanctae Mariae et Pelagio, Gallo autem suo et Otmaro villam Chollinchovin super tabulam lecti solito iure canonum pro animae requie disponens dedit; multum rogans nostrates, quatenus ecclesiam ab eo in loco sancti Galli in honore sanctae crucis sanctique Magni constructam et sub regiae auctoritatis privilegiis dotatam tuerentur ibique servitium canonicorum minui non paterentur. In vigilia dein Theophaniae confidentissimus in Domino diem obiit. In ecclesia sedis suae ad parietem dexterum multis suorum lacrimis fletus sepultus est.

In cruce quaesitam pretioso sanguine vitam
des cui, Christe, locis in paradisiacis.

28. Raro autem deinceps homo videndus est, in quem largitor omnium bonorum tantum suorum congerat donorum. Erat enim homo praeter decorae faciei dotem et staturae procerae doctus et disciplinatissimus. Scribendi lingua manuque artifex. Lineandi et capitulares litteras rite creandi prae omnibus gnarus, ut in apicibus l et c longi evangelii

and so spent the day in rejoicing. However, on the following day when his sickness got worse, he sent his servants all around to gather with all speed priests, monks, and canons, especially our brothers. On the eighth day after the feast of Saint John he was propped up to celebrate the Mass, and having confessed his sins in public, he asked everyone for absolution and granted it to everyone. Afterward, writing on the tablet he used in bed, he made arrangements for the peace of his soul in accordance with the statutes of canon law: some places not yet given as gifts, he bestowed on Saint Mary and Pelagius, while to his beloved Gall and Otmar he gave the estate called Köllikon. He earnestly besought our monks to protect the church dedicated to the Holy Cross and Saint Magnus that he had built in Saint Gall and endowed with special royal privileges and not to let the service of canons decline in it. Then on the day before Epiphany he died, trusting with the greatest confidence in the Lord. With many tears of grief from his people, he was buried in his cathedral church near the right wall.

Grant him, Christ, the life in paradise
that you won with your precious blood on the cross.

28. Rarely since then would you see a man whom the generous giver of all that is good would shower with so many of his gifts. In addition to being endowed with a handsome face and tall stature, he was a learned and extremely well-disciplined man. He showed artistry in his writing both in the words he chose and with the hand that wrote them. More than any other he was skilled at drawing and delineating capital letters in the proper manner, as you can see in the first letters *L* and *C* of the Long Gospel. He drew those

primis videre est. Quas episcopus, ut aiunt, probans, quid in talibus adhuc posset, lineans aurificabat. Metro primus et coram regibus plerumque pro ludicro cum aliis certator. Dicendi, praeter quod naturalis ei commoditas inerat, artifex erat. In palatinis et synodicis aeque valens conciliis. In eo loco, quo apostolus prophetas ponit, nemo nobilior illo, adeo, ut raro in gradibus stans orator ille vehemens auditoribus promptis lacrimas non eliceret. Favoribus quia aures interdum adhibere solebat, se ipsum arguebat. Hoc malum, inquiens, esse, quod et iusti et optimi vix vitare valeant: "Quis enim tam sanctissimus," ait, "qui non dicta et facta sua recipi malit quam abici? Ilicoque adest pestis illa, quae Graece dicitur 'doxa,' *aurium inflatio magna.*" Post eleemosynarum cottidianas et pedum lavacri exhibitiones commessator pro tempore, loco et personis hilaris erat et iucundus, prodigus numquam. Mariae et Pelagii et Galli sui et Otmari, ut dicere solebat, singularis dilector, in quorum etiam, ut aiebant, nominibus deficiens exspiravit.

29. In calce tandem opusculi et reticenda hominis tangere indecorum non puto. Adolescens quidem et adhuc scholaris gratia amicos visendi hospitio cuiusdam nobilis viri receptus, privignam eius virginem latenter agnovit. De qua semel tantum, ut aiunt, cognita filiam habuit. Quem lapsum paenitentia multa secuta est amborum. Velum sacrum utique ipsa Turegi sibi imponi expetens, vitam agebat

letters and delineated them with gold when he was bishop to prove, so they say, that he could still do it. He was superb at composing metrical verse and often competed with others before kings for amusement. He showed mastery at public speaking that went beyond inborn talent and was influential at court councils and synods. At the level where the apostle puts prophets, there was no one more celebrated, so much so that only on rare occasions would this ardent orator fail to move to tears the audience before him when he was standing on the steps before the altar. He would censure himself because he inclined his ear now and then to words of praise. Pronouncing that this was an evil that even the best and most righteous could hardly avoid, he said, "Who is so very saintly that he would not choose that his words and deeds be welcomed rather than rejected? At that very moment there appears this pest that is called 'glory' in Greek, which *puffs up our ears.*" After performing his daily practices of almsgiving and foot washing, he was a lively and delightful companion at meals as occasion, locale, and personages required, but he never overindulged. He said he especially loved Mary, Pelagius, and his beloved Gall and Otmar, and he even died, they say, with their names on his lips.

29. Finally, at the end of this section I do not think it inappropriate to mention even things the man wanted to keep quiet. When young and still in school, he was received as a nobleman's guest while he was visiting friends, and there he came to know, in secret, the nobleman's maiden stepdaughter. Although he knew her only once, they say, she bore him a daughter. This transgression was followed by great repentance on both their parts. She insisted on taking the holy veil in Zurich and led an admirable life thereafter. Finally,

laudabilem. Ad ultimum abbatissa inibi eius iuvamine facta, multa fecit pro anima utique ipsius et sua. *Filiam* vero tandem *viro maturam,* cum oblatum sibi velum recusaret, dotatam cum praediis viro tradidit cuidam Notkero de prosapia Waltrammi et Notkeri, de quorum dominio montes nostri nomina habent. Eius quidem feminae generis viros fortes et bonos, clericos praeclaros virtutumque conspeximus monachos. Enimvero ipsa dum Turegi apud matrem educata, aliquantisper etiam litterata, in aetate puellari videretur quidem pulchra, ad *amplexus* Arnolfi regis clam *dum peteretur,* respondisse fertur lenoniae procis: "Eius generis prosapiae nec de matre nec de patre sum," inquit, "ut virginitatem meam me cuidam, vel ipsi regi quidem, deceat prostituere." Sicque amplexus illicitos regis, hac et illac fugitans et latitans, usque dum praedicto viro nuberet, frustraverat.

2 Claruerat autem Salomon sub quinque regibus aeque sibi amicis: Luduwico, Karolo, Arnolfo, item Luduwico, Chuonrado.

30. Hinc de Hisone magistro et discipulis eius Nokero Balbulo, Tuotilone, Ratperto vitas, ut ita dicam, non negligendas aggrediar scribendas.

2 Iso quidem non solum bene natorum, sed et sanctorum filius fuit parentum. Qui, ut crebro solebant victualium aliarumque rerum abstinentia semet ex consensu pro Deo affligere, quadragesimam quandam secreti cubantes, sabbato sancto lavacro tandem utebantur. Ornanturque ambo post

with his help she became abbess there and did many things for her own soul and especially for his. But when her *daughter* eventually became *ripe for a husband,* she refused the veil offered to her. Salomo provided her with estates as a dowry and married her to a man called Notker, from the stock of Waltram and Notker, the local lords from whose domain our mountains derive their names. We have seen brave and good men descended from this woman, famous clerics and virtuous monks. Brought up at her mother's abbey in Zurich and also taught letters for a while, she was considered beautiful as a girl. When she was secretly *approached to become* King Arnulf's *mistress,* they say that she answered the panderers, "I am not from such a family, either on my mother's or on my father's side, that it would be proper for me to sell my virginity to anybody, even the king himself." In this way she escaped the illicit embraces of the king by all sorts of tricks, avoiding or hiding from him until she married the man I mentioned earlier.

Salomo was prominent under five kings who were all 2
equally friendly to him: Louis, Charles, Arnulf, another Louis, and Conrad.

30. From this point on I will embark on writing about master Iso and his students, Notker the Stammerer, Tuotilo, and Ratpert, for their lives, if I may say so, should not be passed over.

Iso was the son of parents who were not only of noble 2
birth but also saintly. Since they often abstained, by mutual agreement, from food and other things, mortifying their flesh for the love of God, once during Lent they slept in separate beds and finally on Holy Saturday they took a ritual bath. After the ashes and penitential sackcloth, they dressed

cineres et cilicia ad processionem cum civibus, prout bene natis copia erat. Ibat mulier vigiliis convicta dormitum in lectum, nobilius quidem tunc pro tempore stratum, post lavacrum. Temptatoris ductu vir eius in conclave ipsum fortuitus intraverat. Accedensque ad illam, ipsa quidem non recusante, eo sancto die concubuit. Fit post facinus patratum tantum amborum in ipso conclavi lamentum, ut familia superveniens, quid factum sit, non quaereret, cum Deum
3 inclamando, quid fecerint, ipsi palam fecerint. Inter lacrimas ambo iterum abeunt lavatum, induuntur item ciliciis per tot hebdomadas tritis. Cineribusque aspersi presbyteri loci nudipedes coram omnibus civibus vestigiis procidunt. Ille vero pie discretus paenitentia eorum accepta, populo Deum pro eis inclamante, indulgentiam eis dedit allevatosque pro foribus basilicae eo die et nocte punitionis gratia incommunicatos iusserat stare. Ibant tandem officio diei peracto ad proximae villae presbyterum, fama quidem sanctum, et eodem habitu ipsi et civibus eius lapsum suum fletibus nudant et, ut crastina eis communicare liceat, permissum eius rogant. Quos ille severe invectus temeritatis arguebat; benedictione tamen illius accepta redeuntes in sua, ieiuni vigilem flentes duxerant noctem.

4 Dies paschae illuxerat; matutini pro foribus stabant, cruce ante missas exportata extremi sequuntur. Presbyter

up as best they could, given their noble status, for the procession with the townspeople. Exhausted by her vigils, after
the bath the woman went to sleep in her bed, which was also
rather splendidly decked out for the occasion. Lured by the
Tempter, her husband happened to enter this room. He
came up to his wife and, since she did not protest, lay with
her on that holy day. After the evil deed was done, they both
started wailing in the room so loudly that their household
staff came running and did not even ask what had happened,
because by crying out to God the spouses themselves made
clear what they had done. In tears, both spouses once again 3
went to the bath, and again put on their penitential sackcloth, which they had worn for so many weeks. Sprinkled
with ash and barefoot, they went to the local priest and before all the townspeople fell at his feet. The kindly, discern-
ing priest accepted their repentance and, because people
were calling upon God on their behalf, he granted them absolution and after raising them to their feet, he ordered
them, as a punishment, to stand in front of the church doors
on that day and night without taking the Holy Communion.
Finally, when the service of that day ended, they went to the
priest at a nearby village, who was known as a holy man, and
dressed in the same way, they tearfully revealed their sin to
the priest and to the people and begged him for permission
to take Communion on the following day. He severely chastised them and denounced their grave offense; still, they received his blessing and went back home, where they kept
vigil through the night, fasting and crying.

Easter Day dawned; early in the morning they were 4
standing at the church doors and, when the cross was
brought out before the Mass, they followed at the end of the

autem illos populi totius adnisu inter kyrieleison induxerat, extremos locaverat. Communionem, quia presbytero illi iam dicto non placeret, non petebant. Communione autem finita quasi presbyter ille festinus tamquam populo suo adhuc officium facturus ingreditur, manibus apprehensos ad aram duxit. Pyxide communionis aperta fletu perfusos communicavit et festinans quasi ad suos rediturus, revestiri eos et epulari pace et osculis datis edixit, et rediit. Laetati quoque sunt omnes talis viri auctoritate illos communicatos. Diem tandem in laetitia et eleemosynis agentibus partesque presbytero illi sancto et eulogia per equitem mittentibus, inventum est eum nusquam eo die a suis descendisse, sed angelum Dei, quod factum est—quod etiam in synodo propalatum est—totum fecisse. Agebant ambo illi gratias deinde die et nocte Deo, et virtutum operibus, quibus assueverant, tunc artius insistebant.

31. Sed mulier illa concubitu illo cum esset gravida et tempore labente propinqua iam partui, ericium peperisse somniaverat, puerulosque plures, ut stimulos ei eruerent, accurrisse et parietes eis caraxasse viderat. Evigilans nimis stupida somnium viro narrat. Qui in Deo confisus somnium illud nihil mali portendere, ad inclusum in Monte Victoris Eusebium pergens, coniectorem eius fore rogavit. "*Filium,*" inquit, "*uxor tua pariet,* quem sancto Gallo votabis. Apud illum

procession. Moved by the entreaties of all the people, however, the priest invited them in during the Kyrie Eleison and placed them in the back. They did not seek Communion, because the abovementioned priest would dislike that. But when Communion ended, that other priest appeared to hurry in as if he was still about to say Mass for his people, took the couple by the hands, and led them to the altar. He opened the pyx and gave the tear-drenched couple Communion. Then in a hurried manner, as if he was about to return to his people, he told them to change their clothes and to feast again, gave them a blessing and a kiss, and went home. Everyone rejoiced that the couple had received Communion under the guidance of such a man. They ended that day in festivities and almsgiving, but when they sent a horseman to deliver items from their feast and their gifts to the saintly priest, it turned out that he had never left his people on that day, but that it was an angel of God who had done all that had happened, and this was even made public at a synod. Afterward both spouses gave their thanks to God day and night and persisted in performing their usual good works even more assiduously.

31. When Iso's mother became pregnant from that intercourse and, as time went on, came close to labor, she dreamed that she gave birth to a hedgehog and that many little boys had run up to it in order to pluck out its needles and had used them to scribble on the walls. She woke up in great amazement and related her dream to her husband. Trusting in God that the dream did not portend any evil, he went to Victorsberg, to the anchorite Eusebius, and asked him to interpret the dream. The anchorite said: "*Your wife will bear a son* whom you will dedicate to Saint Gall. He will

enim educatus, doctor erit magnificus et multos pueros, ipse asper disciplinis, stilis armaturus."

2 Factum est, ut vir ille, spiritu Dei plenus sanctique Galli compatrianus, praedixerat. Per cuius praeter haec praesagia Dominus multis revelaverat multa; sed et ipsi Karolo quidem, qui eius petitione, ut et Rapertus scribit, ipsum illum Victoris Montem sancto Gallo contradidit. *Puer natus,* educatus, sancti Galli fit monachus doctissimus docuitque, ut in gestis eius iam scripsimus, Salomonem cum ceteris quam plurimis. Sed Hartmuotus noster, Ruodolfo Burgundionum regi notissimus, cui et cognatus, cum magistrum aliquem nostratium Grandivallensium coenobio peteret, ipsum illum regi ad annos tres a Crimaldo expetiit condicto in manus pacto, uti ter in anno sumptibus sibi regis monasterii sui daretur invisere claustrum. Ibi vas illud spiritus sancti cum devenisset, provinciis diffamatum et regnis sancti Galli dulcissima suffecerat pocula.

3 Fulsit autem ibi sancti Galli lucerna illa interdum quidem per miracula. Nam uti plurima doctus, cum unguenta quidem facere nosset, leprosos et paralyticos, sed et caecos curaverat aliquos. Quod quidem, dum id diu celasset, virtute sanctitatis suae magis fecisse, vellet nollet, tandem patuit. Nam dum pauperculum quendam caeculum mendicare audisset ad hostium, misericordia tantilluli motus, unguentum afferri iubens egreditur ad videndum. Cuius cum digitis

be educated at Saint Gall and become a distinguished teacher, and being sharp himself in the arts, he will arm many boys with pens."

It happened just as that man, filled with the spirit of God 2
and a fellow countryman of Saint Gall, had predicted. Besides this, through Eusebius's prophecies the Lord revealed many things to many people, even to Charles himself, who, as Ratpert also writes, handed that same Victorsberg over to Saint Gall at Eusebius's request. *The boy was born,* educated, and became the most learned monk of Saint Gall. As we have already mentioned when writing about Salomo's deeds, he taught Salomo along with a great many others. However, when King Rudolf of Burgundy, who knew our abbot Hartmut very well and who was also his relative, sought among us a teacher for the monastery of Grandval, Hartmut specifically asked Grimald, on the king's behalf, to let Iso go for three years, with an agreement, confirmed by a handshake, that Iso would be granted leave to visit the cloister of his monastery three times a year at the king's expense. When that vessel of the Holy Spirit arrived there, acclaimed throughout the provinces and kingdoms, he provided the sweetest elixirs of Saint Gall in abundance.

Meanwhile, that famous light of Saint Gall shone brightly 3
there by way of his miracles. Learned in many areas, he also knew how to make ointments and he cured lepers, paralytics, and even some blind people. Although he had kept it secret for a long time, it finally came to light, willy-nilly, that he did so more by the power of his holiness. For instance, when he heard that a little blind beggar was asking for alms at the gate, moved by pity for such a small child, he ordered ointment to be brought and went out to see him. After

benedicens tractaret oculos unguentoque linire inciperet, exclamavit puer: "Video," inquit, "domine, video!" Et per aliquot dies convalescens, oculis tandem quidem clarissime vidit. Quod tamen ille, ut caelatum esset, unguenti pretiosissimi, quod manu ferret, factum affirmans virtute, non mentitus est.

32. Talibus vir Dei cum dominum suum sanctum Gallum, ubicumque esset, ornasset virtutibus, stimulos suos pluribus scholaribus acuebat, cum ipse *tantis virtutibus pollens* vellet tamen esse involutus ut ericius. Anhelabant ad illius doctrinam totius Burgundiae nec non et Galliae ingenia. Erant et aliqui, qui inter suos satis haberent, si discipuli Hisonis vel ad horam dicerentur, etiamsi ad stilos eius non acuerentur. Erat enim de illo late fama, quoniam, etsi obtusa inveniret ingenia, ipse eis daret acumina. Libuit tandem et ipsum vel propter gratas consuetudines discipulorum vel propter *minam dandam ad mensam,* ut post tres annos regi concessos aliorum annorum moras sibimet ab abbate suo per se ipsum expeteret. Mansit itaque in benigna peregrinatione sua per plures tandem annos, ratisque sibi temporibus claustrum suum, abbatem et fratres visitans, benedictione illorum roboratus, discipulos iterum aegre exspectatus revisit.

2 Disponente vero tandem eo, qui posuit *terminos, qui praeteriri non poterunt,* morbo correptus, plurimis hinc inde dolentibus, bene validae adhuc aetatis diem obiit, multum

blessing him, he touched the boy's eyes with his fingers and started to spread ointment on them. The boy exclaimed: "I see, my lord, I see!" After recovering for several days, he did finally see very clearly. However, in order to keep it secret, Iso, in claiming that what had happened was due to the power of the very precious ointment that he applied with his hand, did not tell a lie.

32. After the man of God had added luster to his lord Saint Gall with miracles such as this wherever he was, he began to sharpen his needles for many students, for although *prolific in such miracles,* he wanted to be curled up like a hedgehog. The sharp minds in all of Burgundy, and Gaul as well, were eager for his teaching. There were even some among his pupils who were quite happy to be called Iso's students just for a short time, even if they did not get sharpened to his stylistic level. In fact, there was a widespread report about him that even if he encountered dull minds, he would give them sharp edges. In the end, whether because of the agreeable ways of his students or because of the *money to be deposited in the bank,* it pleased him personally to seek permission from his abbot to stay for some additional years beyond the three years conceded to the king. As a result, he ended up remaining in his altruistic sojourn abroad for many years, and after visiting his monastery, his abbot, and brothers at times prescribed for him, he was reinvigorated by their blessings and went back again to see his students who were eagerly awaiting him.

But finally, in accordance with the destiny fixed by the 2
one who *set the limits that cannot be passed,* Iso, while still in the prime of life, succumbed to illness and died. While large numbers of people grieved in different areas, he himself was

dolens, quod claustro suo procul sit et in coemeterio sancti Galli sepeliri non licuit. Collectis autem undequaque discipulis eius sepultus est in ecclesia sancti Germani. Ubi cum tandem coruscaret miraculis, corpus eius furto, ut aiunt, in Burgundiam in quandam hominis potentis translatum est ecclesiam. Quod etsi dubie roboretur, praeterire tamen noluimus. Constat autem id in tumulo, quo conditum est, non haberi.

33. De Notkero, Ratperto, Tuotilone, discipulis eius et Marcelli, quoniam quidem *cor et anima una erant,* mixtim, qualia tres unus fecerint, quantum a patribus audivimus, narrare incipimus. Hi quidem ab Hisone cum in divinis non mediocriter essent praelibati, Marcello, ut iam diximus, sunt coniuncti. Qui in divinis aeque potens et humanis, septem liberales eos duxit ad artes, maxime autem ad musicam. Quae cum ceteris naturalior et, quamvis difficilius apprehensa, usu quidem sit iucundior, tantum in ea tandem valuerant, quantum in operibus singulorum, quae iam ante quiddam tetigimus, apparet. Enimvero hi tres quamvis votis essent unicordes, natura tamen, ut fit, erant dissimiles.

2 Noker corpore non animo gracilis, voce non spiritu balbulus, in divinis erectus, in adversis patiens, ad omnia mitis, in nostratium acer erat exactor disciplinis; ad repentina timidulus et inopinata praeter demones infestantes erat, quibus quidem se audenter opponere solebat. In orando, legendo, dictando creberrimus. Et ut omnes sanctitatis eius in

very upset that he was far from his monastery and could not be buried at the cemetery of Saint Gall. But after his students gathered together from all parts, he was buried in the church of Saint Germanus. Because his presence there achieved scintillating fame thanks to the miracles he brought about, his body was stolen, they say, and moved to a powerful man's church in Burgundy. Although this information is supported by dubious evidence, I did not want to omit it. It is generally agreed that the body is not in the grave where it was buried.

33. I will now begin to relate all that I have heard from the fathers about Notker, Ratpert, and Tuotilo, the students of Iso and Marcellus, a combined account, because *they were of one heart and soul,* so that the three made one. After getting a significant foretaste of divine learning from Iso, they were assigned to Marcellus, as I have already said. Equally strong in divine and secular learning, he guided them toward the seven liberal arts, but most of all to music. Since this art is more natural than the others and, although more difficult to learn, brings more joy when practiced, they eventually became as good at it as the work each of them produced demonstrates (but I have already touched upon this earlier). Although these three were like-minded in their goals, they were, as often happens, very different in their nature.

Notker was slight in body but not in soul, stumbling in 2
speech but not in spirit, upright in divine matters, patient in adversity, generally mild but a keen enforcer of discipline among our own; he was timid when something happened suddenly and unexpectedly, except when demons attacked, in which case he usually confronted them boldly. He was assiduous at praying, reading, and composing poetry. And, to

brevi complectar dotes: sancti spiritus erat vasculum, quo suo tempore abundantius nullum.

34. At Tuotilo longe aliter bonus erat et utilis, homo lacertis et omnibus membris, sicut Favius athletas eligere docet. Erat eloquens, voce clarus, celaturae elegans et picturae artifex. Musicus sicut et socii eius, sed in omnium genere fidium et fistularum prae omnibus; nam et filios nobilium in loco ab abbate destinato fidibus edocuit. Nuntius procul et prope sollers, in structuris et ceteris artibus suis efficax, concinnandi in utraque lingua potens et promptus natura, serio et ioco festivus: adeo, ut Karolus noster aliquando ei maledixerit, qui talis naturae hominem monachum fecerit. Sed inter haec omnia, quod prae aliis est, in choro strenuus, in latebris erat lacrimosus; versus et melodias facere praepotens, castus ut Marcelli discipulus, qui feminis oculos clausit.

2 Ratpertus autem inter ambos, quos diximus, medius incedebat, scholarum ab adolescentia magister, doctor planus et benevolus, disciplinis asperior, raro praeter fratres pedem claustro promovens, duos calceos annum habens; excursus "mortem" nominans, saepe Tuotilonem itinerarium, ut se caveret, amplexibus monens. In scholis sedulus plerumque cursus et missas negligebat: "Bonas," inquiens, "missas audimus, cum eas agi docemus." Qui cum labem maximam

briefly sum up all the gifts of his holiness in a few words, he was a vessel more abundantly filled with the Holy Spirit than any other in his time.

34. As for Tuotilo, he was good and effective in a very different way. His arms and all parts of his body were just as Fabius instructs for choosing athletes. He was eloquent, had a loud voice, carved elegant reliefs and was skillful at painting. Like his comrades he was a musician but better than anyone at playing any kind of string or wind instrument; he even taught the sons of nobility to play string instruments at a place designated by the abbot. A careful courier to destinations far and near, handy at building and other crafts useful for his fellow monks, he was also naturally capable and quick at composing verses in both languages, lively at work and play, so much so that our Charles once cursed the person who made a man of such talents a monk. But along with all these qualities, and, what was most striking, he was a vigorous participant in the choir, but tearful in the darkness of his cell; he was extremely good at making verses and melodies, and he was chaste as fitting for a student of Marcellus, who used to shut his eyes before women.

Between those two whom I have described, Ratpert 2
steered a middle course. A schoolmaster from a young age, clear and benevolent as a teacher, he was rather strict in disciplinary matters; setting foot outside the cloister more rarely than other brothers, he had one pair of shoes a year; calling a trip outside "death," he often embraced Tuotilo as he prepared for a journey, urging him to be careful. Diligent at school, he mostly neglected daily assemblies and Masses, saying: "We hear good Masses when we teach how to conduct them." Although he called impunity the greatest bane

claustri impunitatem nominasset, ad capitulum tamen nonnisi vocatus venit, cum sibi officium capitulandi et puniendi gravissimum, ut ait, sit traditum.

35. Tales cum essent tres isti nostrae rei publicae senatores, quod semper doctorum est et utilium, ab otio vacantibus et *in levitate ambulantibus* detractiones et dorsiloquia patiuntur assidua, sed maxime, quia minus refellere solebat, sanctus, ut vere asseram, domnus Nothkerus. Tuotilo quidem et Rapertus, acriores talibus minusque ad contumelias habiles, rarius ab eis laedebantur. Notkerus autem, hominum mitissimus, quid iniurie essent, in semet ipso didicit.

2 De quibus pluribus unum aliquem, ut, quantum satanas in talibus praesumat, *ab uno discas omnes,* introducere volumus. Erat hic quidem refectorarius nomine Sindolfus, postremo autem, fictis obsequelis, cum alias in nullo esset utilis, accusans fratres criminibus coniectis, a Salomone operariorum positus est decanus. Enimvero cum esset refectorarius, pro commodis incommoda, quibus ausus erat, exhibebat, prae ceteris autem Notkero. Salomone autem in plurimis occupato nec attendere ad singula sufficienti, alimonia interdum fratribus cum aut detraheretur aut depravaretur, clamabant plures pro iniustitia; inter quos aliquando etiam tres, quos dicimus, isti aliqua locuti parebant. At Sindolfus, discordiae semper fomes, sciens antiquam condiscipulorum *odii facem* et causam, accommodat se auribus Salomonis,

of the monastery, he only went to the chapter when summoned, because, as he said, he was already entrusted with the heaviest duty of conducting the business of the chapter and administering punishment.

35. Such were the qualities of the three senators of our republic, but, as always happens to the learned and capable, they endured constant disparagement and backbiting from those spending their time in idleness and *walking in levity.* But most of all Master Notker, a truly holy man, suffered, because he usually put up less of a fight. Tuotilo and Ratpert, on the other hand, sharper with such people and less susceptible to insults, were more rarely wounded by them. But Notker, the gentlest of men, learned the meaning of injustice firsthand.

Of those many tormentors I will present only one *so that* 2
from the one you may learn the extent to which Satan takes control of all such people. There was this man by the name of Sindolf, who was in charge of the refectory, but later, though he was useless in other respects and kept accusing the brothers of supposed crimes, he was made dean of all the workers by Salomo thanks to feigning devoted service. In fact, while he was in charge of the refectory, he caused discomfort instead of comfort for those whom he had the audacity to treat this way, and above all for Notker. Salomo was preoccupied with many responsibilities and could not look into the details when food for the brothers was sometimes either withheld from the brothers or spoiled. Many cried out because of the injustice; among those, the three friends I have described were thought at some point to have said something. But Sindolf, who was always fomenting discord and knowing *the source* and cause *of the* long-standing *hatred* that

quasi pro suo honore rem sibi sit dicturus. Ille vero etsi nihil nocivius scisset praelatis a subditis quam susurros audire, quid novi afferret, quaesivit. Ille vero tres illos semper super se verba iacere solitos hesterno, quae Deo importabilia sint, mentitur locutos. *Credidit* ille *sermoni* et nihil mali opinantibus rancorem portavit, tandem et ostendit. At illi cum nihil ab eo reatus sui *exsculpere possent,* Sindolfi se technis hariolantur fuisse circumventos. Re tandem coram fratribus discussa, cum ipsi, testantibus cunctis nihil omnino se contra episcopum dixisse, cum ceteris eum vincerent, vindictam super falsidicum quisque sibi rogant. Quod ille cum dissimulasset, taciti quieverant.

36. Erat tribus illis inseperabilibus consuetudo, permisso quidem prioris, in intervallo laudum nocturno convenire in scriptorio collationesque tali horae aptissimas de scripturis facere. At Sindolfus sciens horam et colloquia quadam nocte fenestrae vitreae, cui Tuotilo assederat, clandestinus foris appropiat aureque vitro affixa, si quid rapere posset, quod depravatum episcopo traderet, auscultabat. Senserat illum Tuotilo, homo pervicax *lacertisque confisus,* latialiterque, quo illum, qui nihil intellegeret, lateret, compares alloquitur: "Adest ille," inquid, "et aurem fenestrae affixit. Sed tu, Notker, quia timidulus es, cede in ecclesiam! Ratperte autem mi,

the three fellow students had for him, attuned his words to Salomo's ears, by sounding as if he was about to tell him something to protect Salomo's honor. Even though Salomo knew that nothing was more harmful than for superiors to listen to whispers from subordinates, he asked Sindolf what news he brought. Sindolf lied that those three were always in the habit of speaking out against Salomo and the day before had said something intolerable before God. Salomo *believed the story* and harbored resentment toward those who thought no ill of him, and finally he showed it. Because they *could not get out of* Salomo any sense at all of what their fault was, they guessed that they were victims of Sindolf's scheming. Finally, when the affair was discussed before the brothers and, with everyone testifying that they had never said anything whatsoever against the bishop, the three, with the help of the rest, defeated Sindolf, each of them asked for punitive action against the liar. But when he made no comment, they silently let it rest.

36. The three inseparable friends would usually get together with the abbot's permission in the scriptorium at night in the break between the services to discuss the scriptures, an occupation most suitable for such an hour. One night Sindolf, who knew the time of their meetings, crept up outside to the glass window by which Tuotilo was sitting, pressed his ear to the glass, and listened intently, to see if he could catch something that he might later twist and report to the bishop. Tuotilo, a determined man, *confident in his strength,* noticed him and said to his companions in Latin, to keep it secret from Sindolf, who would understand nothing: "He is here, with his ear glued to the window. Now you, Notker, because you are a bit timid, go into the church! And

rapto flagello fratrum, quod pendet in pyrali, deforis accurre! Ego enim illum, cum appropinquare te sensero, vitreo citissime redaperto captum capillis ad meque pertractum violenter tenebo. Tu autem, anime mi, *confortare et esto robustus,* flagelloque illum totis viribus increpita et Deum in illo ulciscere!"

2 Ille vero, sicut semper erat ad disciplinas acutissimus, modeste exiens, rapto flagello cucurrit celerrimus hominemque intro capite tractum totis viribus a dorso ingrandinat. Et ecce ille *manibus pedibusque* renisus, flagellum incussum capiens tenuit. At ille virgam propius aspectam rapiens ictus ei validissimos infregit. Cum autem parci sibi *male* iam *mulctatus* incassum petisset: "*Voce,*" inquit, "*opus est,*" et exclamans vociferavit. At fratrum pars, voce audita tali tempore insolita, stupens accurrit luminibus et, quidnam esset, quaesivit. Tuotilo autem diabolum se cepisse creber ingeminans, lumen adhiberi rogat, ut, in cuius illum imagine tene-
3 ret, certius inspiceret. Capite autem inviti hac et illac ad inspicientes versato, si Sindolf esset, quasi nescius interrogat. Omnibus autem vere ipsum esse clamitantibus et, ut illum dimitteret, rogantibus, relicto eo: "Me miserum," ait, "in auricularem et intimum episcopi manus misisse!" Rapertus vero fratribus accurrentibus in partem cedens clam se subduxit. Neque enim ipse, qui passus est, a quo cederetur, scire poterat. Quaerentibus autem aliquibus, ubinam domnus

you, my dear Ratpert, grab the brothers' whip that hangs in the warm room and run back inside! As for me, when I hear you coming, I'll very quickly open the window, grab him by the hair, drag him in, and hold him by force. Then you, my dear friend, *be strong and courageous:* thrash him with all your might and take vengeance on him for God's sake!"

So Ratpert, always the strictest in matters of discipline, 2
quietly left the room, grabbed the whip, promptly ran back, and when Tuotilo had dragged the man inside headfirst, Ratpert flogged him on his back with all his might. And now, look, Sindolf, fighting him off *with his hands and feet,* caught the whip when it struck him and held on to it. But Ratpert spotted a rod lying nearby, grabbed it, and gave Sindolf a terrific thrashing. *After this severe punishment,* vainly begging for mercy, Sindolf said, "*I need to shout!*" and loudly cried out for help. But some of the brothers, astonished to hear shouting at such an inappropriate hour, came running with lamps and asked what on earth was going on. Tuotilo, insisting again and again that he had caught the devil, asked the brethren to hold the light closer so that he could see more clearly in whose shape the devil was as he now held
him. Tuotilo turned the head of the resisting man to this 3
side and that to face the onlookers and pretending that he did not know, asked whether it was Sindolf. So when they all shouted that it *was* Sindolf and asked Tuotilo to release him, he let him go, saying: "What a wretch I am, to lay hands on the bishop's counselor and intimate friend!" As for Ratpert, he stepped aside and quietly moved away from the scene when the brothers came running. Not even the monk who suffered it could know who had done the thrashing. When some brothers asked where Master Notker and Ratpert had

Notkerus Rapertusque abissent: "Ambo," inquit, "ad opus Dei, diabolum sentientes, abierunt meque cum illo *in negotio perambulante in tenebris* dimiserunt. Vere autem omnes scitote angelum Domini ictus ei manu sua incussisse!"

4 Discedentibus tandem fratribus a partium sectatoribus surgunt, ut fit, multiloquia. Alii Dei iudicio, ut auscultatores clandestini publicarentur, factum dicebant; alii autem tali viro, nisi quod "angelum Dei" praetendit, tale opus non decuisse. Occultabat autem se confractus ille corporis pariter et mentis dolore. Interrogatque tandem episcopus post aliquos dies, ubinam tamdiu moraretur suus famidicus—sic enim hominem nominare erat solitus nova semper aliqua sibi clam apportantem. Re, ut erat, veraciter comperta, quoniam tantae auctoritati pro tam turpiter reo nihil imputare volebat, consolatur accitum: "Quoniam," inquit, "illi a pueritia mei semper invidi male tibi fecerant, ego quidem, si vixero, melius tibi facere habebo." Data est post non multum temporis occasio, et plerisque omnibus, ne rem loci tam praeclaram in tali homine deiceret, contradicentibus, ut supra praelibavimus, operariorum factus est ab ipso decanus.

37. Erant illo in tempore sancto Gallo et alii coenobitae quidem sancti, quorum iustitiae *apud Deum non sunt in oblivione,* quorum quidem opera multa audivimus praeclara. Inter quos Hartmannus et ipse doctissimus, abbas coenobii post

gone, Tuotilo said, "They both felt the presence of the devil and went off in order to perform divine office and left me alone with the one who *stalks in the darkness.* You should all know, though, that it was truly an angel of God who struck him with his own hand!"

When the brothers finally left, there was much discus- 4
sion, as generally happens, between the adherents of different groups. Some said that it was God's judgment that made it happen, so that secret eavesdroppers might be brought to light; others said that for such a man an action of this kind would have been unseemly had he not used "an angel of God" as a pretext. Sindolf, for his part, was hiding, racked by physical and mental pain in equal measure. Finally, several days later, the bishop asked what was keeping his tattletale away for so long (this is what he usually called Sindolf, who always brought him news in secret). When the bishop found out what had really happened, he did not want any blame to be attached to such an authoritative figure for such a sordid affair and so summoned Sindolf and consoled him. "They have always been jealous of me ever since boyhood, and since they have wronged you in this way," he said, "I will surely make it right for you, as I live." An opportunity arose not much later, and even though practically everyone argued that such a distinguished position would be wasted on such a man, the bishop appointed Sindolf dean of workmen, as I mentioned earlier.

37. At that time Saint Gall also had other holy monks whose acts of righteousness *before God are not forgotten* and about whose many glorious deeds I have heard tell. Among them was Hartmann himself, also a very learned man, who became abbot of our monastery after Salomo, and Waltram,

Salomonem, Waltrammus vero, cuius etiam melodiae, quis fuerit, non celant, Ruodkerus, cuius supra meminimus, et alii quidem multi, *cum sanctis sancti, cum electis electi.* De quibus, quia longum est operi audita prosequi, tres solos, quos assumpsimus, in exemplum posteris sufficere credamus.

2 Notkerus vero in his, quae in capitulo suo praelibavimus, dies noctesque *semper idem* et novus, quod Ratpertus in scholis, hoc ipse in claustro praeter verbera omni caritatis egit censura. Nam priorum permisso, magis autem et ortatu, iuveniores ad hoc idonei noctes diesque, quando ab orationibus quiesceret, velut *in insidiis erant.* Neque enim hora incompetens dicebatur, si codice in manibus quis cum domino Notkero loquebatur. Ipse autem cum propter regulae tenorem sibilis eos interdum et strepitu absturbaret, ab abbatibus ei per oboedientiam, quod refutarat, iniunctum est. Quam autem mellifluus in responsis fuerit, lacrimae eorum, qui hominem viderant, testantur. Enimvero etiam in spiritu Dei multa bonis et malis aut fortunia praedixit aut infortunia. Sicut, ut gratia exempli superiora repetam, cuidam Karoli elati animi capellano.

38. Nam rex idem cum ob caritates agendas fratribus, ut solebat, coenobio veniret totumque triduum gratia reverentiae conversantium ibidem moraretur sanctisque nostris, ut et Ratpertus scribit, munificus, abbate iam mutato abire parasset, ille quidem elati animi capellanus virum Dei

whose very melodies reveal what kind of man he was, and Ruodker whom I mentioned above, and also many others, *saints with the saints, elect with the elect.* It would take too long to tell you everything I have heard, but the three of them I have taken up, I believe, will suffice as models for posterity.

As for Notker, day and night he stayed *always the same* and 2
yet different in those situations that I have already described in his own chapter, and he followed the same policy in the cloister as Ratpert did in the school, except for his total regard for love rather than rods. With the permission or rather the encouragement of the elders, young men who were so inclined *lay in ambush,* as it were, day and night, waiting for him to take a break from his prayers. No hour was considered inappropriate if someone with a book in his hands started talking to Master Notker. But when at times, because of the tenor of the Rule, he hissed or mumbled words of disapproval to chase them away, he was ordered by the abbots to do as a matter of obedience what he had refused to do. As for how mellifluous he was in reciting responses—the tears of those who saw the man bear witness to that. He also accurately predicted, by means of God's Holy Spirit, many fortunate or unfortunate events for good people and bad people, as, for example—to go back to what I said earlier—he did for a certain haughty chaplain of King Charles.

38. When King Charles came to the monastery to give a love feast for the brothers as he was accustomed to do, he stayed there for three full days out of respect for the community and gave generously to our saint, as Ratpert also wrote. With the new abbot installed, the king was getting ready to leave when the haughty chaplain walked by and

psalterio, ut solebat, assidentem praeteriens conspexit. Agnitoque, quod is esset, qui Karolo multa quaerenti pridie quaesita resolveret, comitantibus ait: "Ecce, inquam, iste est, quo neminem aiunt in regno Karoli doctiorem. Sed ego, si vultis, illum tam praecellentissime doctum ad irrisionem vobis temptabo et, quod tantae famae vir omnino nesciat,
2 interrogabo." Illis vero, ut hoc faceret, curiose rogantibus accedunt pariter, salutant eum. Humilis ille assurgens, quid petant, quaerit. At ille infelix, quem diximus: "Scimus," inquit, "homo doctissime, omnia te nosse. Quid autem Deus in caelo nunc faciat, a te cupimus, si nosti, audire." "Scio," inquit ille, "et optime scio. Nunc enim facit, quod semper fecit, utique et tibi quam mox facturus est. *Exaltat* enim *humiles et humiliat superbos.*" Abibat temptator ille et irrisor a suis irrisus, parvipendens, quod sibi futurum dixisset. Sonatur continuo ad concursum et laudes caesaris abituri. Arripit ille infelix futurus labarum eo die ordinis sui dominum antecedendi. Et equo superbo invectus, ante portam civitatis offendens cecidit et misere in facie collisus crus confregit.
3 Committitur abbati novo, Hartmuoti suffecto, Perinhardo procurandus. Cui ipse tandem praesagium Notkeri omnemque huiusmodi rem cum aperuisset, desiderabat viri Dei, si

noticed the man of God who was sitting at his psalter as usual. When the chaplain recognized him as the man who the day before had resolved many of the queries posed by Charles, he said to his companions: "I say, look, that is the man who, they say, is more learned than anyone else in Charles's kingdom. But if you want, I will try to make a laughingstock out of him, as superbly learned as he is, and ask him something that he, a man of such renown, is entirely
ignorant about." His companions were curious and asked 2
him to do it; they all came up to the monk together and greeted him. The man humbly got up and asked what they wanted. Then that wretch I have mentioned said: "We know, my dear and highly learned fellow, that you know everything. We long to hear from you, if you know, what God is doing now in heaven." "I do know," the monk answered, "and I know it very well. It's this: at the moment he is doing what he has always been doing, that is to say, he is going to do it to you in just a moment. *He exalts the humble and humbles the haughty.*" That devilish mocker walked away, mocked by his own men, belittling the assertion that the monk had predicted his future. Immediately after that, the signal was sounded for assembling and honoring the departing emperor with acclamations. That man, who already had his misfortune in the making, gripped the banner of his company that was to ride before his lord on that day. Riding on his high horse, he stumbled at the city gate, fell wretchedly
on his face and broke a leg. He was taken to the new abbot 3
Bernhard, Hartmut's successor, for treatment. When he finally related to the abbot Notker's prediction and the whole story, he begged to receive absolution and blessing from the

se invisere dignetur, absolutionem et praesentis benedictionem. Quod cum ille despective de Notkero audiens, nihil sibi mali eius vaticinio assereret contigisse, coagulari fractura illa nullis fomentis, nullis adunari valuit ligamentis. Supplicatur tandem media quadam nocte a miserantibus clamores eius Notkero. Qui dum adveniens crus contrectasset, confestim conbullire illud sensit confractus didicitque severe de cetero humilia sentire.

39. Et ut ad ordinem redeamus Sindolfumque sub Salomone licenter bacchantem prosequamur: quadam die, quod erat refectorarii, Notkero et Ratperto simul ordinariis mensuram potus, ut officii sui erat, considentibus cum in uno vase non poneret, sed maledicta submurmurans absentibus adhuc quasi proiceret, vas illud quasi de mensa lapsum in terram cecidit operculoque procul rotante in latus iacuit vinumque, tamquam si subrectum esset, solide continuit.
2 Quod ille morose reversus—nam per passus aliquot festinus abscesserat—cum levasset, accurrentibus, qui procul viderant, et, si quicquam de vino effusum sit, terram conspectando quaerentibus: "Ne miremini," inquit, "si diabolus, a quo nigros libros noctibus discunt, fascinatorum suorum calices, ne effunderentur, continuit." Quod Hartmannus post a dicentibus cum audisset protervoque illi occurrisset: "Vide, bone vir," inquit, "ne in tales viros iniurias tuas tam

man of God in person if he would deign to visit him. After listening to the story about Notker with utter contempt the abbot assured the man that no evil had befallen him because of Notker's prophecy; yet he was unable to stop the bleeding caused by the fracture, by any poultices or bandages. Finally, supplication was made one night to Notker by monks who took pity on the chaplain's shouted pleas. Notker came and, as soon as he touched the broken leg in order to examine it, the injured man felt it immediately start to heal, and he learned the hard way how to feel humble in the future.

39. Now, to get back to the chronological order, let me continue telling you about Sindolf and his uncontrolled behavior under Salomo. One day, when Notker and Ratpert were both servers for the week, Sindolf in his capacity as a refectorer did not set down their measure of drink in a jug for them when they were seated, as it was his duty to do, but murmuring curses under his breath, he practically tossed it to them before they reached their seats; the jug apparently slipped off the table and fell to the floor, landing on its side, and although its lid rolled away, yet it still held all the wine
as if it were upright. Sindolf sullenly turned back (he had 2
hastily retreated a few steps) and picked up the jug. Then those who saw this from a distance ran up to him and, looking at the floor, asked if any of the wine had spilled out. Sindolf said to them: "Don't be surprised if the devil, from whom they learn the black arts at night, restrained the cupfuls of wine for his enchanted followers from spilling out." Hartmann heard about this later from brethren who told him about the incident, and when he ran into that insolent man, he said: "Watch out, my good man, that you do not finally do something exceedingly stupid to such worthy men

patienter ferentes nimium tandem desipias!" Cui ille cum sibi solita usque ad convicia respondisset protervia, Waltrammus, tunc decanus, in proximo fratrum capitulo *regulari* illum *vindictae subiecit.*

3 Tuotilo vero abbatum, sub quibus militaverat, permissis plerumque et praeceptis multas propter artificia simul et doctrinas *peragraverat* ut in suo capitulo tetigimus, *terras.* Picturas etiam et anaglyphas carminibus et epigrammis decorabat singulariter pretiosis. Tantaeque auctoritatis, ubicumque moraretur, apparuit, ut nemo, illum qui vidisset, sancti Galli monachum dubitasset. Erat autem in divinis et humanis ad responsa paratissimus et, si quid incondecens, maxime in monachis, usquam vidisset, pro loco, tempore et persona zelator erectus, ut in uno de pluribus dicere habebimus.

40. Enimvero quoniam homo erat itinerarius lateque terrarum et urbium gnarus, missus est aliquando pro communi causa Mogontiam utique pro pannis laneis emendis, quos "sericales" vocant aut "tunicas." In ingressu ergo civitatis circa sancti Albani monasterium hospitium petens, hominibus suis statim propter pabula et victualia mercatum missis, ipse super sedile se lassus, ut paulisper quiesceret, locaverat. Erant autem dies vindemiae, quibus fratres ad oboedientias dimissi sunt per vineas. Et ecce primo signo ad vesperas pulsato circator fratres collecturus, asino pro religione insidens, hostio domus hospitii iam dicti quasi aliquem et ibi quaesi-
2 turus appropiat. Latenter autem, si commatrina sua domi

who have borne your insults so patiently!" When Sindolf, in his usual fashion, responded with insolent words that bordered on insults, at the next chapter meeting Waltram, who was then dean, *meted out his punishment in accordance with the Rule.*

Regarding Tuotilo, I have already mentioned in a chapter 3
about him that he *traveled far and wide* to share his technical skills and learning and that the abbots under whom he served allowed, and often ordered, him to do so. He even decorated his paintings and relief work with poems and inscriptions of unique value. Wherever he stayed, he displayed such authority that no one who saw him doubted that he was a monk of Saint Gall. In matters human and divine he was always quick and ready to answer any question, and if he ever saw something unbecoming, especially in monks, he conducted himself with zeal and rectitude with regard to place, time, or person, as in the one case out of many that I am going to tell you about.

40. Because Tuotilo was a courier and familiar with lands and cities far and wide, he was sent to Mainz once on the community's business, specifically to buy woolen shirts that are called "serge" or "tunics." There he sought out an inn at the entrance to the city near the monastery of Saint Alban, and after promptly sending his men to purchase food and fodder, he lay down, exhausted, on a bench to rest for a little while. It was the time of the grape harvest, when brothers were sent out to the vineyards to tend to their estates there. At the first sound of the bell for Vespers, here came a roundsman to gather the monks and, sitting on a donkey out of reverence for God and seemingly looking for someone, drew near to the entrance to the aforementioned inn.
Stealthily he rode up to the house to find out if his special 2

sit, sciscitando domum inequitat. At illa de camera egressa salutans compatrem, hospitem illum dormire putans, optulit viro mustum. Quo ille *impigre hausto* vaseque reddito mammam feminae titillat assentientis. Hospes vero viso facinore exilit, illum scelestum inclamitans, comis apprehensum in terram deiecit flagelloque, quo ad equum usus est, adhuc manu habito acriter hominem cecidit adiciens: "Hoc," inquit, "tibi sanctus Gallus, sancti Albani frater, dedit!" Ille vero quamvis pro reatu sit tristis et passus, timidus tamen sui venia petita, uti se celatum habere vellet, hominem rogat. Hospes illi: "*Ne* modo *adicias peccatum peccato,* quantum in me est, bene celaberis."

3 Intimatur abbati fratrem de sancto Gallo ante portam hospitari. Vocatur in claustrum. Nomen sciscitati agnoscunt hominem diu fama vulgatum. Caritativeque tractato ipsi exhibebant Martham. Ille autem capacibus exhibebat Mariam. Rogaturque ibi morari, usque dum thronum Dei in bractea altaris aurea celaret. Cui similem anaglypham raro usque hodie videre est alteram. In circulo scribens hunc versum:

Ecce *polo potior solio terraque scabello.*

4 Cum autem ibi aliquantum tardasset, non celatum est ex parte, quid deforis egerit. Rogatus dicere: "Fratrem," inquit,

friend was at home. Thinking that her guest, Tuotilo, was asleep, she came out of her room, greeted her dear friend and offered him new wine. *He eagerly drank it up,* gave the mug back to her, and began to play with the breast of the willing woman. As for the guest, when he saw this evil deed, he leaped up and loudly denouncing him as an abomination, grabbed him by the hair, threw him to the ground, and as he was still holding in his hand the whip that he had used on the steed, he vehemently struck the man, adding these words: "It is Saint Gall, a brother of Saint Alban, who has given you this!" As for the man, although he was dejected about his crime and had suffered for it, he fearfully begged for his forgiveness and asked Tuotilo to be good enough to keep the matter secret. The guest said to him: "Just *don't add sin to sin,* and as far as I am concerned you can count on it staying secret."

The abbot of Saint Alban received word that a brother 3
from Saint Gall was staying before the city gate. He was invited into the monastery. When they learned his name, they recognized him as the man who had long been famous far and wide. Treating him with loving charity, they rendered him the service of Martha, while he to those who understood played the role of Mary. They asked him to stay there long enough to carve the throne of God on the gold leaf of the altar. You can hardly see another relief like that to this day. Encircling it he wrote the following verse:

> Behold! *I have the sky for my throne and the earth for my footstool.*

After he had lingered there for a little while, what he had 4
done outside partly came to light. When asked about it, he

"ibi indisciplinatum vidi, quem, ut ferirem, flagellum levans intentavi, quod illi et mihi indultum quidem rogo." Sic ille fidei memor veritati parcens, non tamen mentitus est.

Dixerant autem de illo unum aliquid, quod, quamvis monachi non fuerit, propter naturam tamen hominis dicere volo. Ibat aliquando per silvam *latronibus aptam* duobus suis comitatus, uno scutato cum lancea, altero sine. Et ecce a duobus audacissimis invasus, ambos istos uterque suum equo deiecerat. Interea ille, utroque in spolio occupato, robur quoddam validum circumspectum arripuit et terrore magno minax super illos venit. At illi videntes *hominem forti assimilem* spolia omittunt, scuta dorso reiecta contra illum vergunt. Lanceasque ille latronum prae securitate procul abiectas suos citissime rapere iussit et, ut se defenderent, acer verbis emonuit. Quas cum deiecti celeres raperent, tanti ducis violentiam minime se perpeti posse videntes, hostes ab eo exarmati divertunt. Sic isti lancea etiam sua levata, ut, si illi reverterentur, domino eam darent, silvam *imperterriti* transeunt.

41. Notkerus autem spiritualiter, ut diximus, fortis, quantum Tuotilo in homines, tantum ipse valuit in daemones; alias autem corpore, ut ieiunans et vigilans, tener, ut diximus, et macer. Accidit autem, ut quadam nocte in ecclesia

said: "I saw a brother there who lacked discipline and I raised my whip threatening to strike him, and for this I truly ask forgiveness on his and my behalf." In this way he remained true to his promise but compromised the truth, and yet he did not lie.

They also told another story about him that I want to tell you because even though it may not befit a monk, it shows the man's character. Once, he was going through a forest, *a likely place for robbers,* accompanied by his two men, one of them bearing a shield and a lance and the other unarmed. Behold! Two very bold robbers attacked him and threw both his companions off their horses. In the meantime, while each of the two robbers was busy collecting his spoils, Tuotilo grabbed a sturdy oak branch that he spotted nearby and came at them, a threatening figure in a terror-inspiring attack. Seeing *a valiant-looking man,* they dropped the spoils, shifted their shields from their backs, and moved against him. Tuotilo ordered his men to seize with all speed the lances that the robbers had carelessly thrown aside at some distance and sharply urged them to defend themselves. When the unhorsed men quickly seized the lances, the enemy saw that they could by no means withstand the power of such a commander. Disarmed by him, they turned and ran. Tuotilo's men also picked up their master's lance, ready to hand it over to him should the robbers return, and they passed through the forest *utterly unafraid.*

41. As for Notker, he had spiritual strength, as I said, and was just as effective in fighting demons as Tuotilo in dealing with men; but in other respects, as I mentioned, he was physically frail and emaciated as a result of fasting and keeping vigil. One night it so happened that he *rose before dawn,*

praeveniens in maturitate altariaque circumiens, ut solebat,
clamaret. In cryptam vero veniens XII apostolorum sanctique Columbani, acriores de post aram *oculi eius* cum *dedu-
cerent lacrimas,* quasi canem audierat mussitantem. Cumque
interea suis vocem grunnientis mixtam sentiret, intellexit
temptatorem: "Esne tu," inquit, "iterum ibi? Quam *bene tibi,
miser, contigit* nunc mussitanti et grunnienti post gloriosas
2 voces illas, quas in caelis habueras!" Accensoque lumine, quo
angulo lateret, quaesivit. Ille vero sinistro angulo appro-
piantem tamquam canis rabidus vestes lacerat. "Eia," inquit
ille, "servitium tuum foris cryptam satagere habeo; neque
enim poenae illae valent, quas, ut aiunt, iam pateris: acrius
tibi aliquid paraturus sum. Praecipio tibi autem in nomine
istorum sanctorum et Domini mei, ut me in eodem, quo
nunc indutus es, canino corpore exspectes." Et ille: "Faciam," inquit, "si volo." Et Notkerus velocius abiens:
"Confido," ait, "in Domino, quia, velis nolis, me exspectabis." Festinato autem aram sancti Galli adiens, cambotam
suam et magistri eius, multarum virtutum operatricem, cum
sphaera illa sanctae crucis notissima rapuit et, in introitu
cryptae dextero sphaera posita, cum baculo sinistrorsum
3 caninum illum aggressus est diabolum. Cum autem illum
baculo sancto caedere coepisset, voces suas anteriores altius
gannitu edidit et grunnitu. Tandem vero cum ad sphaeram
sanctissimam cedendo cedentem fugiens venisset, ultra iam

and as he walked around in the church, from one altar to another as was his custom, he was *chanting out* his prayers. When he entered the crypt dedicated to the twelve apostles and Saint Columban and as *tears were falling* more profusely *from his eyes,* he thought he heard a dog growling from behind the altar. When he detected, mixed with the growling, the sound of a pig grunting, he realized that it was the Tempter. “Is that you there again?” he said, “*You wretch,* how *fittingly it has turned out for you* now to be grunting and growling, after the glorious sounds that you once made in
heaven!” Lighting his lantern, Notker searched around to 2
find in which corner he was hiding. As he approached the corner on his left, the devil tore at his clothes like a rabid dog. “Well then!” Notker said. “I will have to deal with your service outside the crypt; the punishment that they say you now suffer is insufficient; I’m going to arrange something harsher for you. In the name of these saints and my Lord, I command you to stay and wait for me in the same canine form that you have assumed.” He replied: “I’ll do it if I feel like it.” Notker quickly said as he moved away: “I put my trust in the Lord that you will wait for me, whether you feel like it or not.” He hastily walked up to the altar of Saint Gall, grabbed the staff (it had belonged to the saint and his teacher and had worked many miracles) together with the much-acclaimed sphere of the Holy Cross, placed the sphere on the right of the entrance to the crypt and came at
the canine devil with the staff from the left. When Notker 3
started beating him with the holy staff, the devil raised his voices, snarling and grunting even louder than before. He retreated, fleeing from Notker’s beating, and finally stopped when he reached the holy sphere, unable to proceed farther;

progredi non valens constitit, et tot iam ictus et incussiones
ferre non sustinens, barbarice clamans: "*Auwê mir wê!*" vociferavit. At interea aedituus cum basilicam intrasset vocesque
horridas audisset, lumen velox in manibus sumpsit et ad
cryptam acceleravit. At ille cum ei ictum ultimum fecisset,
baculum sanctum in locis confregit. Et nisi aedituus sphaeram videns allevasset canemque sic abire permisisset, adhuc
4 eum caedere habuisset. Aedituus vero baculo inspecto atto-
nitus: "Baculumne sanctum, domine mi, in cane foedasti?"
Illo conticente addidit: "Quisnam ille erat," inquit, "qui
'*awê*' vociferavit?" Putansque illum pro pietate furem aliquem celare, ivit in pedes per totam ecclesiam, furem
comprehendere cupiens. Sed cum neque furem inveniret
neque canem, graditur *secum mirans,* quia ecclesiam post se
introiens clauserat, quidnam esse posset, quod contigerat.
Virum denique regularem iam semel sibi tacitum amplius
alloqui non ausus est praesumere.

5 Et ille, secundum quod humilis erat et prudens, aedituo foras ire significans, in partem eum sumpsit benedictioneque praelata: "Quoniam baculum," inquit, "fili mi, confregi, nisi tu iuveris, secreta mea habent efferri. Sed quoniam meum non est *ambulare in magnis et in mirabilibus super me,* silentio fidei tuae, quod factum est, committo." Sicque ei rem, ut facta est, enucleavit. At ille baculo per fabrum latenter reparato, quod factum est, ad tempus occultavit. In temporis autem processu res, ut erat, in medium venit.

he could no longer stand all the beating and pummeling and cried out loud in the vernacular: "Alas for me!" Meanwhile the sacristan, who entered the church and heard horrible noises, quickly picked up a lantern, and hurried to the crypt. When Notker struck his last blow at the devil, he broke the holy staff in several places. But he would have kept up the thrashing had not the sacristan seen the sphere and picked
it up, thus letting the dog escape. The sacristan, for his part, 4
examined the staff and said in astonishment: "Did you pollute the holy staff by using it on a dog, sir?" When Notker remained silent, he added: "Who was it who called out 'alas'?" Thinking that Notker was concealing some thief out of the goodness of his heart, the sacristan carefully walked around the entire church, eager to catch the thief. But he found neither a thief nor a dog and continued walking around, *wondering to himself* what on earth could have happened because he had locked the church when he came in. In the end, he did not dare to presume to talk further to a man who was guided by the Rule and who had already answered him with silence once.

Notker, being a humble and prudent man, signaled to the 5
caretaker to step out, took him aside, gave him a blessing, and said: "My son, since I have broken the staff, my secret will come out unless you help me. But since it is not my way *to occupy myself with things too great and too marvelous* for me, I put my trust in your loyalty to keep silent about what has transpired." On this condition, he explained to him in detail exactly what had happened. The staff was quietly repaired by a workman, and he at first kept what had happened a secret. But in the course of time the whole affair, as it truly happened, came to light.

42. Et ut videas loci nostri religionem etiam in psalmodiis, tredecim sedilia cum psalteriis aut auro inpictis aut alias nobilibus habebat; praeter alias et habet illa sancti Galli basilica capellas. In quorum uno angulari foribus proximo Notkerus psallere erat solitus. Accidit autem, ut quadam die ad nonae synaxim non veniret neque eam per se caneret. In illo autem solio cum post completorium *clara adhuc die* precibus insisteret, videt super se in laquearii interrupti trabi-
2 bus diabolum consedisse et stilo in tabula scribere. Quem cum, quid scelus scriberet, interrogasset: "Nonam," inquit, "quam tu scelus hodie supersederas, scribo." At ille dicto citius: "*Deus, in adiutorium meum intende!*" prosecutus, videt eum manu celerrima, quod scripserat, planasse. Cumque ad preces synaxis se in terra prosterneret, tabulam laquearii disrupti super eum deiecerat. At ipse videns, ut ictum declinaret, citus exsiliit. Cachinnans tandem ille: "Tamen mihi ut assurgeres," inquit, "effeci." "Enimvero," ait et Notker, "si tu ut nuper caninus fueris, iterum tecum habeo operari."

3 Tandem cum evanuisset, fratres aliqui in extremis templi orantes, sonum tabulae vocesque audientes mirati, quid esset, citi aderant. Videntesque eum, ut solebat, prostratum, nolebant illum, quod etiam incompetens hora esset, impedire. Tandem tamen Tuotilo, unus ex ipsis, signo dato amice

42. So that you may appreciate the religious devotion of
our monastery in the singing of psalms too, it had thirteen
seats furnished with psalters that were decorated either
with gold or with otherwise precious elements; also, the
church of Saint Gall has more chapels than other churches.
In one of those seats, the corner one closest to the door,
Notker was accustomed to sing psalms. One day it so happened that he neither came to the assembly at None nor
sang by himself. When he was intent on his prayers at that
seat after Compline, *while it was still clear daylight* he saw the
devil sitting on one of the crossbeams of the ceiling above
his head and writing with a pen on a tablet. When Notker 2
asked him what evil deed he was writing down, the devil
said: "I am writing down the None that you, wicked man,
skipped today." Notker immediately responded by praying,
"*O God, come to my assistance!*" and saw that the devil, moving
his hand very quickly, erased what he had written. When
Notker prostrated himself on the ground for the prayers of
the divine office, the devil tore a plank out of the paneled
ceiling and threw it at him. Notker saw this and quickly
leaped out of the way to avoid being hit. Finally, the devil
said with a cackle: "I still made you stand up for me." "Yes,"
Notker answered, "and if you become a dog, as you did not
long ago, I will have to deal with you again."

When the devil finally vanished, some brothers who were 3
praying at the other end of the church and who had heard the voices and the noise made by the plank quickly came over wondering what was going on. They saw Notker prostrate as usual on the floor and did not want to disturb him because the time was still inappropriate. Finally, Tuotilo, who was with them, gave him a friendly sign, inviting him to

illum foras evocans, silenter in aurem: "Magnas," inquit, "inquietudines tu et daemones tui fratribus facere soletis." At ille: "Audierantne, mi anime, fratres omnia?" "Non omnia," inquit; "sed mihi, velim, quae haec turba fuerit, per *singula pandas.*" Ipse vero id cum abnueret ab eoque se concitus, tabulam ibi cecidisse dicens, subtraheret, erant alii, qui viderant et factum, ut erat, non celabant.

43. Erat eodem in tempore in loco adolescens quidam monachus admodum litteratus, comitis cuiusdam filius nomine Wôlo, inquietus et vagus, cui propter aversionem cum nec decanus ipse nec domnus Notkerus seu ceteri imperare potuissent crebroque esset verbis verberibusque coercitus nihilque proficeret, omnes pro talis ingenii viro dolebant. Nam cum numquam sanctus Gallus nisi libertatis monachum habuisset, nobiliores tamen saepius aberrabant. Advenerant in monasterium parentes eius pro eo solliciti; per quorum monita cum parumper proficeret, iterum post habitum eorum idem erat. Diabolus autem quadam die domno apparuit Notkero diluculo: "Malam tibi," inquit, "et fratri-
2 bus tuis facturus sum noctem." "Mala avis," ait ille, "malam famam prodere solet." At ille fratribus, quae audivit, uti die illo se caverent, praenotuit. Wôlo vero cum hoc et ipse a dicentibus audisset: "*Senes,*" inquit, "semper vana *somniant.*" Erat autem dies ipse, quo sibi a decano, ne quoquam, ut solebat, claustro progrederetur, interdictum esse omnes noverant. Et cum sederet ad scribendum, ultima eius scriptura

step outside, and quietly whispered in his ear: "You and your demons have a habit of creating great disturbances for the brothers." Notker asked: "Did the brothers hear everything, my dear friend?" "Not everything," Tuotilo said, "but I'd like you *to explain to me in detail* what this commotion was about." Although Notker refused to do so, saying that a plank had fallen down there, and quickly withdrew from Tuotilo, there were others who had seen what had happened and did not keep it secret.

43. At the same time there was in our monastery a young
monk well educated in the liberal arts; he was the son of a
count and called Wolo. He was restless and given to wandering, and neither the dean himself, nor Master Notker, nor
the others could control him because of his resistance. He
was often disciplined with reprimands and rods, but nothing worked, and everybody felt sorry for him because of his
character. You see, although Saint Gall had never had a monk
who was not freeborn, those more nobly born more often
went astray. Wolo's parents, worried about him, came to the
monastery; although he improved slightly as a result of their
admonitions, after they left he again became the same as before. One day at dawn the devil appeared to Master Notker
and said: "I am going to make it a bad night for you and your
brethren." Notker replied: "A bad bird usually brings bad 2
news." But he told the brothers what he had heard and
warned them to be on their guard that day. As for Wolo,
when he, too, heard people talk about it, he said: "*Old men*
always *dream* false dreams." But it was the very day when, as
everybody knew, the dean had forbidden Wolo his usual
walk outside the cloister. When Wolo sat down to copy
scriptures, the last words he wrote were: "*For he was at the*

erat: *Incipiebat enim mori.* Ilicoque exsiliens, ceteris illum inclamantibus: "*Quo nunc,* Wôlo, *quo nunc?*" in campanarium sancti Galli per gradus ad hoc quidem nobis paratos ascendere incipit, uti oculis, quia gressu non licuit, montes camposque circumspiciens vel sic animo suo vago satisfaceret.

3 Ascendens vero cum super altare virginum venisset, impulsu, ut creditur, satanae per laquear cecidit collumque confregit. Plurimis autem, qui viderant vel audierant, accurrentibus, cum viaticum ei properanter afferrent, confessione dicta communicavit. At illi cum eum efferre voluissent et ad domum infirmorum portare: "Sinite me," inquit, "sanctas virgines prius inclamare! Ipse enim sciunt, quia, quamvis alias nefandissimus, mulierem tamen non novi." Interea cum alte eiulasset, Notkero accurrente, manus illi porrexit: "Tibi," inquit, "domine mi, et sanctis virginibus, quas semper amabas, animam peccatricem commendo." At ille iactans se circa eum: "Sanctae," inquit, "virgines, in vobis confisus fratris istius crimina super me tollo et ambos nos vobis committo." Et haec dicens flebat et eiulabat. Cumque ille efferretur, pro foribus ecclesiae quiete petita, Notkerum manu artissime stringens, omnibus preces effundentibus, emisit spiritum.

44. Inter exsequias Notker eum lavit, in feretrum collocavit, obsequium faciens totam eius sepulturam ipse

point of death." He immediately leaped out of the room, and while the others were calling out to him: "Where are you going now, Wolo, *where now?*" he began climbing up to the bell tower of the church of Saint Gall by the stairs that had been put there for us to use for this very purpose: that he might let his eyes wander over the mountains and fields and at least appease his restless spirit this way, because he was forbidden to go on foot.

But as he climbed up above the altar of the Virgins, he 3
fell, knocked by a beam pushed by Satan, it is believed, and broke his neck. Many people who saw or heard this ran up to him; they hastily brought him the viaticum, and he made his confession and received the last Communion. When they tried to pick him up and carry him to the infirmary, he said: "Let me call upon the Holy Virgins first, for they know that although I have been very sinful in other respects, still I have not known a woman." In the meantime, since he had been moaning loudly, Notker came running up and Wolo said, reaching out his hands to him: "My master, to you and to the Holy Virgins whom you always loved I entrust my sinful soul." Notker threw himself down next to Wolo and said: "Holy Virgins, I trust in you, and I take this brother's sins upon myself and commend us both to your care." As he said this, Notker was crying and moaning. When he was being carried out, Wolo asked them to stop at the church door and, tightly squeezing Notker's hand, he drew his last breath, surrounded by the brethren who poured out their prayers.

44. Performing the funeral rites, Notker washed Wolo, placed him on a bier, conducted the funeral Mass and took care of the entire burial, and as long as he lived always

procuravit semperque, quoad vixit, duo in se monachi officia testatus est solvenda. Completorium ipso obitus viri die dum finiretur, patrum quidam simplicior precem, in qua inest "*Ut sicut laeti duximus diem, ita noctem quoque laeti transigamus,*" dum recitasset, exsiliens vir Dei: "Quid petis," inquit, "frater admirabilis, quid petis? *Sufficeret hodie diei malitia sua* et superabundaret; tu autem et nocti eadem precaris?"

2 Septima vero obitus hominis die cum pernoctans in ecclesia permansisset, circa tempus laudis nocturnae parumper super genua pausans, videt quasi Rapertum suum se excitantem et dicentem: "*Dimissa sunt ei peccata multa, quia dilexit multum.*" At ille evigilans: "Unde, anime mi, unde hoc nosti?" cum subiunxisset, quasi modesto gradu ille exiit. At ipse putans eum ecclesiam, ut ibi licentius loqueretur, exire, dum eum extra velum prosequitur, neque ipsum neque gres-
3 sus eius ullum sentire poterat sonum. Cereoque accenso quaesivit eum in lecto. Quem invenit surgentem, ut et ipse, sicut solebat, *praeveniret in maturitate et clamaret.* Cereo extincto ecclesiam rediit. *Te Deum laudamus* prae gaudio flens silenter cantavit. Die autem dato, quaerente Ratperto, utrumne ad excitandum se nocte venisset, quod viderat, amabili suo aperuit. Tandem quoque et ceteros fratres spes tanta non latuit.

declared that he was to fulfill the duties of two monks all by himself. On the same day that Wolo died, as Compline came to an end, one of the fathers who was a bit simple said a prayer that included the following words: "*May we pass the night in joy, just as we spent the day in joy.*" As he was reciting this, the man of God leaped up and said: "What are you asking for, my admirable brother, what are you asking for? *Let the day's own trouble be sufficient for the day* and more than sufficient; are you now praying for the same thing to happen at night, too?"

On the seventh day after the man's death when Notker 2
had remained in the church for a night vigil around the time of the night office and was resting on his knees for a while, he thought he saw his friend Ratpert rousing him and saying: "*Many sins are forgiven him, because he has loved much.*" But when Notker woke up and asked: "How do you know this, my dear friend, how do you know?" the other man seemed to walk out with a soft step. Thinking that Ratpert was going out of the church so that he could talk to him more freely there, Notker followed him behind the curtain, but he could neither see him nor hear any sound of his footsteps.
He lit a candle and went to look for Ratpert in his bed. He 3
found him getting up, because he, too, would usually *rise before dawn and chant out his prayers.* He put out his candle and went back to the church. He quietly sang "God, we praise you," weeping for joy. When the day began and Ratpert asked Notker if he had come during the night to wake him up, Notker revealed to his beloved friend what he had seen. Eventually such a good reason for hope did not stay hidden from the rest of the brothers as well.

4 Ratpertus vero et ipse sanctus circa claustrum sancti Galli cum languidus iret nec tamen docere desineret, XL discipulis quondam suis, canonicis tunc quidem presbyteris, loco propter festum advenientibus animam singulis in manibus commisit, quorum quisque ei XXX missas obituro promiserat. Sicque ille laetissimus Deum, uti se diutius morbo coqueret, rogans, panis nitidus factus inter discipulorum manus in paradisum, ut credimus, transiit. Pro quo Notker et Tuotilo praeter ceteros fratres dolentes, qui post eum relicti sunt, multa fecerunt.

45. Tuotilo vero cum apud Metensium urbem caelaturus
satageret, peregrini duo sanctae Mariae imaginem caelanti
astiterant eleemosynamque petebant. Quibus cum nummos
clam tribueret, divertentes ab eo clerico cuidam astanti
aiebant: "Benedictus Domino vir iste, qui nos hodie bene
consolatus est. Sed estne soror eius," inquiunt, "domina illa
praeclara, quae ei tam commode radios ad manum dat et
docet, quid faciat?" Ille vero miratus, quid dicerent, cum
nuperrime ab eo digressus nil tale vidisset, revertitur et,
quod dixerant, velut *ad momentum et in ictu oculi* contempla-
2 tur. Ait autem illi clericus et peregrini: "Benedictus tu pater
Domino, qui tali magistra uteris ad opera!" Qui cum ipsos,
quid dicerent, nescire assereret, vehementer in *illos invectus,*
ne cui tale quid dicerent, interminatur. In crastinum autem
cum gloriam talem de se plures audiret dictitare, subtrahens
se cessit de medio neque iam ultra in urbe illa operari
volebat. In bractea autem ipsa aurea, cum reliquisset circuli

As for Ratpert, who was also a holy man, he still did not 4
stop teaching even when he was feebly walking around the cloister of Saint Gall. When forty of his former students, by then actually canons and priests, arrived at the monastery for a feast, he entrusted his soul to each of them, and every one of them promised him thirty Masses after his death. And so, greatly rejoicing and asking God to bake him longer with illness, he became shining bread and through the hands of his students passed, we believe, into paradise. Notker and Tuotilo, who survived him and grieved more than the other brothers, did much for his soul.

45. As for Tuotilo, when he was working on carving reliefs in the city of Metz, two pilgrims stood near him as he was carving out an image of Saint Mary and begged for alms. He secretly gave them money; they turned away from him and said to a cleric standing nearby: "That man who has consoled us well today is one of God's blessed. But is that his sister," they said, "that beautiful lady who so helpfully puts tools in his hands and teaches him what he should do?" The cleric, surprised by what they said because he had just left Tuotilo and seen nothing of the kind, turned around and, as if *in a moment, in the twinkling of an eye,* he beheld what they
were talking about. The cleric and the pilgrims said to Tuo- 2
tilo: "Father, you are blessed by God, enjoying, as you do, the assistance of such a teacher in your work!" He assured them that they did not know what they were saying, vehemently *reprimanded them, and forbade them to tell such a tale to anyone.* On the next day, however, since he heard many people spreading this account of his glory, he withdrew from their midst and departed, and thereafter refused to do any more work in that city. Later on, however, the following

planitiem vacuam, nescio cuius arte postea caelati sunt apices:

Pan <ana>thema pia caelaverat ipsa Maria.

Sed et imago ipsa sedens quasi viva cunctis inspectantibus adhuc hodie est veneranda.

3 Dicebant autem nobis patres, quod ipse vir Dei iter agendo in quandam villam, ubi ad missas sonatum est, properans daemonem ab homine in ecclesia bacchantem invocatione sancti Galli eiecerat. Sunt vero et alia, quae de illo audivimus, multa; sed et de aliis nostro in loco Dei viris, quibus quia, ut nunc saeculum est, diffidi putamus, tacere quam scribere maluimus. De obitu autem eius, quia nihil constans comperimus, hoc solum, quod ad gaudia eum migrasse confidimus, indubitanter asserimus.

46. De Notkero, quae reliqua sunt, audenter narrabimus, quoniam illum spiritus sancti *vas electum* nequaquam dubitamus. Remansit ille sanctissimus uterinis in spiritu viduus et orbus. Tandemque malum illi, quo *dolore cordis intrinsecus tactus* est, accidit. Epistolas canonicas Graecas a Luitwardo Vercellensi episcopo petitas multis sudoribus ille exemplaverat. Et ecce Sindolfus, magnus iam et praepotens in loco, ut diximus, codicem illum delicate scriptum casu incurrens furatus est, et singulas quaternionum, sicut hodie videre est, cultro excisas discerpsit atque depravavit et iterum conplicatas in locum, ubi eas fuerat furatus, reposuit . . . arus sponte . . . velut haec miraculis factam, ne maturitas tanti viri umquam huic assenserit levitati . . .

words were carved by someone on the golden plate, where he had left a circular surface empty:

> Mary carved out this votive offering herself.

The image of Mary sits there as if she were alive to this day, to be worshiped by everyone who looks upon it.

The fathers also used to tell us that when that man of 3
God was on the road, after hurrying into a village where the bells rang for Mass, by invoking Saint Gall he cast out a demon from a man who was running wild in the church. There are also many other things that I have heard about him and also about other men of God in our monastery; but since our age is such that I think I will not be believed, I prefer to keep silent rather than to write about them. Regarding Tuotilo's death, since I have found no certain information, this is the only indubitable assertion I can make: I am confident that he passed away to joy.

46. I will proceed with confidence to relate what remains to be said about Notker, because I have absolutely no doubt that he was a *chosen vessel* of the Holy Spirit. That holiest of men remained, orphaned and bereft of his brothers in spirit. Finally, there was a malicious act against him, which left him *stricken with grief to his heart's core.* With much effort he had copied Greek canonical Epistles that he had borrowed from Liutward, the bishop of Vercelli. Along came Sindolf, who, as I said, had by this time become an important and very powerful figure in the monastery. He chanced to come across that exquisitely written codex, furtively removed it, cut out some gatherings with a knife, pulled them apart, then put them back in a jumbled order (as we can see today), and returned the codex to the place he had stolen it from . . .

2 Quae autem Tuotilo dictaverat, singularis et agnoscibilis melodiae sunt, quia per psalterium seu per rottam, qua potentior ipse erat, pneumata inventa dulciora sunt, ut apparet in *Hodie cantandus* et *Omnium virtutum gemmis.* Quos quidem tropos Karolo ad offerendam, quam ipse rex fecerat, obtulit canendos. Qui rex etiam, *Viri Galilei* offerendam cum dictasset, Tuotiloni versus addere iniunxit, ut aiunt: *Quoniam Dominus Iesus Christus* cum ceteris, *Omnipotens genitor fons et origo* cum sequentibus, *Gaudete et cantate* et alios quidem; sed istos proposuimus, ut, quam dispar eius melodia sit ceteris, si musicus es, noris.

3 Waltrammus autem, quem supra diximus, decanus, sed et Hartmannus, qui abbas noster factus est, quas fecerant laudes, sua nomina quia preferuntur in cantilenarum libellis, studiose transimus, praeter quod Waltrammi sequentia *Sollemnitatem huius devoti filii ecclesiae* sine eius nomine scribitur. Fecerat et Hartmannus minor quaedam, quae utrius sint, aequivocatio dubia facit. Erant vero et alii quidam nostratium, qui sequentias et tropos nec non et alia quaedam plura pro studio quisque suo fecerant opera, quos loco suo memoraturi singulorum singula narranda servamus.

47. Hartmannum post Salomonem privilegio electionis patres acceperant abbatem. De quo, quoniam proprium eius sui temporis libellum habemus, plura scribere supersedemus. Erat tamen, ut a patribus audivimus, praeter sapientiae

As for Tuotilo's compositions, they have a unique and distinctive melody, because notes are more delightful when played on a psaltery or a rotta (which he himself played quite masterfully), as manifested in *Today We Must Sing* and *Adorned with the Jewels of All the Virtues.* He offered those very tropes to Charles, to be sung in the offertory that the king had written himself. When this king also composed the offertory *Men of Galilee,* they say he prevailed upon Tuotilo to add these verses: *Since our Lord Jesus Christ,* together with the others *Father Almighty, the Fount and Source,* and those that follow, *Rejoice and Sing* and also some others; but I have mentioned these compositions so that, if you know about music, you can understand how much his type of melody differs from those of other composers. 2

As for Waltram, the dean whom I mentioned earlier, and also Hartmann, who became our abbot, I intentionally pass over the hymns they composed because their names appear in the hymn books, except that Waltram's sequence *Feast of this Devout Son of the Church* has been copied without his name. Hartmann the younger also composed some hymns, but the ambiguity in their names makes it uncertain which hymns are whose. There surely were also other composers among us who wrote, each according to his inclination, sequences and tropes as well as many other pieces. We will consider them in their own place, saving a detailed description of the individual works of each for later. 3

47. After Salomo, the fathers chose Hartmann as abbot by the privilege of election. I refrain from writing much about him because we have a short book about his time that he wrote himself. He was, however, as we have heard from the fathers, quite apart from his scholarly gift of wisdom,

doctrinalem dotem religionis tenacissimus, claustro saepius manens, quae deforis in locis suis agerentur, minus sollicitus. Magisque suos habere passus quam se, quae sibi suppares in manus dare vellent, regratiando contentus, solius disciplinae patrum more investi<ga>tor et severus exactor. Doctrinas vero ita amabat, ut inter scholas et claustrum aut nihil aut parum intersit. In victu fratrum et vestitu Hartmuoti statuta secutus; maxime autem authenticum antiphonarium docere et melodias Romano more tenere sollicitus. De quo antiphonario altiora repetere operae pretium putamus.

2 Karolus imperator cognomine Magnus cum esset Romae,
ecclesias cisalpinas videns Romanae ecclesiae multimodis in
cantu, ut et Iohannes scribit, dissonare, rogat papam tunc
secundo quidem Adrianum, cum defuncti essent, quos ante
Gregorius miserat, ut item mittat Romanos cantuum gnaros
in Franciam. Mittuntur secundum regis petitionem Petrus
et Romanus, et cantuum et VII liberalium artium paginis ad-
3 modum imbuti, Metensem ecclesiam ut priores adituri. Qui
cum in Septimo lacuque Cumano aere Romanis contrario
quaterentur, Romanus febre correptus vix ad nos usque venire potuit. Antiphonarium vero secum, Petro renitente, vellet nollet, cum duos haberet, unum sancto Gallo attulit. In tempore autem Domino se iuvante convaluit. Mittit imperator celerem quendam, qui eum, si convalesceret, nobiscum stare nosque instruere iuberet. Quod ille quidem

extremely steadfast in his piety, more often staying in the cloister and less concerned about how his lands were being managed on the outside. He allowed his monks to have more than he had himself, grateful and content with whatever his subordinates were willing to hand him, and only cared about establishing and strictly enforcing discipline according to the custom of the fathers. Learning, however, he loved so much that he made little or no distinction between school and cloister. In the matters of food and clothing for the brothers he followed Hartmut's statutes; but most of all he applied himself to teaching the authentic antiphonary and keeping the melodies in the Roman style. I think it worthwhile to go into that antiphonary in more depth.

When the emperor Charlemagne was in Rome, he real- 2
ized that chanting in the churches this side of the Alps deviated in many ways from that in the Roman church (as John also wrote) and for the second time asked the pope (by this time Adrian) once again to send Romans who were expert in chants to Francia, because those sent earlier by Pope Gregory had died. In response to the king's request, the pope sent Peter and Romanus, who were very knowledgeable both in chanting and in the texts of the seven liberal arts. Like their predecessors, they were due to arrive at the
church in Metz. But when at the Septimer Pass and Lake 3
Como they were afflicted by air unfavorable to Romans, Romanus, sick with fever, could barely reach our monastery. Since he had two copies of the antiphonary, he was determined to bring one to Saint Gall and did so, although Peter was against it. In time, with the Lord's help, Romanus recovered. The emperor sent a courier with the request for Romanus to stay with us and teach us if he recovered. This

patrum hospitalitati regratiando libentissime fecit: "Quattuor," inquiens, "*mercedes* vos, sancti Domini, in me uno *acquisistis. Hospes erat, et in me eum collegistis; infirmus, et visitastis. Esurivit in me, et dedistis mihi in eo manducare; sitivit, et dedistis ei bibere.*"

4 Dein uterque, *fama volante* studium alter alterius cum audisset, emulabantur pro laude et gloria naturali gentis suae
more, ut alterum transcenderet. Memoriaque est dignum,
quantum hac emulatione locus uterque profecerit et non
solum in cantu, sed et in ceteris doctrinis excreverit. Fecerat
quidem Petrus ibi iubilos ad sequentias, quas Metenses vocat. Romanus vero Romanae nobis econtra et Amoenae de
suo iubilos modulaverat. Quos quidem post Notker, quibus
videmus, verbis ligabat. Frigdorae autem et Occidentanae,
quas sic nominabat, iubilos, illis animatus, etiam ipse de suo
5 excogitavit. Romanus vero, quasi nostra prae Metensibus
extollere fas fuerit, Romanae sedis honorem sancti Galli
coenobio ita quidem inferre curavit. Erat Romae instru-
mentum quoddam et theca, ad antiphonarii authentici publicam omnibus adventantibus inspectionem repositorium,
quod a cantu nominabant cantarium. Tale quidem ipse apud
nos ad instar illius circa aram apostolorum cum authentico
locari fecit, quem ipse attulit exemplato antiphonario. In
quo usque hodie, in cantu si quid dissentitur, quasi in spe-
culo error eiusmodi universus corrigitur. In ipso quoque

Romanus most willingly did out of gratitude for the fathers' hospitality. He said: "Holy men of God, just by getting me, *you have secured* a fourfold *reward. He was a stranger, and you took him in, in me; he was sick, and you visited him. He was hungry, in me, and you gave me, in him, to eat; he was thirsty and you gave him to drink.*"

Later on, when *the news spread* and each of them heard 4
about the other's efforts, they began competing with each other for praise and glory, as is the natural bent with their people, so that each tried to outdo the other. It is worth mentioning how much both places benefited from this competition and how much stronger they grew, not only in chanting but also in other areas of learning. For Peter wrote music there for sequences that he called the Metz sequences. As for Romanus, he in his turn composed for us his own music for the *Romana* and *Amoena.* Afterward Notker combined these melodies with the words that we now see. They also inspired Notker for his part to compose his own melodies for the *Frigdora* and *Occidentana,* as he called them.
Romanus, as if it was his duty to exalt our place over Metz, 5
managed to bring the honor of the Roman see to the monastery of Saint Gall in the following way. There was in Rome a certain device, a case that allowed all visitors to examine the authentic antiphonary, a repository, that is, that they called a *cantarium,* from *cantus,* a chant. Romanus also had a device similar to theirs placed in our church, near the altar of the apostles, together with the authentic copy of the antiphonary that he himself had brought. To this day, if there is any disagreement about chant, all errors of this kind are corrected by it, as if in a mirror. In this very antiphonary, Romanus was also the first to devise the system of assigning

primus ille litteras alphabeti significativas notulis, quibus visum est, aut susum aut iusum, aut ante aut retro assignari excogitavit. Quas postea cuidam amice quaerenti Notker Balbulus dilucidavit, cum et Martianus, quem de Nuptiis miramur, virtutes earum scribere molitus sit.

48. Hartmannus autem paucos annos cum praefuerit, in maximo nostratium luctu diem obiit. Claustrumque nostrum disciplinae patrum tenacissimus sectator doctrinaeque assiduus inculcator reliquit celeberrimum, praeter quod terras colentium et secularis rei curas gerentium non sine damno loci nimis exilis exactor erat. Enimvero eo claustri solius gubernacula curante et praepositis religionem, quam docuit, etiam deforis in sancta simplicitate artissime servantibus, maiores locorum—de quibus scriptum est, quia servi, si non timent, tument—scuta et arma polita gestare inceperant, tubas alio quam ceteri villani clanctu inflare didicerant; canes primo ad lepores, postremo etiam non ad lupos sed ad ursos et ad *Tuscos,* ut quidam ait, minandos aluerant *apros.* "Cellararii," aiunt, "curtes et agros excolant. Nos beneficia nostra curemus et venatui, ut viros decet, indulgeamus!" His bonis florentem rem publicam nostram hisque malis Hartmannus obiens reliquerat periclitantem.

49. Defuncto Hartmanno Engilbertus eligitur Chuonradoque dirigitur. Quem ille omni honore dignatum sancti Galli fecit esse vicarium, brevique supervivens tempore defunctus est et ipse. At Engilbertus loca foras monasterium

significative letters of the alphabet to the neumes as necessary, either above or below, or before or behind. Later Notker the Stammerer elucidated the significance of these to someone who had asked him as a friend, since Martianus, whom we admire for his *On the Marriage,* also endeavored to describe their benefits.

48. After he had ruled for a few years, Hartmann died, greatly mourned by our brothers. Because he very tenaciously followed the discipline of the fathers and assiduously inculcated learning, he left our monastery a place of great renown, except that he was an inadequate manager of those who worked our land and conducted our worldly affairs, not without damage to the monastery. While he attended only to the management of the cloister, and the provosts, in their holy simplicity, very strictly observed, even outside the monastery, the ways of devotional life that he taught them, the stewards of the estates, about whom it is written: "If servants have no fear, they get puffed up with arrogance," started carrying gleaming shields and arms, learned how to play their horns with a sound different from that of the other peasants; they reared hounds, at first to chase after hare and as time went on not only wolves but bears and *Tuscan boars,* as someone said. "Let the cellarers work on their farms and fields," they said. "As for us, let us attend to our benefices and indulge in hunting as befits men!" At his death, Hartmann left our community flourishing by these blessings and imperiled by these woes.

49. After Hartmann died, Engilbert was elected abbot and sent to Conrad. The king deigned to receive him with every honor and made him the vicar of Saint Gall but lived only a short time thereafter and then he too died. When

minus culta colere incipiens, maiores, quos diximus, talium desueti minus ei obtemperabant. Atque ille his atque aliis multis afflictus infortuniis, quae et sibi per se et defuncto Chuonrado totius regni imminebant cervicibus, domi residens tristis finem rei ieiunans cum suis et orans exspectabat. Cuius rei seriem breviatim dicere ad tragoediam nostram explicandam utile duxi.

2 Chuonradus rex virili prole carens, Eburhardum autem
fratrem habens ad regni gubernacula, si sibi superviveret,
aspirantem, sensit eum nec regno virtute quidem habilem
nec populo moribus acceptum. Rogantemque, cum ipse iam
senesceret, ut se populo commendaret, crebro frustravit.
Incipiens autem mori clam loquitur fratri: "Video," ait, "ger-
mane mi, et semper vidi te a populo nolle accipi; ideoque,
quod saepe rogaras, ne te contristarem, tacite distuli. Consilium autem meum si nunc feceris, ut in Deum spero, inglo-
3 rius non eris. Est in Saxonia, cui neminem in regno equipa-
rem scio: Henrich quippe comes, Mathilda coniuge clarus.
Sumens ergo coronam et sceptrum, noctu dieque accelera
ad ipsum; teque et regnum ei meis verbis in manus dato, et
mei in te memores fore ambos rogato." Fecit igitur, ut
rex iusserat, veniensque secretum comitis petiit alloquium.

Engilbert began attending to the largely uncultivated estates outside the monastery, the stewards I have mentioned, unaccustomed to such interference, did not obey him at all. Distressed by these and many other misfortunes that were hanging over his own head and, after Conrad's death, over the entire kingdom, he stayed in the monastery in sorrow and waited for the end of the troubles, fasting and praying with his brethren. To relate our tragedy in detail, I have considered it useful briefly to describe the sequence of these events.

King Conrad lacked male progeny, but he had a brother, 2
Eberhard, who aspired to rule the kingdom should he survive the king; Conrad felt, however, that Eberhard possessed neither the moral character needed for a ruler nor a disposition that would be acceptable to the people. As Conrad grew older, Eberhard asked his brother to commend him to the people, but the king continually frustrated his hopes. However, when the king was *at the point of death,* he talked to his brother in private. "I see, brother," he said, "and I have always seen it, that the people are unwilling to accept you; and so, because I did not wish to make you sad, I have quietly delayed doing what you often asked of me. But if you follow my counsel now, as I hope to God you will, you
will not end up without glory. There is a man in Saxony who, 3
to my knowledge, has no equal in the kingdom: it is Count Henry, ennobled by his wife Mathilda. Take the crown and the scepter, therefore, hurry to him, riding day and night, put yourself and the kingdom in his hands with words I give you, and ask them both to be mindful of me in their dealings with you." Eberhard did as the king had ordered, and when he arrived, he asked for a private audience with the count.

Eliminatis omnibus ipse hostium clausit clamideque exuta ad pedes viro corruens nimis stupenti coronam et sceptrum detegit et, quae iussus est, narrat. Cui ille inter cetera, si secum in fide, qua dixerat, sentire vellet, omnia, quae tanto nuntio decerent, facturum spoponderat. Et ne per *longas ambages* vadam: fit colloquium publicum, Henricus Saxonum et Francorum consensu elevatur et ungitur in regnum.

50. Sed postea dux Lotharingorum Kisilbertus Eburhardum castigatum, cur honorem suum alieno dedisset, regi Saxonico rebellare secumque sentire persuasit. Surgunt ambo in arma. Ducibus Suevo et Norico litteras mittunt. Quibus secum sentire iam motis, quadam die cum collectas in armis apud Prisacham copias navibus transposuissent ipsique interea in litoris planitiae luderent tabula, Chuono quidam regii generis, Churzibolt a brevitate cognominatus, fortuitu xx militibus stipatus viros incurrit, Kisilbertum cum omnibus, qui in nave erant, quam insilivit, lancea infixa submersit, Eburhardum levitatis increpatum gladio in litore
2 occidit. Erat quidem *angusto in pectore* audax et fortis. Qui leonem cavea effracta se et regem solos inventos in consilio insilientem—rege, grandi quidem viro, gladium, quem Chuono tunc, ut moris est, gerebat, arripere volente—ipse

After everybody departed, he locked the door. Taking off his mantle, he sank down at the man's feet, and, to the count's utter astonishment, uncovered before his eyes the crown and the scepter and related what he had been ordered to tell. The count promised him, among other things, that he would do everything that befits such an important envoy if Eberhard was willing to ally with him faithfully, as he had said he would. To cut *a long story* short, there was a public assembly and with the agreement of Saxons and Franks Henry was anointed and raised to the kingship.

50. Later on, however, Giselbert, the duke of Lotharingia, reprimanded Eberhard for giving his title away to a foreigner and persuaded him to join his side and rebel against the Saxon king. Both rose up in arms. They sent letters to the dukes of Swabia and Bavaria. One day, after these dukes had been persuaded to join the rebels, the armed force they had raised had been transferred to ships near Breisach, and the commanders were playing a board game on the level ground at the shore. A certain Chuono, a man of royal descent, nicknamed Churzibold for his short stature, who happened to have twenty fighting men with him, attacked the men. Giselbert jumped onto a ship, but Chuono drove him through with his spear and drowned him together with all the others who were on board the ship he leaped onto; Eberhard he killed on the beach with his sword, after upbraiding him for being fickle. Although *narrow chested,* Chu- 2
ono was bold and strong. Once a lion escaped from a broken cage and came upon him and the king just as the two of them were taking counsel in private and leaped upon them; the king, a large man himself, sought to grab the sword that Chuono was then carrying, as was the custom, but Chuono

praesiliens incunctanter occidit. Diffamatur longe lateque Henrici regis militem leonem se insilientem gladio occidisse. Mulieres ille et mala arborum naturali sibi quodam odio adeo execratus est, ut, ubi in itinere utrumvis inveniret, mansionem facere nollet. Multa sunt, quae de illo concinnantur et canuntur, quae, quia ad nos redeundum est, praeterimus, nisi quod provocatorem Sclavum, giganteae molis hominem, e castro regis prorumpens novus David lancea pro lapide straverat.

3 Purchardus autem dux Suevorum, Sueviam quasi tyrannice regens, praestationes Engilbertum abbatem primo militibus suis petivit; postea, utique quod cum rege Saxonico sentiret insimulatum, quaecumque loca sancti Galli sui rapere vellent, patienter tulit et, nisi pretiis gazophylacii eius redempta, nulla reddi fecit; inter quae calicem illum aureum, Adalberonis episcopi donum, cum dari sibi consentiret, et crucem, a sancta Wiborada correptus uxori verbis simulatis, ut aiunt, uti redderet, iussit; reque infecta ad Italiam, ut et eius regem secum sentire faceret, properans, beata illa ei mortem pro avaritia praesagiente, equo ruens periit. Quae quia alibi plenius sunt scripta, hic libasse sufficiat.

51. Engilbertus vero—ut, unde digressi sumus, redeamus—ad Henricum venit, abbatiam ab eo suscipiens fidem iuravit. Omnique honore ab eo dimissus domum ad maiora

leaped up before him and killed the lion instantly. The stories spread far and wide about King Henry's fighting man who killed with his sword a lion leaping onto them. Out of some innate hatred in him, he swore off women and apples, to the extent that when he traveled he did not want to stay at places where he might come across either of those. There have been many songs and stories about him, but since we have to return to our story, we shall pass over them here. I shall only mention that once he dashed forth from the king's camp and like a new David with a spear in place of a stone struck down a Slavic challenger, a man of giant physique.

Now Burchard, the duke of Swabia, who ruled Swabia 3
like a tyrant, at first requested land allotments for his fighting men from Abbot Engilbert; in any case, later on, because he heard the abbot was siding with the Saxon king, he indulgently let his men seize any of Saint Gall's lands they wanted and made them give nothing back unless it was ransomed by precious objects from Saint Gall's treasury. Among these precious objects were a golden chalice, a gift from Bishop Adalbero, and a cross. When he consented to accept them, he was reprimanded by Saint Wiborada, and so he gave a feigned order, they say, to his wife to return them. This was not done, and when he rushed off to Italy to convince its king to join his side, with that blessed woman foretelling that he would die for his greed, he tumbled down from his horse and died. Because these events are described elsewhere at more length, let it suffice merely to have touched on them here.

51. But to return to where we were before digressing, Engilbert went to King Henry, received the abbey from him, and swore an oath of fidelity. The king sent him off with every honor, and Engilbert came back home to even greater

adhuc infortunia rediit. Nam Ungri auditis tempestatibus regni Noricos *rabidi invadunt* et vastant, Augustaque diu obsessa, precibus Oudalrici episcopi, sanctissimi quidem inter omnes tunc temporis viri, repulsi Alemanniam nemine vetante turmatim pervadunt. At Engilbertus, quam idoneus ad
2 mala toleranda quidem fuerit, impiger ostendit. Nam malis his imminentibus, militum suorum unoquoque pro semet ipso sollicito, validiores fratrum arma sumere iubet, familiam roborat; ipse velut Domini *gigans lorica indutus,* cucullam superinduens et stolam, ipsos eadem facere iubet. "Contra diabolum," ait, "fratres mei, quam hactenus animis in Deo confisi pugnaverimus, ut nunc manibus ostendere valeamus, ab ipso petamus!" Fabricantur spicula, feltris loricae fiunt, fundibula plectuntur, tabulis compactis et vannis scuta simulantur, sparrones et fustes acute focis praedurantur. Sed primo fratrum quidam et familiae famae increduli fugere nolunt.

3 Eligitur tamen locus velut a Deo in promptu oblatus ad arcem parandam circa fluvium Sint-tria-unum. Quem sanctus Gallus quondam sanctae trinitatis amore de tribus fluviis in unum confluentibus sic equivocasse fertur. Praemunitur in artissimo collo vallo et silva excisis locus fitque castellum, ut sanctae trinitati decuit, fortissimum. Convehuntur raptim, quaeque essent necessaria. Haec in vita Wiboradae per scriptorem eius minus dicta a fratribus, qui haec noverant, docti praestrinximus. Capella citata fit oratorium, in quod

misfortunes. When the Hungarians heard about unrest in the kingdom, they *ferociously invaded* Bavaria and laid waste to it. After besieging Augsburg for a long time, they were driven back thanks to the prayers of Bishop Ulrich, surely the saintliest man of all at that time, and then, meeting no opposition, in roving bands they swarmed through Alemannia. But Engilbert quickly showed how adept he was at cop-
ing with adversity. With disaster looming over them and 2
each of his knights only looking out for himself, he ordered the stronger brothers to take up arms and equipped the dependents. He himself, like *a giant* of the Lord, *put on a breastplate,* covering it with his cowl and stole and ordered the monks to do the same. "My brothers," he said, "just as we fought the devil with our hearts, trusting in God, so now let us ask that we be able to show the same power with our fists!" They made javelins, cut breastplates out of felt, wove slings, joined together boards and baskets to fashion shields, and sharpened spears and cudgels and hardened them in fire. Initially, however, some of the brothers and dependents did not believe the rumors and refused to flee.

A place was chosen near the river *Sint-tria-unum,* as if spe- 3
cially designed by God for building a fortress. It is said that at one time, out of love for the Holy Trinity, Saint Gall made up this appropriate name for the three rivers flowing into one. The place was fortified at its narrowest neck of land by a rampart, and with cuttings from the forest, and it became a fortress, a very strong one as befitted the Holy Trinity. Everything that was needed was brought there without delay. These details are not mentioned at all by the author of the life of Saint Wiborada; I have briefly related what I learned from the brothers who knew about this. A chapel was

invehuntur cruces et cum diptychis capsae, nec non et paene omnis praeter libros repositorios ecclesiae thesaurus. Illos abbas Augiam, non satis tuto tamen, commiserat. Nam cum reportarentur, ut aiunt, numerus conveniebat, non ipsi. Senes cum pueris in Wazzirburc tuitioni dedit, quam cum familia, quae trans lacum erat, sollicite firmavit. Quibus etiam, ut navibus quidem crebrius inessent, victualia secum assumere iussit.

52. Ibant exploratores per nota sibi loca nocte dieque, adventum hostium fratribus, sanctum Gallum umquam a barbaris invadi nimis incredulis, ut ad castellum fugerent, praedicturi. Engilbertus enim et ipse talibus assentiens paene sero carissimas sancti Galli res castello intulit. Unde et ciborium Otmari relictum est hostibus. Nam hostes non simul ibant; sed turmatim, quia nemo restiterat, urbes villasque invaserant et spoliatas cremaverant, ideoque improvisi, qua vellent, imparatos insiliebant. Silvis quoque centeni vel minus interdum latentes eruperant. Fumus tamen et caelum ignibus rubens, ubi essent turmae quaeque, innotuit.

2 Erat autem tunc inter nostrates frater quidam simplicissimus et fatuus, cuius dicta et facta saepe ridebantur, nomine Heribaldus. Huic, cum ad castellum fratres primo

quickly built to serve as an oratory, and crosses and chests with lists of the dead were brought there, as well as almost all the treasure from the church except the library books. Those the abbot entrusted to Reichenau, which however did not prove to be a safer place: they say that when the books were carried back to Saint Gall, their number was right but the volumes were not the same. For safekeeping Engilbert put the old men and boys in Wasserburg, which he prudently manned with dependents who lived on the other side of the lake. He even ordered them to bring provisions with them, so that they could more frequently stay on the ships.

52. Day and night, scouts roamed over places they were familiar with; when the enemy approached, the scouts were to warn the brothers to flee to the fort, for they were extremely incredulous that Saint Gall would ever be overrun by barbarians. In fact, Engilbert himself shared this opinion and was almost too late in moving Saint Gall's most precious possessions into the fort. As a result, the canopy from the altar of Saint Otmar was left behind for the enemy. The enemy, you see, did not come all at once; rather, because no one resisted, they attacked cities and villages, in bands, pillaging and burning them down, and so they would fall unexpectedly upon the unprepared inhabitants wherever they pleased. At times, too, they hid in the woods and then sallied forth in companies of no more than a hundred men. However, smoke and a fiery-red sky indicated where individual bands were.

At that time there was a brother among us, by the name 2
of Heribald, very simple and dull witted, and people often made fun of what he said or did. As the brothers began to

pergerent, ut et ipse fugeret, cum terrore quidam dicerent: "Enimvero," ait ille, "fugiat, qui velit; ego quidem, quia corium meum ad calceos camerarius hoc anno non dedit, nusquam fugiam." Cum autem illum fratres, ut secum pergeret, in novissimo articulo vi cogere vellent, multa reluctatus, nisi annotinum corium sibi ad manus daretur, nusquam se iuravit iturum. Sicque Ungros ingruentes *imperterritus* exspectabat. Fugiunt tandem paene sero fratres cum aliis incredulis, horridis vocibus hostes instanter irruere perculsi; sed ipse intrepidus in sententia permanens otiose deambulabat.

53. Ingruunt tandem pharetrati illi, pilis minantibus et spiculis asperi. Locum omnem perscrutantur solliciti; nulli sexui vel aetati certum est misereri. Inveniunt solum illum in medio stantem intrepidum. Quid velit curque non fugerit, mirati, *ferro* interim *parcere* necatoribus iussis, primipilares per interpretes interrogantes, fatuitatis monstrum ubi sentiunt, omnes illi risibiles parcunt. Aram lapideam sancti Galli, quod prius crebro talibus frustati nihil intus nisi ossa vel cineres cum invenissent, nec tangere curant. Requirunt
2 tandem a fatuo suo, ubi thesaurus loci sit conditus. Quos cum ille alacer ad gazophylacii duceret occultum ostiolum, effracto illo nihil ibi nisi candelabra et coronas deauratas reperientes, quas in *fugam festinantes* reliquerant, deceptori suo

hurry to the fort, some of them called in alarm that he should run too. "Sure," he said, "whoever wants to can run. But I won't run anywhere, because this year the chamberlain didn't give me leather for my shoes." When, at the very last moment, the brothers tried to force him to come along with them, he fiercely resisted, swearing that he would go nowhere unless his year's supply of leather was handed over to him. So he waited for the aggressively advancing Hungarians *without a trace of fear.* Finally, the brothers and other holdouts fled, almost too late, panic-stricken by the savage cries, as the enemy at once burst in. But Heribald was leisurely walking back and forth, undaunted and firm in his resolution.

53. Finally, the Hungarians broke in, armed with quivers and bristling menacingly with spears and spikes. They scrutinized the entire place warily; it was clear that there was going to be *no mercy shown* to anyone of either sex or any age. They found Heribald standing alone and undaunted in the middle of the courtyard. Wondering what he might want and why he had not run away, the captains ordered the men doing the killing to hold their weapons for a while and interrogated Heribald through an interpreter; when they grasped his monstrous foolishness, they all laughed and spared him. They did not bother to touch the stone altar of Saint Gall, because they had often broken such Christian altars before and never found anything inside but bones or ashes. Finally, they asked their fool where the treasure of the monastery was hidden. When he eagerly led them to the secret little 2
door of the treasury, they broke it down and found nothing inside but candlesticks and gilded crown chandeliers that the brothers had left *in their haste to flee;* then they threat-

alapas dare palmis intentant. Duo ex illis ascendunt campanarium, cuius cacuminis gallum aureum putantes deumque loci sic vocatum non esse nisi carioris metalli materia fusum, lancea dum unus ut eum revellat, se valid<i>us protendit, in atrium de alto cecidit et periit. Alter interea in dedecus fani dei ipsius, ad summum pinnaculi orientalis veniens, dum ad alvum se parasset purgandum, retrorsum cadens totus confractus est. Quos ambos, ut Heribolt post retulit, inter postes valvarum dum cremassent rogusque flammivomus superliminare et laquear vehementer invaderet contisque incendia certatim plures miscerent, nequaquam templum Galli sicut nec Magni incendere quiverant.

3 Erant autem in cellario fratrum communi duo vasa vinaria usque ad sigillos adhuc plena. Quae, quia in articulo illo nemo boves iungere aut minare est ausus, ita sunt relicta. Haec vero, nescio quo loci fortunio, nisi quod talibus in vehiculis praedarum abundaverant, hostium nullus aperuit. Nam cum quidam illorum ascia vibrata unum retinaculorum succideret, Heribaldus inter eos iam domestice versatus: "Sine," inquit, "vir bone! Quid vis vero, ut nos, postquam abieritis, bibamus?" Quod ille per interpretem audiens et cachinnans socios, ne fatui sui vascula tangerent, rogavit. Sicque usque ad abbatis conspectum Ungris locum deserentibus sunt servata.

ened to slap Heribald for deceiving them. Two of them climbed the bell tower, thinking that the weathercock on top was made of gold and that the god of the place, called by this name, Gallus, would only be cast from the most precious metal. As one of them reached out more strenuously with his lance to tear it off, he fell down to the court from the high roof and perished. Meanwhile the other one, intending to dishonor the very sanctuary of the god, headed for the top of the eastern spire, and as he had readied himself to empty his bowels, he fell backward and was smashed to pieces. As Heribald related later, when they burned the bodies of those two between the doorposts, the funeral pyre spewed out flames, which greedily fell upon the lintels and roof panels, and some Hungarians eagerly stoked the fire with pikes, but they managed to set neither the church of Saint Gall nor the church of Saint Magnus on fire.

In the brothers' communal cellar there were two wine 3
barrels, still full almost up to their bungs. They were left behind because at the moment of flight no one dared to harness and drive the oxen. By some chance that favored the monastery none of the enemy opened them, maybe because they already had such an abundance of wine loaded on their carts that were filled with loot. When one of them brandished his ax and was going to cut off one of the barrel hoops, Heribald, who by then felt at home with them, said: "Leave it alone, there's a good man! Really, what do you want us to drink after you leave?" The man heard this in the interpreter's translation, gave a roar of laughter and asked his companions not to touch their fool's little barrels. This is how they remained unharmed right up to the abbot's inspection after the Hungarians had left the monastery.

54. Exploratores autem, qui silvas et quaeque latentia sollicitissime scrutarentur, certatim illi mittunt; eos, si quid novi referant, opperiuntur. Sparguntur tandem, Wiborada iam passa, per atrium et prata ad prandia copiosa. Ciborium quoque sancti Otmari argento vestitum nudant, quod repente invasi fugientes asportare non poterant. Primipilares quidem claustri planitiem tenentes omni copia convivantur.
2 Heribaldus etiam coram illis plus quam umquam, ut ipse postea dicebat, saturatus est. Cumque more suo *super viride faenum* singuli ad prandendum absque sedilibus recumberent, ipse sibi et clerico cuidam praeda capto sellulas posuit. Ipsi vero cum armos et ceteras victimarum portiones semicrudas absque cultellis dentibus laniando vorassent, ossa obesa inter se unus quidem in alterum ludicro iecerant. Vinum quoque plenis cubbis in medio positum sine discretione, quantum quemque libuerat, hausit.

3 *Postquam* vero *mero incaluerant,* horridissime diis suis omnes vociferabant. Clericum vero et fatuum suum id ipsum facere coegerant. Clericus autem linguae bene eorum sciolus, propter quod etiam eum vitae servaverant, cum eis *valenter clamabat.* Cumque iam satis lingua illorum insanisset, antiphonam de sancta cruce, cuius postera die inventio erat, *Sanctifica nos* lacrimans inceperat. Quam Heribaldus cum eo, quamvis voce raucosus, et ipse decantabat. Conveniunt

54. Meanwhile, the Hungarians were eagerly sending out
scouts to search the woods and all hiding places with complete thoroughness and waiting to hear if they reported any
news. Eventually, soon after Wiborada suffered martyrdom,
they spread themselves around the courtyard and over the
meadow for a rich feast. They also stripped the canopy from
the altar of Saint Otmar, which was decorated with silver:
attacked so suddenly, the brothers had not been able to
carry it away as they fled. The captains claimed the inner
court of the cloister, where they had a plentiful feast. Herib- 2
ald, as he used to say later, also stuffed himself in their company more than he had ever done. When the Hungarians
reclined without benches, one by one *upon the green grass* for
the meal, as was their custom, he put out little stools for
himself and for a cleric who had been taken captive. The
Hungarians meanwhile, after devouring shoulders and other
portions of slaughtered animals' meat half raw and, without
knives, tearing at them with their teeth, playfully threw the
bones, picked clean, at each other. Full cups of wine were
placed in the middle, and everyone without exception drank
as much as he wanted.

Warmed up by the wine, they all cried out to their gods in 3
the most horrifying manner. They forced the cleric and their
fool to do the same. The cleric, who knew their language
well—and it was because of this that he had been spared—
shouted loudly along with them. Then, after enough insane
shouting in their language, he tearfully began singing *Bless
Us,* the antiphon in honor of the Holy Cross, whose discov-
ery was to be celebrated on the following day. Heribald, too,
sang along with him, although he was hoarse. Everybody

omnes, qui aderant, ad insolitum captivorum cantum, et ef-
4 fusa laetitia saltant coram principibus et luctantur. Quidam etiam armis concurrentes, quantum disciplinae bellicae nossent, ostenderant. Interea clericus ille pro relaxatione sua rogandi tempus opportunum in tali alacritate arbitratus, sanctae crucis implorans adiutorium, provolvitur miser principum cum lacrimis pedibus. At illi nimis effero spiritu sibilis et quasi grunnitu horrido satellitibus, quid velint, insinuant. Illique rabidi advolant, hominem dicto citius corripiunt, cultellos, ut ludicrum, quod Teutones *picchin* vocant, in coronam eius facerent, antequam capite illum plecterent, exigunt.

55. Interim dum talia parant, exploratores in silva, quae <in> castellum vergit, subitanea tubarum et vocum significatione accelerant. Castellum cum armatis legionibus obfirmatum improximo sibimet esse asserunt; clerico ibi et Heribaldo relictis solis in claustro, celeres pro se quisque viri foras festinant et, ut assueti erant, priusquam quisquam
2 credat, parati in acie stabant. Audita autem castelli natura, quod obsideri non possit, locum autem longo collo et artissimo impugnantibus maximo damno certoque periculo adibilem, tutores eius suae multitudini, dum victualia habeant, modo viri sint, numquam cessuros, monasterio, eo quod

who was there came closer to listen to the captives' unfamiliar song, and they danced and wrestled with joyful abandon
before their leaders. Some of them even clashed weapons 4
with others to demonstrate how great their mastery of martial skills was. Meanwhile the cleric decided that, in the midst of such merrymaking, the moment was ripe for asking for his release. So the wretched man prayed to the Holy Cross for help and fell in tears at the feet of the leaders. But the leaders, in a most savage manner, indicated to their attendants what they wanted by hissing and a horrible kind of grunting. The attendants dashed up in maddened rage, seized the cleric sooner than you can say the word, and bared their knives in order to use the tonsured crown of the cleric's head in a game that the Germans call *picchin,* intending next to behead him.

55. Just as the Hungarians were getting ready to do this, their scouts rushed in from the forest that slopes down toward the fort, with sudden blasts of their horns and shouting. They reported that there was a fort nearby, guarded by an armed force. Everyone, each man of his own accord, hastened outside, leaving the cleric and Heribald in the monastery on their own, and, faster than anyone would believe, the Hungarians were standing ready in their battle array, as
they were trained to do. They heard the news that the fort, 2
due to its situation, could not be besieged, and that its location could only be reached by way of a long and extremely narrow neck, which would mean certain danger and great casualties for an attacking force; they also learned that the defenders, provided they were men of courage, would never yield to the enemy's superior numbers as long as they had sufficient supplies; and so, in the end the Hungarians left

Gallus *deus* eius *ignipotens* sit, tandem omisso, villae domos, ut videre possint—nam nox proxima erat—aliquas incendunt et silentio tubis et vocibus indicto via, quae Constan-
3 tiam ducit, abeunt. Castellani autem cum monasterium ardere putassent, abitu eorum comperto per compendia eos insecuti, exploratores de longe multitudinem prosecutos in faciem aggressi, quosdam occidunt, unum autem vulneratum captum avehunt; ceteri vix fuga lapsi multitudini tubis, ut caveant, significant. At illi campos et planitiem, quam citissime poterant, obtinentes aciemque, prout copia esset, alacriter instruentes vehiculis et ceteris impedimentis circumpositis noctem vigiliis partiuntur fusique per herbas vino et somno taciti indulgent. Mane autem prima villas proximas incurrentes, si quid fugientes reliquerint, investigant et rapiunt, cunctaque quae praetereunt aedificia exurunt.

4 At Engilbertus, hostium invasionis primicerius, castellum repetere ceteris dimissis, cum paucis aeque audacibus monasterium vitabundus inambulat; si aliqui ad insidias relicti sint, explorat. Heribaldi fratris fatuitatem, bene quidem nati, miserans, si vel corpus eius ad sepeliendum inveniant, sollicite investigant. Illo quidem nusquam reperto—nam cacumen proximi montis, vix a clerico persuasus, cum ipso occupans inter arbusta et frutecta latuit—miserebatur

the monastery because they thought that its *god* Gall was *ignipotent.* They set fire to some houses in the town so that they could see better (because night was falling), had their horns and voices observe silence, and retreated by the road that leads to Constance. The fort's garrison thought that 3
the monastery itself was burning, but after learning of the enemy's retreat they pursued the Hungarians by a shortcut, launched a frontal attack against the scouts who followed the main force at a distance, killed some of them, captured one wounded man, and took him away; the rest of the scouts who had only just managed to escape sounded their horns to alert the main force, which then as fast as it could reached level ground and promptly set the army in battle order as best they could. After placing their carts and other travel gear all around them, they divided the night into watches, and stretched out on the grass and quietly indulged in wine and sleep. Early the next morning they hurried on to the nearest villages and, checking to see if the fleeing inhabitants had left anything behind, seized what was still there, and burned the houses they passed on their way.

Meanwhile Engilbert, the chief commander in the war 4
against the enemy's invasion, took a few equally daring men, sent the rest back to the fort, and cautiously prowled around the monastery to find out if the Hungarians had left an ambush. Feeling sorry for Brother Heribald's folly, for he was wellborn, they carefully searched to see if they at least could find his body for burial. But Heribald was nowhere to be found because the cleric had, with great difficulty, persuaded him to run, and they were both hiding in the bushes and trees on the top of the nearest mountain. Engilbert pitied him even more when he thought that the enemy may

adhuc, si tantae simplicitatis mancipium hostes quidem secum abegerint. Miratus etiam vini vasa ab hostibus nimium bibulis vitata, gratias Deo egit.

56. Matutinas deinde laudes cursim de sancta cruce, prout silentissime poterant, persolventes, ianuas et laquear praeustum mirantur. Locoque celerrime abeuntes, si Wiborada vivat, ad clausulam eius silentio scissitantur. Compertoque, quod passa sit, tardare non ausi, montem proximum superant castellumque per avia nota celeres tandem revisunt: timentes, ut fit, ne aut in insidiis relicti aut ad alia circumquaque spolia sparsi, socios in locum secuti superveniant; parati tamen, *quoniam res eis pro anima erat,* aut fortiter emori aut manibus quidem viriliter defendi.

2 Et clericus Heribaldo assumpto—castellum enim de monte conspexerant—matutini adveniunt. Sed custodes de longe illos et adhuc in tenebris prospicientes, exploratores putantes sociis clamabant. At illi agiliter erumpentes, Heribaldo agnito de clerico primo haesitant, in munitionem tamen eum recipiunt et omnem tragoediam eius audientes hospitaliter tum pro Christo sed et pro captivo suo, cuius linguam noverat, tractant curando. Tandemque per illos
3 duos omnes insolentiae *hostium didicerant mores.* Ungar

have forcibly led this simple man away with them as a slave. Engilbert was also amazed to see that the enemy, all heavy drinkers, had ignored the wine barrels, and he gave thanks to God.

56. Then they sang the morning Lauds for the Feast of the Holy Cross, quickly and as quietly as possible, and looked in amazement at the scorched doors and paneled ceiling. They left the monastery in great haste and quietly went to Wiborada's cell to find out if she was still alive. When they learned that she had suffered martyrdom, they did not risk lingering, but quickly climbed over the nearest mountain by unfrequented paths known to them and finally returned to the fort. As often happens in such cases, they were afraid that the enemy might be waiting in ambush, or scattered in search of further booty all around, or had followed their fellow monks into the monastery and attacked them. However, *because their lives were at stake,* the men of Saint Gall were prepared either to die bravely or to use their hands to defend themselves like men.

In the morning the cleric, accompanied by Heribald, hav- 2
ing noticed the fortress from the mountain, approached the
gate. When the watchmen spotted them from a distance it
was still dark, so they took them for spies and shouted out
to their companions. They promptly dashed outside and
recognized Heribald, but they were hesitant at first about
the cleric. Nevertheless, they let both men inside the fortifi-
cation, and when they heard the story of the cleric's ordeal,
they treated him hospitably for Christ's sake but also for
the sake of dealing with their prisoner whose language he
knew. Eventually they *learned* from those two men *about the*
excessive *ways of the enemy.* The Hungarian was baptized, got 3

baptizatus uxorem duxit, filios genuit. Dein, quoniam reverti eos interdum solere didicerant, arbores silvae iterato contra castelli aditum latius succidunt fossasque altius fodiunt. Puteum, ubi scirpus ante crescere solebat, altissime fodientes certi aquae, purissimam inveniunt. Vinumque, quod Heribaldo Ungri diviserant, languenis et, quibuscumque possent, vasculis clandestini die noctuque curraces reportant. Sicque degentes Dominum assidui invocant.

4 De sancta Wiborada autem, quia liber per se est eius, amplius non loquemur, praeter quod in sanctam eam levari iam bis nostris temporibus per duos papas decretum est et sub Norperto tandem impletum.

57. De sancto Oudalrico autem, qualiter nobiscum egerit, dicta patrum quaedam audivimus, quae quidem in vita eius vel tertio iam scripta non invenimus. De nobilibus enim ille, ut et ab aliis iam dictum est, natus, apud nostrates educatus est et doctus. Hic viam, qua in caelos volavit, subvolare didicit. Hic virtutibus, quas nunc operatur, praeludium fecit.
2 Sanctorum enim nostrorum Galli et Otmari, quos puerulus patres elegit, se monachis iungens *cum sanctis sanctissimus et cum electis* ingreditur *electissimus.* Hartmanni enim iunioris discipulus divina prae omnibus spiritu sancto praelibatus hausit. In refectorio coram patribus, ubi vel in puncto

married and had sons. Since the defenders of the fort had learned that the Hungarians were sometimes inclined to return, later on they once again cut down the forest trees over a wider area in front of the entrance to the fort, and they dug the ditches to a greater depth. At the place where rushes usually grew before, they dug out a very deep well, and found the purest water, as they had been certain they would. Quickly and secretly, by day and night, they brought over the wine that the Hungarians had put aside for Heribald, carrying it in jars and whatever other containers they could find. While engaged in these activities, they kept calling upon the Lord.

About Saint Wiborada we will say no more because there 4
is a book specially devoted to her; I shall only mention that
before our present times two popes decided that she should
be elevated to sainthood and that this was finally accomplished under Norbert.

57. On the other hand, concerning Saint Ulrich and the
life he lived with us, we heard some stories told by the fathers that we have not found in his *Life,* even though it has
now been recorded three times. He came from a noble family, as other authors have also said, and he was brought up
and educated among us. Here he learned how to soar up to
the path by which he flew to heaven. Here he first demonstrated the miraculous powers that he exercises today. In 2
joining the monastic community of our saints, Gall and Otmar, whom as a little boy he chose as fathers, he entered it as
the holiest among the holy and the most elect among the elect. As a
student of Hartmann the Younger, he imbibed divinity more
deeply than the other students for he was touched by the
Holy Spirit. In the refectory in the presence of the fathers,

peccare capitale erat, lector inoffensus creber erat quamvis canonicus. Quod tamen illi progenitorum suorum indultum est gratia.

3 Wiboradam inclusam, coaevulis se licentia data ad ludos
parantibus, feriatis diebus furtim visitare assolitus, divinis
ab illa interdum verbis et exemplis instructus est paginis.
Nam quadam die cum illum ante fenestellam clausulae
stantem levissimo videret cingulo praecinctum, de suo ei
paratum offerens: "Castitatis," inquit, "fili mi, tibi cingulum
per hoc lineum meum a Deo accipe! Continentiaeque strophio ab hac deinceps die per Wiboradam tuam te praecinc-
4 tum memento! Cave autem me tibi a Domino meo edictum
ferente, ne ullis abhinc colloquiis vanis mulierculis miscea-
ris! Et si, ut facillime fit, aliquo carnis igne incensus fueris,
loco in quo fueris mutato: *Deus, in adiutorium meum intende!*
Domine, ad adiuvandum me festina! mox cantaveris. Sin autem
sic pacem aliquo alio lapsu tuo vetante non habueris, titionem sive candelam ardentem, quasi aliud aliquid agas,
quaerens, digitum vel leviter adure eodemque versu dicto
securus eris." Sic magistra praedurata discipulum sanctissi-
mum futurum, ut ipse patribus narrabat, contra ignem igne
praeduraverat.

58. Multa sunt, quae de doctrina nutricis suae—sic enim etiam vetulus eam nominare solebat—patribus ille dixerat, quae, quia austera huius temporis sanctis videri possunt et impossibilia, ne quid eis suboleat, praeterimus.

2 De cilicio etiam, quo ipsa utebatur, cuius hodie asperita-
tem pro reliquiis id habentes horrescimus, pulvillulum filio

where making even a small mistake was a capital offense, he often acted as a flawless lector even though he was a canon. He was indulged in this because of his noble birth.

On feast days, when the other boys were getting ready to 3
play, having received permission to do so he usually visited
the recluse Wiborada in secret, and she sometimes taught
him scripture by words and examples. One day, when she
saw him standing in front of the small window of her cell,
girded with a very light belt, she offered him one that she
had made herself: "My son," she said, "accept a belt of chas-
tity from God with this piece of linen! And remember from
this day on that you have been girded with a band of conti-
nence by your friend Wiborada! I bring you this command 4
from my Lord: from now on be careful never to engage in
vain conversations with silly women! And if, as very easily
happens, you get incensed with a fire of the flesh, get away
from that place at once and chant: '*O God, come to my assis-*
tance! O Lord, make haste to help me!' But if some other sin pre-
vents you from finding peace in this way, get a firebrand
branch or candle, as if you were about to do something else,
and burn your finger only slightly; and after you say the same
verse, you will be safe." Thus, as he himself related to the fathers, the fire-hardened teacher had hardened one who was
to become her holiest student with fire against fire.

58. There are many stories that he told the fathers about the teachings of his nurse—that is what he usually called her even as an old man—but we will omit them because the holy men of our times may think that something is amiss, finding her precepts harsh and impossible to live up to.

Out of the hair shirt that she had worn herself she even 2
sewed a pillow for her son, as she called him, for his use in

suo—ut et ipsa eum nominabat—in abstinentiae diebus utendum conneverat. Quod interdum in sinu gestans noctibus ille maxillis lapide supposito aptare solebat. Tali ille lectisternio pro deliciis usus coram ianuis ecclesiae nocturnorum sonitum aut in sedili aut nuda quidem exspectare terra solebat. His et aliis similibus eum a pueritia assuescentem, cum et feminarum alloquia et solita sociorum fugitasset ludicra, "sanctulum" illum derisorie iam abinde coeperant vocitare.

3 Audivimus etiam de eo, quod quidem pro nihilo ab rigidis corde duci soleat, quod cum ei graphium coaevulorum quidam furatus sit, per nescio quam sub cappula incuriam sibimet ipsi manum transfixerit. Quam cum ille dolore clamans exereret, diu quaesitus et saepe peieratus Oudalrici proditur stilus. Hoc tamen ille et alia de se similia cum tegere nosset, illius meritis fieri praeter altioris aliquos ingenii quis credere nollet?

4 Nam figuratis et interdum etiam risum moventibus, non tamen falsis et *inanibus* crebro usus est *verbis.* Ut cuidam scholarium elato et glorianter agenti, cum, Constantiae diaconatu pretio empto, inter processores nostros progredi parans, stola indutus sibi evangelium eo die nobis lecturo non sine gloria assisteret: "Eia," inquit, "mi sodes care, quam decenter tibi clipei fascia insidet!" Id ipsum tamen etiam sibi

the days of penance: nowadays we regard it as one of his relics, and its roughness makes us shudder. He sometimes carried that pillow close to his chest and at night he would put it on a stone and snuggle his cheek against it. Such was the congenial bedding he generally used, when he stretched out on a seat or even on the bare ground before the church doors, as he waited for the call to Nocturns. Because he became accustomed to these and similar hardships from boyhood onward, and because he shunned conversations with women and the usual games his companions played, people even then began mockingly calling him "little saint."

I have also heard the following story about him, which of 3
course hard-hearted people usually consider of no account. One of his fellow students stole his stylus and while holding it under his cape without due care, the thief pierced his own hand with it. He cried out in pain, stretched out his hand, and the stylus that Ulrich had long been searching for and had been repeatedly lied to about was discovered. Although Ulrich knew how to conceal this episode and others like it that concerned him, who, except some people of higher understanding, would refuse to believe that they happened thanks to his miraculous powers?

His *speech* was often elaborate and sometimes even pro- 4
voked laughter, yet it was never false or *meaningless.* For instance, this is what happened to a certain haughty and preening student. After he had purchased a deacon's position in Constance, this man wanted to walk at the head of our procession; dressed in a stole, he positioned himself beside Ulrich with considerable arrogance. Ulrich, who on that day was to read the Gospel to us, said to him: "Look, my dear friend, how nicely the shield strap fits you!"

pro reverentia sui, ut nobis canonicus evangelium legeret, concessum est. Nam frater conscriptus tum vocis pulcherrimae gratiam habebat.

59. Diutius autem quam ceteri coaevi sui tum pro gratia loci tum pro Wiborada sua scholis inhaeserat. Quas tamen tandem relinquens suique iuris in possessionibus factus, Augustae, ubi canonicus ab infantia erat, in virtutum exemplis clarissimus, Gallum suum crebro visitabat. Fratres suos conscriptos ter in anno ipse minister paverat. De conviviis autem ipsis, quamvis multa dictu dulcia patres, qui intererant, narrare soleant, unum ego miraculum etiam sibimet ipsi grande visum in memoriam posteris memorabo.

2 Est non longe a monasterio pons altus, sic quoque vocatus, super praecipitium arduum, ut videre est, situs alteque profundum, inevitabilis quidem Gallum illac petentibus. Ducitur vas vinarium Oudalrici, tunc quidem episcopi, boum paribus copiosis longoque tractu minatis per ipsum montem illum ad caritatis fratrum, ipso iam in loco manente, convivium. Et ecce, horridum dictu, vehiculum illud onustissimum exorbitans cecidit et paria illa super se con-
3 volvit. Clamatur viciniae circumquaque ad auxilium. Conveniunt undique; integra omnia et sana invenientes iumenta prostrata disiungunt acuto ingenio; et anxio labore, quia alias non poterant, ad pontem ipsum item omnia reportant.

Although he was a canon, Ulrich was granted the honor of reading the Gospel to us out of respect. He was then actually an enrolled brother, blessed with the most beautiful voice.

59. He stayed at school longer than other students of his age, in part out of love for the monastery, in part for the sake of his beloved Wiborada. However, he finally left both. Later, when he had come of age and into full possession of his property, and after his miraculous powers had won him great fame in Augsburg, where he was a canon from early childhood, he often visited his beloved Saint Gall. Three times a year he provided a meal for his enrolled brothers and served them personally. Although the fathers who were there told many stories about those feasts that are pleasant to relate, I will only mention one miracle for posterity to remember, one that even Ulrich himself found important.

Not far from the monastery, there is a high bridge—this 2
is also what it is called; as one can see, it crosses a precipitous and deep ravine, and cannot be avoided by those who travel to Saint Gall from that direction. A barrel of wine that Ulrich, by now a bishop, sent for the brothers' love feast, was being transported over that same mountain by many pairs of oxen yoked together in a long train; Ulrich himself was already staying at the monastery. Suddenly (horrible to relate) the very heavily loaded cart slipped off the road and fell rolling down, dragging the train of oxen with it. People from around the neighborhood were called on for help.
They gathered from all over; finding everything intact and 3
in good shape, they ingeniously managed to unyoke the prostrate animals and by feverish effort brought everything back to the same bridge, for there was nothing else they

"*Kyrie eleison*" vero cantantes paucaque iumentis, quia perculsa erant, adiumenta nectentes, episcopo Bozanarium suum exspectanti deferunt et integra omnia et sana ostendunt. Laudes Deo cum fratribus tandem vir Dei publice persolvens, exemplo Benedicti et Mauri ipse hoc signum fratrum meritis, ipsi autem impossibile illud virtutum eius possibilitati attribuunt.

4 Egerat quidem aliquando in loco sancti Magni etiam
diem sibi semper amabilem. Reliquiasque eius, ut mos nobis
est, cappa illa aquilifera indutus vespere diei sancti ipse domum reportabat. Et cum infirmus tunc esset, ut saepe quidem erat, paralyticus quidam adiutorio suorum in viam se,
ut ipse super eum graderetur, prostraverat. At ille homini
appropians, quasi de obstaculo indignatus: "Surge," ait,
5 "quia et ego pedibus infirmus super te progredi nequeo." At
ille tamquam ad increpantis verbum velocissime surgens in-
columis abiit. Secutusque fratres sine ullius adiutorio sancti
Magni ecclesiam cum ceteris sanus introiit. Et episcopus
capitio cappae imposito cum anhelus stetisset et de via lassus, audiens sanitatem hominis, acriter in dicentes invectus,
super cancellos tandem innititur, signumque tam manifes-
tum ab se excutiens, sancti Magni virtutem, quam manibus
gerebat, hanc esse astantibus praedicans asseruit. Neque tamen sic eis, ut hominem ab ipso sanatum esse discrederent,
persuadere quidem ullo modo potuit.

could do. Then, singing "*Kyrie Eleison*" and lending some help to the animals because they were exhausted, they delivered his Bolzano wine to the waiting bishop and showed him that everything was intact and in good shape. When finally the man of God together with the brothers sang the hymns of praise to God in public, he himself, following the example of Benedict and Maurus, attributed this miracle to the brothers' merits, but the brothers believed that this impossible occurrence was made possible by his miraculous powers.

Also, once he celebrated the Feast of Saint Magnus, al- 4
ways especially dear to him, at our monastery. And as is our custom, on the evening of the feast day, dressed in that eagle-bearing cape, he was carrying the saint's relics back home. Although he was sick then, as indeed he often was, a certain paralytic, helped by his people, prostrated himself in his path so that Ulrich might step on him. Ulrich approached the man and said, as if angry at the obstruction: "Get up, because my legs ache, too, and I am unable to step
over you." As if responding to the reproach the paralytic im- 5
mediately got up and walked away safe and sound. Following the brothers, he entered the church of Saint Magnus along with the others, healthy and with no assistance whatsoever. The bishop meanwhile pulled the hood of his cape over his head and stood there gasping, tired from walking; when he heard about the man's healing, he reprimanded those who were talking about it. Then, leaning against the chancel railing, he denied his part in what was so obviously a miracle and declared to those present that it was due to the power of the relics of Saint Magnus which he was carrying in his hands. However, he could by no means make the people stop believing that the man had been healed by Ulrich.

60. Haec de pluribus, quae apud sanctum Gallum commanens gessit, tribus vitae eius scriptoribus non praeiudi-
cantes scripsimus. Neque enim miramur eos, cum quibus in
saeculo versatus est, ea, quae cum spiritalibus gessit, quia
minus sciverant, non scripsisse. Sed plura eos, quae de eo
concinnantur vulgo et canuntur, tacuisse, cum infima quaedam eius magna fecerint, etiam miramur. Neque enim, quia
interdum ridenda, ut diximus, non inaniter loqui solebat et
2 facere, ea dici ab eis quaeramus. Ut abbati nostro Ymmoni,
verecundo homini et talia semper detestanti, cum incudem
noviter sub terra repertam sibi dari peteret, feminam de
mercato dorso validam inferri iusserat. Sed et Hettinum ca-
merarium suum, in effuso Lico flumine iam mergi visum,
quomodo *ad se* festinum *vocaverit* fluctusque illum coram
pedibus suis in litus eiecerit. Sed et ipsam urbem suam Au-
gustam quidem in Ungrorum invasione sub Henrico, ut iam
diximus, rege, quomodo meritis suis liberaverit ab ipsis,
prius illam, quam ad nos venerint, arta obsidione cingenti-
3 bus, nec uno verbo tetigisse miramur. Nam imminente ir-
ruptionis illorum iam facili introitu, infantulos urbis univer-
sos ab uberibus matrum raptos circa se coram altaribus nuda
terra iactari iusserat, vagitibusque illorum lacrimas cum eiu-
latibus miscens infestissimos illos alter Ezechias abegerat
hostes. Nam nulla nisi talium precum existente causa, efferi
illi urbe relicta ad alia dispersi sunt loca.

60. I have written about these deeds among many others that he performed while staying at Saint Gall without wishing to pass judgment on the three authors of his *Life*. I am not surprised that those with whom he came in contact in the secular world were less aware of what he did in the monastic community and so did not write about it. But I am still surprised that they said nothing about the many episodes of his life widely celebrated by the people in stories and songs, even though they make much of mere insignificant incidents. Nor should we expect them to report the amusing but not pointless things, as I have remarked, that
he sometimes said or did. For instance, when our abbot 2
Immo, a venerable man who always detested such tricks, asked for an anvil that had recently been found under the ground, Ulrich had a market woman with a strong back brought to him. There is also the incident, when he saw his chamberlain Hetti on the point of drowning in the flooded waters of the river Lech, Ulrich *called out to come to him* in all haste, and the current cast Hetti out on the riverbank at his feet. I am surprised that they have not even said a single word about how, during the Hungarian invasion under Henry, as I have already recounted, he saved, by his miraculous powers, his own city of Augsburg from the Hungarians,
who had besieged it before they came to us. At the moment 3
when the enemy attack was imminent and it was clear that they would easily enter the city, Ulrich ordered all the infants in the city to be torn away from their mothers' breasts and cast on the bare ground around him before the altars. Mingling his tears and wailing with those of the babies, he, like a second Ezechias, drove a very dangerous enemy away. These prayers were the only reason why those savages left the city alone and scattered, heading to other places.

61. Hugo etiam quidam, regii generis homo primarius, propter sororem viri Dei, virginem sacram, incestu agnitam ab ipso quia saepe inclamatus est, insolenter ei inimicus, quadam die carrae vehiculo, ut erat infirmitatis suae, occurrit invecto. Quem cum milites episcopi praecessores, uti ei non occurreret, praemonerent: “Carrucarium,” inquit, “il-
2 lum ab itinere meo numquam declinabo.” Quod ille a dicentibus post audiens: “Carrucae,” inquit, “vehiculo, scitote filii mei, ipse plus quam ego indigus erit.” Nec post multum nocte quadam sanus sopori se tradens cum evigilasset, lumbos, in quibus peccaverat, acerrime dolens in inferioribus ab illa nocte ita decreverat, ut praeter cutem et ossa gracilia nihil haberet. Sicque longaevitatis tempora, numquam cogi valens, ut pacem a viro Dei peteret, perduxerat. Ipsa autem sanctimonialis illa sanctorum exemplorum post visa est femina, quippe quam frater novis sententiis, dum vixit, annuatim puniverat.

3 Ungris autem a se recedentibus, cum Puochouvam illos, ubi soror ipsa erat, partesque nostras, ubi Wiboradam matrem sciebat, invadere velle comperisset, orasse fertur: “Domine, miseram istam adhuc impunitam mihi dona, ut gladio non pereat! Sed et illam gladio semper paratam, ut palmam martyrii mereatur, confortans robora! Cellam quoque Galli tui integram cum sibi famulantibus, *pie et misericors,* conserva!” Atque ita precibus eius sanctis effectum Deus undique dedit.

61. There was also a certain Hugo, a high-ranking man of
royal stock, whom Ulrich often reviled for having had unchaste relations with the man of God's sister, a consecrated
virgin, and the man was unusually hostile to Ulrich. One day
Hugo came across Ulrich as he was riding in a cart because
of his illness. When the bishop's guards who were riding
ahead of him warned Hugo so that he could avoid meeting
Ulrich, he said: "I'll never get out of the way of that cart
rider." After Ulrich heard about this from the people who 2
were talking about it later, he said: "My sons, let me assure
you that he will soon have more need of a cart than I." One
night not long afterward Hugo settled down to sleep in good
health and woke up with extremely severe pain in his loins,
those by which he had sinned, and after that night his lower
body shrank so much that nothing remained but skin and
fragile bones. In this state he spent the long years of his life,
never able to bring himself to ask the man of God for peace.
As for that nun, afterward she seemed to be a woman to be
held as a holy example since her brother imposed new pen-
alties upon her every year as long as he lived.

After the Hungarians retreated from him, Ulrich found 3
out that they planned to invade Buchau, where his sister
was, and our lands, where he got to know Mother Wiborada,
and they say that he prayed as follows: "Lord, spare this
wretched woman, still unpunished, for my sake, so that she
not perish by the sword! Also comfort and give strength to
that other woman who is always ready for the sword, so that
she may deserve the palm of martyrdom! *Lord of compassion
and mercy,* keep safe the cell of your Saint Gall along with all
those who serve him!" God granted his holy prayers in all
respects.

62. At Engilbertus noster, circumquaque omnibus igne caelo nocte dieque relucentibus, exploratores iam emittere non ausus, castellum suum cum suis immanens tuebatur. Raro autem in monasterium magis animo fidentibus, ut missas ibi agerent, missis, spiritum inter eorum reditum vix habere potuit. Multum autem socios roborabat inter timorem et spem Heribaldi et clerici assidua de hostibus relatio. Mirabantur tandem altioris ingenii fratres pium Deum tam amicum simplicitati, ut eum etiam fatuos et hebetes tueri non pigeat inter medios hostium gladios et contos.

2 Quaerentes autem ab Heribaldo inter otia, quomodo
sibimet tam numerosi hospites sancti Galli placerent: "Eia,"
inquit, "quam optime! Numquam ego, credite mihi, hila-
riores in claustro nostro homines vidisse me memini; cibi
enim potusque datores sunt largissimi. Quod enim ego ante
cellararium nostrum tenacissimum vix rogare poteram, ut
vel semel sitientem me potaret, ipsi mihi affluenter roganti
3 dabant." Et clericus: "Et si bibere," inquit, "nolles, alapis
cogebant." "Non nego," ait; "id enim unum valde displice-
bat, quod tam indisciplinati quidem erant. In veritate dico
vobis: numquam in claustro sancti Galli tam indisciplinatos
vidi. Neque plus in ecclesia et in claustro, quam si foris in
prato essent, ferales illi," inquit, "egerant. Nam cum eis semel manu signum darem, ut Dei ipsius memores vel in ecclesia silentius agerent, grandes mihi collo infregerant. Atque

62. To return to our account: the sky all around was ablaze day and night from reflected fire, and our abbot Engilbert, not daring to send out any more scouts, remained at the fort and guarded it with his men. Occasionally, however, he would send the more courageous of the monks to the monastery so that they might conduct Mass there, and he could barely draw breath until their return. The incessant reports of Heribald and the cleric about the enemy strengthened the confidence of their companions who lived between fear and hope. In the end, the brothers who had a deeper understanding of things kept marveling how merciful God showed kindness toward simplicity and took the trouble to protect even fools and the dull witted in the midst of the enemy's swords and pikes.

When they asked Heribald in a quiet moment how he 2
had liked Saint Gall having such a large number of guests, he said: "It was really great! Believe me, I can't remember ever having seen a happier group in our monastery, and they are very generous providers of food and drink. Before, I was hardly able to ask our very stingy cellarer to give me a drink when I was thirsty, but when I asked them, they gave me
plenty." The cleric said: "And if you refused to drink, they 3
would box your ears and force you." "I don't deny it," Heribald said. "One thing I really didn't like was that they were so undisciplined. *In truth, I tell you:* I've never seen such undisciplined people in the monastery of Saint Gall. Whether in the church or in the cloister, those savages behaved no better than if they were outside in a field. For example, when I once signaled with my hand for them to be quiet out of respect for God at least in the church, they punched me in the neck. But right away they made up for the wrong they had

ilico, quod in me peccaverant, vino oblato, quod nemo quidem vestrum faceret, emendabant."

63. Taliter *imperterriti* illi, Deum semper invocantes, miseriis suis se pascebant, dum otia haberent. *Fama* vero *volante,* ut fit, reversos hostes iterum in coenobio versari, emitti se fatuus, ut ad caros suos veniret, enixe rogabat. Sicque per aliquot dies ipsi et Wazzirburgenses in navibus tamen saepius agentes, quas hostes nullas habebant, finem hostice tempestatis exspectabant.

2 Audiunt tandem, Constantia foris muros cremata, intus armis defensa, Augia quoque navibus subductis armatis multis in circuitu fulgida, hostes saevos cis citraque Rhenum omnia igne cedibusque pervadentes transisse. Ausi tandem monasterium securi intrare, oratoria purgant, officinas perscopant. Episcopo Notingo tunc accito, aqua benedicta cuncta spargi rogantes, vim daemonum omnem eliminant.
3 Atque sic Engilbertus armis relictis, militiae caelesti se suosque iterum assuefaciens, in utrisque frugi hominem se exhibuit. *Oves* enim dispersas velut *humeris reportans ad gregem,* regulae eas redocuit tenorem. Pabula eis, quae cara tunc quidem omnibus erant, omni industria undequaque corradere sollicita curavit sollertia; neque enim erat emere omnibus

done me by immediately offering me wine, which none of you ever did."

63. By this means the *undaunted* brethren, who never stopped calling upon God, found strength in their misfortunes, when they had time to spare. But then came a *rumor, flying* fast as rumor does, that the enemy had returned and were once again based at the monastery, and the fool began insisting that they let him out so that he could join his dear friends. For this reason, the brethren and the men of Wasserburg spent several days, often on ships because the enemy had no ships at all, waiting for the time of hostilities to pass.

Eventually they heard that Constance had been burned 2
down outside the walls, but inside had been defended with arms, while the island of Reichenau glittered with the protection of a large number of armed ships surrounding it; the savage enemy had crossed the Rhine and brought fire and slaughter everywhere they went on both sides of the river. Finally, the brethren took courage and safely entered the monastery; they purified the places of worship and swept through the domestic buildings. Then they summoned Bishop Noting and asked him to sprinkle holy water everywhere so that they might eradicate all demonic forces.
So it was that Engilbert laid his arms aside and once again 3
turned to training himself and his monks in the service of heaven, showing himself as an effective leader in both the military and spiritual spheres. He *carried* the scattered *sheep back to the fold on his shoulders,* as it were, and he taught them again the intent of the Rule. Everyone placed a high value on food. Engilbert spared no effort in carefully and tirelessly searching everywhere to scrape together provisions, expensive for all, for the monks. There was none for sale and no

profligatis neque spes verni fructus hostibus arare vetantibus.

4 Sic ille VIII post hanc tempestatem annis loci sui provisor, decessoris sui disciplinam deintus tenuit, protervam deforis servorum naturam frangens emendavit. Tandemque infirmans, fatigatus corporis malis, Thietoni venerando abbati electo a fratribus regimen suum, regi supplicans, reliquit. Ipse autem loca abbatum, quae diximus, non diu supervivens tenuit.

64. De Ungrorum quoque infortuniis tragoediae nostrae non piget ascribere. Erat ea tempestate in pago, quem Friccouve dicunt, Hirminger quidam, vir non adeo praepotens, sed manu et animo validus filiorumque Machabeorum sex sicut Mathathias quondam pater fortissimus. Iste enim turmam illam, quae cis Rhenum nos quoque—a sociis, qui ultra R<h>enum erant, disiuncta—invaserat, ita circumve-
2 nerat. Enimvero cum Sechingensem sanctae crucis locum illi invasuri, in arto Rheni pontem parantes, inspectivi sociis consedissent seque invicem super flumen allocuti securius iam agerent, ipse istos cum filiis, copiis pro tempore undecumque corrasis, intempesta noctis *somno vinoque sepultos* tribus partibus impetu facto improvisos invaserat et paene omnes, praeter qui Rhenum fuga transnataverant, aut occiderat aut merserat. Nam et villani quidam praedocti, ollis prunas

prospects for spring crops because everything had been destroyed and the enemy had prevented plowing.

Thus Engilbert managed his monastery for eight years af- 4
ter this disturbance; he upheld the discipline of his predecessor within the community and improved it beyond the cloister by subduing the violent behavior of the serfs. Finally, frail and exhausted by illness, he petitioned the king and yielded his governance to Thieto, a venerable man, who was elected abbot by the brothers. For the remaining short time of his life, Engilbert held the abbots' estates that I have mentioned.

64. After the account of our tragedy, it would not be amiss to tell you also about the misfortunes of the Hungarians. In a district called Frickgau there lived at that time a certain Hirminger, who did not belong to the highest ranks of power but was strong in body and mind; his main strength, moreover, lay in the fact that like Mattathias of old, he was the father of six Maccabees. Hirminger fell upon the same enemy band that had come to our side of the Rhine and attacked and surrounded us, separating itself from their
comrades on the other side of the Rhine. In preparing for an 2
attack on the monastery of the Holy Cross in Säckingen, the Hungarians were building a bridge over the narrow part of the Rhine. They had sat down in view of their comrades, chatting with them across the river and feeling quite safe. Together with his sons, Hirminger, who had raised an army for the occasion from all around, in the dead of night launched a three-sided assault on the unsuspecting Hungarians, who were *buried in sleep and wine.* Almost all the enemy were slaughtered or drowned, except those who escaped by swimming across the Rhine. Some of the villagers had been

in proximo monte paratas habentes, tumultu audito faces
accensas levabant et, ut discretionem sociorum et hostium
3 nossent, quasi perlustrium fecerant. Spectabant sociorum
internecionem transfluminales hostes otiosi. Iraque armati
accurrunt ad profluentis litus rabidi. Missilia furori satisfa-
cientes plurima iaciunt caninoque ululatu voces horridas
miscent. At Irminger cum suis spolia in facie hostium col-
lecta basilicae triumphans intulit et per omnes circumquaque munitiones dispertivit. Et quia naves praeter eius
urbis defensaculo subductas nullas in Rheni viciniis sciverat,
suadebat urbanis navibus ipsis pontibus iunctis armatas legiones transponere, se duce, qui *illorum mores in armis iam*
nosset, quantocius confligere.

4 Dum haec sataguntur, navibus Ungri de Swarzwalde multis paratis in Alsatiam ipsi priores suas legiones transponunt et a Luitfrido quodam, terrae illius potentissimo, bello suscepti plurimo damno sui tandem cruentam victoriam sunt adepti. Senserant iam mitius sibi agendum inter Teutones et in terra illorum minus fore tardandum. Alsatia tandem, qua ierant, vastata et cremata, Hohfeldi montem Iurisque silvam festinanter transeuntes Vesontium veniunt.

65. Erat tunc Burgundionum rex Chuonradus, adolescens

told of the plans in advance and had set jars with burning coals on the nearest mountain, and when they heard the sounds of battle, they lit torches and raised them to provide illumination, so that the combatants could tell friend from
foe. The enemy on the other side of the river helplessly 3
watched their comrades being slaughtered. Incensed, they ran up to the bank of the flowing river in a mad rage. To satisfy their fury, they hurled a huge number of missiles and mingled their horrendous shouting with doglike howls. Hirminger together with his men collected the spoils before the eyes of the enemy, brought everything to the church in triumph, and distributed it among all the forts round about. Because he knew that there were no ships in the neighboring stretches of the Rhine other than those brought for the defense of the fortress, Hirminger persuaded the garrison to join those ships together to form bridges, transport his troops to the other side, and join battle as soon as possible under his leadership, since *he was now familiar with the enemy's ways of fighting.*

While these preparations were underway, the Hungarians 4
outfitted a large number of ships in the Black Forest and began transporting their troops to Alsace before them. Liutfrid, the most powerful lord of that land, engaged them in battle, but in the end the Hungarians obtained a bloody victory, with great losses to their own side. By this time the Hungarians understood that they should behave more peaceably among the Germans and that they should not linger in their land. Finally, after sacking and burning Alsace, where they had gone, they quickly crossed the Vosges mountains and the Jura forest, and came to Besançon.

65. The king of the Burgundians at that time was Conrad,

floridus, sanctae Adelheidae quidem frater. Venerant quondam Saraceni navibus in Burgundiam belloque omnia disturbantes, tandem victi in valle Fraxnith angustiis tutissima, invito qui tunc erat rege, consederant. Paceque petita uxores filias gentis ducunt. Vallem maximae ubertatis parvis regi reditibus datis incolunt. Ad quorum ducem Chuonradus, nobili astutia usus, legatos dirigit his verbis: "Ecce Ungri, fillones illi fugitivi, nuntiis me fatigant, ut sibi pace mea vos
2 quidem a tantae ubertatis terra armis expellere liceat. Sed vos, si viri estis, obviam illis me iuvante quantocius pergite! Enimvero si vos eos in faciem invaditis, ego eos a latere involabo. Sicque illos, ut confido, profligatos exterminabimus." Misit autem et ad Ungros qui dicerent: "Quare, viri fortissimi, mecum armis agere vultis? Expedit enim utrisque nostrum magis, ut pacifici simus. Venite ergo mecum, et hostes meos illos eradamus de terra uberrima, vosque ibi considite! Sed et insuper provinciam proximam terrae illi, si mecum in fide senseritis, libens vobis tribuam."

3 Consenserant utrimque legationi regiae. Erumpunt Saraceni e valle Fraxnith confertissimi. Die et loco condictis occurrere parant Ungri. Rex suis undecumque collectis aciem ordinat, specie velut his et his futurus subsidiis. "Quam acute," inquit, "incidant lanceae et gladii, hodie ostendite,

in the bloom of youth, Saint Adelheid's brother. Sometime in the past, Saracens came to Burgundy on their ships, made war, and threw everything into confusion. But they were finally defeated and settled down in the valley of Fraxinetum, which is safely protected by ravines, against the wishes of the king at the time. The Saracens asked for peace and married the daughters of the local people. They lived in a very fertile valley but gave little of their revenues to the king. Conrad, with remarkable cunning, sent envoys to their leader with these words: "See how the Hungarians, those ne'er-do-well runaways, tire me out by sending envoys, asking my permission to drive you away from this fertile land by
force of arms. But if you are brave men, make a move against 2
them, with my help, as soon as possible! To be sure, if you attack them head-on, I will swoop on their flank. This way, I firmly believe, we will destroy and eliminate them." But he also sent envoys to the Hungarians, to say: "Why do you, strongest of men, choose to go to war with me? It is more convenient for both of us to make peace. So come with me and let us root out my enemies from this very fertile land, and settle there yourselves! In addition, if you keep faith with me, I will also gladly grant you the province next to that land."

Both sides agreed to what the royal envoys proposed. 3
The Saracens sallied forth from the valley of Fraxinetum in close array. On the day and at the place previously agreed upon, the Hungarians were ready to confront them. The king arranged his men, gathered from all around, in battle formation, as if to provide reinforcement for one side or the other. "My very brave comrades," he said, "show today how sharply your spears and swords can cut! Let no one worry

socii mei fortissimi! Tam diversorum daemonum utra pars
vicerit, nemini sit curae! Victores esse qui coeperint, tribus
4 vos partibus insilite! Parmis reiectis ferro utimini! Nullo
discrimine trucidetur Sarracenus et Ungar! Neminis illorum
misereri certum est, quia mei quidem ipsorum miseret
nemo." Confligunt tandem in conspectu regis in acie pro-
spectantis electissimi satanae milites et filii. Neutris cedentibus trucidantur utrimque ut victimae. Tandemque rex
animose pugnantibus veritus, ne utra pars ad ultimum aufu-
geret, signo dato gradatim velut subsidians supervenit et
undique ad hos et illos prosternendos turmatim omnes cir-
cumdedit. Fugaeque locum non habentes, quos non occidit,
captos Arelato vendidit. Ipse vero paucis amissis Deo et
sancto Mauricio, in cuius ense et lancea ita pugnabat, laudibus triumphabat.

66. Et ut ad nos redeamus: Thieto tandem fratribus ad
prospera et adversa aequanimiter ferenda in praedictis tempestatibus acerrime praeduratis et ad spiritalia ab Engil-
berto reformatis initio gubernaculi sui facile praefuit. Sed
infortuniis maxime dolendis in processu temporum suorum
prosecutus, lacrimandae tragoediae materiam posteris reliquit. Nam monasterium sub illo crematum est ita.
2 Laetania maior dominicam incidit; fratribus cruces alias

about which side of those different demons should win!
Whichever side begins to get the upper hand, attack them
on three sides! Throw away your shields and use your blades!
Let Saracen and Hungarian be slaughtered without distinc- 4
tion! I have decided to show mercy to none of them, because none of them would show mercy to me." Finally, Satan's finest warriors and their sons clashed together in view
of the king, who stood watching in the front of his troops.
With neither side giving way, men on both sides were slaughtered like sacrificial animals. Finally, as they were battling
fiercely, the king, fearing that one side would eventually flee,
gave a signal and gradually approached as if to lend support.
He surrounded them all entirely with a body of troops with
the goal of destroying both armies. There was nowhere to
run, and those he did not kill, he captured and sold into slav-
ery in Arles. Meanwhile the king himself, having lost only a
few men, celebrated his triumph by singing praise to God
and Saint Maurice, under whose sword and lance he fought
so successfully.

66. To return to our own community: the beginning of his abbacy was easy for Thieto, because by that time the brethren had been thoroughly seasoned by the previously mentioned upheavals to face prosperity and adversity alike with equanimity and had been restored to spiritual pursuits by Engilbert. However, in the course of his abbacy he was plagued by especially grievous misfortunes, and what he left to posterity resembles the plot of a tearful tragedy, for the monastery burned down during his rule, and this is how it happened.

The Greater Litany fell on a Sunday. Because the broth- 2
ers' procession following the crosses took a different route,

sequentibus officinae loci, ut moris est, non sunt benedictae. Et abinde morem patres statuunt, ut, quocumque loci cruces sequamur, presbyter diei, si dominica sit, claustrum circumiens benedicat. Erant disciplinae loci ut semper et tunc severe, non modo in claustro, sed et in scholis exterius. Unde etiam praeter clericos, qui apud nos saepe nutriti sunt, clarissimos, ecclesiis variis multoties dedimus et episcopos.
3 Et ut tragoediam, quam dicturus sum, consoler: vidi egomet ipse Chuonrado imperatore Ingilinheim pascha agente, sancti Galli monacho scholas Magontiae curante, officium, ut solitum est, in medio chori crebro coronati inspectu agere. Cumque manum ille ad modulos sequentiae pingendos rite levasset, tres episcopi, hominis quondam discipuli, imperatori in throno proximi: “Ibimus,” aiunt, “domine, et
4 magistrum in eo, quod ipse nos docuit, iuvabimus.” Illo hoc gratum fore dicente, descendentes sociantur sancti Galli monacho, inclinantes inclinato, opus Dei, quod docuit, reverenter cum eo perficiunt. Flebat homo cum gaudio, gratias referens sancto Gallo. Post missas peractas vix ille coactus pedes imperii, ut moris est, petere, auri uncias in eis positas sustulit. Ad imperatricem autem ridente imperatore per vim tractus, et ibi aurum eius sumpsit e pedibus, Mahthilda quoque, soror eius, anulum illi in digitum, vellet nollet, inseruit.

the domestic buildings of the monastery were not blessed as
is customary. Thereafter the fathers established a custom
that in the future, by whatever route our procession was to
follow the crosses, the priest of the day, if that fell on a Sunday, should walk around the cloister and bless everything.
The monastery rules then were strict as always, not only
within the cloister but also outside in the school. This is why
besides clerics, who have often been fostered by us, we have
also frequently given very distinguished bishops to various
dioceses. To alleviate the tragedy I am about to relate, when 3
Emperor Conrad was spending Easter at Ingelheim and a
monk of Saint Gall was in charge of the school at Mainz, I
saw them with my own eyes conducting divine office, as
they were accustomed to do, in the middle of the choir under the watchful eye of the tonsured monk. When he duly
raised his hand, to reflect the melody of the sequence, three
bishops, his former students, who were standing next to the
emperor sitting on his throne, said: "My lord, we shall go
and help our master in the skill that he himself has taught
us." The king said that this would please him, and they 4
stepped down, came up to the monk of Saint Gall, bowed to
him who had bowed to them, and together with him reverently conducted the divine service that he had taught them.
That man wept with joy, giving thanks to Saint Gall. After
Mass had been completed, they barely persuaded him to
kneel at the emperor's feet, as is customary, and to accept
the ounces of gold placed there. Then they practically
dragged him toward the empress, as the emperor laughed,
and at her feet he picked up some more gold. Her sister
Mathilda also slipped a ring on his finger, whether he wanted
it or not.

5 Haec ergo nequaquam *aurium inflationi* satagens dixerim, sed ut honorem doctrinae et disciplinae loci nostri praememorans, damna, quae a scholaribus pro disciplinis pertulimus, quamvis importabilia fuerint, portabilius audiantur.

67. Erat, ut diximus, dies sancto Marco solemnis; et ut
solent scholasticuli diebus festis, ut cras vapulent, saepe me-
reri, veniam per precatores vel inducias, ut verius scribam,
secunda feria habuerant. At tertia feria exactoribus, quos
circatores vocamus, culpas eorum magistro rememoranti-
bus, omnes exuere iubentur. Mittitur unus vapulatorum in
2 superiora domus pro virgis ibi repositis deferendis. At ille,
ut se et socios liberaret, titionem de fornacula quadam citissime rapiens aridis lignis tecto proximis infixit et, quantum
otii erat, conflavit. At exactoribus illum, cur tardaret, inclamantibus, domum ardere vociferans reclamavit. Sicque tegulis aridis, aquilone quoque flante, incendia rapientibus
domus tota flammis conluxit.

3 Revestiti dicto citius omnes magistro spreto prosiliunt, tecta conscendunt. Tegulas disiectas cum igne aquilo rapuit et in turris cuiusdam culmina ecclesiae sancti Galli proxime volantes portavit. Erat turris ipsa ab Hartmoto quondam ad hoc ipsum ignis discrimen tribus muri obvoluta tegminibus, ut thesaurus ecclesiae, si casu locus ardescat, in hanc per cryptam *pervium* illac *usum* habentem raptim portetur. Haec

I would never tell you this *in order to boast;* rather, I re- 5
mind you about the high esteem in which our monastery is held for learning and discipline so that hearing the account of the unbearable harm that we suffered at the hands of students because of disciplinary issues might be more bearable.

67. It was, as I said, the feast day of Saint Mark. The
schoolboys did, as schoolboys often do on feast days, something that merited flogging the next day; on the Monday
they received pardon, or rather a postponement, to be more
precise, thanks to intercessors. On the Tuesday however,
when the enforcers whom we call roundsmen reminded the
master about their transgressions, the students were all ordered to take off their clothes. One of those who were to be
flogged was sent to the upper floor of the building to bring
the rods that were kept there. In order to save himself and 2
his friends, he very quickly grabbed a burning branch from a
hearth, thrust it into a pile of dry wood close to the roof, and
blew on the wood for as long as he could. When the enforcers called out to him, asking why he was taking so long, he
loudly shouted in response that the building was on fire.
The roof shingles were dry and the north wind was blowing,
and so the entire building lit up in flames.

They all instantly put their clothes back on, rushed out 3
without paying attention to their master, and climbed up to the roof. The north wind and the fire loosened and carried off shingles, sending them flying to the top of a tower that was very close to the church of Saint Gall. It was the very tower that Hartmut had once surrounded with three protective walls for just such a fire emergency, so that if the monastery caught fire, the church treasury would be speedily carried to the tower by the crypt which had *a passageway*

vero tegulis ligneis super lapideas tecta ignem, ut diximus,
rapuit absideque sanctarum virginum imminens eam, ut ad-
4 huc videre est, mordacius igne cremavit. Mira, ut a senibus,
qui tunc iuvenes aderant, audivimus, mora erat incendii,
priusquam superius tectum ignesceret. Campanas enim omnes depositas cum universo ecclesiae suppellectili evehunt. Cancellos confractos circum et super aram sancti Galli convolvunt, ne ossa eius quidem igne solverentur. Sancti Otmari tandem corpus exportant; cunctaque, quae exportant, in domiciliis curtis abbatis, quae incendium vix evaserant, sub custodibus locant. In talibus miseriis et infortuniis Thieto spectator anxius circumcursabat.

68. Incendio postea finito cineres parietibus ecclesiae proximi caute collecti in profluente purgantur, Hartmuotique *aurea talenta* guttatim micantia eruuntur. Varietas hominum de viciniis, ut fit, concurrentium multa fraudibus auferunt. Enimvero, ut aiebant, nec ipsi custodes rerum fidem tenebant. Libri multi rapiuntur, tum cetera.

2 Post talia ambustorum infortunia fratribus nec tecta nec
victualia per spatia aliqua temporum habentibus fit occasio temptationibus. Per montes enim et valles proximasque

into it. But in fact the tower, covered by wooden shingles laid over its stone tiles, caught fire, as I said, and since it stood directly over the apse of the Holy Virgins, angrily
snapping flames burned the apse, as one can still see. There 4
was a surprising delay in the progress of the fire, I have heard from old men who were there as young men at the time, before it spread to the higher part of the roof. The monks were able to take all the bells down and carry them along with all the furnishings of the church. They broke off the chancel screens and enfolded them above and around the altar of Saint Gall so that his bones would not be destroyed by the fire. Finally they carried out the body of Saint Otmar; everything that they carried out they placed under guard in the buildings of the abbot's courtyard that had barely escaped the fire. In the midst of such sorrows and misfortunes, Thieto kept running back and forth, an anxious witness.

68. Afterward, when the fire stopped, they carefully gathered the ashes closest to the church walls, rinsed them off in a stream, and drop by drop Hartmut's *golden talents* emerged, shining. As generally happens in such circumstances, a wide-ranging mix of people from round about had come running to the monastery and had fraudulently carried off quite a lot. In fact, they said, even those who were guarding the property did not keep faith. Many books were snatched away, as well as other things.

After this terrible misfortune of the fire, the brothers had 2
neither shelter nor food for some period of time, and this provided opportunity for temptation. Since there was no way to prevent the brothers from seeking places to stay wherever they could in the mountains, valleys, and nearest

villas, quaqua poterant, fratres dum loca manendi quaerere
non erat inhiberi, tum vere tum false, ut fit, oriuntur infa-
miae. Thieto enim, ut necessitas erat, tum per se tum per
nuntios de fratribus idoneos, si quos compati sperabat, mi-
3 seriis loci consulere rogabat. Relicti sunt circa ambusta et
cineres Galli senes cum iunioribus non adeo ad imperia parentibus. Conveniunt, qui et quando volunt, ad tuguria in
ambustis ad hoc ipsum contexta. Fiunt disciplinae per con-
cordes, refelluntur per discordes. Quidam cnim disciplinas
detrectantium, in quibus in tali tempestate et spes utique
esset, *excusso iugo* recalcitrant.

69. In quibus erat Victor quidam Retianus, doctus prae ceteris, sed iuvenis insolens et minus oboediens. Erat tunc Craloh, abbatis quidem frater, decanus, homo antiquae disciplinae et severitatis—et, ut aiebant, interdum pernimie—et rigidus in ultionibus. Fit Victor reus; invehitur Craloh in hominem severius. Victor autem rebellio factus, inter convitia illum insilire parans alapam minatur. At ille pertinacem devitans, equo ascenso fratri foras agenti turbam nuntiat. At Anno, frater et ipse quidem, homo mitissimus, Victori et propter generis et propter ingenii nobilitatem semper amicus, in gratiam eum reducere frustra parat. Nam abbatem animosum supervenire Victor audiens loco cessit.

villages, evil rumors started circulating, as generally happens, some true, some false. As necessity dictated, Thieto
approached any people whom he expected to show compassion, either personally or by appropriate messengers chosen
from among the brothers, and asked them to take thought
for the monastery's distress. In the charred debris and ashes 3
of Saint Gall, there remained only old men together with
the younger ones, who were not much inclined to obey orders. Whenever they wanted, those who were willing gathered in the huts that had been built out of charred debris for
this very purpose. Discipline was obeyed by the compliant
and rejected by the contentious. In fact, some of the brethren who resented the discipline and were the very people
who should have been reliable in such troubled times, *cast
off the yoke* and started resisting control.

69. Among them was a certain Rhaetian, Victor, a young man who was more learned than the others but also insolent and disobedient. Craloh, the abbot's brother, was then dean; a man of the discipline and strictness of old—even excessively so at times, they said—and harsh in punishment. Once Victor committed an offense, and Craloh reprimanded him very severely. Then Victor became rebellious: shouting abuse, he was about to attack Craloh and threatened to slap him. But Craloh got away from the persistent monk, climbed on a horse, and reported the commotion to his brother who was then outside the monastery. Anno, also his brother and a very mild man, who had always been friendly to Victor because of his noble birth and intelligence, vainly tried to have Victor forgiven. When Victor heard that the abbot was coming back and was very angry, he left the monastery.

2 At Thieto aetate iam gravescens laborumque pertaesus, veritus etiam, ne iuventus soluta licentia insolesceret, ecclesia et claustro vicinorum iuvamine tectis, quosque fratrum valuit, ut Cralohum abbatem pro se eligerent, sollicitavit idque Victore avulso proclivius effecit. Ottonem adiit, germanum ipse pro se abbatem fecit, iussum quidem, ut, si Victor ad se supplex venerit, suscipiatur. Nam propinquorum eius quidam per regem, quae vellent, effecerant. Quibus ille versus et epistulas, quibus se imperio innotescerent, conquestivas dabat. Rediit Craloh domum. Quo festive suscepto Thieto caminatam quandam, veterum seniorum angulum vocatam, introiit. Loca, quae abbatibus supra diximus dicata, in finem vitae retinuit.

70. Tandem Victor cum propinquis suis, viris potentibus, venit. Supplex, ut iussum est, recipitur. Ipsi tamen propinqui hominis, ut ei abbatiam Favariensem traderet, pretia et praedia Craloho porrigentes, frustati sunt iratique recedunt minati, si umquam copia fuerit, ultionem.

2 Compulit tandem Craloh fratres, errovagari post arsuram solitos, claustro stabiles vivere, silere et loqui pro tempore, regulam cottidie audire et facere, licentias interdum, quae etiam irregulares essent, tamquam noviciis dare, *arcum tendere et laxare,* tandem vero et acrius, quoniam sic homo erat, in aliquibus commissa punire, unde etiam, ut fit, odio

As for Thieto, he was weighed down by age and worn out 2
by his labors and also afraid that the young monks would become insolent given wider latitude. Accordingly, after he had the roofs of the church and monastery rebuilt with the neighbors' help, he persuaded as many brothers as he could to elect Craloh abbot in his stead, and this was easier for him to accomplish in Victor's absence. He went to Otto, and Otto made his brother abbot in his stead. The new abbot, however, was ordered to take Victor back if he came to him begging forgiveness. It was some of Victor's relatives who had achieved what they wanted by way of the king. To bring his plight to the king's attention, Victor had been sending his relatives poems and plaintive letters. Craloh returned home. He was received with ceremony, and Thieto entered a heated cell, called "the elders' corner." Until the last day of his life he remained in possession of the estates designated for the abbots that I mentioned above.

70. Victor eventually arrived with his relatives, who were powerful men. He begged forgiveness and was taken back, as ordered. His relatives offered Craloh money and estates in exchange for giving Victor the abbey of Pfäfers, but they were rebuffed and went away in anger, threatening revenge at the first available opportunity.

Craloh eventually forced the brothers, who had taken to 2
wandering after the fire, to live a stable life in the cloister, to observe silence and to speak at appropriate times, to hear the words of the Rule daily and to observe it—sometimes allowing them liberties that were even against the Rule, as if they were novices—and *to draw and release the bow.* But because this was the kind of man he was, he also punished some monks very severely for their offenses, and, as gener-

patuit. Cuius scintillas, quaqua potuit, Victor inflammavit, propter quod et ipsi in scholis, quas ei commiserat, plura incommodasset severius inconsulto eo cum pueris agendo. Sed et prima utrisque discordia *manet alta mente reposta.*

3 Surgit tandem in abbatem pluralis querela tum a familia tum a fratribus iugum eius propter insolentiam detrectantibus. Nam et Enzilinum quendam, Victoris patruum, Favariensium praepositum, ad se accitum, cum reum fecisset, verberatum deposuit. Qui tamen, cum esset astute acutus, ultioni se, quam loco suo dicere habebimus, nepote acuente praeparavit.

71. Erat his temporibus tempestas illa pluribus nota inter Ottonem quidem et Luitolfum, patrem et filium. Sed Luitolfus per Suevos secum tum sentientes Italiam petens, locum sancti Galli minax abbati propter insolentiae querelas adiit. Craloh autem audito adventu eius, clam assumpto Waningo fratre et paucis servitoribus ad Ottonem in Fran-
2 ciam *profugus venit.* Paraturas vero sanctuarii ille, quas secum inconsiderate carissimas sumpsit, furto amisit. Cum autem et ipse rex de eo non bene sentiret, pro fide tamen, qua fugiens venit, sancto Oudalrico, condiscipulo quondam suo, qui tunc aulae aderat, pro eo loquente, cum gratia receptus

ally happens, therefore laid himself open to hatred. Victor fanned the sparks of this hatred into flames by whatever means he could, because Craloh had distressed him a great deal in the school too, which he had entrusted to Victor, by treating the boys severely without consulting Victor. Moreover, each of them still kept their earlier quarrel *harbored deep within his heart.*

In the end, because of his arrogance the abbot caused 3
much grumbling, both among the dependents and among the brothers who resented his yoke. For instance, he summoned a certain Enzelinus, who was Victor's paternal uncle and the provost of Pfäfers, found him guilty, and had the man flogged and deposed. Enzelinus, however, was a sharp and smart man, and, incited by his nephew, he prepared for his revenge, about which I will tell you in its proper place.

71. It was in those days that that stormy dispute well known to many arose between Otto and Liudolf, father and son. When Liudolf, heading to Italy, was passing through Swabia, at that time allied with him, he came to the monastery of Saint Gall, a threatening figure for the abbot, because he had heard complaints about Craloh's arrogance. When Craloh heard about Liudolf's approach, he fled in secret, taking with him Brother Waning and a few servants
and *came* to Franconia *to seek refuge* with Otto. He had rashly 2
taken some very costly vestments from the sanctuary and had lost them to theft. Although the king himself did not think well of him, Craloh was still graciously received because he had shown his loyalty to the king by coming to seek refuge, and also because Saint Ulrich, a former fellow student of his who was then present at the court, had spoken on his behalf. In the meantime, though the order was given

est. Et cum de privato regis interea pasci iuberetur, magnam cum suis penuriam pertulit propinquis Enzelini et Victoris, mensae regiae et victualium oeconomis, qui ei et in hoc et in aliis, quaqua poterant, gravi incommodo erant.

3 Luitolfus igitur monasterio biduum immoratus, electione fratrum Cralohum detestantium Annonem quidem, fratrem eius, abbatem eis posuit, pluraque gratiae et dilectionis signa ostendens, fausta sibi clamantium vocibus prosecutus recessit. Anno vero, homo dignissimus, si digne esset electus, frugi abbatis egerat opera et virtutes apud Deum et homines; et anno regiminis sui uno et fere dimidio, quibus advixerat, inter praeclara, quae passim accelerans effecerat, opera vallos urbis, sicut per saecula videre est, miro conatu effoderat; muros ipsos cum turribus tredecim fundans, supra terram ultra genu altos obiens reliquit.

72. At Craloh cum rege duos fere annos exsul ducens, ab oeconomis, quos diximus, frequenter turbatus infortunia multa perpessus est. Venit interea et Enzelinus in aulam, quem diximus. Coepitque cum propinquis suis oeconomis et aliis, quos plurimo, ut aiebant, auro oberaverat, amicis ubi otiose versari—vitabundus tamen, ne Craloh se videret—sollicite agere, versibus etiam regi se per amicos conqueri. Nam et ipse utique, velut apud sanctum Gallum educatus,

that Craloh was to be supported at the king's personal expense, he and his men experienced circumstances of extreme poverty because relatives of Enzelinus and Victor, who were the stewards in charge of the royal table and provisions, tried to inconvenience him in whatever way they could in this and in other respects.

Liudolf stayed at the monastery for two days; the monks 3
who detested Craloh elected his brother Anno, and Liudolf made him their abbot. After showing the monks his favor and affection in many ways, Liudolf departed amid acclamations and wishes of good fortune. Anno, a very worthy man, if he had only been properly elected, capably attended to the tasks of abbot, exhibiting the necessary virtues before God and men. During his rule as abbot—about the last year and a half of his life—he speedily accomplished many outstanding projects, including ditches that, with amazing energy, he had dug out around the fortress as posterity can see. He also laid the groundwork for the walls themselves together with thirteen towers and at the time of his death the walls stood knee-high above the ground.

72. As for Craloh, he lived in exile at the royal court for almost two years, often harassed by the abovementioned stewards, and suffered many misfortunes. In the meantime, Enzelinus, whom I have mentioned, also arrived at the court. At first, he lived there in peace, spending time sociably with his relatives, the stewards, and other friends, whom, as they said, he had bribed with a great amount of gold, taking care nevertheless to avoid being seen by Craloh, and writing versified complaints that his friends passed on to the king. Enzelinus was certainly very learned, just as if he had also received his education at Saint Gall, and when the

admodum erat litteratus. Et cum elegos eius rex legisset, flosculis verborum delectatus querelis compassus est.

2 Tandem vero aliquandiu bene celatus casu Cralohum incurrit. Cui ille: "Vae tibi, Enzeline!" ait; "*Quid tibi hic negotii?* Per coronam meam istam," inquit, "malo tuo venisti!" Econtra ille, quod risum multis moverat, Rhetianus et minus Teutonus: "*Cot ilf, erro*" respondit, id est: "Deus adiuvat, domine." Locoque quantocius cedens minas ipsas in lacrimabiles elegos transtulit et regi eos ipse ostendit. Quibus item ille delectatus hominemque intuitus osculari se iubet, regratiandum pro versibus, si ambo viverent, pollicitus: "Cum abbate tuo te," inquit, "quem iam domum regredi pace reddita volo, ubi primum copia fuerit, pacificabo et, si quid rei tuae cum ipso moliri potero, libens agam." Nam Luitolfus in Italia mortuus erat. Sed et Anno lacrimandus suis obierat.

73. Mane sequente Craloh in alloquium regis vocatus assedit. Sed et Hartperto Curiensi episcopo assedente rex ait: "Quoniam quidem, abba mi, *ad caulas* redire paras, *ovem* tibi quandam, non tamen *perditam, in umeris pono reportandam.* Enimvero non dubito, quin noveris, quem dico." Cum autem ille aliquamdiu sederet ovemque tandem recipere nollet, motus est rex. Sed episcopus ita est quasi pro nobis locutus: "Vide, rex, animum subditis non ferendum, qui et tibi

king read his elegies, he was delighted by the flowery rhetoric of Enzelinus's language and responded favorably to his complaints.

Eventually, however, after successfully avoiding Craloh 2
for a while, Enzelinus ran into him by chance. Craloh said to him: "Woe to you, Enzelinus! *What is your business here?* I swear by this tonsure of mine," he said, "it is to your own misfortune that you have come here!" Enzelinus responded, as a Rhaetian rather than a German, making many people laugh: "*Cot ilf, erro,*" that is "God helps, my lord." He moved away as quickly as he could, rendered those threats into tearful elegiac verses and personally presented the poem to the king. The king was again delighted and, looking at Enzelinus, invited the man to kiss him and promised that if they both lived, he would return his thanks to Enzelinus for his poems. "I will reconcile you with your abbot," he said," and I want him to return home at the first opportunity once peace has been made; and if there is anything I can do to help resolve your quarrel with him, I will gladly do it." By this time Liudolf had died in Italy, and Anno, too, had passed away, mourned by his monks.

73. The following morning Craloh, summoned for an audience with the king, sat down before him. With Hartpert, bishop of Chur, also present, the king said: "My lord abbot, since you are preparing to return *to the fold, I am going to place a sheep on your shoulders to be carried back,* even though it has not been lost. I have no doubt that you know whom I mean." After Craloh had sat there for a while still refusing to take the sheep back, the king became angry. But it was the bishop who said the following, apparently on our behalf: "Your Majesty, look at the arrogance of this man, intolerable

post gratiam clementer exhibitam resultare non metuit."
2 Et acute subiunxit: "Neque enim, si iustitiam, mi rex, ipse mihi feceris, eius est ovis illa, quoniam meae sedis semper erat illa abbatia, quousque Salomonis episcopi technis inde est subducta." At oeconomi astantes: "In fide," inquiunt, "qua tibi, rex, iuravimus, neminis est iustius Favariensis abbatia quam fiscaliter tua." Quibus dictis aulici omnes attestando assultant. Rex vero in ira consurgens consessum diremit. Craloh autem in veniam frustra cecidit, vehementer frustratus gratia domini.

3 Sanctum autem Oudalricum audiens supervenientem, nocte in occursum eius, qui ei infortunia sua panderent, misit ita mandans: "*Adiutor in opportunitatibus,* accelera quantocius, quia famulus ego tuus sum *in tribulatione.*" At aulici adventum sancti ut praevenirent, regem mane primo, ut conventu edicto de abbatia decerneret, rogant timentes, quia Ottoni intimus erat, sancti hominis praesentiam. Capita autem conventus, ut abbatiam fisco regio attestando addicerent, praestruunt, aurum Enzilini, quod plurimum, ut dixi, attulerat, oberando eis dilapidantes. Rege tum assidente pari consessus testimonio fisco eius addicitur abbatia. Quam ipse ilico Enzilino ferula tradidit.

4 Venit tandem episcopus sanctus, nil contradicere valens sancti Galli damnis optimumque ducens, si vel in gratiam

among your subjects, for after he has been mercifully shown favor, he does not fear to defy you." Shrewdly he added: "Ac- 2
tually, my king, if you allow me to say so, that sheep is not even his, because that abbey always belonged to my diocese until it was taken away by Bishop Salomo's machinations." Then the stewards who were standing nearby said: "By the fealty we have sworn to you, our king, the abbey of Pfäfers in all fairness belongs to no one but you, as part of the royal fisc." When they said this, all the courtiers jumped up to confirm it. The king, however, rose from his seat in anger and dissolved the assembly. Craloh then fell at his feet, seeking forgiveness in vain, completely deprived of his lord's favor.

When Craloh heard that Saint Ulrich was arriving, he 3
sent his men to meet him at night to relate his misfortunes to him and convey the following message: "*You who bring assistance at the right time,* hurry as quickly as you can, because I, your servant, am *in serious trouble.*" Meanwhile the courtiers, in anticipation of the holy man's arrival, asked the king first thing in the morning to convene the council and make a decision about the abbey, for they feared Ulrich because he was close to Otto. The leading men of the council, for their part, planned that their testimony would bring the abbey within the royal fisc, by deploying as bribes Enzelinus's gold, which, as I said, he had brought in large quantities. Then in the king's presence and with the unanimous consent of the council the abbey was added to the royal fisc. The king immediately handed the abbey over to Enzelinus together with the staff.

The saintly bishop finally arrived and since he could not 4
undo the loss suffered by Saint Gall, he thought that the

amicum reducere posset. Quod tamen tandem consiliorum artificio sollicite perfecit, rege quidem ante datam gratiam iurante, nisi quod sibimet in tempestate bellica fidei specie advenerit, tam immitis animi abbas iam non foret. Commissusque ipsi Dei viro redeunti, ut eum in sedem suam auctorabiliter reponeret, fratres quoque, quibus invisus erat, reconciliaret, Craloh cum illo domum revertitur.

74. Sed in monasterio in adventu illorum acerba fuit confusio. Ad recipiendum enim episcopum cum evangelio, etiamsi frater conscriptus non fuerit, equum esse, ut pariter occurrant, omnes concordant, sed non sic quidem invisam Cralohi quidem insolentiam. Suscipitur episcopus. Victor evangelium obtulit ipsi. Quod ubi ille osculatur, Victor revertitur. At episcopus currax post illum veniens, a capillo hominem capiens regyravit. At ille evangelium in episcopum
2 reiciens furibundus abscessit. Sed ipse codice suscepto abbati porrigit. Quem abbas osculatum suscipiens per se ipsum usque ad altare gestavit. Victor autem—sonorae enim vocis erat—responsorium *Deus qui sedes* levat. Quod fratres ceteri, quoniam ipse inter eos magni momenti erat, lugubriter percantantes, claustrum spretis illis introeunt et, totum illud super se quidam claudentes, partim de nocte partim palam recessuri opportunitatem exspectant. Erat autem, ut a patribus, qui intererant, audivimus, inter primam et tertiam confusio ista.

best he could do was at least to bring his friend back into favor. He finally achieved this by careful and skillful diplomacy, even though before granting his favor the king swore that had Craloh not come to him in the guise of a loyal supporter amid the turmoil of war, a man of so harsh a disposition would not now be abbot. He was entrusted to Ulrich, that man of God who was going back, so that thanks to his authority he would reinstall Craloh in his seat and also reconcile him with those brothers who were so hostile to him. Craloh returned home with Ulrich.

74. At the time of their arrival there was bitter turmoil in the monastery. Everyone agreed that it was fair that they should together meet the bishop to welcome him with the Gospel, even though he was not an enrolled brother, but there was to be no such welcome for Craloh's outrageous behavior. The bishop was welcomed. Victor offered him the Gospel. When Ulrich kissed the book, Victor turned away. Then the bishop quickly came up behind him, grabbed the man by the hair, and turned him around. Victor threw the
Gospel back at the bishop and stormed out in fury. The 2
bishop caught the book and handed it to the abbot. The abbot kissed the book, took it, and carried it to the altar himself. Meanwhile Victor who had a sonorous voice, raised up the responsory *God, You Who Sit.* Since he was a man of great importance among the brothers, the others sang it in somber tones to the end and entered the cloister without paying attention to the bishop and the abbot. Some of them locked it behind them and waited for an opportunity to go back, some at night, some in plain sight. As I heard from the fathers who were present there, this commotion took place between Prime and Terce.

3 Venit episcopus cum suis et abbatis militibus ad ostium
ecclesiae, quod claustri est introitus. Pulsans vero nominatim condiscipulorum quondam postulat alloquium, hominum, qui, quaqua opus foret, singulares loci sui columnae
quidem essent. Inter quos erant, de quibus loco suo Deo
dante dicturi sumus magnalia: Ekkehardus, post doctrinas
decanus; Notkerus, quem pro severitate disciplinarum Piperis Granum cognominabant, doctor pictor medicus; Geraldus, ab adolescentia usque senilem vitae finem semper scho-
4 larum magister; Burchardus, post abbas, praeter singulares
scientiae et virtutum dotes nobilitate, qua et ceteri pol-
lebant, regalis. Hi quattuor praelecti a fratribus ianuae aec-
clesiae clausae appropiant et episcopum, si ad se intrare
dignetur, Amalungum ut secum solum sumeret, rogant. Erat
autem hic Ekkehardi frater, laicus admodum litteratus, orator in conciliis facundissimus, consilio magnus, religione
paene monachus. Qui et dulcis ad omnia erat et iucundus, in
quodcumque rem, ut aiebant, vertere vellet, potentissimus.
Huic soli, ut audivimus, laico ab ullius memoria capituli domum intrare permissum est.

75. Operae pretium erat dicere, si memor sim, quae a diversis diversa audivi, quantus utique Dei spiritus die illa tonuerit, quae ratio et confessionis fratrum humilitas: reos

The bishop, accompanied by his fighting men and those 3
of the abbot, came up to the church door that serves as an entrance to the cloister. He knocked and asked to speak to his former fellow students, mentioning them by name, men who would be outstanding pillars of their monastery, wherever there was a need. Among these men—and in the appropriate place I will tell you great things about them, God willing—there were the following: Ekkehard, who became dean after some time spent teaching; Notker, whom they nicknamed Peppercorn for his severity in enforcing discipline, a scholar, painter, and physician; Gerald, who always served as a schoolmaster from the time of his youth until he died in
old age; and Burchard, who later became abbot and besides 4
his singular gifts of learning and the virtues, was distinguished, like the others, by his noble birth, in his case by royal ancestors. These four, chosen in advance by the brothers, approached the locked door of the church and asked the bishop that if he saw fit to enter the cloister, he bring only Amalungus with him. This man was Ekkehard's brother, a well-educated layman, a very eloquent orator in assemblies, a wise counselor, and almost a monk in religious observance. He was charming and cheerful in every situation and, as they said, very adept at turning an issue into whatever he wanted. According to what we have heard, he was the only layman in living memory who was permitted to enter the chapter house.

75. It would be worthwhile to tell you, if I can recall them, the different things I have heard from different people: how loudly the Spirit of God thundered on that day, and the good sense and humility of the monks' confession. They confessed that they had indeed been guilty, for they could not

se quidem esse, quod dominum insolentem minus perpeti possint, et, quod is, quem liberi patrem elegerint, pro liberis se servos fecerit, equanimius non tolerarint; evangelicae patientiae esse *usque ad mortem oboedire:* sed hoc, si in persecutione tyrannus infestet, carnifex laniet; se quidem in pace ecclesiae patrem, qui filios diligere non odire, *pastorem,* quem *oves tondere non glutire* libeat, privilegii iure elegisse.
2 Illum vero lupo veniente noctu nemini ovium verbum dantem fugiisse, se lupis reliquisse; insuper thesauros ecclesiae clam se raptos perdidisse. "Tandemque, postquam abbatiam sancto Gallo honoram incautela sui amisit, *quasi re bene gesta,* super nos tamquam pastor et pater," aiunt, "venit, quibus utique nec amicus est, post et quam nos desertor aufugit neque per litteras neque per nuntium umquam uno verbo consolatus est."

3 Et Walto decanus: "Sed, o sancte Dei, frater noster tanto tempore, quoniam per te nobis desertorem ipsum imperii iussu iterum imponendum audivimus, tibi episcopo et fratri honorem debitum impendere non dubitavimus, sed illi non ita. Tu quoque insolentia, qua volebas, usus es in fratrem nostrum et tuum. Scias autem nobis animo firmissime sedisse, reo, aperto claustro, quod quidam inconsultius clauserunt, quoniam quidem nostrum est nemini manu resistere,

endure an insolent master, nor could they calmly put up with the fact that the man whom they, as children, had elected to be their father turned them from children into slaves. They also said that although it was the nature of endurance as described in the Gospel *to be obedient unto death,* this was applicable if a tyrant were relentlessly persecuting them or an executioner were tearing them limb from limb. They, on the contrary, exercising their privilege in the peaceful setting of the church, had elected a father to love his sons, not hate them, and *a shepherd to shear his sheep, not swal-*
low them. Craloh, however, when the wolf came in the night, 2
had fled without saying a word to any of his sheep and left them to the wolves; moreover, he had lost the church treasures that he had secretly seized. "Finally," they said, "after losing the illustrious abbey of Saint Gall due to his rash behavior, he comes back to rule us as our pastor and father *as if he has done a good job* of managing things; although in no way is he our friend after running away and deserting us, and never sending us a single word of consolation, either by letter or through a messenger."

Dean Waldo said: "But, holy man of God, since we heard 3
that it was you, our longtime brother, who would, by imperial decree, reinstall as our abbot this man who deserted us, we did not hesitate to extend honors due to you as a bishop and a brother, but not so to him. You, too, have acted presumptuously toward our brother who is also your brother. You should know therefore our firm decision: we will open the doors of the cloister that some brothers have rather unadvisedly closed, and we will not forbid entry to the offender because it is not our way to resist anyone by force. But you should also know that no matter what we endure at

introitum non vetare; domicilium autem, quod per sanctum Gallum nidus noster est, usque ad querelas regi dirigendas, quoquo modo illum patiamur, etiamsi alapas incusserit, velle fovere. Quorundam autem animos, qui eum fugere et, ut ipsi aiebant, tyranno cedere cogitabant, aegre sedavimus et, quicquid Deus de nobis fieri pro peccatis permiserit, nobiscum pati persuasimus."

4 Postquam sic per Waltonem decanum, hominem praeter dotes generis et virtutum verbo potentem, omnium assensu peroratum est, episcopus lacrimatur. Et Amalunch: "Nobis duobus," inquit, "qui ad tantae molis causam introducti sumus, nunc non est flendum, sed solaciis, si quae possumus, et consiliis in articulo hoc commodis, sancte pater, agendum." Optimum autem videri in aurem dixit, ut ipsum primum fratris, in quem manum misit, animum nec non et omnium fratrum, quantum posset, leniret, *ne tristitiam* hanc *super tristitiam habentes* minus parerent consiliis. Surgens vero episcopus, veniam quidem ab omnibus sibi quidem assurgentibus petens, Victori per se prosternitur. A quo sublevatus pacem, decano monente, viro sanctus obtulit et recepit. Purpuram vero magni pretii, quam ipse protinus sancto Gallo dedit, fratri laeso postea tradidit.

76. Consilio tum breviter habito, concordiae cedere omnibus persuasis, Victor tantum solus condiciones quasdam cum abbate agendas instrepitat. Cui animo saniores resultant. Introductoque in claustrum abbate episcopus cum

his hands, even if he were to slap us, we will take care of our home, our nest, thanks to Saint Gall, right up to the point of sending a letter of complaint to the king. Some brothers have nevertheless considered running away from him and, as they put it, yielding to the tyrant; with difficulty we have calmed them down and persuaded them to endure with us whatever God allows to happen to us for our sins."

When Dean Waldo, who besides possessing the gifts of 4
noble birth and the virtues was also very eloquent, had finished his speech in this vein to the approval of all, the bishop started crying. Amalungus said: "Holy father, now both you and we have become caught up in a very distressing situation, but now is not the time for crying; rather, we should be providing whatever we can in the way of solace and counsel appropriate to the moment." He also whispered in the bishop's ear that he thought it best for the bishop to start out by appeasing, as best he could, the brother on whom he had laid a hand and then all the brothers, so that they would not *add this grievance to previous grievances* and refuse to follow his counsel. Then the bishop stood up and asked forgiveness from all the brothers, who rose in response, and he prostrated himself before Victor. Victor raised him up, and at a sign from the dean, the holy man offered Victor peace and received it in return. After that he gave the offended brother a purple vestment of great value, which he immediately donated to Saint Gall.

76. They held a short council after this, and although everybody had been persuaded to agree to a settlement, Victor was the only one who loudly insisted that certain conditions needed to be worked out for the abbot. Those who were more reasonable opposed him. When the abbot was brought

Amalungo, in partem illum sumentes, tragoediam fratrum pandunt, qualemque se inter eos veniens exhibeat, praemonent. Enimvero nisi rigori solito verbis et gestu, prout tempus tunc erat, aliquantulum cederet, *novissima peiora*
2 *prioribus futura* praesagant. At ille, quaecumque duo illi suadeant—tamen, ne abbatis nomen in se vilesceret, videant—facere spondet. Et episcopus: "Sunt," inquit, "inter ipsos viri, ut nosti, quibus hoc regnum maioris consilii non habet, regi ipsi noti et grati, quibus te placet primitus pacificari et eorum consulto rem aggredi." "Bene," ait, "sanctissime, monuisti; id ambo, ut agatis, postulo." Ingreditur tunc solus persuasor fratrum episcopus. Quibus lenitis cum decanum assumere regrediens vellet, sine capite se inveniri nolle ce-
3 teri inquiunt. Quattuor autem illos, quos diximus, cum illo progredi sanxerunt. Quibus ille in aurem consulto quaedam locutus cum ipsis egreditur, abbatem dux talibus aggressurus commilitonibus. Et subridens dixit: "*Prima coniunctio acerrima* est." Amalunch autem ubi germanum vidit cum illis, surgens occurrit viris. Et silentio: "Benedictionem ab illo," ait, "non adhuc petatis; sed *patientes estote et confirmate corda* et taciti, usque dum, quid sentiat, ab ipso audiatis, consistite! Sicut silva," inquit, "personet, sic echo resultet."

4 Appropiantibus vero abbas assurgens: "*Benedicite!*" praetulit. Quibus tacitis Amalunch: "Quantum mihi," inquit, "de

to the cloister, the bishop and Amalungus took him aside, explained to him the nature of the brothers' grievance and gave him advice on how he should behave toward them. They predicted, in fact, that if in the present circumstances he did not somewhat soften the habitual harshness of his speech and demeanor, *the situation would be worse than before.*
The abbot promised to do everything the two men sug- 2
gested, urging them, however, not to let his authority as abbot be diminished. The bishop said: "As you know, there are men among them whom the king himself knows well and favors, and the kingdom possesses no others *more valued for their counsel;* you should first of all make peace with them and then do as they advise." Craloh said: "Holiest of men, you have advised me well; now I ask that you two arrange it." Then the bishop entered the cloister alone in order to win the brothers over. When he had calmed them down and, on his way back, was intending to take the dean with him, the others said that they did not want to be left without a leader. The monks decided instead that the four broth- 3
ers I have mentioned should go with him. The bishop deliberately whispered something to them and led them out like a military commander, about to attack the abbot with these comrades-in-arms. He said with a smile: "*The first contact is the fiercest.*" When Amalungus saw that his brother was with them, he got up and ran to meet the men. He quietly said: "You should not ask the abbot for a blessing yet; instead *be patient, and strengthen your hearts,* and stand in silence until you hear what he has to say! As the wood fills with sound, so the echo responds."

But when they approached, the abbot rose and was the 4
first to say: "*Bless me!*" They remained silent, and Amalungus

regula innotuit, minores a maiore benedictionem habent pro tempore petere." Et episcopus: "Magna," inquit, "donaria tibi, frater, offerimus." Et ille: "Utinam mihi," inquit, "ut ego ipsis offerar, Dominus donet!" Factum est utrimque silentium; parantur alloquia. Quae Amalunch, ne forte commotionem parerent, pertimescens: "Eia," inquit, "domini, consilium meum facessere utrimque dignamini! De simultatibus, rogo, nullum iam verbum hinc inde loquamini; sed in pace Domini omni fastu deposito utrimque veniam petentes osculemini!" Placuit episcopo et utrisque consilium in venias *et in oscula ruendo.* Post pauca paucis verba utrimque semet anticipantes considunt unanimes. Conferuntur consilia, qualiter totum corpus capiti et caput corpori restituatur.

5 Stat consilium patrem filiis oblatum in sancti Benedicti, cuius imago appicta sedebat, ponere solium. Inducitur manu episcopi locatusque parumper residet. Tandemque assurgens lacrimando in veniam corruit; sed et episcopo secum ruente fratres omnes econtra ruebant. Erat facietenus videre spiritum sanctum opus suum ibimet agere. Osculatis singulis unanimitas in domo solidatur. Amalunch vero, homo iucunditatis grataeque vox dulcedinis, sequentiam *Laus tibi sit, O fidelis Deus* gratulanter incipiens, episcopo et abbate cunctisque iuvantibus consummavit. *Agitur dies in laetitia;* longos rancores caritas fregit.

Non tulit hanc speciem furiato pectore Victor.

said to them: "According to what I know of the Rule, it is the subordinates who have to ask their superior for a blessing." The bishop said: "Brother, we offer you great gifts." Craloh replied: "If only God would grant that I be offered to them!" Silence fell on both sides as they were preparing to speak. Fearing that this might lead to an altercation, Amalungus said: "My dear lords, may both parties be good enough to follow my advice! I ask you not to speak of disagreements from now on but rather to lay all self-righteousness aside in the spirit of the Lord's peace, ask forgiveness from each other, and kiss." This advice pleased the bishop and both parties, and they *hastened* to ask forgiveness and *to exchange kisses.* After conversing for a short while, with each side anticipating what the other one wanted to say, they all sat down in agreement. They discussed plans for restoring the whole body to its head and the head to its body.

They made a decision to install the father offered to his 5
sons in the seat of Saint Benedict, whose painted image was placed there. The bishop led the abbot by the hand to the seat, where he sat down and remained sitting for a while. Finally, he got up and sank to the ground in tears, seeking forgiveness; the bishop, too, sank down, and so in their turn did all the brothers. It was obvious that the Holy Spirit was then and there at work. After they all exchanged kisses, harmony in the house was strengthened. Then Amalungus, a cheerful man who possessed a sweet and pleasant voice, joyfully began the sequence *Praise Be to You, O True God,* and sang it to the end with the support of the bishop and abbot and everybody else. *The day was spent in joy;* love destroyed old grudges.

Victor, *maddened in his heart, could not bear this sight.*

6 Abbatem quippe in sede sua cum vidisset, turbidus exsiliit et quasi loco cessurus capituli domo exivit. Quem tamen episcopus, prout potuit, revocatum delinivit et in abbatis gratiam reductum ad tempus compescuit, quod tamen post abscessum eius minus quidem profuit. Egreditur post aliquot dies loco episcopus ad suos iturus, Victoremque, ut putabat, in gratia stabilitum reliquerat.

77. Accidit autem tempore labente, ut ad amicos foras eundi a decano licentiam Victor peteret, re vera Enzelinum modernum abbatem, ut Cralohi damnis insultaret vel etiam cum illo penitus persisteret, petiturus. Insinuatur abbati, deforis tunc agenti, Victorem quidem abscessum non parvis impensis se celato parare. Mittit ille secretius ad militem suum quendam viae eius contiguum, ut eum custodiret claustroque suo invitum reduceret. Nemo enim de familia Galli tanti generis viro vim inferre auderet. Custoditus invaditur; ut redeat, primo rogatur; tandem, cum nollet, hasta-
2 rum impulsibus compellitur. At ille robur quoddam e proximo rapiens, militem ipsum capite incutiens equo cadere fecit seminecem. Eo autem cadente omnes pariter sui Victorem invadentes equo deiciunt oculosque illi, pro dolor, furibundi eruunt. Miles autem ille cum refocilatus, illo

When he saw the abbot installed in his seat, he leaped up 6
in agitation and ran out of the chapter house as if intending to leave the monastery. The bishop, however, called Victor back, calmed him down as best he could, restored him to the abbot's favor, and held him in check for the time being; this, however, was of little help after the bishop's departure. A few days later the bishop left the monastery to return to his congregation, thinking that he had left Victor safely returned to favor.

77. After some time had passed, however, it happened that Victor asked permission from the dean to travel outside the monastery to visit his friends. In reality he intended to go to Enzelinus, newly made abbot, in order to make fun of Craloh's woes or even to stay with Enzelinus outright. The abbot, who was at that time doing business outside the monastery, was informed that Victor, at considerable expense, was getting ready to leave without telling him. He sent a secret message to one of his knights who lived near the route Victor would be traveling, telling him to watch out for Victor and to bring him back to his monastery even against his will. No dependent of Saint Gall, you see, would dare to use force against a man of such noble birth. They spotted Victor and seized him: at first they asked him to go back to the monastery but he refused, and they finally
started forcing him with their spears. Victor, in his turn, 2
grabbed the first stick he could find and hit the knight on the head, causing him to fall from his horse half-dead. When the knight fell down, all his men came at Victor together, threw him off his horse and, alas, gouged out his eyes in their fury. When the knight began to recover and regain

iam caecato, ad se rediret, multum doluit, quoniam sibimet deinceps domo propria exulandum non dubitavit. Nam aliquanto post haec elapso tempore amicis viri obvius occiditur; armiger quoque eius, qui facinori intererat, in arbore suspenditur.

3 Deportatus per silvam ad proxima armentariorum coenobii magalia, caecus intimatur in claustro fratribus. Fitque in monasterio non ferenda confusio, paene omnibus in abbatis insolentiam facinus vergentibus. At discipuli hominis pluresque de fratribus celeres ad illum venientes, luctus tali orbo inspecto miscent et in caelum eiulatus. Re tandem abbas audita monasterium in tali confusione ingredi distulit; sine armis autem non esse fidelium consilio curavit, quo-
4 niam propinquorum caeci minas saevas audiverant. Misit tandem nuntium decano Waltoni, uti fratrem illum sollicite curaret. At ille severus etiam et ipse: "Alius," inquit, "dum ego decanus sum, curet. Dic ergo illi, quod ante me decani semper infirmos curabant non iussi, sed talem numquam. Raroque quisquam abbatum monachum, quem caecari fecerit, decano curandum commisit." Talibus ille responsis tanti viri auditis, ut Waningum, in omnibus tempestatibus suis capellanum eius, dicere audivimus, tantum contabuit, ut vix loqui residens valeret.

consciousness, by which time Victor had already been blinded, he became extremely upset because he did not doubt that after this he would be exiled from his own home. After some time had passed, he encountered Victor's friends and was killed; his armor-bearer who was also involved in the crime, was hanged from a tree.

Victor was carried through the woods to the nearest huts 3
where the monastery's herdsmen lived, and word was sent
to the brothers in the cloister that he had been blinded. A
terrible turmoil arose in the monastery, and almost everyone was inclined to attribute the crime to a shameless act of
the abbot. Victor's students and many of the brothers
quickly came to him, and when they saw him so terribly deprived of his sight, their lamentations mingled with howls
reached up to the sky. When the abbot finally heard what
had happened, he delayed his return while the monastery
was in such turmoil; on the advice of those loyal to him, he
took care never to be without armed protection, because he
had heard about the savage threats issued by the kin of the
blinded man. Eventually he sent a messenger to Dean 4
Waldo, asking him to provide the best care for that brother.
But Waldo, a severe man too, said: "Let someone else treat
him while I am dean. Tell the abbot that deans before me always treated patients without being asked, but never for
this kind of injury. Rarely did any abbot entrust a dean to
care for a monk whose blindness the abbot himself had
caused." When the abbot received this response from so
venerable a man, as we have heard from Waning, the abbot's
chaplain during all those turbulent times, he was so over-
whelmed that he sat down and was barely able to speak.

78. Victor dein per Notkerum medicum orbibus in brevi sanatus, in bonis postea operibus semet exercuit. Et ut ea, quae de eo audiveram, brevi perstringam: Argentinensis, quidam Erchinbaldus nomine sanguinis sui, episcopus sub Burchardo abbate propter doctrinas et miseriae consolationem permisso ipsius ad se hominem traxit et urbem suam doctrinis eius floridam fecit. Tandem autem episcopo defuncto cellam quandam heremiticam intra Hohfeldinos montes, Longum Mare vocatam, solitario defuncto ingressus per multos annos tenuit. Multasque virtutes, ut ibi celebre est, in extremis suis faciens, sanctissimus circumquaque habitus diem senex obiit.

2 Veni autem et ego ipse in locum ad quendam tunc temporis magni nominis solitarium, vidensque inter colloquia sepulchrum quoddam plus ceteris honoratum, cuiusnam id esset, quaesiveram: sancti Victoris esse ait. Et cum breviter mihi vitam eius et casus utique plus notos panderet, nihil venenatum super illum tumulum vivens progredi posse asseruit. Serpentes autem enormes ibi videre est plures et reptilia informia. Usque huc de Victore.

79. At Craloh quasi corpore tristitia effeto et doloribus incedere coepit in dies amplius languidulo. Nam et fama erat venturos quantotius ab imperio, qui eum ob vindictam facinoris deposituri erant a regiminis solio. Nam regem procul contra Danos Sleswic agentem factum non latuit.

78. Victor's eye sockets were soon healed thanks to Notker the Physician, and afterward he dedicated himself to good works. To summarize briefly what I have heard about him, the bishop of Strasbourg, who was called Erchinbald and was Victor's kinsman, with the permission of the next abbot, Burchard, took Victor in, both to console him in his misfortune and because of his learning, and Strasbourg flourished thanks to Victor's teaching. In the end, after the bishop died, Victor entered a hermit's cell in the Vosges mountains, whose recluse had passed away; it was called Long Lake and he lived there for many years. Because in the last years of his life he performed many miracles, as is well known in those parts, by the time of his death in old age he was regarded all around as the holiest of men.

I myself also visited this place to see a hermit, greatly re- 2
nowned at the time; while talking with him I noticed a grave that seemed more venerated than the others and asked whose it was; the hermit said it was Saint Victor's. He briefly told me about his life and about its most famous events, and he assured me that no poisonous creature could pass over Victor's grave and live. But in fact many enormous snakes and hideous reptiles can be seen there. So much about Victor.

79. As for Craloh, day by day he became more feeble, seemingly worn out by sorrow and pain. In addition, there was a rumor that envoys would very soon come from the emperor who would strip Craloh of his abbacy in punishment for his crime. Even though the king was then far away, fighting the Danes in Schleswig, what had happened did not escape his attention.

2 Ingresso tandem monasterium variae ei res erant cum variis. Quadam autem die quorundam quasi fidelium consilio,
fratribus sed et Victore praesentibus, rogat licere sibi con-
scientiam in ara sancti Galli iuramento purgare de eo, quod
in Victore patratum est, facinore ita: uti sic sibi Deus lumen
aeternum daturus sit, sicut ipse in privatione luminum eius
3 hominis reus fuerit. Ad quae Gerhaldus, ad responsa, ut aiebant, semper paratissimus: "Praetermisso," inquit, "quod
manus in illum mittere, domine mi, iusseras, ne sic quidem
tanti facinoris, ut aiunt, causa fueris." Tandem vero nemini
iam fratrum animo sedit illum iureiurando reatum ipsum a
cervice sua excutere posse. Differtur tamen causa propter
honorem eius in posterum, propter quod etiam ipsa die virginem Kerhildam, Notkeri Balbuli neptim, apud sanctum
Magnum circa Wiboradae clausulam includere ipse condix-
4 erat. Nam et antea quidem, Rachilda post Wiboradae passionem vigesimo primo anno ad Deum assumpta, Perhterat,
quaedam vidua sancta, cum et ipsa includi apud nos optasset
et, clausula eius sibi oblata, paene annum in probatione lau-
dabilis appareret, vulgi visitationes crebras et inanes devitans, in cella Salomonis circa parietem tituli sancti Georgii
includi rogaverat, magnarum virtutum operatrix plures inibi
annos exegerat.

5 Obiit quoque cum omnium dolore Walto decanus, et in
locum eius subrogatur Purchardus. Et anno elapso velut comitiis post illum fit Ekkehardus decanus. In quo tandem

When Craloh finally returned to the monastery, a variety 2
of things happened to him involving a variety of people. One day, at the suggestion of some people seemingly loyal to him, he asked, in the presence of the brethren including Victor, that he be allowed to clear his conscience concerning the crime committed against Victor by taking an oath before the altar of Saint Gall, in this vein: that God would give him eternal life, just as he had been guilty in depriving this man of his eyesight. At this point Gerald, who was al- 3
ways, as they said, very prompt to respond, said: "My lord Abbot, except for the fact that you ordered your men to lay hands on Victor, you were not responsible for so horrible a crime, as they say." In the end none of the brothers was convinced that Craloh could escape blame by swearing an oath. Yet out of respect for him the decision in this matter was postponed because Craloh had determined that on that day he would enclose the virgin Gerhilda, the niece of Notker the Stammerer, in a cell near Wiborada's cell at Saint Magnus. Sometime earlier, twenty years after Wiborada had suf- 4
fered her martyrdom, Rachilda was summoned by God, and Bertrada, a saintly widow who had also wanted to become a recluse at our monastery, received Rachilda's cell. She lived there for almost a year as a trial period, avoiding frequent idle visits from the public, proving herself to be worthy of praise. Bertrada asked then to be enclosed in Salomo's cell near the wall of the church of Saint George, and she spent many years there performing great miracles.

Dean Waldo died too, to everybody's sorrow, and Bur- 5
chard was appointed in his place. After a year passed, Ekkehard succeeded Burchard as dean, as if elected by popular

Craloh plus quam in semet confisus, loco, quoniam imbecillior in dies erat, interdum cedens Herginisowam pro pausatione creber adierat. Fratribusque absentiam eius non aegre ferentibus ibi manebat.

80. Nam in Ekkehardo, natura et studio caritatis dulcedine pleno, spiritus cunctorum quieverat. Qui de Ioniswilare, quod, ut diximus, ipse requisivit et tenuit, hebdomadam septem cottidie victualium statuit cum pane abundo et quinque mensuris de cervisia. Quarum quintam, nonalem quidem, vino comparari voluit.

2 Hic aliquando Romam pro voto pergens, papae intimus factus aliquamdiuque apud illum propter doctrinam detentus, aeris terrae vitio morbo corripitur perque sex hebdomadas lecto tenetur. Papa vero saepe eum visitans impensorum copiam dabat. At ille quadam die, satis iam tarde quidem, eum rogat, ut, quando proxime se visitet, Iohannis Baptistae reliquias secum ferat. Erat enim semper assertor eius et amator validus. At ille mane proxima ad eum cum reliquiis cum accederet, aeger in amplexus ipsarum et papae assurgens, ex illa hora melius habere coepit. Et cum in brevi convalesceret, reliquiis Baptistae et multorum ab apostolico donatus sanctorum sospes domum rediit, et permisso Burchardi, tunc abbatis, et dote ecclesiam illis decoram paravit.

3 Multa de eo post dicenda sunt; sed prius, a quo spiritu ductus sit, ex verbis ipsius nosci licet. Scripsit enim doctus

vote. After that Craloh, who had more confidence in Ekkehard than in himself and was getting weaker by the day, began leaving the monastery from time to time, and often went to Herisau to rest. And since the brothers had no problem with his absence, he remained there.

80. Thanks to Ekkehard, who by nature and by application was full of the gentleness of love, everyone calmed down. Using the proceeds from Jonswil, the property which, as I said, he had himself acquired and retained, he established seven daily rations a week with plenty of bread and five measures of beer. He allowed every fifth of these measures (the Nones, so to speak) to be of wine.

Once Ekkehard went to Rome to fulfill a vow; he became 2
close to the pope and was invited to stay with him for a while in view of his learning; because of the region's bad air, he fell ill and was confined to bed for six weeks. The pope often visited him, bringing numerous gifts. One time, quite late in the day, Ekkehard asked the pope on his next visit to bring the relics of John the Baptist with him. Ekkehard had always been a great advocate and admirer of that saint. On the next morning the pope came to Ekkehard with the relics. The sick man rose from his bed to embrace the relics and the pope, and from that moment on Ekkehard began getting better. In a short time he recovered, and the pope gave him the relics of the Baptist and of many other saints. Ekkehard returned home safe and sound, and after receiving permission and an endowment from Burchard, then abbot, he erected a beautiful church for the relics.

There is much to be said later about Ekkehard; but before 3
that, his own words allow us to see the nature of the spirit that guided him. This learned man wrote the sequences

ille sequentias *Prompta mente canamus, Summum preconem Christi, Qui benedici cupitis, A solis occasu.* De sancta Afra antiphonas, ut reliquias eius mereretur, Luitoldo episcopo et sequentiam dictavit. Hymnum *O martyr aeterni patris,* antiphonas *Ambulans Iesus, Adoremus gloriosissimum.*

4 Scripsit et in scholis metrice magistro—vacillanter quidem, quia in affectione, non in habitu erat puer—vitam Waltharii manufortis. Quam Magontiae positi, Aribone archiepiscopo iubente pro posse et nosse nostro correximus; barbaries enim et idiomata eius Teutonem adhuc affectantem repente Latinum fieri non patiuntur. Unde male docere solent discipulos semimagistri dicentes: "Videte, quomodo disertissime coram Teutone aliquo proloqui deceat, et eadem serie in Latinum verba vertite!" Quae deceptio Ekkehardum in opere illo adhuc puerum fefellit, sed postea non sic, ut in Lidio Charlomannico: "*Mole ut vincendi ipse quoque oppeteret.*"

5 Obtulit autem ille sancto Gallo ad monachatum quattuor ex fratribus vel sororibus nepotes suos: duos sibi equivocos, Burchardum quoque post abbatem, Notkerum magistrum nostrum. Quorum quisque ecclesiae dicendus sit speculum. De quibus loco suo memoralia sua dicemus. Unusquisque enim ipsorum libro suo sufficeret. Tales palmites dum vitis illa iam mitteret, bene matura in die Felicis in Pincis vindemiata est ipsa. Talis autem luctus de obitu hominis erat, ut

Let Us Sing with Ready Heart, Let Us Praise the Supreme Herald of Christ, You Who Wish to Be Blessed, and *From the Setting of the Sun.* He composed antiphons and a sequence about Saint Afra for Bishop Liutold so that he might deserve her relics. He also wrote the hymn *O Martyr of the Eternal Father* and the antiphons *While Jesus Was Walking* and *Let Us Praise the Most Glorious One.*

In school Ekkehard also wrote for his master a metrical 4
Life of Waltharius the Strong Armed, although his meter was shaky because he was still a boy emotionally, though not in overall character. When I lived in Mainz, I corrected this composition at Archbishop Aribo's request to the best of my ability and knowledge, for barbarisms and native idioms often prevent a striving German, trying hard to be a Latinist, from suddenly becoming one. This is why half masters do a bad job of teaching when they tell their students: "Imagine how it would be spoken most eloquently before a German and translate the words in the same order into Latin!" This error led Ekkehard astray in this work as a boy, but not so later on, as we can see, for instance, in the song of Carloman: "*He too died from the massive weight of victory.*"

Ekkehard also gave four of his nephews, sons of his broth- 5
ers or sisters, as oblates to Saint Gall. Two of them were his namesakes, one was called Burchard and later became our abbot, and one was called Notker, who was my own master. Each of them deserves to be called an exemplary figure of the church. I will tell you memorable things about them in an appropriate place. Each of them deserves his own book. By the time this vine produced these branches, it had fully ripened and been harvested on the day of Saint Felix in Pincis. Such was the mourning over his death that when

decanus post illum Immo postque abbas ipse ad sanctum Michaelem, ubi liberius eiulare posset, corpore eius in feretro posito secederet, ita vociferans: "*Vide, Domine, et considera, quem vindemiaveris ita!*"

81. Et his quidem per digressionem dictis ad Cralohum redeamus. Enimvero Ekkehardum hic defunctum ad facta sua insignia mox resuscitabimus. Craloh autem, cum in dies viribus deficeret et iam saepe Victoris amicis milites sui securitatem frustra pro eo porrigerent, armis infra forisque commanens custoditur. Tandem vero communi consilio responsa totius abbatiae committit Ekkehardo. Ipse autem in Herginisowam exercitii gratia equitans ibi in lectum decidit. Videns autem finem vitae adesse, Ekkehardum cum fratribus *sanioris consilii* evocans *disposuit domui,* et ipse, <illum> pro se abbatem eligere facile omnibus persuasis, viam omnium ingressus est reportatusque coenobium honorifice sepelitur.

2 At Ekkehardus—Ottone apud Anglos cum Adaltage rege ipsorum, socero suo, aliquamdiu agente, ut iunctis viribus Chnutonem Danorum debellaret regem—habenas abbatiae, sicut sub abbate vivo solebat, usque ad cognitionem imperii strenue regebat. Accidit autem, ut quadam die foras iturus, ante portam equo in glacie lapso tibiam pedemque confringeret hisque non recte coagulatis postmodum

Ekkehard's body had been laid out on the bier, Immo, who succeeded Ekkehard as dean, later becoming abbot himself, withdrew to Saint Michael's. There he could more freely raise his voice in lamentation, and he cried out, "*Behold, O Lord, and consider what vine you have so harvested!*"

81. After these remarks by way of a digression let us now return to Craloh. We shall even bring Ekkehard back to life to tell you about his remarkable deeds. As for Craloh, because his strength ebbed away day by day and his knights had been unsuccessful in the repeated offers of security they made to Victor's friends on his behalf, he remained protected by arms both inside and outside the monastery. In the end, on the unanimous advice of the monks, he entrusted the running of the entire abbey to Ekkehard. As for Craloh himself, he rode to Herisau for exercise, and took to his bed there. Perceiving that the end of his life was near, Craloh summoned Ekkehard and the *wiser* brothers, and *set his house in order,* and, after easily persuading them to elect Ekkehard in his place, then went the way we all go. His body was brought back to the monastery and given an honorable burial.

Ekkehard held the reins of the abbey firmly in his hands, 2
just as he had been doing while the abbot was still alive, until he was recognized as abbot by the emperor. Otto had for some time been waging war in the land of the Angles after joining forces with their king, Adaltag, who was his father-in-law, to defeat Cnut, king of the Danes. One day, when Ekkehard was about to set out from the monastery, it happened that his horse slipped on ice in front of the gate and Ekkehard broke his foot and his shinbone. Because they did not heal properly, he limped thereafter. For this reason, with

claudicaret. Qua causa electionem suam omnium fratrum concordia in Purchardoum unanimem suum transtulit, de quo supra diximus. De quo etiam adhuc altius quaedam repetere habemus.

82. Oudalrich quidam, comes de Karoli prosapia, Wendilgartam, Henrici regis de filia neptim, uxorem accipiens, Adalhardum, qui Gallo Altstetin post tradidit, de ea et filiam procreavit. Hic nuntio Puochorn, ubi habitavit, accepto Ungros Noricum, ubi praedia ei erant, irruere, hostes cum ceteris bello aggressus, victus capitur et in Ungariam captivus asportatur. Qui autem Ungros Agarenos putant, longa via errant.

2 Wendilgarth vero quasi—viro, ut fama erat, occiso—vidua, ad nuptias petita, nutu Dei nubere noluit. Sed Salomone rogato ad sanctum Gallum concessit, ubi sibi iuxta
Wiboradam caminata constructa de suo vixit, fratribus et
pauperibus pro anima viri quasi defuncti multa largitur. Dul-
ciaminum autem cum esset avida et novitatum semper ap-
petens, uti delicate nutrita et his assueta, increpata est a
Wiborada, quoniam non esset signum pudicitiae in femina
appetere varia cibamina. Quadam autem die ante clausulam
virginis cum sedisset ad colloquia, poma sibi dari ad vescen-
3 dum, si dulcia ibi haberet, petiverat. "Quibus pauperes
utuntur," illa ait, "habeo pulcherrima," proferensque mala

the approval of all the brothers he handed over his office to Burchard, his close associate whom I mentioned above. Concerning him I need to go back to an episode from an even earlier period.

82. A certain Ulrich, a count of Charlemagne's lineage, married Wendilgart, a granddaughter of King Henry through his daughter, and fathered Adalhard, who later handed Altstätten over to Saint Gall, and a daughter. When Ulrich received a message at Buchhorn, where he lived, that the Hungarians had invaded Bavaria, where he had estates, he along with others fought a battle with the enemy and was defeated, captured, and taken to Hungary as a prisoner. By the way, those who believe that the Hungarians are Hagarenes are far off the mark.

Wendilgart, apparently a widow because her husband had 2
been reported dead, received proposals of marriage, but a
sign from God caused her to refuse them. Instead she petitioned Salomo and retreated to Saint Gall, where she had a
little heated chamber built for her near Wiborada. Wendilgart lived there drawing on her own funds and making large
donations to the brothers and the poor on behalf of the soul
of her husband, whom she believed to be dead. Since she
was always craving delicacies and eager for something new,
as she had been raised in luxury and accustomed to such
treats, Wiborada often rebuked her on the grounds that
seeking variety in food signaled a lack of a sense of propriety
in a woman. One day when Wendilgart was sitting in front
of the virgin's cell talking with her, she asked Wiborada
to give her some apples to eat if she had any sweet ones.
Wiborada said: "I have some very nice ones that the poor 3
eat," and she offered some very sour wild apples and left

de silva acidissima inhianti et de manibus ei rapienti reliquerat. At illa vix unum dimidium ore et oculis contractis vorans, cetera proiciens: "Austera es," ait, "austera sunt et mala tua." Et cum esset literata: "Si omnia," inquit, "mala factor talia creasset, numquam Eva malum gustasset." "Bene," ait illa, "Evam memorasti; enimvero quomodo et tu, sic deliciarum avida erat, ideo in escula unius mali peccaverat."

83. Abscessit femina nobilitatis rubore perfusa per virginem humilitatis. Vimque post haec sibimet inferens, dulcia-
mina occursantia ligurire abstinuit. Tantaque monitrice in
brevi adeo excrevit, ut sacrum velamen, quod antea detrec-
tavit, a iam dicto episcopo imponi sibi synodo favente roga-
verit. Quo facto laicali in tantum exuta est animo, ut virtutibus cum inclusis assuefacta post Rachildam, quae passim in
corpore et maxime mamillis ulcerosa cottidie emori visa est,
2 includi optaverit. Et quia vere et ipsam quidem martyrem
incidimus, levius ei erat cum magistra semel *cerebrum disper-
gendum* optulisse, quam xxi post illam annis *testa saniem* cum
sancto Iob inclusam *rasisse,* cum tamen interea ieiunare et
orare—vigilare enim dolores dabant—et eleemosynas dare
non taederet. Ut de illa Ekkeharth, qui supra, consobrinus
eius, cecinit:

them with the eagerly waiting woman, who snatched them out of her hands. Wendilgart, however, had barely eaten half an apple when she made a face with her mouth and eyes and threw the rest away, saying: "You are sour, and your apples are sour, too." Because she was an educated woman, she said: "Had our maker created all apples in such a way, Eve would never have tasted the apple." "It is fitting," Wiborada said, "that you have mentioned Eve, for she craved delicacies just like you, and it was because of this that she sinned by taking a bite of an apple."

83. The noble lady departed, made to blush with shame
by the humble virgin. Thereafter Wendilgart forced herself
to abstain from sweets when they were offered to her to
taste. Guided by such a counselor, she made so much progress in a short time that she asked the aforementioned
bishop to place on her head, with the synod's approval, the
sacred veil, which she had earlier spurned. After this was
done, she so completely cast off secular preoccupations
that, having grown accustomed to a virtuous life among the
recluses, she chose to be enclosed in a cell after Rachilda,
who had sores all over her body and especially on her breasts
and seemed to be at death's door every day. Since we have 2
touched on Rachilda, a true martyr, it would have been easier for her if she had offered her *brains to be splattered* with
her teacher Wiborada, at a single stroke rather than living as
a recluse, scraping off the *pus with a potsherd* like Saint Job
for twenty-one years after Wiborada's death. Even though
the fasting, praying, or giving alms did not weary her, the
nightly vigils caused her pain. As Ekkehard, her cousin,
whom I mentioned earlier, put it in verse:

Hanc Satan, hanc laesit, cum Iob saniem sibi rasit.
Ieiunans flevit; tormenta dolens vigilavit.

3 Neque enim vitam vel passionem votivae martyris lucidius succingere potuit. Ad cuius sepulchrum in repentinis
angustiarum motibus, *experto credite,* multum valet orasse.

84. Venerat quarto anno initiante anniversarius, ut cre-
debat, viri sui amarus, et Wendilgarth Puochorn adiens
dispersit, ut solebat, *dedit pauperibus.* Et ecce Oudalricus
captivitate fortuito elapsus, eam, inter ceteros pannosos
clandestina arte se celans, ut sibi vestem daret, inclamat.
Quem illa, quod improbe audaciusque mendicaret, increpi-
2 tans, vestem tamen ei velut indignans dedit. At ille manum
dantis cum veste stringens, ad se tractam amplexatus, vellet
nollet, osculatus est. Capillisque prolixis in collum manu
reiectis, cum etiam aliqui alapas minitassent: "Parcite,
quaeso," ait, "tandem alapis, quas multas pertuli, et Oudalricum vestrum recognoscite!" Audita tandem voce domini,
milites stupidi vultuque quondam noto inter crines re-
cognito clamose salutant; familia gratulans vociferatur.
Wendilgarth autem dum quasi dedecus ab aliquo passa stupida residisset: "Nunc demum," ait, "Oudalricum mortuum
3 sentio, cum talem ab aliquo pertuli violentiam." Ille autem
cum ei manum de vulnere aliquo quondam notissimo ad
allevandum porrigeret signabilem, *quasi de somno evigilans:*
"Dominus meus," ait, "omnium hominum carissimus!
Salve," ait, "domine; salve, semper dulcissime!" Et inter

Satan tormented her, and she scraped her boils like Job.
She fasted and wept; she suffered torments keeping vigil.

By no means could he have described more clearly and 3
succinctly the life and passion of this devoted martyr. Praying at her tomb has proved very effective in sudden bouts of distress; *trust one who has experienced it!*

84. At the beginning of the fourth year there came, as Wendilgart believed, the bitter anniversary of her husband's death, and she went to Buchhorn and *distributed freely and gave to the poor* as usual. Suddenly Ulrich, who had, by lucky chance, escaped from captivity and secretly hidden himself among the other beggars, loudly called on her to give him clothes. She rebuked him for begging immodestly and all too boldly, but despite her indignation she gave him a garment nonetheless. He grasped her hand together with the 2
garment as she gave it, drew Wendilgart willy-nilly into his embrace and kissed her. When some of her men even threatened to slap him, he pulled his long hair back to his neck and said: "Please spare me the slaps; I suffered many of them; and recognize your Ulrich!" When they heard the voice of their lord and recognized amid the hair the face well known of old to them, the astonished fighting men loudly greeted him with acclamations; the dependents shouted their joy. Wendilgart, however, sat as if stunned by the disgrace she had suffered at someone's hands, and said: "I see that Ulrich really is dead now that I have suffered such violence from
some man." Then he reached out his hand to raise her up, a 3
hand marked by a scar from an old wound, so familiar to her; she said, *as if awaking from sleep:* "My lord, dearest of all men! Greetings, my lord, greetings, my beloved!" She kissed and

oscula et amplexus: "Induite," inquit, "dominum vestrum, donec ei lavacrum ad horam acceleretis!" Indutus vero: "Eamus," inquit, "ad ecclesiam!" Et inter eundum: "Quaeso," ait, "quis capiti tuo velum illud imposuit?" Audito, quod in synodo episcopus, tacitus sibimet: "Nec ego te iam nisi eius permisso amplecti," ait, "habeo."

4 Laudes a clericis tandem, qui plures ad diem convenerant, incohantur, a plebe persolvuntur. Missas pro vivo, non pro defuncto in gaudiis celebrant. Itur lavatum. *Fama volans,* ut fit, multos adduxit. Convivio diei opipare peracto dies multi laetificantur.

85. In proximo fit synodus. Repetit uxorem, quam Deo ille subarraverat, ab episcopo Oudalricus. Velum manu episcopi ablatum in scriniis ecclesiae synodi decreto servandum locatur, ut, si vir eius prior obierit, vidua illud reinduat.

2 Nuptiae tandem aguntur a principio. *Concepit mulier.* Gallumque suum et inclusas sanctas viro comite votive adiens, si masculum pepererit, sancto Gallo monachum devovit. Abeunt igitur domum. At tempore labente appropinquans partui, pregnans periclitatur et ante quattuordecim temporivi partus dies emoritur. Infans excisus et arvinae porci recens erutae, ubi incutesceret, involutus, bonae indolis cum in brevi apparuisset, baptizatur et Purchardus nominatur.

embraced him, and said to the servants: “Dress your lord and run at once to prepare his bath.” When he had been dressed, he said: “Let us go to the church!” On the way there he said: “Please tell me who put that veil upon your head.” When he learned that it was the bishop who had done it at the synod, he quietly said to himself: “And I am not to embrace you without his permission.”

Then the clerics who had gathered in great numbers on 4
that day began chanting the hymns of praise, and the people joined in and sang them to the end. Mass was joyfully celebrated for the living man instead of a dead one. The husband and wife went to the bath. *Word spread quickly,* as generally happens, and drew many people. A splendid feast was had on that day, and many days thereafter were spent in rejoicing.

85. Soon after this the synod convened. Ulrich asked the bishop for the return of his wife, whom the latter had pledged to God. The bishop removed Wendilgart’s veil with his own hand, and by decree of the synod it was placed in the church chests for safekeeping, so that if her husband died first she could put it on again as a widow.

Finally, the nuptials were held anew. *The woman conceived.* 2
Accompanied by her husband, she came to her beloved Saint Gall and to the holy recluses to give a vow that if she bore a male child, she would offer him to Saint Gall as a monk. Then the couple went home. Time passed, and when she was approaching the end of her term, Wendilgart became dangerously ill and died fourteen days before her due date. The baby was cut out of her womb and wrapped in freshly abraded pig fat so that his skin could properly form; in a short time he showed great promise and was baptized

Pater illum tandem nutricis sinu adductum Gallo, ut cum
matre voverat, super aram ipsius ponens cum terris in
Hosten et decimis, multum matrem plorans, iniciaverat.
3 Educatur puer in monasterio delicate pulcherrimus. Solebant autem fratres eum cognominare ingenitum. Et quoniam immature est editus, nec musca illum sine sanguinis eruptione postea mordebat. Ideoque et virgis in eo magister parcebat. Vir quoque factus virtutes sibi ingenitas, quamvis carne imbecillis fuerit, semper amabat et animo bene maturo immaturae praeerat carni. Tali ac tanto patri, virtutes longa consuetudine in naturam iam vertenti, Ekkehardus honores sibi oblatos omnium assensibus obtulerat.

86. Dirigitur tandem cum fratribus allectis magno Ottoni, Mogontiam Chnutone rege victo Sleswich revertenti. Qui illum ante notissimum ut eminus aspexit: "Accelera," ait, "nepotule, et osculare!" Pusillus quidem erat et pulcher facie. Stringensque illum sub chlamyde delicate tractavit. Videns autem ferulam: "Estne mortuus," ait, "monachorum suorum ille caecator?" "Defunctus," inquiunt, "abbas noster est, O rex; in Deo nunc solo est, quid fuerit." Dein singulos osculatus: "Quid velitis," ait, "video; sed quem velitis, nescio." "Eum ipsum," aiunt, "O rex, quem amplexaris, dominum nostrum Purchardum." Quo dicto procidebant pariter.

and named Burchard. Eventually, his father took him from a wet nurse's breast, brought him to Saint Gall, placed his son on the altar of Saint Gall, as he and the mother had vowed to do, and, while weeping profusely for the child's mother, dedicated him to Saint Gall together with estates in Höchst and tithes. The boy, who was very beautiful, was raised in the 3
monastery with great indulgence. The brothers' nickname for him was "the unborn." Because he was born prematurely, later even a fly could not bite him without causing him to bleed. For this reason his teacher spared the rods in his case. When he grew up, he never lost his love for the virtues that were innate with him, even though he was physically weak, and he controlled his underdeveloped body with a well-developed mind. Such was this great father, who had turned the virtues, through long practice of them, into second nature, and to whom, with the consent of all, Ekkehard offered the office that had earlier been offered to him.

86. Eventually he was sent off with selected brothers to Otto the Great, who had returned to Mainz after defeating King Cnut at Schleswig. The king recognized him from afar because he had gotten to know him very well before this and said: "Hurry up, my little nephew, and kiss me!" Burchard was, in fact, very small and handsome in appearance. The king gently pulled him closer and embraced him under his mantle. Then, seeing the abbot's staff, he said: "So he is dead, that man who blinds his monks?" "Our abbot has died, Your Majesty," they said, "and God alone will now judge what he was." The king kissed each monk in turn and said: "I see what you want, but I do not know whom you want." "This very man, Your Majesty," they said, "whom you are embracing, our lord Burchard." With these words, they all

2 Surgere iussi: "Sed et pater noster Ekkehardus precator noster orationem vobis," aiunt, "mandat et salutem, et promissorum frequentium in hoc uno vos memorem postulat." "Vereor," ait ille, "ne disciplinarum severitates, quas patres vestri prae omnibus amaverant, exosi ad hunc tantillum, mitem quidem vobis et consensibilem, concesseritis. Et quare illum ipsum, quem dicitis, virum magnanimum non elegeratis?" Dein omni serie electionis per ordinem propalata: "Ad hoc etiam non adeo mitis, O rex," inquiunt, "hactenus fuit in disciplinis, ut earum neglector quidem ullo modo sit fore putandus."

3 Quibus auditis dum quiesceret, conversus ad illum, *a mento* virum *manu tenuit* et delicatis verbis: "Tune eris," inquit, "abbatulus meus? Si Domini voluntas sit, fiat et mea!" Deinde illum secum duxit in ecclesiam ad Otigebam reginam. "Nepotem meum hunc," inquit, "mox abbatem te iuvante futurum ad tuam offero gratiam." Collectaque continuo facta ferulam exigens, tribuit ei verbis, quibus solitum est, abbatiam. Ipse autem *Te Deum laudamus* incohans, omnes, qui aderant, laudibus instare monebat.

4 Quibus ita finitis cum abbatem novum regina in partem sumptum amice haberet, calicem sancti Galli magni pretii aureum dare, si ei Favariensis abbatia reddi possit, pollicetur. "Regii iuris," ait illa, "ambo sunt, et calix et abbatia. Sed petitionem tuam opportunius forte alia quam nunc vice ego quidem domino meo intimabo. Quapropter, quia nunc unam accepisti, domum redito, et cum proxime adveneris,

sank down at his feet. When they had been ordered to rise, 2
they said: "Our father Ekkehard, our intercessor, also sends you his prayers and greetings and asks you to be mindful in this instance of what you have frequently promised." The king said: "I fear that because you hated the severity of discipline, which your fathers had loved most of all, you approved this tiny little man who is surely mild toward you and compliant. Why did you not elect that high-minded man you mentioned?" Then they described the entire process of election, step by step, and said: "Besides, Your Majesty, Burchard has not so far been so mild in enforcing discipline that he would in any way be considered likely to neglect it."

When he had heard this in silence, he turned to Bur- 3
chard, *took* him *by the chin* and tenderly addressed him as follows: "So you are going to be my little abbot? If this is God's will, may it also be mine!" Then the king led him into the church to meet Queen Otigeba. "I present to Your Grace," he said, "this nephew of mine, who will soon, with your support, become abbot." As soon as the prayer was finished, he called for the staff and with the customary words granted him the abbey. The king began singing *God, We Praise You* and invited all those present to join him in chanting the hymn of praise.

After they had finished, the queen took the new abbot 4
aside, treating him in a friendly manner, and he promised to give her the very valuable gold chalice of Saint Gall if the abbey of Pfäfers could be restored to him. "Both the chalice and the abbey are royal property," she said. "But I shall perhaps more opportunely bring your request to my lord's attention on some other occasion than now. So return home because you have just now received one abbey, and I believe

pro altera, puto, commodius interpellare tunc habebis." Missione dein hilariter sibi ab imperatore data domum rediit.

87. Qualem autem se consiliis Ekkehardi quantumque exhibuerit, pauperes nec non fratrum et familiae pars multa,
quam videmus adhuc hodie quidem, interdum cum lacrimis
testari solet. Delicatus autem cum esset, ut diximus, episcopi, tunc quidem Chuonradi, iussu carnes edebat. Quod tamen pace novitatis monachorum, qui *irritare* nunc Deum
solent *in adinventionibus suis,* ut *multiplicetur in eis ruina,* nequaquam dixerim. Quibus tamen licentius erat carnes cru-
das laniare, quam infanda plura, quae quasi religiosi super-
2 stitione quadam schismatica assolent, facere. Nimia est
tamen, si ausim dicere, varietas vestis ecclesiae, qua scribitur induere, si utrosque, quos dicimus, suo quidem colore in
eam dignatur intexere aut deforis, ut interdum solet, poly-
mitare. Relinquamus, necesse est, Deo soli iudicium suum,
cum tamen id audenter et veraci argumento possimus asse-
rere: si aliqui apud nos in his schismatum tempestatibus caelum, ut vere quidem faciunt, adipisci nituntur, acrius quam
in patrum serenitatibus, ut aciem satanae perrumpant, *as-
surgere* habent *in clipeum,* validius *torquere spicula, acutius* iacere *tela.*

3 At Purchardus eleemosynas, ut ab infantia solebat, quia
nunc copia maior foret, agere nimium laetatus, non egenis

that when you come back next time, you will find it easier to plead for the other." Then the emperor affably gave him leave, and he returned home.

87. As to the sort of person he was and how great he proved himself to be under Ekkehard's guidance, the poor often bear witness, sometimes with tears, as well as a great many of the brethren and dependents we still see today. Because of his delicate constitution, mentioned above, he used to eat meat thanks to an edict of Conrad, who was bishop at that time. I would never declare this, however, by way of justifying the novel behavior of monks who nowadays often *provoke God to anger* with their newfangled ways *so that more and more disasters befall them.* It would be better for them to tear at raw flesh rather than to perform the many unspeakable acts, which, in the name of piety, they practice in accordance with some schismatic superstition. Yet, if I may ven- 2
ture to say so, the rich variety of vestments at church, where they are supposed to be worn, is excessive, if it allows for both techniques that I mention here, each with its own color, to be woven into the fabric or to be stitched on the outside, as is sometimes done. We should leave judgment on this to God alone—we have to—although I can make the following assertion boldly and on good evidence: if in these troubled times of schisms there are some among us who strive to gain entrance to heaven, as there certainly are, then in order to break through Satan's battle lines, they need *rise up and take up their shields* more vigorously, *hurl their spears* more forcefully, and *shoot their arrows more accurately* than in the serene days of the fathers.

Burchard, delighted that now he had more scope to give 3
alms, as he had done since childhood, *distributed them freely*

solum et peregrinis, sed passim tam fratrum quam familiae palam et clam *dispersit, dedit pauperibus.* Cumque hoc sedulus dies et noctes agens subnudus interdum domum redisset vel nudipes, camerarius suus Richere, fratris quidem filius, incusabat illum crebro secretius, quasi camera sua dispersiones eius ferre non posset, cum unis distractis semper alia
4 reposceret. Cumque ille aliquando nepotem, ne sibi molestus esset, secretius argueret: "Enimvero," ait, "si tu non dederis, quae postulo, alium scio"—decanum dicens—"qui in quantiscumque poterit, me quidem adiuvabit. Nam ille saepius, quae egenis dem, quam tu, roccos videlicet et camisias, caligas et calceos et cetera usque ad cingula mihi clam suggerit, sed et sub opertorio lectuli, ut ibi inveniam, abscondit."

88. Cum autem etiam Ekkehardus ipse per se esset eleemosynarius, iucundum quiddam de eo dicemus. Hominem quendam domesticum cum ad hoc quidem destinaverit, ut, si quos ei pauperes vel peregrinos diceret, clam in domo ad hoc decreta lavaret, raderet, vestitos reficeret et noctibus iussos, ut nemini dicerent, a se emitteret: accidit quadam die, ut ei contractum, Gallum genere, carruca advectum, ut
2 solebat, committeret. Quem ille grossum quidem et crassum cum toto virtutum adnisu, clauso super se solos, ut iussus est, ostio, vix in vas lavacri provolveret, maledicens (erat enim irascibilis): "Vere," ait, "simpliciorem quam dominum meum hodie nescio hominem, qui, cui bene faciat, discernere nescit, mihi quoque tam pinguem helluonem dorso sustollere iniunxit." At contractus, cum aqua sibi lavacri

and gave not only to the needy and strangers, but openly and
secretly *to the poor* among both the brothers and the dependents. Since he persisted in doing this day and night and
sometimes returned home almost naked or barefoot, his
chamberlain Richer, his brother's son, often quietly reproached him, saying that his treasury would be unable to
support his distribution of alms because after distributing
one lot he would always ask for more. Burchard occasionally 4
rebuked his nephew discreetly for causing him trouble, saying, "If you don't give me what I ask for, I know another
man"—meaning the dean—"who will help me as much as he
can. He secretly brings me things to give to the needy more
often than you do: coats and shirts, boots and shoes, and everything else, even belts, and he hides everything under my
bed covers where I can find it."

88. Since Ekkehard took it upon himself to act as an almoner, I will relate an amusing story about him. He assigned
a certain domestic servant to the task of bathing, shaving,
clothing, and feeding any poor people or strangers he indicated, secretly in a house designated for this purpose, and to
send them off at night with orders not to tell anyone. One
day it so happened that Ekkehard entrusted to him, as usual,
a lame man, a Gaul by birth, who had been brought there on
a cart. The lame man was big and fat and the servant, after 2
locking the door behind the two of them, as he had been ordered to do, barely managed, struggling with all his might,
to push him into the bathtub; being an irascible man, the
servant cursed him and said: "Really, I don't know of a sim-
pler man alive today than my master who makes no distinction regarding the people he helps, for he ordered me to
carry this fat glutton on my back." Since the cripple felt that

nimis videretur calida, rustice: "*Cald, cald est!*" ait. At ille, quoniam id Teutonum lingua "Frigidum est" sonat: "Et ego," inquit, "calefaciam!" Haustamque de lebete ferventi lavacro
3 infudit aquam. At ille cum clamore horrido: "Ei mi! *Cald est, cald est!*" ait. "Enimvero," ait ille, "si adhuc frigidum est, *ego hodie, si vixero,* tibi illud caleficabo!" Et hauriens adhuc ardentiorem infudit. At ille bullientis aquae fervorem ferre non sustinens, oblitus contracturae citus assurrexit, lavacro exsilivit, ad ostium recludendum, ut fugeret, velociter currens, cum pessulo aliquamdiu luctatur. Sed et hominem ubi deceptorem vidit, titionem semiardentem ab igne dicto citius rapiens, grandes sine numero nudo infregit.

4 At Ekkehardus turbam et voces in superiori domo audiens, acriter in utrumque, cum citius descenderet, Teutonice et Romanice invectus est; hunc, cur falleret, illum, cur sibi ad puniendum hominem non reservasset, increpitans. "Eia," ille ait, "mi domine severe, tute ei corniculum abmorderes et plures quam ego nunc illius ori infringeres. Enimvero longe aliud ageres: scelestum hunc vestitum et saturum noctu a te deosculatum dimitteres, quod, ut te novi, et hodie facturus es." Et ille: "O servum," ait, "*furciferum!* An *non licet mihi facere, quod volo?*" et cetera. His peractis castigatum quidem verbis hominem et, ne facinus tale umquam repeteret, iurare coactum abire permisit.

89. Et quoniam hic locum aptum puto de Ekkehardo,

the water in his bath was too hot, he said in his rustic way: "Hot, it's hot!" Since in German that sounds like "It's cold, cold," the servant said: "I'll warm it up!" and he poured some water from a boiling kettle into the bath. The lame man 3
gave a horrible shriek: "Ouch! It's hot! It's hot!" "Well," the servant said, "*as I live,* if it is still cold, *I'll heat it up for you right away!*" And he got some water that was even hotter and poured it in. Then the man, no longer able to bear the heat of the boiling water, forgot his lameness, quickly got up, sprang out of the bathtub and raced up to the locked door to escape, and wrestled with the bolt for a while. But when the servant realized that the man was a fraud, he grabbed a half-burned branch from the fire, faster than anything, and beat the naked man severely with countless blows.

Ekkehard, who was on the upper floor of the house and 4
had heard the commotion and the shouting, quickly came downstairs and rebuked them, angrily asking, in German and in Romance, the one why he had deceived them and the other why he had not left it to him to punish the man. "Look, my stern master," said the servant, "would you really hurt a hair of this man's head and punch this man's face more than I just did? In reality, you would do something completely different: you would send this rogue away at night, clothed and well fed, with a kiss, which very thing—I know you—you were about to do just now!" Ekkehard said: "Oh, *you gallows rogue of a servant! Don't I have the right to do what I want?*" and so on. After saying this, he chastised the man verbally, made him swear that he would never again commit such an outrage, and gave him permission to leave.

89. Since this is the right place, I think, to write about

sororis eius filio, quem et ipse et Geraldus docuerant severe,
<scribere>, rem arduam aggredior: quoniam, cum tales viri
aut nulli aut nunc rarissimi sint, discredi mihi vereor. Erat
hic facie adeo decorus, ut *inspicientes,* sicut Iosephus de
Moyse scribit, *gratia* sui *detineret.* Ut Otto Saxonicus Rufus
de illo: "Nemini umquam," ait, "Benedicti cuculla decentius
insederat." Statura procerus, forti assimilis, aequaliter gros-
sus, oculis fulgurosus, ut quidam ad Augustum ait: "*Quia
fulmen oculorum tuorum ferre non possum.*" Sapientia et elo-
quentia, maxime autem consiliis nemini id temporis post-
2 ponendus. In aetate florida gloriae, ut talis facturae vir, hu-
militati proximior, sed postea non ita, quia disciplina, cum
qua nihil umquam participii superbia habuit, in ipso erat
spectaculo digna. Doctor prosper et asper: nam cum apud
suum Gallum ambas scholas suas teneret, nemo praeter
exiles pusiones quicquam alteri nisi Latine ausus est proloqui. Et quos ad litterarum studia tardiores vidisset, ad scribendum occupaverat et lineandum. Quorum amborum ipse
erat potentissimus, maxime in capitularibus litteris et auro,
ut apparet in versibus fornicis Galli, quos fecit:

Templum, quod Gallo Cozpertus struxerat almo,
hoc abbas Immo picturis compsit et auro.

3 Has ille litteras cultello concisas illic liniverat. In litteris autem studiose mediocres et nobiles aeque erudiverat. Quorum tamen numerosos Gallo et aliis ad summum evexerat.

Ekkehard II, Ekkehard I's sister's son, who had been given a rigorous education by both Ekkehard I himself and Gerald, I shall embark on this difficult task, although I fear that no one will believe me because nowadays such men are either exceedingly rare or do not exist at all. Ekkehard was so handsome in appearance that his *attractiveness made people stop and stare,* just as Josephus writes about Moses. The Saxon, Otto the Red, said about him: "The cowl of Benedict has never looked so good on anyone." He was tall and proportionally broad like a strong man, with shining eyes, as someone said to Augustus: "*Because I cannot bear the lightning flash of your eyes.*" He was second to none at that time in
wisdom and eloquence, especially regarding counsel. Given 2
such natural gifts, he was inclined to pride more than to humility in his youth, but not so later on, because his sense of discipline in which pride never played any part might well serve as a model. As a teacher he was both supportive and stern, for when he was in charge of both schools at his beloved Saint Gall, no one except little boys dared to say a word to anyone else except in Latin. If he saw that some of his students were too slow in studying letters, he put them to copying and delineating. He himself was very capable at both, especially at forming capital letters and decorating them with gold, as is evident in the verses that he made on the arch of Saint Gall:

> This church that Gozbert erected for kindly Saint Gall,
> Abbot Immo adorned with pictures and gold.

He carved out those letters with a knife and delineated 3
them. He carefully taught letters to those of noble and middling birth with equal attention. He guided a great number of his students to the very top ranks at Saint Gall and other

Eorum enim plures ipse vidit episcopos. Ut quondam Mogontiae in generali concilio, cum consessum adveniens intrasset, sex ei quondam discipuli, tunc episcopi, assurrexerant et magistrum salutabant. Et Wilegisus archiepiscopus digito accitum osculatus: "Digne, fili mi," ait, "et tu quandoque cum talibus inthronizaberis." Cuius pedes cum peteret, manu eum delicate erexerat. Et quoniam praepostere fortunam hominis praelibavimus, ad altiora eius acta veniemus.

90. Hadawiga, Henrici ducis filia, Suevorum post Purchardum virum dux vidua cum Duellio habitaret, femina admodum quidem pulchra, nimiae severitatis cum esset suis,
longe lateque terris erat terribilis. Haec quondam parvula
Constantino Graeco regi cum esset desponsata, per eunu-
chos eius ad hoc missos litteris Graecis adprime est eru-
2 dita. Sed cum, imaginem virginis pictor eunuchus domino
mittendam uti simillime depingeret, sollicite eam inspiceret, ipsa nuptias exosa os divaricabat et oculos. Sicque
Graeco pervicaciter repudiato, litteris post Latinis studen-
tem Purchart illam dux multipliciter dotatam duxit; et cum
iam esset decrepitus, thalamo, ut aiebant, secum nequic-
quam cubantem, in proximo moriens, quamvis non intac-
tam, incognitam, ut celebre est, cum dotibus et ducatu reliquit puellam.

places. He even saw many of them become bishops. So it was that one day during a general council at Mainz, when he entered the assembly, six of his former students, who had by then become bishops, stood up and greeted their master. Archbishop Willigis beckoned Ekkehard with his finger, kissed him, and said: "My son, some day you, too, will sit as you deserve on a bishop's throne along with these men." When Ekkehard tried to sink down at his feet, the archbishop affectionately raised him up with his hand. Since I have jumped ahead and given you a foretaste of the man's good fortune, we shall now turn to what he did earlier.

90. Hadwig, Duke Henry's daughter and duchess of Swabia after the death of her husband Burchard, lived as a widow in Hohentwiel; she was a very beautiful woman, and since she was excessively severe with her household, she was feared in lands far and wide. Sometime earlier, as a very young girl, she was betrothed to Constantine, the Greek king, and received excellent instruction in Greek letters from his eunuchs who had been sent there for this purpose.
However, when a painter eunuch began studying her care- 2
fully in order to convey a very close likeness of the maiden in a portrait that was to be sent to his master, Hadwig, who hated the prospect of this marriage, contorted her face and rolled her eyes. In this way the Greek was firmly rejected, and Duke Burchard married her, richly endowed as she was, at a later date when she was studying Latin. Since by then he had become decrepit, she lay with him in their marriage bed to no avail, so they said, and when he died very soon after the wedding, he left her a maiden, not known, albeit not untouched, as is widely reported, with the dowry and the duchy.

3 Haec sanctum Gallum vidua orandi aliquando petiverat causa. Quam Purchardus abbas festive susceptam utique neptim donis cum prosequi pararet, ipsa se alia dona nolle, ait, praeter Ekkehardum sibi doctorem si Duellium ad tempus concederet. Nam cum portanarius esset, de voluntate ipsius ipsa cum eo pridie secreta condixerat. Quod dum abbas ingrate quidem concederet et avunculus dissuaderet, ille tamen nihilominus, quae petitus est, facere pertenderat.

4 Duellium die condicto cum aegre exspectatus veniret, ultra, quam ipse vellet, susceptum in conclave suo proximum, suum, ut ipsa ait, manu duxit magistrum. Ibi nocte et die cum familiari aliqua intrare solebat ad legendum pedisequa, foribus tamen semper apertis, ut, si quis etiam ausus, quid esset, nihil, quod diceret, sinistrum haberet. Illic quoque crebro ambos ministri et milites, principes etiam terrae lectioni aut consiliis invenerant agentes. Moribus tamen illa suis severis et efferis saepe virum exasperans, domi interdum quam secum mansisse multo malle fecerat. Ut in dorsipallio et cortina lecti sui, quae humilia sentiens ipse iussit deponi, deponentem illa iussit verberari et magistro multa rogante vix concessit non decapillari.

5 Domum ille aut festis aut quandolibet visere iret, opinabile erat, quantas homini impensas navibus Steinaham

After she had become a widow, Hadwig once visited Saint Gall to pray. She was ceremoniously received by Abbot Burchard because she was his niece, and when he was about to give her parting gifts, she said that she wanted no other gifts from him than Ekkehard if he would permit him to come to Hohentwiel for a while as her teacher. For since Ekkehard was the doorkeeper, she had talked with him about her intentions in secret the day before. Although the abbot agreed without enthusiasm and his uncle advised against it, Ekkehard nonetheless persisted in doing what was asked of him. 3

When, eagerly awaited, he came to Hohentwiel on the appointed day, his reception was much warmer than he could have wished. Hadwig led her master, as she called him, by the hand to a chamber next to her own. Night and day she would go in there in order to read, accompanied by a maidservant, but the door always stayed open, so that even if anybody dared to wonder what was going on, that person would have nothing suspicious to report. State officials, knights, and even princes of the land often found the two of them in this room engaged in reading or discussions. She often irritated him, however, with her severe and cruel behavior, and at times made him very much wish that he had stayed at home rather than be with her. This was the case with the back cushion and bed curtain, which he asked to be removed out of humility: she ordered the servant who was removing them to be flogged and when her teacher begged repeatedly, she barely agreed not to have the servant's hair shorn off. 4

When he went back home for a visit, on feast days or at any other time, it was remarkable how many presents she sent ahead for him by ship to Steinach; she herself with her 5

praemiserit, novum illi semper aliquid in paraturis aut sibimet utendum aut Gallo offerendum acutissima ipsa Minerva praestrui faciens. Inter quae praeter casulas sericas, cappas et stolas alba est illa philologiae nuptiis auro insignis; praeter quae dalmatica et subtile paene aurea, quae postmodum, Immone abbate sibi antiphonarium quendam petitum denegante, acutia sua versipelli resumpserat.

91. Patuerant his temporibus ora invidorum ut semper in monachos quasi pro libitu viventes. Positus est, ut ceteros relinquamus et nostra fortunia tangamus, Augensibus abbas de fratribus ipsorum nomine Ruodmannus. Qui cum suis tyrannice praeesset, pellem vellicare nesciens perscinderet, linguam quoque malignam in sancti Galli monachos quasi minus regulares, quaqua poterat, dilatabat.

2 Erant adhuc sancto Gallo praeter Ekkehardum hunc,
quem dicimus, iunioresque, quos patres nutriverant, multos:
Ekkehardus decanus bene validus, Gerhaldus, Notkerus,
Chunibertus Altaha post abbas, Walto secundus. Qui iussu
abbatis sui Ruodmannum per Ekkehardum internuntium
3 convenientes, *linguae parceret,* fraterne rogabant. Quod ille
cum minimi penderet, nuntium tamen et personae honore
et ducis severe, ad quam etiam ille tunc ibat, timore tractabat
condigne. Ipse vero Ekkehardus cum hominem ad omnia
adversativum prudenti facundia crebro inter agendum

finest skill was always having some new, luxurious vestments prepared for him beforehand, either for his own use or as an offering to Saint Gall. Among these vestments were not only silk chasubles, copes, and stoles but also that alb that depicts the Marriage of Philology in gold; in addition to those, a dalmatic and a subdeacon's liturgical garment made almost entirely out of gold, which she recovered later by means of a clever trick when abbot Immo denied her the antiphonary that she asked for.

91. At that time, as always, the mouths of the envious opened up to accuse monks of living for pleasure. There was appointed abbot of Reichenau—to leave other personages aside and deal with events in our area—a man called Ruodmann, one of the Reichenau brothers. He ruled his own monks like a tyrant: not knowing how to shear his sheep's fleece, he shredded it, and he also deployed his malignant tongue against the monks of Saint Gall wherever he could, as though they were not observing the Rule.

In addition to the Ekkehard whom I have been talking 2
about and many younger men whom the fathers had brought up, Saint Gall also had Ekkehard the very capable dean, Gerald, Notker, Cunibert, later the abbot of Niederaltaich, and Waldo the Second. At the behest of their abbot, they met with Ruodmann, employing Ekkehard as a mediator, and in a brotherly fashion asked him *to moderate his tongue.*
Although Ruodmann paid very little attention to this, he 3
still treated the mediator appropriately, both out of respect for his position and out of fear of the harsh duchess, to whom he, too, was then going. As for Ekkehard himself, he tried in the course of negotiations, repeatedly but to no effect, to convince by his prudent eloquence the man who

frustra convinceret, minis eius validissimis motus, ad monasterium clam rediit et, qui obstaculum adventus sui duci rediceret, in montem propinquum remisit, et missionem Ruodmanni dedignans abivit.

4 At Ruodmannus ad ducem eum abisse arbitratus, equite
ascenso sanctum Gallum noctu invadens, claustrum clandestinus introiit, ut, si quid reatui proximum invenire posset, furtive perspiceret. Et cum claustrum sibi notissimum
circumiens undique speculatus fuisset, nihil voti sui inve-
niens, e parte ecclesiae dormitorium ascendit secessumque
5 fratrum pedetemptivus ascendit et occulte resedit. E ves-
tigio illum Ekkehardus, homo ad omnia circumspectus,
strato surgens consequitur, nescius eius. Solumque hominem nactus miratur, quisnam fratrum noctibus nobis inso-
litam ita iret viam illam vitabundus. Lumine enim ille officinae obscuro sedebat occultus. Aliquamdiu autem cum, quis
sit, haesitasset, runcore narium, quo commotus solebat,
Ruodmannum esse persenserat. Ilicoque accensam, quam
fratrum quendam clam afferre monuit, abbatis lanternam
coram illo statuit, et stramina apponens pro capellano pro-
6 cul constitit. Accedentesque solito fratres silentium nutibus
monuit miratos, cui lanterna steterit; nam abbas, cui soli
lanterna geri solita est, loco afuit. Tandem diu exspectatus

resisted all his attempts to persuade him. Becoming alarmed by Ruodmann's powerful threats, he secretly returned to the monastery, sent a messenger to the nearby mountain to explain to the duchess what prevented him from coming, and went away disdaining to take leave of Ruodmann.

Meanwhile Ruodmann, believing that Ekkehard had 4
gone to the duchess, mounted a horse and made his way into
Saint Gall at night, secretly entering the cloister so that he
might furtively look around and see if he could find anything
approaching an offense. After going around the cloister,
which was very familiar to him, spying everywhere, and finding nothing that he wanted to find, he climbed up to the
dormitory from the side of the church, climbing cautiously
to the brothers' latrine, and sat down there hiding. Ekke- 5
hard, a man attentive to all things, immediately got up out
of bed and followed his footsteps, unaware of his identity.
He came across a man on his own, and Ekkehard wondered
which of the brothers could be taking such an evasive route
in this way, so unusual for us, at night. The man was sitting
hidden from view in the dim light of the room. Although for
a while Ekkehard was not sure who the man was, by the
snorting sound that the man usually made with his nose
when agitated he recognized that it was Ruodmann. Ekkehard immediately had the abbot's lantern, which he had
asked one of the brothers to bring secretly, lit and set before
the man, and putting straw down beside him, he stood at a
distance, playing the role of a chaplain. He made signs to the 6
brothers, who approached as usual, to be silent, as they were
wondering for whom the lamp had been set, since the abbot, for whom alone the lantern was usually brought, was
absent from the monastery. Finally, after a long wait, when

cum nescius ille, quidnam facere posset, surgeret, Ekkehardus lanterna levata abeuntem eadem, qua eum venisse senserat, praeivit via. Et cum ad introitum ecclesiae, ubi locus auditorii est, venissent, sedere ibi, quoad eum decano avunculo et fratribus intimaret, ut hospitem tantum non ignorarent, silenter monuit.

92. Et ecce fratrum pars, maxime iuvenum, novitate rei stupidi cum appropiassent, quidam ipsorum re agnita, flagello de pyrali rapto, scelestum illum incurrens clamitat et, nisi animis saniores ei erecto ad ictum bracchio occurrissent, grandes incussisset. At ille se in angustia esse tandem sentiens: "Si fugae," inquit, "copiam haberem, iuvenum optimi, profecto fugerem; nunc autem in vestris quia, velim nolim, sum manibus, mitius mecum quidem vos condecet agere, sed et decanum vestrum et ceteros patres exspectare."

2 Decanus tandem consilio in brevi petito supervenit cum patribus. At Notker medicus Piperis Granum animosior in illum: "Malo tuo, versutissime hominum, *leo quaerens, quos devores,* fratrum, quos alter satanas accusas, manus," inquit, "incideras!" Ille vero tanti viri verbis tremefactus, decanum animi piissimi non ignarus: "Vide," ait illi, "pater prudentissime, ne me aequivoci tui artibus circumventum

the man, not knowing what on earth he could do, stood up, and as he was leaving, Ekkehard raised the lantern and went ahead of him by the same route that he had noticed him using before. When they came to the church entrance where the reception room is, he made a silent sign to the man to sit down there until Ekkehard informed his uncle the dean and the other brothers, so that they would not be unaware of the presence of such an important guest.

92. At this point some of the monks, particularly the young ones, came on the scene, stunned by the strangeness of the incident. When they drew near, one of them, realizing what had happened, grabbed the whip from the warm room, and rushed in, loudly proclaiming Ruodmann a scoundrel; if those of sounder judgment had not intervened as his arm was raised to strike, he would have thrashed the man severely. Then Ruodmann said, finally feeling that he was in a tight spot: "Excellent youths, if I had an opportunity for flight, I would surely be fleeing. As it is, since I am in your hands whether I like it or not, it would surely be appropriate for you to treat me more gently and wait for both your dean and the other fathers."

After a brief consultation, the dean finally arrived with 2
the fathers. Notker the Peppercorn, the physician, quite outraged at Ruodmann, said: "It is to your own destruction that you, the craftiest of men, you, like *a lion seeking someone to devour,* have fallen into the hands of brothers whom you—a second Satan—accuse!" Ruodmann, reduced to quivering at the words of such a great man and not unaware that the dean was a man of the most kindly disposition, said to him: "See to it, most prudent father, that you do not allow me, who have been outmaneuvered by the devices of your

3 dehonestari sinas et te postea intemporive paeniteat!" Tandemque procidens: "Ecce," ait, "veniam ab omnibus peto, ut
in gratiam vobiscum rediens deinceps talibus quidem absti-
neam." Moverat animis saniores repentina rerum in tam
potente mutatio. At alii, ut fit, aliud fremebant. Tandem
consulto Ekkehardi lenitis patribus et per ipsos omnibus re-
conciliatus, ipso comite ad suos, ubi iussi exspectabant, est
egressus. Laetaque coram suis locutus abibat, obnixe Ekkehardum, ut, quando proxime Duellium pergeret, se non
praeteriret, inter cetera rogans. Fratribus vero duo vasa vini
per ipsum pollicitus, nave Steinaham in proximo misit.

93. Sed Purchardus foris turbam audiens, nimis, cum adveniret, doluit, quod tam securus et liber abivit, querelasque inauditae rei episcopo mandat. Et ecce Ekkehardus aequivoco diacono, post decano, et Purchardo puero, post abbate, consobrinis, comitatus, Duellium pergens item Augiae Ruodmannum, ut condixerant, alloquitur. Inter colloquia versutus ille artibus suis abusus imparem non invenit. Nam festinantem, ne serus feminae severae adveniret, equo decoro donat. Quem ille parte comitatus cum praemitteret,

namesake, to be dishonored, and that it does not make you
repent afterward, when it is too late." Finally prostrating 3
himself, he said: "Look, I beg all of you for forgiveness, so that I may be restored to your favor and abstain from such actions from now on." The sudden change in circumstances of so powerful a man moved those of sounder judgment. But, as usually happens, some people muttered this and some that. Finally, when Ekkehard's counsel had calmed the fathers and through them Ruodmann was reconciled with everyone, he departed, accompanied by Ekkehard himself, to join his men at the place where they were waiting for him as ordered. He made cheerful remarks before his men and went away, persistently asking Ekkehard among other things not to pass by without stopping the next time he went to Hohentwiel. Moreover, Ruodmann promised the brothers, through Ekkehard, two barrels of wine, which he shortly sent by ship to Steinach.

93. But Burchard, who heard about the disturbance when he was outside the community, was very unhappy when he arrived to learn that Ruodmann had departed unconcerned and without penalty, and he sent a complaint to the bishop about the unprecedented incident. And look, when Ekkehard was making for Hohentwiel, accompanied by his cousins, that is, his namesake Ekkehard the deacon, later dean, and the little boy Burchard, later abbot, he spoke with Ruodmann at Reichenau, as they had agreed to do. During their conversation the crafty abbot deployed all his skills but met his match. When Ekkehard was hurrying so that the demanding woman would not find him arriving late, Ruodmann gave him a beautiful horse as a gift. When Ekkehard sent it on ahead with some of his companions, his

paulisper inter verba laetitiae et familiares astutiae ictus
2 sciolus tardat. Tandemque cum inter amplexus et oscula dimitteretur, supplantator ille hospiti suo in aurem: "Fortunate," ait, "qui tam pulchram discipulam docere habes grammaticam!" Ad quod ille, quasi caro assensu subridens, talia in aurem adversario reddit "amico": "Sicut et tu, sancte Domini, Kotelindam monialem pulchram discipulam caram docuisti quidem dialecticam." Dictoque citius, cum ille nescio quid resibilare vellet, ab eo divertens equo ascenso indignanter abivit. At Otkerus, frater et miles abbatis, cum motum sensisset: "Illum equum, domine mi, ut mihi videtur, penitus perdidisti."

3 Fratres autem, quos diximus, duo illi, sicut ab ipsis audivimus, cum missionem peterent inclinati, aversus ab illis ait fratri: "Utinam," inquit, "post illum celeres, qui equum illum nobilem mihi reducant, mittere velles!" Et ille: "Enimvero," ait, "illam petit ille cum suis nunc feminam, ut cuiquam meorum quicquam illius tangere iubere non praesumam." Sic illi duo equis ascensis post magistrum modeste perrexerant. Ascendentes autem montem apparuerunt duci ad vesperas eunti. Quibus salutatis (nam turbam Ruodmanni iam priorem audiverat): "Enimvero," ait, "ut audio, magister mi, non percommodus lanternifer fuisti *lupo* illi *aliunde caulas intranti.*" Cumque ille quidem surrisisset: "Per Hadewigae,"

cunning host deliberately held him back for a while with
merry words and friendly witticisms. As they were finally 2
taking leave of one another with embraces and kisses, the trickster whispered in his guest's ear: "You lucky man, who have to teach grammar to such a beautiful female student!" At those words Ekkehard smiled as if in affectionate agreement and replied by whispering the following in the ear of his "friendly" adversary: "Just as you too, holy man of the Lord, taught the nun Kotelinda, your beautiful female student, your beloved dialectics!" Just as the other man was ready to hiss something in response, faster than you could say anything, Ekkehard turned away from him, mounted his horse, and went away in indignation. So Otker, the abbot's brother and bodyguard, sensed his agitation and said: "It seems to me, my lord, you gave away that horse for nothing."

Meanwhile, as the two brothers I mentioned bowed and 3
asked permission to leave, Ruodmann turned away from them, as I heard from them themselves, and said to his brother: "I wish you would send swift men after him, to bring me back that splendid horse!" The brother said, "He is now headed for that woman with his companions, so that I cannot presume to order any of my men to touch anything of his." And so the two brothers mounted their horses and discreetly set out after their master. As they were riding up the mountain, they were seen by the duchess who was going to Vespers. After greeting them—she had already heard about the earlier brush with Ruodmann—she said: "I hear, my master, you were not a very accommodating lantern carrier for that *wolf that got into the sheepfold by another way.*" When Ekkehard laughed, she said: "By the life of

illa ait, "vitam"—sic enim iurare solebat—"si imperitorum aliquis claustri illius invasori grandes infregisset, non ego curassem."

94. Altera dein die cum diluculo, ut ibi solebant, silentium regulae, cuius et ipsa exactrix erat sollicita, de more persolvisset—nam iam monasterium in monte statuere coeperat—magistrum lectura adiit. Et cum sedisset, ad quid puer ille venerit, ipso astante inter cetera quaesivit. "Propter Graecismum," ille ait, "domina mi, ut ab ore vestro aliquid raperet, alias sciolum vobis illum attuli." Puer autem ipse *pulcher aspectu,* metro cum esset paratissimus, sic intulit:

Esse velim Graecus, cum sim vix, domna, Latinus.

2 In quo illa, sicut *novarum rerum cupida,* adeo est delectata, ut ad se tractum osculata scabello pedum proximius locaret. A quo, ut repentinos sibi adhuc versus faceret, curiosa exegerat. Puer vero magistros ambos intuitus, quasi talis osculi insuetus, haec intulit:

Non possum prorsus dignos componere versus,
nam nimis expavi duce me libante suavi.

3 Illa vero extra solitam severitatem in cachinnos versa, tandem puerum coram se statuit et eum antiphonam *Maria et flumina* quam ipsa in Graecum transtulit, canere docuit ita:

Hadwig"—that was how she was accustomed to swear—"if one of those youngsters had given that cloister intruder a thrashing, I would not have minded."

94. Next day at dawn—as was customary there, she had obeyed the command for silence according to the Rule, of which she too was a meticulous observer, for she had already begun erecting a monastery on the mountain—she went to her master for reading. When she sat down, among other things she asked the reason why the little boy had come, as he stood there nearby. "My lady, I have brought him here to you for Greek," Ekkehard said, "so that he might pick up something from your lips; he knows a little already." Then the boy himself, *lovely to look at,* offered the following since he was always ready with a verse:

> I would like to be Greek, my lady, although I am barely
> Latin.

As she was always *eager for new things,* she delighted in 2
those verses so much that she drew the boy to herself, kissed him, and sat him down on the footstool at her feet. Full of curiosity, she demanded that the boy make more improvised verses for her. But the boy looked at both his masters, as if unused to such a kiss, and offered this:

> I can by no means compose proper verses,
> for I've become terrified from the kiss of the sweet
> duchess.

But she broke into laughter, contrary to her usual sever- 3
ity, and finally she put the boy facing her and taught him how to sing the antiphon *Seas and Rivers,* which she had herself translated into Greek:

Thalassi ke potami, eulogiton kiryon;
ymnite pigon ton kyrion alleluia.

Crebroque illum postea, cum vacasset, ad se vocatum, repentinis ab eo versibus exactis, graecissare docuit et unice dilexit. Tandem quoque abeuntem Horatio et quibusdam aliis, quos hodie armarium nostrum habet, donavit libris.

95. At Ekkehardus minor ille interea cum puero ad alios, ut solebat, quosdam ducis capellanos, quos illa nullo modo in corte sua otia tenere est passa, erudiendos secesserat; nam et ipse erat idonee litteratus. Remanserant solito soli ad legendum illi. Vergilius erat in manibus, sed et locus ille: "*Timeo Danaos et dona ferentes.*" "Locum hunc," Ekkehardus
2 ait, "commode heri ego, domina mi, memorare habui." Et cum ei, quomodo se abbas Augiam invitatum equo honorabili donaverit, versutis tamen sermonibus inter dona non abstinuerit, insinuasset, ultima tamen utrimque in aures susurria celavisset, "Vellem," ait illa, "*omnem* illam, quae nuperrime inter vos accidit, *a principio audire* tragoediam, quoniam, si eam vere quidem audierim, ignoro. Miror etiam, me imperii vicaria tam prope assidente, duo mei ducatus monasteria, me equidem spreta, tanta miscuisse infortunia. Enimvero nisi consiliarii dissuaserint, ubi reatum invenero,
3 iuste vindicare habebo." Et ille: "Infidum est," ait, "serena mi, ut ego quidem, qui reconciliationis post avunculum *pars*

Seas and rivers, praise the Lord;
streams, sing glory to the Lord, alleluia.

Afterward, when she had time, she often called for the boy, demanded spontaneous verses from him, and taught him to speak Greek; she was exceptionally fond of him. Finally, as he was leaving, she gave him a copy of Horace and some other books which our library holds to this day.

95. Meanwhile the younger Ekkehard withdrew with the
boy, as he usually did, to teach some chaplains of the duchess, whom she under no circumstances allowed to be at leisure at her court, for he was also suitably learned himself.
Hadwig and Ekkehard II were as usual left alone to read.
They were engaged in reading Virgil, specifically the passage
"*I fear the Greeks even when they bear gifts.*" Ekkehard said,
"My lady, yesterday I had occasion to remember this passage." He revealed to her how the abbot invited him to 2
Reichenau and gave him a handsome horse, yet did not refrain from adding some sly remarks to his gifts; however, he
kept from her the last exchange they had whispered in each
other's ears. Then she said: "I would like *to hear from the beginning the whole* tragic story that has most recently been
played out between you, because I do not know if I have
heard it right. I am also amazed that two monasteries in my
duchy could have become entangled in such a series of unfortunate events with utter disregard for me, a representa-
tive of the emperor whose seat is so near. I can assure you,
unless my counselors dissuade me, when I find the guilty
party, I will deliver just punishment." Ekkehard said: "It 3
would be disloyal, my serene duchess, for me, who *played a
great part* in the reconciliation, a part second only to that of

maxima fui, accusative tibi quicquam, quia aliter non potero, post pacis oscula dicam. Quamvis enim me ille heri in multis, ut ipsa hominem nosti, cum et dona steterint, clam stimulaverit, meum tamen nequaquam est tantorum virorum pactam pacem scindere, cum et ego propter hoc non omittam, quin paci, prout ipse quidem vult, cum illo assentiam." Placuit mulieri ratio et rectilinium magistri. Colloquium tamen publicum postea pro his et pro aliis regiminis causis Walewis villa edixit. Illuc quoque episcopum et abbates venire iusserat.

4 Ruodman autem Ekkehardum verba illa in aures dicta duci propalasse suspicatus, animo contabuit litterasque in montem ei per peregrinum sagacem quendam direxit. Haec post reparandae inter se gratiae litteras verba: "Miror enim amicum meum ad omnia acutissimum, si novissima illa in aures susurria domnae ductrici effuderat. Quod si forte feceras, renunties, rogo." Eius autem econtra per eundem gerulum haec post aliqua verba: "Neque enim tantae apud formosissimam meam umquam fui fiduciae, ut severitatis eius auribus haec ausim ingerere" Haec de mediis amborum brevitatis ego gratia excerpseram brevibus.

96. Absolutus tandem timore maximo eius, quam maxime timuisset, ad Kaminoldum tunc episcopum se primo per nuntios vertit. Qui cum et ipse ei pro fraude claustri

my uncle, to tell you something in an accusatory vein after a kiss of peace, because I could not do otherwise. Although that man covertly goaded me yesterday in many ways, even in the midst of gift giving—you know the man yourself—nevertheless, it is by no means my intention to tear apart the peace that such men have agreed upon; for this reason I will also not fail to agree to make peace with him, as long as he himself wants it." The woman liked the good sense and straightforwardness of her teacher. She proclaimed, however, a general assembly afterward at the village Walewis, to deal with these and other matters of governance. She also ordered the bishop and the abbots to be in attendance.

Ruodmann, suspecting that Ekkehard had divulged to 4
the duchess the words whispered in their ears, was deeply troubled and dispatched a letter to him on the mountain with a clever pilgrim. After some lines about repairing their friendship there followed these words: "I would be surprised indeed if my friend, who is extremely sharp in all respects, had poured those recent whispers into the ears of the lady duchess. If by any chance you have done that, report back, I beg you." Ekkehard's response, sent with the same bearer, after some remarks contained these words: "I have never had so much confidence in the presence of my fairest lady as to dare to inflict these things upon her stern ears." For the sake of brevity I have selected these statements from the correspondence of both men to summarize their content.

96. Finally released from his overwhelming fear of the woman he had feared above all, Ruodmann first turned to Kaminold, the bishop at the time, by means of envoys. Since the bishop himself was also hostile to him because of his

invasi infestus fuerit, ratis donariis eum pacificavit. Dein ipsum in montem duosque cum eo ad ducem de suis misit causidicos. Episcopus quidem, quod in se peccasset, dimissum coram ea pronuntiat. Causidici vero: "Si ab episcopo liber est, gratia vestri," aiunt, "immerito, dux optima, caret."

2 Quibus illa: "Sancti Galli," inquit, "locus imperialis libertatis cum sit meique regiminis, immunitatis privilegio pollet. Quam ei prae illo sub abbatis nomine vere tyranno obtinebo, si potero. Legatur mulcta immunitati inscripta; et quoniam, episcope mi, pro eo venisti, sicut ius postulat, sancto Gallo eam et abbati resolvat. Et quoniam mei iuris est, si laicus laicum, ut id ipsum iuridicialiter proloquar, involaverit, coram comite meo lege multetur; multo magis, si regiae libertatis abbatem tyrannicus abbas nocturnus invaserit, regali coram me sententiae subiacebit. Attamen maiestatis reo, nisi quod tanti viri vos quidem, qui pro illo loquimini, estis, si vel respondere iam absque praesentia imperii me deceat, nescio."

3 Tandem post plura, cum consiliarios, inter quos et Ekkehardum, adhibuisset, vix actum est, ut—abbate nostro per mulctam immunitatis prius in praesentia suorum, quos ad

offense of invading the cloister, Ruodmann placated him with well-chosen gifts. Then Ruodmann sent the bishop along with two of his own advocates to the duchess on the mountain. The bishop proclaimed in her presence that he had forgiven Ruodmann's transgression against him. The advocates then said: "If he has been cleared by the bishop, excellent duchess, he does not deserve to remain withdrawn from your favor."

She replied to them: "Since the monastery of Saint Gall 2
enjoys imperial liberty and lies within my jurisdiction, it draws its strength from its privilege of immunity. I will defend its immunity, if I can, in the face of one who is really a tyrant under the guise of abbot. Let the fine be read out as prescribed in the charter on immunity, and since you, my bishop, came here on his behalf, let him pay the fine to Saint Gall and to the abbot as the law requires. Given that it lies within my jurisdiction—to put this matter in legal terms—if a layman attacks another layman, he should be fined before my count according to the law; it follows, even more emphatically, if a tyrannical abbot makes a nocturnal incursion against another abbot who enjoys royal protection, he will be subject to royal jurisdiction before me. Yet I do not know if it would even be proper for me to be responsible for someone charged with high treason at this moment without imperial presence, were it not for the fact that you who speak for him are such important men."

The duchess called in her counselors, Ekkehard among 3
them, and after prolonged deliberations a decision was reached with difficulty: our abbot was first to be reconciled with Ruodmann, in the presence of his own men appointed for this purpose, by the payment of the immunity fine for

hoc direxerat, pro invasione illa numquam inter monachos audita reconciliato—die dato centum libras ante portas Duellii, ut se deceret, Ruodmannus ostenderet tandemque tunc gratiam suam haberet. Dieque dato, quinquaginta abbati episcopi gratia remissis, cetera recipi iussit.

97. Misitque post dies istos dux ipsa Purchardo nostro,
cognato videlicet et amabili suo, ambulatorem valde decibi-
lem et alacrem, ut animum suum laesum et ipsa leniret—audivit enim eum delicatis equis delectari nimium—sed et ne
pro se pigeret quidem orare. Ricchunbach invento equus
praesentatur laetanter se continens. Quem ille continuo
2 amore tantae datricis sellari sibi iubens abiturus ascendit. At
equus exaltanter eum gestans, in postem valvarum curtis
hominem teneritudinis, ingeniti tamen ardoris et alacritatis,
impegit et femur ei disiungens vertibulo coxae evulsit. Qua
plaga cum per Notkerum pro posse sanaretur, postea tamen
absque geminis sustentaculis ingredi non potuit. Et cum talia diu sit passus, Richero iam dicto curtis suae camerario,
homini pro virtutibus vix comparando, Ekkehardi decani
iam senescentis ut ageret consiliis et abbatiam pro se rege-
ret, communi fratrum iniunxit consensu. Raroque coenobium aliud iucundius quam Galli tunc floruit.

98. Assumptus est interea in aulam Ottonum, patris et filii, Hadewiga agente Ekkehardus, ut capellae semper immanens doctrinae adolescentis regis nec non et summis dexter

that unprecedented intrusion among monks; then on the appointed day, as his duty required of him, Ruodmann was to present one hundred pounds before the gates of Hohentwiel and would only then regain the duchess's favor. On the appointed day she ordered that as a favor to the bishop fifty pounds was to be returned to the abbot and the rest brought into the castle.

97. Sometime after this the duchess sent a very handsome
and lively ambling horse to our Burchard, who was her relative and dear friend, so that she, too, might soothe his hurt
feelings—she had heard that he was greatly interested in
fine horses—but also so that it would not displease him to
pray for her. They found him at Rickenbach and the horse,
cheerfully restraining itself, was presented to him. Out of
love for so generous a benefactress, he immediately ordered
the horse saddled for himself and mounted it in order to
ride off. But the horse, eagerly carrying Burchard, who had a 2
delicate build but an innate enthusiasm and zest, smashed
him against a post of the courtyard gate and caused his thigh
to be wrenched from its joint with the hip. Although Notker did his best to heal the wound, he still could not walk afterward without two crutches. After suffering such a condition for a long time, with the consent of all the brothers
he bid the aforementioned Richer, the chamberlain of his
court, a man of almost incomparable ability, to proceed with
the counsel of Dean Ekkehard, who was already getting old,
and rule the abbey on his behalf. Rarely did any other monastery flourish more happily than Saint Gall did then.

98. Meanwhile thanks to the efforts of Hadwig, Ekkehard was admitted to the court of the two Ottos, father and son, so that as a permanent member of the court chapel he would use his skills to teach the young king and be his

esset consiliis. Ibique in brevi tantus apparuit, ut in ore omnium esset summum eum aliquem exspectare pontificatum. Nam et Adalheida regina illum, nunc sancta, per se diligebat. Cumque ei ita aliquamdiu agenti abbatia Elewangensis quasi ad exspectandum, ut aiebant, offerretur a regibus et ipse eam suscipere ingratus non esset, regina cum duce, quoniam adhuc aulae prae omnibus esset necessarius, fortunam distulerant, usque illum episcopio magno donarent.

2 At Ruodman, cum et ipse quidem multa dando aulicis esset intimus et Ekkehardus aliquando, fratres suos ut viseret, palatio ad tempus cessisset, susurrabat contra eum sed et adversus ceteros, ut solebat, sancti Galli monachos, quasi ipse et quidam alii ex ipsis multa possidentes delicatius viverent, ceteri autem famelici inediam paterentur, abbas vero in infirmitate detentus minus eis consulere posset: se vero Coloniae monachum regularissimum nosse, Sandratum nomine, cui si copia daretur, tam potentes viros humiliando Benedicti viam ingredi cogeret.

99. Perveniunt ad aures imperii verba, et ecce Ekkehardus reversus supervenit. Secreto Ottones illi infamiam narrant ab ipsoque, quidnam videatur, quaerunt. At ille amborum provolutus pedibus, privilegii nostri modo memores sint, rogat; de cetero, quoscumque velint, ad perspiciendum,

right-hand man in high councils. In a short time there he so distinguished himself that everybody was saying that he might expect one of the highest bishoprics. Even Queen Adelheid herself, now a saint, also thought highly of him. Since he had been performing his duties in this manner for a while, he was offered the abbacy of Ellwangen by the kings, as a step toward what was to be expected, so people said, and he would have been quite grateful to accept it, but because he was still needed at the court more than anybody else, the queen and the duchess delayed his promotion until they could present him with an important bishopric.

As for Ruodmann, he too, by giving numerous gifts, was 2
on intimate terms with the courtiers. On one occasion, when Ekkehard had left the palace for a while to visit his brothers, Ruodmann spread evil rumors about him and also about the other monks of Saint Gall, as he was accustomed to do, saying that Ekkehard himself and some other monks had many possessions and lived a soft life while the rest went hungry and were suffering from starvation, while the abbot, incapacitated by illness, could do little to provide for them. Ruodmann also said that he knew a monk in Cologne by the name of Sandrat, a strict observer of the Rule, who, if given the opportunity, would humble these powerful men and force them to follow the path of Benedict.

99. These words reached the emperor's ears, and this was what Ekkehard encountered when he returned. The two Ottos secretly told him about the slander and asked what he himself made of it. Ekkehard threw himself down at their feet and begged them only to be mindful of our privilege; as for the rest, they should send whomever they wanted to investigate what monastic life at Saint Gall was like, and if

quae religio in loco sit, dirigant et, si quid ibi devium reperiatur, consilio perspicientium tunc quidem emendent. Otto vero pater: "Neque enim," ait, "ut nepotem meum, privilegii vestri abbatem, deponam, facile, etsi etiam clinicus fiat, animo erit. Infamiam tamen, quam audio, aboleri vobis ipsis petendum erat." Rogat ille tandem, uti, quoscumque praeter Ruotmannum solum vellent, in locum dirigerent: "Quoniam haec ipsa," inquiens, "infamia technis ipsius est in aula vestra."

2 Audita quoque et ipsius odii causa, nihilominus tamen consilio inito, inter episcopos et abbates ad hoc electos sedecim in locum Galli dirigunt. Et Otto filius in consessum eorum a patre missus: "Ite," inquit, "vos nominati episcopi cum abbatibus, coenobii sancti Galli monachos, qui infamantur, correcturi! Et quia repentina rerum mutatio saepe *novissimum errorem priori facit peiorem,* ideo tot *magni consilii angelos*—pater meus dicit—dirigimus, ut prudentia omnium vestrum collata, si qua nimis ibi contra Deum senserit esse, manere non sinat; si qua autem portabilia viderit, ipsis quidem cum ratione vos monentibus stare patiamini. Scimus enim, quocumque modo vivant, virtutum tamen sancto Gallo non defore viros. Si autem *scientia,* quae *inflat,* elatos ibi senseritis et nuntii vestri, ut fit, in aliquo contradictores, nobis tales in aulam adducite, ut ex eis, si idonei sint, scholis aliquibus, quae in regno vacillant, praeponamus, sin autem, in regularia claustra includamus."

anything out of order was found there, they should then correct that with the help of the investigators' counsel. Otto the father said: "Deposing my nephew, an abbot you chose to elect, will not be easy for me, even if he becomes bedridden. However, it is you yourselves who should bring an end to this slander that I hear of." Ekkehard finally asked the kings to send to the monastery whomever they wanted with the sole exception of Ruodmann, adding "because it is thanks to his scheming that this slander is found at your court."

Having learned the cause for the hatred, after delibera- 2
tion they nevertheless sent to the monastery of Saint Gall sixteen men, chosen for this task from among bishops and abbots. Otto the son, who was sent by his father to their assembly, said: "You who are the bishops and abbots we have named, go and correct the monks of Saint Gall whom rumor is giving a bad name. It is because sudden changes often make *the most recent error worse than the original one,* that we are sending so many *angels of great counsel,* as my father says. Should the combined wisdom of all of you find anything there that is contrary to God, it should not allow such practices to continue; but should your wisdom see some usages as acceptable, you should let them stand, with your reasonable recommendations. We know that there will be no lack of virtuous men at Saint Gall, however they live. But if you see men who are arrogant due to their *knowledge* that *puffs up* and who object to your mission in any way, as often happens, bring such men to our court so that we may put some of them, if they are suitable, in charge of some schools in our kingdom that are faltering, and if they are not suitable, we may confine them to monasteries that conform to the Rule."

100. Huic edicto Ekkehardus consulto cum non interesset, sed nec Ruodmannus quidem, Arnolfus Tullo episcopus: "Rem arduam, domine mi rex," inquit, "aggredi habebimus; et ut ego suspicor, infamia talis invidiae fonte orta est. Ego enim nuperrime votivus quidem locum illum adiveram, et similem caritatem in regno patris tui nescio, si invenerim. Sed et cetera in opere Dei, quae videram, incomparanda di-
2 cebam. Quapropter quantum in me est, sine magnae causae occasione tanti meriti et nominis viros non aio impetendos. Neque enim unius tramitis et regulae via caelum et *regnum Dei* scanditur. Quod, quia *intra nos est,* aliis sic, aliis vero sic ascendere conceditur. Novit enim Deus, in omni ordine hominum qui sunt eius. Et quot *mansiones in regno patris quidem sunt,* tot viae in eam, mi rex, ni fallor, ducunt."

3 At Hiltebaldus Curiensis episcopus: "Omnia, quae ibi noscuntur, pie rex, laude digna sunt," ait, "praeter quod habent ibi quaedam sua et carnium aliqui illorum utuntur eduliis. Et haec ipsa quidem abbatum suorum, ne deficerent, semper egerunt permissis. Quod autem proprietates habent, tale est," ait: "Idonei, qui inter eos semper fuerunt, semet ipsos sed et reliquos minus lingua vel manu validos sub disciplinae severitate a patribus stringunt inolita. In refectorio autem minus, ut loci penuria est, curatos in locis ab abbate infra claustri saepta destinatis, quibuscumque

100. By design, Ekkehard was not present when this proclamation was made, but neither was Ruodmann. Arnolf, the bishop of Toul, said: "My lord king, we will have to embark on a difficult task; this slander, I suspect, has originated from a wellspring of envy. I visited that monastery very recently, to fulfill a vow, and I do not know if I could find similar charity elsewhere in your father's kingdom. I would say that other practices also pertaining to the service of God,
which I saw there, are without comparison. For this reason, 2
as much as it is in my power, I say that men of such great merit and reputation should not be accused without very serious cause. For it is not by a single path or rule that we climb our way to heaven and to *the kingdom of God.* Because *it is within us,* it is granted to some to ascend by one way but to others by another. God knows who are his own in all kinds of men. As many *mansions* as there are *in the Father's kingdom,* so many are the ways, my king, that lead to one of them if I am not mistaken."

But Hildebald, the bishop of Chur, said: "Everything 3
there that we know of, merciful king, is worthy of praise, except the fact that some of them there have personal property and consume meat dishes. They have always had these very practices with the permission of their abbots so that they would not be found at fault. As for the reason why they hold property, it is this: Those who have the right qualities, those who have always been there among them, restrain themselves and also the others who are less capable with their speech or their hands, by the severe discipline ingrained in them by the fathers. Because of the poverty of the monastery, the poor monks are not being taken care of in the refectory but being nourished with whatever food

4 possunt, indigos cibariis pascunt. Si autem id habentibus
habere inhibebitur et interdum labore manuum, qui inibi
semper pretiosissimus erat et est, recipere vetabitur vel
etiam a cognatis et amicis emendicata contrahere, locus ille
semper nutritor virtutis virorum in nihilum redigetur. Et
si de memet ipso pace imperii quicquam," inquit, "adicere
audebo, hoc veraciter inferre potero: quoniam si iustus ipse
sibimet est lex, magis regulares in vestro regno monachos
5 non habetis. Ego enim inter illos nutritus et propter virtutes
adhuc eos interdum visitans scio, quod assero." "Enimvero si de suo, ut asseritis," rex ait, "vivunt, id ipsum secundum regulam Benedicti ut faciant, quantum potissime poteritis, ut agatis, vobis omnibus iniungimus. Et quoniam et nos quidem aliquos de ipsis venerabiles agnoscimus, non hostiliter eos aggredi libet; sed tot consultores amicissimos quidem dirigimus, ut infirmo fratri meo abbati—quoniam pater meus filium eum vocat—adminiculo sitis, ut bona multa, quae faciunt, ad Benedicti regulam deinceps," inquit, "vergant."

101. Praemittitur tandem Ekkehardus nimis pro patria anxius, qui abbati nostro adventus tot hospitum diem et causam denuntiet, multum a patre et filio, ut, quae regulae sint, sentiant, adiuratus. Cui cum Ruodmannum, ut petiverat, legationis exsortem relictum dicerent, gaudentior ibat,

they can find in places designated by the abbot within the
monastery walls. But if having property is denied to those 4
who have it and if they are forbidden to acquire it from time
to time by their handiwork—which was always highly valued
there and still is—or even to gather resources that they have
obtained by begging from relatives and friends, this monastery, which has always nurtured men of virtue, will be reduced to nothing. If I dare, with the emperor's permission,
to add a personal note," he said, "I can truthfully say this: if
the just man is a law to himself, you do not have monks in
your kingdom who are more observant of the Rule. I was 5
raised among them and still visit them from time to time because of their virtues and I know what I am talking about."
The king said, "If they live on their own means, as you maintain, we command all of you to take steps as best you can to ensure that they do so in accordance with Benedict's Rule. Since we also are aware that some men among them are venerable, we wish you to approach them in a manner that is not hostile; rather, we are sending so many very friendly advisers to lend support to my ailing brother, the abbot—my father calls him his son—so that afterward they may direct the many good things they do to comply with Benedict's Rule."

101. Ekkehard, who was very anxious for the well-being of his home monastery, was eventually sent ahead to inform our abbot about the day of and the reason for the arrival of so many guests, and both father and son repeatedly beseeched him to see that they abide by the Rule. When they told him that Ruodmann, as Ekkehard had pleaded, had been left out of the group selected, Ekkehard went away in a happier mood; but he also asked both kings that he be

permitti tamen sibimet ab ambobus postulans, ut, si quid pro loci qualitate consulere nosset, liceret.

2 Abbas autem et *sanioris consilii* patres audito nuntio primo stupent; postmodum vero orationum instantia roborati erant confidentissimi. Pro impensis tandem receptionis illorum cum fluctuasset, litteras abbas regibus dirigit in haec verba: "Dominis meis terrarum potentissimis Purchardus suus caelorum sine fine potentiam. Scio, domini mei, saepe me sanguinis vestri abiectum et degenerem delicatius, quam optare habuerim, ab utroque vestrum tractatum. Nunc autem cum in manu Domini summi plagatus quidem affligar, insuper a vobis tam repentinis motibus concuti numquam
3 speraverim." Et post pauca de Ruodmanni prius inimica invasione et de hac ipsa technis eius in se tot hospitum immissione: "Acuat, ait, oro, spiritus sanctus ferulam meam sibi in gladium et, memet Ruodmanni iacula retundere non valente, ipse retundat. Videat tandem super omnia maiestas vestra, si in immissione illa mihi parcere noluerit, quibus tantus populus apud nos vivat obsoniis. Enimvero si victualia ipsa, quae in regularibus meis vix in annum reposueram, fuerint absumpta, non aliam quam penuriam postea habebunt regulam. Tandemque necesse erit, ut coacti male vivant."

4 Inito tandem consilio iniungitur Ruodmanno, velut annuorum fructuum repositori quidem quaestuoso, legatos

permitted to allow anything he saw that would contribute to the betterment of the monastery.

The abbot and the fathers of *sounder judgment* were at first shocked at hearing the news; but afterward, strengthened by constant prayers, they were filled with confidence. Because the abbot was uncertain about the expenses involved in receiving the guests, he sent a letter to the kings that included these words: "To my lords, masters of the world, their servant Burchard wishes the power of heaven without end. I know, my lords, that you both have often treated me, a lowly and unworthy person of your blood, more gently than I could have hoped for. Now, however, when I am in the hand of the highest Lord, afflicted and cast down, I would never have dreamed that in addition to that I would also be troubled by such unexpected developments coming from you." After saying a few words about Ruodmann's ear- 3
lier hostile intrusion and about this descent of so many guests upon him due to Ruodmann's machinations, the abbot wrote: "I pray that the Holy Spirit may sharpen my staff into a sword for himself and since I myself am not strong enough to repel Ruodmann's spears, that the Holy Spirit may blunt them himself. Finally, if Your Majesties do not wish to spare me that shower of missiles, may they consider above all what supplies such a crowd will live on. In the event that the provisions that I usually store up for my rule-abiding monks for almost a year are consumed, the monks will have no other Rule but penury thereafter. The outcome will be inevitable: they will be compelled to live wretchedly."

A decision was finally reached that Ruodmann, as an ac- 4
quisitive steward who stored up enough produce to last a year, would be charged with taking care of the royal envoys

regios in locis nominatis euntes procurare et redeuntes; in coenobio autem nostro octo sibi nominatos Purchardus susciperet, octo Ruodmannus. Cum autem Chuonradum episcopum nostrum in praesentia ipsius sui in talibus participem fore ipse regibus suaderet, raucosa voce, ut erat, ille reclamabat: "Nequaquam!" inquiens; "tu solus *intrivisti, tibi* soli *edendum est.*" Omnibus autem in risum motis: "Neque enim," ait, "cum *accusatore fratrum* in caelis nec in terris participari libet."

102. Indicta tandem die, quae erat feria tertia dominicae tertiae post pascha—Desiderio tunc, propter quod Gallus eius reliquias loco ipse intulerit, apud nos celeberrima—adveniunt omnes. Festive receptis *Cives apostolorum* responsorium canitur. Abbas in auditorio debilis residens introductis quidem eis assurgit. Legitur consedentibus lectio de caritate et de pedisequa eius discretione. Qua finita assurgunt omnes in abbatis et fratrum oscula. Deinde abbas, "*Benedicti vos Domino*" et fratres, "*Qui fecit caelum et terram.*"

2 At Henricus Treverensis, *cui summa rerum commissa erat,* circumspecto claustro: "Enimvero," ait, "talis nidus bonas aves decet." Et Kebo Lorisham abbas, vir nominis reverendi prae multis et eo die pro nobis plus ceteris sentiens, sed et crebro nos postea donis et consiliis iuvans: "Si placet," ait, "ipsarum avium hunc nidum, qualis per omnia sit, primitus ab abbate audiamus, ut, de ceteris quid agamus, integrius

at appointed places on their way there and back; Burchard would receive eight men assigned to him in our monastery, and Ruodmann eight. But when Ruodmann proposed to the kings in the presence of our bishop Conrad that the bishop should have a share in these arrangements, the latter loudly protested in that rasping voice he had: "Never!" he said. "*You* alone *cooked this up and you* alone *must eat it.*" When everybody burst into laughter, the bishop said: "I have no wish to have anything in common with *an accuser of brethren,* either in heaven or on earth."

102. Finally they all arrived on the appointed day, which was the Tuesday after the third Sunday after Easter, the day to honor Desiderius, most solemnly celebrated by us at that time because Saint Gall himself had brought his relics to our monastery. The visitors were festively received, and the responsory *Fellow Citizens of the Apostles* was sung for them. When they were brought in, the frail abbot, sitting in the reception room, rose to greet them. They sat down and the section from scripture about Charity and her handmaiden, Discretion was read to them. After the reading ended, they all rose to kiss the abbot and the brothers. Then the abbot said, "*May you be blessed by the Lord,*" and the brothers responded, "*Who made heaven and earth.*"

Henry of Trier, *to whom leadership of the delegation had been* 2
entrusted, looked around the cloister and said: "Such a nest befits good birds." And Kebo, the abbot of Lorsch, a man with a more revered reputation than many, who on that day favored us more than the others, and who later on also often helped us with gifts and counsel, said: "If it pleases you, let us first of all hear the abbot describe this nest of birds in all its details so that we can more fully understand how we

3 scire valeamus." Et Kerho Wizzinburgensis abbas, magni nominis et ipse, qui nos post hanc tempestatem ad aquaeductum, quem ipse primus nobis excogitavit, fistulas terebrare docuit, et semper amavit, episcopum nostrum interea et abbatem cum fratribus—quorum reverentia illum, ut post asseruit, vehementer movebat—in capituli domum comitatus, quae congrua nosset, praemonuit.

4 At illi pervagatis Ekkehardo duce officinis, adhuc post arsuram vix quidem quibusdam vel tectis, penu fratrum paene vino vacuum mirantur. Aperiri autem sibi etiam privatorum repositoria cum Ekkehardus ductor eos, iureiurando nihil celaturum, iubere moneret, cuncta perspiciendo sollicite peragrant. Quaerentibus autem etiam de abbatis proprio penu: "Haec," ait, "quae monstravi, fratrum privata eius semper sunt ad nutum parata. Neque enim ipse, quia sic homo est, alio cellario assolet. Nam omne debitum in fratrum quot annis congerit cellarium."

103. Et Poppo Wirziburgensis episcopus conversus ad ceteros: "Enimvero," ait, "si ita se res inter monachos et abbatem habet, non nos hodie meliorem regulam neque vitam plus communem, etiamsi in loco *pleno* sit *copia cornu,* statuere poterimus. Abbas, ut audivimus, congerit fratribus; fratres ad hoc idonei congerunt abbati, et nihil sine eius permisso sibi. Omnis autem ab utrisque congestio neutris sufficere posse videre est." Et Palzo Spirensis episcopus, in loco

should deal with the rest." Kerho, the abbot of Weissenburg—he was also a man of great repute who after this tempestuous episode taught us how to bore water pipes for the aqueduct that he was the first to devise for us, and who always loved us—while accompanying our bishop, our abbot, and the brothers to the chapter house, gave them preliminary notification about matters he deemed appropriate: their respect, as he later maintained, deeply moved him. 3

But when, with Ekkehard as a guide, they passed through 4
the domestic buildings, some of which were barely roofed after the fire, they were amazed to see that the brothers' cellar was almost empty of wine. When their guide Ekkehard, swearing that he would hide nothing, advised them to order that even individual storage spaces be opened for them, they went through them all, carefully inspecting everything. When they asked about the abbot's personal cellar as well, he said: "These individual storage spaces of the brothers that I have shown you are always, at a sign from him, made available. It is not his custom to have any other cellar, because this is the kind of man he is. You see, every year he stores all proceeds in the brothers' cellar."

103. Poppo, the bishop of Würzburg, turned to the others and said: "If this is how matters stand among the monks and the abbot, we could not establish a better rule or a more communal life today even if *Abundance* were here at the monastery *with her full horn.* The abbot, we have heard, collects supplies for the brothers; the brothers who are suited for this collect them for the abbot and nothing for themselves without his permission. It is evident, however, that the total collected by both parties can be sufficient for neither." Palzo, the bishop of Speyer, who had been brought up

nutritus, quo nemo fama ferente tunc eruditior: "Si sciretis," inquit, "mores et vim disciplinae illorum districtam, *experto credite,* ultra omnes, qui in regno sunt regulares sub copia, eos laudaretis sub inopia." Dein Henricus archiepiscopus, *cui summa rei* huius *commissa est,* ut diximus, assumptis consortibus, proelium se initurum dicens, consessum collegii nostri signifer aggressus est.

2 Thietericus vero Metensis episcopus adolescens, Kerhaldi nuper in loco discipulus, regulae librum manu gerens apertum, cum magistrum suo loco stantem transiens praeteriret, his ille velut discipulum silentio hominem invehitur: "Tune librum," ait, "contra me infers, quem ego clausum quam tu apertum melius novi? Claude illum!" At iuvenis voce magistri coloratus, inclinans librum ocius clausit et residens iuxta se reposuit. Et haec quidem, ut vim disciplinae nostrae panderem, dixi.

104. Cunctis tandem residentibus primas, quem dixi, ita incohavit: "Benedictus Domino iste sancti Galli coetus," ait, "pater cum filiis." Et abbati: "Nostis," ait, "tu fratresque tui, carissimi nostri, quare rerum domini pro vobis solliciti tot dilectos suos ad vos direxerint. Nisi enim vos diligerent, tot electos ad consulendum vobis numquam dirigerent." Et ille: "Scimus enim, quod ad consulendum nobis peccatoribus directi estis, ideoque sancto spiritui, summo hodie consultori utrimque nostro, acceptissimi sitis. Sed tamen unum me maximum movet inter alia miraculum, quod unus ex vobis

at the monastery and who was rumored to be more learned than anyone else at that time, said: "If you knew their ways and their strict discipline *(trust one who knows)* you would praise them in their poverty above all who observe the Rule in this kingdom and live amid abundance." Then Archbishop Henry, *to whom,* as I said, *leadership of the delegation had been entrusted,* gathered his colleagues, said that he was about to enter the fray, and marched as a standard-bearer into the assembly of our community.

Then as Dietrich, the young bishop of Metz and a recent 2
student of Gerald's at our monastery, while holding the book of the Rule open in his hand, was walking past his teacher who was standing in his usual place, Gerald quietly rebuked him as if he were still his student: "Are you bringing this book forward against me, this book that I know better closed than you do open? Close it!" The young man blushed at his teacher's words, bowed, quickly closed the book, sat down, and put the book down beside him. I have told you this to demonstrate the strictness of our discipline.

104. When everybody finally sat down, the archbishop I mentioned began with these words: "Blessed of the Lord is this community of Saint Gall," he said, "the father together with his sons." To the abbot he said: "You and your brothers, who are very dear to us, know the reason why the masters of the realm, out of concern for you, have sent to you so many men dear to them. If they did not love you, they would never have sent so many excellent men to counsel you." The abbot replied: "We know that you have been sent to counsel us sinners, and therefore may you be most acceptable to the Holy Spirit, the highest counselor for both our parties today. But nonetheless, one cause for wonder among others especially

non est missus vel episcopus vel abbas, cui non minus quam vobis omnibus ad omnia, quae ratio possibilia posceret, oboediremus." Et Erpho Wormatiensis: "Tot sancti spiritus, ut hic, abba sancte, videmus, athletis concertare uni nimium fuerit. Sed iam aliquam viam id efficiendi, pro quo missi sumus, mihi placet, aggrediamur!"

2 Monuit tandem Henricus ceteris id suadentibus abbatem, ut aliquem fratrum viam vitae nostrae, qua tunc degeremus, iuberet edicere. Iubet ille Ekkehardum decanum nec non Notkerum medicum, plerisque illis notissimos, surgere et a prima usque ad primam viam vitae nostrae edicere. Quam cum decanus fratre iuvante verissime absolveret, Kebo et abbates episcopis, "Enimvero," aiunt, "haec omnia, quae audivimus, Benedicti sunt regulae praeter hoc solum, quod secundum illam laborant, secundum illam autem non vegetantur. Sed et hoc ipsum eis causa est, ut undecumque quaerant, quo vitam sustentent. Quae quia abbatis permisso quaesita, ubi iusserit, reponunt et ad eius nutum et arbitrium his, quaecumque sunt, utuntur, contra regulam non esse veraciter affirmare valebimus."

105. Et Milo Elewangensis: "Si de carnium esu," inquit, "haesitatis, ego, quod sentio, audentissime dico. Quoniam, quamvis equus in cibo non sit licitus, ambulatorem meum prius vellem monachus meus ederet oboediendo, quam

troubles me, namely that it was not just one of you, a bishop or an abbot, who has been sent to us, for we would no less obey him in everything that reason could make achievable than we would all of you." Then Erpho of Worms said: "Holy father, it would have been too hard for one man to contend with so many champions of the Holy Spirit as we see here. But as things are, it is my view that we should embark on some course of action to accomplish what we have been sent here for."

On the recommendation of the others, Henry finally sug- 2
gested that the abbot tell one of the brothers to explain to all our way of life here, as we then lived it. The abbot instructed Ekkehard, our dean, and also Notker, the physician, both very well known to most of the delegation, to stand up and describe our way of life from Prime to Prime. When the dean, with the help of his brother, finished his very accurate account, Kebo and the abbots said to the bishops, "Everything we have heard is in compliance with the Rule of Benedict, except for a single detail: they work according to the Rule, but their lives are not sustained in accordance with it. This very circumstance is also the reason why they seek everywhere for means to sustain their lives. The fact that they store items they have acquired with the abbot's permission in the place he designates and that they make use of them, whatever they are, in accordance with his decision and judgment, we cannot truthfully confirm to be against the Rule."

105. Milo, the abbot of Ellwangen, said: "If you have doubts about eating meat, I will tell you very boldly what I think. Even though eating horse meat is not allowed, I would rather that my monk, out of obedience, should eat

cetera quaedam, quae regulae sunt, declinaret. Ideoque Benedicti ego vice iudicio decerno: quae abbatis arbitrium iubeat, monachus manducet et bibat; abbas videat, quo arbitrio suo quid iubeat."

2 Cum autem ad verba eius quidam riderent, Henricus intulit: "Mirum," ait, "tam latum lacum hic patere et hic piscium copiam non esse." "Neque totus noster est," Ekkehardus ait, "neque piscium adeo largus, ut interdum domino nostro abbati, quod parce dat, vel soli sufficiat. Si autem emere aliquando invenimus, pretio, quod pro edulio uni nostrum apponendo distrahitur, probum aliquem totam hebdomadam cibare poteramus." "Enimvero," Thietricus ait, "dum ego aliquando hic studui, plures dies aliquando abierunt, quod piscem de pelago illo non vidisse me memini. Sed et maior pars fratrum tunc carnibus non utebatur, quorum quidem parsimonia nimia videbatur. Erant autem alii, qui solis volatilibus, quod unius cum piscibus creaturae sint, licite uterentur. Pauci autem in locis intra domesticos parietes ab abbate permissis quadrupedium quoque usi sunt carnibus. Meliorem autem ego, ut oppinor, numquam monachum videbo, quam eorum aliquis erat, qui interdum carnes edebat."

106. Inclinantur tandem abbates ad episcopos, ut secretis pro legatione sua uterentur consiliis. Quibus morose collatis Henricus surgens abbati nostro ait et fratribus: "Tantae prudentiae, domini nostri, vos novimus, ut legationis nostrae iam effectum in manu arbitrii vestri ponere velimus. Nos enim, ut condiximus, ad horam vobis locum dabimus. Consulite in medium, petimus, ut, qualicumque arte adhuc

my ambling horse than deviate from some other prescriptions of the Rule. For this reason, if I could stand in for Benedict, my view is that a monk should eat and drink what the abbot's judgment prescribes; the abbot should take care with what judgment he prescribes."

When some of them laughed at his words, Henry added: 2
"It is amazing that there is such a large lake here and not plenty of fish." "It is not entirely ours," said Ekkehard, "nor is it very abundant in fish so that sometimes what it sparingly provides is barely enough for even our lord abbot alone. If, on the other hand, we sometimes find fish to buy, for the price it takes to put a dish for one of us on the table we could feed a nobleman for an entire week." "Yes indeed," Dietrich said, "when I studied here in the past, sometimes many days went by when I do not remember seeing any fish from that huge stretch of water. But then, too, the majority of the brothers did not eat meat and their parsimony seemed excessive. There were others who ate only fowl, which is allowed because it belongs to the same class of creature as fish. A few monks also ate meat of four-legged animals, in spaces assigned by the abbot within the house walls. I believe I will never see a better monk than any of those who ate meat now and again."

106. The abbots eventually agreed with the bishops that in the interests of their mandate they should take counsel in private. After protracted deliberations, Henry rose and said to our abbot and the brothers: "My lords, we know that you are men of such wisdom that now we wish to place the outcome of our mission at your discretion. We have agreed to give you the monastery for an hour. We ask you to discuss together as a community how you might, by whatever means

quidem poteritis, bona, quae facitis, regulae sancti Benedicti conformetis. Et quia eius rei legati venimus, ut regularis vitae vobis monitores simus, quidnam hic boni statuerimus, dominis referre habeamus. Et quamvis omnes, qui venimus, bonum vobis testimonium coram eis dare vere habeamus, etiamsi meliora quidem, quae a patribus accepistis, vobis propter consuetudinem sint visa, si ad regulae viliora, ut ita dicam, mutaveritis, infamiam tamen evadetis."

2 Tandem illis pari condicto domo egressis, conferunt consilia abbas fratresque. Placuit omnibus, quicquid quisque privati haberet, in communes officinas in fide deferret, carnibus omnes, praeter quibus regula indulget, abstinendo mensas, etiamsi paupertatis sint, simul habeant. Reliqua vero ordinis, quem audierant, mutare, in quibus Kebo et ceteri abbates suadeant, paratissimi, usque dum, reposita haec si defecerint, litteris abbas regibus intimaverit. Vocantur in consistorium abbates auditisque unanimitatibus Deo gratias agunt. In consuetudine vero, qua degebamus, pauca mutantes, *tempus* se, *quoniam dies mali essent, redimere* aiebant.

107. Properant illi foras alacri animo ad exspectantes. "Enimvero," Kebo ait a longe viris, "spiritus sanctus tardare

are still available to you, bring the good that you do into conformity with the Rule of Saint Benedict. Since we have come here as legates with the task of monitoring your life by the Rule, we have to report to our lords exactly what good practices we have established here. Even though all of us who have come here really intend to provide them with testimony that is favorable to you, nevertheless you will avoid backbiting if you change practices that you have received from your fathers, if they tend to be to the detriment of the Rule, so to speak—even if you have regarded these practices as improvements because they are now customary."

After the delegates finally left the room by mutual agree- 2
ment, the abbot and the brothers discussed what they were to do. Everybody decided that whatever private possessions any monk had, he should bring them in good faith to the communal domestic buildings and that everyone, except those to whom the Rule allowed it, should abstain from meat and take their meals together, even if the food was the fare of a poor man. As for the rest of the items on the list that they had heard, they were very ready to change them insofar as Kebo and the other abbots recommended, until such time as the abbot should inform the kings by a letter if these supplies run out. The abbots were called into the assembly. When they heard about the unanimous decisions, they gave thanks to God. But they altered only a few details in the pattern of observance by which we lived, and they said that that they were *buying time, because these were evil days.*

107. They hastened outside in a cheerful mood to those who were waiting. Kebo called out to the men from a distance, "The Holy Spirit certainly knows no delay. We heard

nescit. Viros virtutum in sancto hoc coenobio esse prius audivimus; nunc re ipsa experiri habemus. Venite iam ipsi et, qui sint, pariter videte!" Iterum considentibus abbas ait: "Quod de meis ego fratribus, domini mei, promittere veraciter audeo, unum hoc vobis dico: quia quod regulae summam scio, dicto paratiores nescio. Ideoque per me peccari non ignoro, si ea, quae perficere nequeunt, eis iniungo. Quapropter a dominis regibus nisi vestro interventu nobis subveniatur, sumptus ad turrim evangelicam aedificandam suppetere non poterunt. Agite ergo! Quicquid meo iussu et vestro monitu facturi sint, in brevi audite!" Et minori Ekkehardo illi palatino: "Surge, fili," ait, "et sicut dominis nostris regibus in praesentia legatorum tantorum et tu quoque dicturus sis, consensum nostrum hic in facie eorum eloquere!"

2 Dictoque ut erat semper paratissimus, surrexit Ekkehardus et ita exorsus est: "In medium, patres et electi Dei, ut monuistis, consulimus. Et ecce qua die vel hora dominus noster et pater dixerit, memores nos sancti patris Benedicti privata nostra, quae tamen eius abbativo permisso habuimus, in medium et ad pedes eius ponemus. Et cetera, quae sancti abbates a nobis consulti in via et modo conversationis nostrae mutanda censebant, quia in nostro arbitrio rem posuistis, eos in participium consilii assumentes mutavimus. Sed quoniam in bono assuetis benefactum aliquod in aeque

earlier that there are virtuous men in this holy monastery; now we can actually experience this ourselves. So come here everyone and see for yourselves who they are!" When they were seated down together again, the abbot said to them: "My lords, I will tell you this one thing that I can honestly venture to assure you about my brothers: regarding what I know to be the essence of the Rule, I know of none keener to obey its requirements. I am well aware that it is my fault if I charge them with responsibilities that they are unable to fulfill. For this reason, had assistance not come to us from our lord kings thanks to your mediation, the resources needed for building the tower of the Gospel could not have been available. Come then! In a few moments listen to what they intend to do in response to my order and your counsel!" To the younger Ekkehard, the courtier, he said: "Stand up, my son, and announce before them the agreement we have reached just as you will also do before our lord kings in the presence of these many envoys!"

Most ready, as always, to comply, Ekkehard got up and be- 2
gan to speak as follows: "Fathers and God's elect, we took counsel together, as you recommended. Here is the result: on the day and at the hour which our lord and father indicates, we, mindful of our holy father Benedict, will lay our private possessions (which, however, we have possessed with the abbot's permission) at the feet of the abbot in the presence of all. As for the other details pertaining to the direction and manner of our life that the holy abbots, consulted by us, deemed necessary to change—since you left the matter to our judgment, we invited the abbots to participate in our deliberations and have made changes. But seeing that it is always burdensome for those accustomed to

bonum aut in parum melius mutare onerosum est semper, nos quidem humiliari assoliti, *ut iumenta fieri apud Deum* non recusamus et onere bis gravari." His et aliis utrimque profligatis gratulantur legati. Surgentesque Deum laudando conventum dirimunt.

108. Postea vero in auditorio convenientes, fratribus se ad missas pro die festo parantibus, Henricus ait consortibus: "Fideles nos nuntios iam nunc, socii, exhibemus, si quisque nostrum pro copia tantis viris in hac mala terra inopibus, ne in promissis deficiant, consulimus." Alacres omnes, prout ipse dictaverit, symbolum fatentur facturos. Et ille: "Non meum est," inquit, "de vestris cuiusque sumptibus dictitare. Pro copia, quam singuli habemus, in charta hic sub nomine quisque suo conferre scribamus." Factum est, et usque ad quadraginta quinque libras symbolus venerat.

2 Interea sequentia *Summis conatibus,* quam Ekkehardus palatinus dictaverat, ipso coram illis stante incohatur et iucunde cantatur. Et Poppo iocose: "Enimvero," ait, "tot hostes viri isti pro nihilo aestimant neque eo minus alacres iucundantur, quod assumus." Et Ekkehardus: "Cantent," inquit, "quam altissime velint; coquina adhuc cuique victum non habet." Quod Henricus audiens alte quidem ingemuit. Et Kebo: "Unum est, domini mei, quod ego mecum cogitans
3 multum vereor, sed et omnibus vobis vereri est: ne, postquam privata, quae quisque sua collaturus est, fuerint

some good to change something that benefits them into something equally good or a little better, we, who are accustomed to being humble, do not refuse to become *like beasts of burden before God* and to be burdened with a double load." When these and other matters were dealt with thoroughly on both sides, the envoys rejoiced. They rose and, praising God, dissolved the assembly.

108. Afterward they gathered in the reception room and as the brothers were preparing for the feast-day Mass, Henry said to his colleagues: "Friends, we prove ourselves today to be faithful envoys if each of us provides assistance, according to his ability, to these deserving men who live in dire need in this harsh land, so that they do not fall short of what they have promised." They all eagerly declared that they would contribute whatever he prescribed. He said: "It is not for me to prescribe how much it will cost you individually. Let each of us write down his contribution, in proportion to the wealth we each possess, under his name here on this sheet." This was done, and the total collected came to forty-five pounds.

Meanwhile they started the sequence *With the Greatest* 2
Effort, which Ekkehard the Courtier had composed, and sang it with joy as he stood before them. Poppo jokingly said: "Truly these men reckon all these enemies of no account and are no less exuberant in their joy because we are present." Ekkehard said: "Let them sing as loudly as they want; the kitchen still does not have food for each of them." Hearing this, Henry gave a deep sigh. Kebo said: "It is the one thing, my lords, that I very much fear when I reflect
upon it, but all of you should fear it too: that after the pri- 3
vate supplies that each of them will bring are consumed,

consumpta, nec de proprio nec de communi habentes, regulam tunc nec unam assequantur nec alteram." Et Henricus: "Dominis nostris id ipsum," ait, "dicere habebimus. Nos vero, quod legatio nostra talem effectum habet, solummodo gaudemus. Enimvero egomet, antequam veneram, aliter evenire putaveram. Neque in *sapientia* tanti *rumoris* et in virtute *operum* viros facile umquam a tam laudabili, qua degebant, vita avelli posse *crediderim*."

109. Abscesserat ab illis iam Ekkehardus. Et ecce quidam fratrum ecclesia egressus sequentiarium manu ferebat. Quem illi assumentes in sequentia diei Notkerum Balbulum laudant. At ille: "Non domini," ait, "haec est Notkeri, sed eius, qui iuxta vos sedit, magistri nostri palatini Ekkehardi." Et Chuonradus: "Insaniat," inquit, "Ruodmannus cum hypocrisi sua in locum hunc, quantum velit, monachos tamen hodie sanctus Gallus habet, quorum similes ipse inter suos numquam simulabit." Et Poppo: "Enimvero," ait, "huic ipsi, cuius haec verba sunt, parem nusquam videmus." Et Palzo: "Dicere," inquit, "habueras, si magistri mei, avunculi eius, verba inspexeras, sed et aliorum plurimorum ex eis verba et opera noveras. Dico enim id sancto Gallo praerogative datum, ut in ornatu verborum praecipuum sui hoc tempore teneant locum."

2 Egressi interea fratres, ut erant palliis parati, stare usque abbas veniat, monentur. Et Poppo interea: "Sanctus Gallus," ait, "tam sonora guttura sua, ne rauceant, dulci hodie vino rigare velit et saturet!"

they will have neither personal nor communal supplies, and then will follow neither the one rule nor the other." Henry said: "We must point this out to our lords. As for us, we are just glad that our mission had such a result. Before coming here I personally thought that it would turn out differently. Nor *would I have believed* that it would ever be possible that men so *renowned for wisdom* and for virtuous *works* could be torn away from so praiseworthy a life as they were leading."

109. Ekkehard had already left them when one of the brothers came out of the church carrying a sequentiary in his hand. They took it and praised Notker the Stammerer for the sequence of the day. But he said: "This is not the work of Lord Notker but rather of the man who sat next to you, our master Ekkehard the Courtier." Conrad said: "Ruodmann in his hypocrisy may rage all he wants against this place, but Saint Gall today has monks whose like he will never pretend to have among his own." Poppo said: "Yes indeed, nowhere else do we see an equal to this very man who has written those words." Palzo said: "You could have said that if you had examined the writings of my teacher, his uncle, but also if you knew the writings and compositions of many others among them. I declare that it has been granted to Saint Gall as a special privilege that in our times his men hold a special place in eloquence."

Meanwhile the brothers had gone outside and as they 2
were clad in their vestments, they were advised to stand there until the abbot arrived. In the meantime, Poppo said: "May Saint Gall ensure that their throats, which are so sonorous, are not hoarse by choosing to moisten them today with sweet wine, and may he fill them up!"

3 Usque huc legationem illam scriptam in verba alia transferens, cartis per impluvium perfusis, quae secuta sunt, conicere non poteram. Quae autem post haec dicturus sum, patrum, qui intererant, relatibus didici.

110. Interea accitus abbas affuit et consedit. Et Henricus parva solacia se collaturos et die condicta daturos fratribus pollicetur. Dein regibus se pro inopia eorum suasuros omnes concordant. Et cum se orationi eorum committerent, abbas intulit: "Immo ut fratres conscripti," ait, "sitis, volo, quia alia vobis dona dare non habemus." Laetis ob hoc omnibus itur in ecclesiam. Recepti manibus abbatis singuli in libro vitae scribuntur.

2 Abbates rogati cum fratribus eo die mensae aderant. De
communi et privatis collectae fiunt et abundam caritatem
faciunt. Cum autem disciplinam loci et morum tenorem
singuli sollicite pervidérent nihilque se quidam illorum, nisi
quod regulae sit, ibi videre silentio sibi dicerent, Milo
3 coclearium sibi afferri signo petiit. Quod cum ministrantium unus manutergio afferret, arte ille sua quasi recipiens decidere sivit. Minister autem continuo non sine rubore in veniam corruit. Surgere autem signo iussus, ut mos loci erat, domo—inclinatus hinc et hinc, nisi a priore signo vel nutu revocaretur—per exitum, qui claustrum ducit, exivit, per

Up to this point I have been putting the report of the del- 3
egation in different words, but because the documents had
been soaked by rain I could not decipher what came next.
So what I am about to say from now on I learned from the
accounts of the fathers who were there.

110. Meanwhile, the abbot was summoned; he arrived and sat down. Henry promised that they would contribute a small amount to help them and give it to the brothers on a day agreed upon. Then they all agreed that they would speak persuasively to the kings about the monks' poverty. When they started to commend themselves to the monks' prayers, the abbot made a suggestion: "Now, I want you to become enrolled brothers, because we have no other gifts to give you." At this, they all rejoiced and went to the church. Each of them, one by one, was welcomed into the abbot's arms and written into the Book of Life.

On that day the abbots sat at the table with the brothers 2
as they had been invited to do. Contributions from communal and personal supplies made for an abundant love feast.
Since all of the abbots had been carefully examining the discipline of the monastery and the tenor of their customs and
some of them were saying quietly to one another that they
saw there only what conformed with the Rule, Milo asked
by a sign that a spoon be brought to him. When one of the 3
servers brought him a spoon in a napkin, as Milo took it
from him, he contrived to let it fall on the floor. The server
immediately blushed and sank down to the ground asking
forgiveness. Bidden to rise by a sign, as was customary at
Saint Gall, he left the room, turning to this side and that in
case he might be called back by a sign or a nod from his superior, going out through the exit that leads to the cloister

4 fores, quae a coquina sunt, mox reversurus. At Kebo, hilari-
tatem machinari artifex: "Vide, Milo," ait, "miser, quid feceris! Frater ille, quem fuco tuo deceperas, exivit; nisi ipse eum
revocaveris, non est reversurus." Ille autem pectus incutiens, uni et alteri signo dato, ut revocaretur, et nemine, quia
Kebo astantibus innuerat, attendente, surgere ipse dum parat, veste eum Kebo detrahit et a coquina regressum digito
fratrem monstravit. Tali hilaritate cum ipsi inter se velut
hospites licentius agerent, nemo quidem loci fratrum motus
est in risum.

III. Surgitur a mensa; itur solitis benedictionum hymnis
in ecclesiam. Et ecce Kebo cum ceteris in veniam corruit
coram fratribus ecclesia egressis: "Nos," inquit, "fratres et
domini, docere vos venimus, et ecce disciplina vestra fracti
stupescimus, cum, nobis effuse solutis in risum, ne unum
vestrum dare viderimus assensum. Talem disciplinam huius
loci semper audivimus praedicari, et quam crebro audivi-
2 mus, nunc oculis inspeximus. Indulgeri tandem rogamus,
quod tantos viros vos impares aggressi sumus et doctissimos
indocti temptavimus. Vere laudis vobis testimonio futuri,
quocumque venerimus." Surgentibus a venia pariter omnes

in order to come back promptly through the door of the
kitchen. Then Kebo, a master at devising occasions for mer- 4
riment, said: "Milo, you wretch, see what you have done!
That brother whom you tricked by your pretense has left;
he won't come back unless you call him back yourself." And
so Milo, striking himself on the breast, made a sign to one
monk and another, that the server should be called back.
Since no one paid any heed (because Kebo had made a sign
to those nearby), Milo was about to stand up himself but
Kebo pulled him back by his robe and pointed his finger at
the brother who had come back from the kitchen. While
the guests interacted quite freely with one another in this
kind of merriment, not one of the brothers of our monastery was tempted to laugh.

III. They got up from the table and went to the church
singing the customary hymns of benediction. When the
brothers came out of the church—lo and behold! Kebo and
the others sank to the ground before them, seeking forgiveness. Kebo said: "My brothers and lords, we came here to
teach you, and here we are, crushed and stunned by your discipline because when we dissolved in unrestrained laughter,
we saw that not a single one of you joined in. We have always
heard talk about the quality of the discipline at this monastery, and what we have often heard about we have now observed with our own eyes. We really beg to be forgiven for 2
the fact that being unequal to the task, we accused such men
as yourselves, and that ignorant as we were, we submitted
highly learned men to a test. We will provide testimony to
your true merits wherever we go." When they got up on
their feet after asking forgiveness, all the brothers together

fratres occurrunt *in amplexus et oscula;* et quoniam incompetens hora esset, abbati decanum dirigunt, ut eis cum hospitibus incompetentia competere permitteret. Venit itaque laetus ipse, ut semper erat dulcissima caritatis anima, abbas; et meridiem usque nonam in sanctae hilaritatis gaudio perduxerant.

3 Sonatur ad nonam. Qua peracta mittit abbas Kebonem, qui episcopos, ut fratres conscripti claustrum intrare iam utique suum non dedignarentur, rogaret. Veniunt omnes, et societati fraternae participandum fore *gaudio gaudent.*

112. Itur in armarium, sed et in angustum sancti Galli the-
saurarium. Prae omnibus autem scriptorum digiti efferun-
tur; gemmarum autem et auri, quorum satis habebant, non
adeo. Versum Ambrosii folio ascriptum: “Nectaris ambrosii
redolentia carpito mella,” memoriter repetebant. Veniunt in
pyrale et in eo lavatorium nec non et proximum pyrali scriptorium, et has tres regularissimas prae omnibus, quas umquam viderint, asserebant esse officinas; et absque dubio,
qui tales dudum incolerent, regulares esse monachos nulli
negandum esset. Invitat tandem abbas omnes pariter ad no-
2 nales fratrum, quibus conscripti essent, biberes. Ibi tanta
hilaritate usque ad vesperum iam paene sonatum comma-
nent, ut senum, qui adhuc hodie talia memorant, recorda-
tionem voluptas sit audire. Ibant pariter ad laudes vespertinas quisque suas, abbate cum fratribus omni dulcedine

rushed *to embrace and kiss* them; and because it was an inappropriate time they sent the dean to the abbot for his permission to make the inappropriate time appropriate for them and the guests. The abbot himself came, delighted, for he was always the sweetest soul of charity; and they spent the midday until None in the delight of holy hilarity.

The bell rang for None. When None ended, the abbot 3
sent Kebo to invite the bishops to feel free to enter their
own cloister as enrolled brothers, which was now assuredly
their own. They all came, *joyfully rejoicing* because they were
now part of the community of brethren.

112. They went to the library, and also to the small treasury of Saint Gall. They praised the skill of the scribes above everything else; less so the precious stones and gold, of which they had enough. They repeated from memory the verse written on a folio of an Ambrose manuscript: "Gather the fragrant honey of the Ambrosian nectar." They went to the heated building, and in it a washing area, and also to the scriptorium next to it, and they declared that these three areas were very much in accordance with the Rule, more so than any they had ever seen; and that undoubtedly nobody could deny that those who had been inhabiting such quarters for some time were Rule-abiding monks. At the end of the tour the abbot invited all of them together for after-
None drinks with the brothers, among whom they were
now enrolled. They stayed there together, almost until the 2
bell rang for Vespers, in such merriment that it is delightful
to hear the recollections of old men who still remember
these events today. After the abbot and brothers bid them a
very affectionate farewell, they went to Vespers at the same
time, each to his own prayers; they agreed that they would

valefactis; condicto quidem, ut cras matutini conveniant et missionis suae responsa regibus reddenda communi disponerent consilio et relatu roborarent concordi et caritativo. Veniunt diluculo in fratrum consessum, et Henrico dictante legationis suae brevem et uniformem ordinant redditionem, ut, quoniam non simul ad aulam sunt redituri, Henricus, cui caput causae a regibus datum est, Kebone comite unum os omnium et lingua foret. "Neque ego," Henricus ait, "si quid de meo adicere potero, confratribus nostris derogare habebo."

113. Assurgunt omnes acclini in gratias. Pergunt tandem in ecclesiam ad dandas abeuntibus prospere viae preces abbas cum fratribus et recipiendas a tot episcopis benedictiones, data prius confessione et a stolatis remissione. Redeuntibus autem in claustrum ad oscula confratrum, Chuonradus noster inter ceteros: "Quoniam ego, filii mei," inquit, "proximior vobis loco sum quam ceteri isti fratres conscripti, pro memoria ipsorum et mea tribus diebus in annis, quibus vixero, caritates me vobis in refectorio factu-
2 rum promitto." Postea etiam hilariter hoc fecit. Et ut, qui intererant, testantur, quotiens ei vacabat, ipse quidem aderat, abbati regio modo proponebat, mensas obambulabat, serio et ioco abbatis assensu colloquia miscebat. Sed et rauca sua naturali voce iucundus lectorem aliquando increpitans: "Numquam etiam conticescis?" ait: "*Tu autem . . .*" Sicque cum vitro purae potionis in medium veniens,

convene the next morning and after a communal deliberation draw up a formal response about their mission to be delivered to the kings and confirm it with a congenial and amicable report. At daybreak they came to the brothers' assembly and at Henry's dictation prepared a brief and consistent report about their mission; since they were not all going to return to the court at the same time, Henry, to whom the kings had entrusted leadership in this matter, with Kebo as his companion, was to be the one mouth and tongue to speak for them all. Henry said, "If I can add something on my own, I will say nothing detrimental to our fellow brothers."

113. They all got up and bowed in gratitude. The abbot and brothers eventually proceeded to the church to offer prayers for the departing guests' successful journey and to receive blessings from these many bishops after first giving confession to, and receiving absolution from, the stole wearers. As they were returning to the cloister to kiss their fellow brothers, our bishop Conrad among the rest of them announced: "My sons, since I am located closer to you than all these other enrolled brothers, in their memory and in my own I promise to give you love feasts in your refectory on
three days each year as long as I live." He quite gladly carried 2
this out afterward. As those who were there testify, whenever he had time, he was present here himself, set out the feast for the abbot in a royal fashion, walked around the tables, and with the abbot's consent added serious and joking comments to the conversation. He once jokingly chided the lector in his own naturally raspy voice: "Do you never keep silent?" and the lector responded: "*The same* could be asked *of you.*" Then he came forward with a glass of unmixed wine

abbatem primo, tum ceteros in sancta caritate bibere rogans, ipsum primosque mensarum osculatus omnibus per eos oscula misit. Talis erat sancti Chuonradi in nos caritas.

3 Henricus vero et Thietericus quosdam cum Ekkehardo decano patrum sumentes in partem, prior, quot annis viveret, decem vasa vinaria, alter totidem salis Spira condixit die dato confratribus mittere. Quod et incunctanter singulis, quibus vixerunt, fecerunt annis. Sicque per oscula mutua valedictione data, utrimque sibi fausta precati ad prandia discedunt, noctem proximam Constantiae simul acturi.

114. Ibat autem et Ekkehardus ipse quidem ad reges unicordes suos, et de his et de aliis mandata abbatis ad illos latu-
rus, sed et, quantum in se sit, causam cum aulicis prospera-
turus. Praeterit autem Ruodmannum die altera Constantiae
pro hospitibus agentem, et cum ei ille: "Benedicite!" arte sua
diceret, quasi ad navem festinans, transeuntem non atten-
debat. At ille constitit et quendam post eum ad navem misit,
qui diceret: "Verum proverbium est: 'Mendacia curta sem-
2 per habent crura.'" Et Ekkehardus: "Verum illud," ait, "esse,
numquam lucidius quam heri et hodie in nobis apparuit. Sed
ne mirum, si me tantillum conviciis prosequitur dominus
tuus, cum mille in regno monachi sint emeriti, qui Deo et
hominibus conquerantur pro conviciis eius. Quapropter et

and asked first the abbot and then the others to drink in the spirit of holy love and kissed the abbot himself and senior monks at the tables, sending kisses through them to all the brothers. Such was the brotherly love that Saint Conrad had for us.

Meanwhile Henry and Dietrich took some of the fathers 3
and Ekkehard, the dean, aside. The former announced that he would be sending his fellow brothers ten barrels of wine on an appointed day as long as he lived, and the other promised the same quantity of salt from Speyer. They fulfilled these undertakings promptly every year as long as they lived. On this note, both sides after exchanging farewell kisses, wished good fortune to one another and went their separate ways for the meal, planning to spend the following night together in Constance.

114. Ekkehard himself also went to his dear friends the
kings, to bring them the abbot's request concerning these
and other matters and also to further our cause with the
courtiers as much as he could. On the following day he
passed Ruodmann, who was taking care of the guests in
Constance, and when Ruodmann in his sly manner said to
him "Bless me!" Ekkehard paid no attention to him, pretending to be in a hurry to get to the ship that was passing
by. Ruodmann stood there and dispatched a man to the ship
after him to tell him: "There is a true saying: Lies always
have short legs." Ekkehard said: "It has never been more 2
clearly demonstrated for us than yesterday and today that
this is true. But it is no wonder if your master pursues one as
insignificant as myself with insults, when there are a thousand monks who have served their time well in this kingdom
and who complain to God and men about his insults. For

3 haec ego cum aliis mille perpetior et quiesco." Sed et quidam ministrorum hominis bene idoneus, cui causa domini
reges interdum erant affabiles: "Enimvero," ait, "etsi dominus meus tacuerit, ego nequaquam omittam, quin talia con-
querar regibus." Rediit nuntius Ruodmanno cuncta, quae
audierat, renuntians. Ille modo non modice stupidus, nequaquam in eum verba haec vertisse care iurans asseruit, sed
magis in eos, qui ipsum et fratres nostros infamassent, falsi-
dicos. Hoc dixit sub obtentu, quasi ipse quidem talium nullus esset.

115. Et Otkerus, quem supra diximus, frater eius et miles:
"Miror te," ait, "numquam hominis pigere, qui astu suo semper tuas exsuperavit acutias. Latere autem te arbitror rumo-
rem, quo apud omnes insigniris: secundam quidem iam te
invasionem loco illi sancto, unam clam fecisse per te solum,
alteram struxisse per tot episcoporum et abbatum collegia.
Hoc in aula tunc musitatum est, sed et proximis diebus a
militibus ipsius abbatis mihi conquestum est. Ideoque ipso
isto homine, cui nunc nuntium tuum misisti, agente, tu so-
2 lus a legatione illa exceptus es. Vereor autem, ne, *quia intimus*
quidem *consiliis est,* apud principes animo, quo nunc est, in-
fortunii tui aliquid conflet." Et ille: "Non nego," ait, "frater;
sed et veraciter assero etiam caput meum abscidendum incunctanter eo pacto me tradere, ut omnes in regno Ottonum monachi vivant secundum regulam sancti Benedicti.
Sed et super ipsos fratres, qui paene sine abbate sunt, a

this reason, I along with the thousand others endure this in-
sult too and keep silent about it." Then one of his atten- 3
dants, a very capable man to whom the kings were friendly
on occasion for the sake of his master, also said: "Even if my
master keeps silent, I will certainly not fail to complain to
the kings about this." The messenger returned and related
to Ruodmann everything that he had heard. Ruodmann,
completely astounded, swore an oath that he had never addressed these words to Ekkehard but rather to the liars who
had defamed him and our brothers. He said this, pretending
that he himself was not one of them.

115. Otker, whom I mentioned above, his brother and
bodyguard, said: "I am amazed that it never bothers you
that this man always gets the better of your craftiness with
his cunning. I think that you are unaware of the rumor everyone repeats about you, namely that you have already in-
truded into that holy place a second time: you made one intrusion secretly on your own, while you engineered another
with all these bishops and abbots. This was whispered at the
court back then, but in recent days, too, complaints about it
have been made to me by the knights of the abbot himself.
Therefore, due to the actions of this very man to whom you
have just sent your messenger, you alone were excluded
from that mission. Because he is *privy to their plans,* I fear 2
that in his present state of mind he may stir up some kind of
trouble for you with our rulers." Ruodmann said: "I do not
deny it, brother; but I also truthfully declare that I would
unhesitatingly submit even to being beheaded if that would
ensure that all monks in the kingdom of the Ottos would
live according to the rule of Saint Benedict. Also, regarding
those brothers who live almost without an abbot, when

dominis invitatus consiliis, quae sensi, fide dixi, qua debui.
Ut autem tot hospitibus invaderentur, crede mihi, neque
consilio interfui, nec umquam placuit mihi, ubi comperi.
3 Sed et hodie laetatus sum et heri, ubi prospera de eis audivi."
"Nollem," ait ille, "frater et domine mi, te pro aliis quam tibi
creditis adeo sollicitari, ut querelas tibi ullas a pari potestate
praeditis compares, sed quantum illi pro tuis, tantum te
quoque *curare* pro suis; et salva sic caritate et pace hinc inde
fueris. Nunc autem te cum tantis viris, qui ad honorem omnia et precibus perducunt et artibus, tam severe discordare
admodum doleo, et maxime cum illo, quem dixi, non parvi
momenti viro."

116. Cum autem Ekkehardus Duellium ipsa die ascen-
deret et Wazemanno ibi abbati, nobis et sibi amicissimo,
omnem seriem rei nostrae, ut ductrici in proximo a Norico,
ubi pascha egit, redeunti insinuaret, et per singula diceret,
in Rotwila legatis Ruodmanno et Otkero comitatis iungitur.
Ubi parum cum eis moratus in Thietingen villam nostram,
ne quicquam Ruodmanni rerum tangeret, vespertinus diver-
tit, quamvis tamen ipse ei per fratrem necessaria abunde
2 promitteret. Ruodmanno autem legatorum quosdam rogante, ut de verbis ad navem male intellectis eum in

invited to do so by my lords, I provided them with the counsel I thought appropriate with the loyalty that I owed them. That so many guests should intrude upon their privacy—believe me, I played no part in this decision nor was I at all pleased when I learned about it. I rejoiced both yesterday 3
and today when I heard things were going well for them." "My brother and lord," Otker said, "I would not want you to concern yourself with monks other than those entrusted to you to such an extent that you bring upon yourself complaints from those endowed with equal power. Rather, I wish you would show the same care about their monks as they show about yours; in this way you would safeguard the love and peace you enjoy in this monastery and elsewhere. As it is, however, I am extremely saddened that you are so very much at odds with those great men who by means of their entreaties and skill conduct all matters to enhance their standing, and especially with that man of considerable significance whom I mentioned."

116. On the same day Ekkehard went up to Hohentwiel and there he told Abbot Wasemann, who was always very friendly to us and to him, about the entire course of our affair in detail, so that the abbot would inform the duchess who was soon to return from Bavaria where she had celebrated Easter; then at Rottweil he joined the envoys, who were accompanied by Ruodmann and Otker. After spending a little time with them there he turned off the road at our estate in Thietingen in the evening so as not to draw on any of Ruodmann's resources although Ruodmann, through his brother, offered to provide in abundance whatever he might need. Ruodmann asked some of the envoys to correct the 2
misunderstandings that had occurred near the ship when

crastinum corrigerent occurrentem, comitatu ille usque Spiram abstinuit ibique eis se, Ruodmanno cis Rhenum regresso, coniunxit. Kebo autem id rogatus, Ruodmannum apud hominem purgare de verbis ipsis aggreditur. Cui ille nihil aliud nisi publicos impulsus et eversiones eius in se et fratres suos, respondit, reservandos. Et ille: "Enimvero," ait, "hesterni diei orisque omnium nostri semper habet, dum homo est, reminisci." Audiunt tandem reges rogationes et ascensionem Mogontiae acturos.

117. Illuc conveniunt praescripti illi, sed et ceterorum aliqui. Vimque omnem legationis suae Ekkehardo astante, quam optime poterant, in brevi per ordinem absolverant. Penuriaque loci conquesta, maxime in vino, et ceteris reculae sumptibus: "Nisi solacio," inquiunt, "iuventur, neque sub regula neque sine regula, cum paupertatulas, quas habent in medium collatas, consumpserint, subsistere non poterunt." "Neque haec ipsa," Kebo ait, "diu durabunt, quae contulerant, quia omne habere omnium illorum sollicite scrutati apud neminem ullius boni copiam praeter caritatis et humilitatis invenimus. Oboeditionem autem illorum, ut vere asseram, Dei virorum laudare mihi non est magnopere, cum et patres nostri episcopi dicto paratiores numquam maiorem vidisse testati sint."

2 Et Otto filius ad patrem: "Enimvero, pater, iucundum est, quod audivimus. Teque decet talium compati penuriis, maxime vero, ut fame eorum invidi et proditores videantur

they saw Ekkehard the next day, but Ekkehard stayed away from their company until he reached Speyer, joining up with them there after Ruodmann had returned to this side of the Rhine. Because he had been asked to do so, Kebo set about trying to clear Ruodmann of responsibility for those remarks. Ekkehard responded to him that it was simply a matter of restraining Ruodmann's public attacks and intrigues against him and his brothers. Kebo said: "Yes, as long as he lives he always ought to remember yesterday and what we all said." Eventually they heard that the kings were going to celebrate the Rogation Days and Ascension at Mainz.

117. The aforementioned men came to Mainz along with some of the others. As Ekkehard stood by, they delivered the gist of their mission as best they could, in a brief and orderly fashion. They lamented the poverty of the place, particularly regarding wine and other small expenses; they said: "Unless relieved by some assistance, they cannot survive either under the Rule or without the Rule once they have consumed the meager supplies they have collected for the community." Kebo said: "Nor will the supplies they have collected last long, because after carefully examining everything that all of them possessed, we found no one with a substantial supply of any goods other than love and humility. But to tell the truth, it is not for me to praise to the skies the obedience of those men of God, because our fathers the bishops, who are more used to issuing orders, have testified that they have never seen greater obedience."

Then Otto the son said to his father: "Truly, father, what 2
we have heard is pleasing. It behooves you to have compassion for the poverty of these men, above all so those envious of their fame and their betrayers might be seen to be

confusi." Et pater: "Si tamen tandem aliquem unum habere consenserint in auxilio, qui regulae peritus aliquantum cum eis conversetur temporis!" Cum autem Kebo, ad haec quiddam ut diceret, surgere coepisset, Henricus illum nutu compescuit. Et ad se accito in aurem: "Noli," inquit, "quicquam contra loqui, quia, quantum eos nunc experti sumus, nemo monachus hodie est in regno, qui in ratione bene vivendi, inter eos veniens, eos praecedere possit. Et forsitan, quisquis ille erit, aut tantae auctoritatis Dei servis manus est daturus aut tandem quoquo modo loco cessurus."

3 At Ekkehardus: "Liceat et nobis," inquit, "O rex, vice abbatis nostri, a quo et ad hoc ipsum missi sumus, quiddam loqui. Bene et optime intulit quidem filius tuus penuriis nostris te decere compati: ne postquam reculae nostrae, quas in medium contulimus, fuerint consumptae, absque omni regula tandem famelicis tuis sit vivere. Quod autem maiestas tua, gloriose mi, subiunxerat peritiorem regulae nobis aliquem auxilio dari, a legatis vestris, abbatibus regulae peritissimis, nunc, ut ita dicam, initiati petimus, pater et fili, ab ipsorum aliquo iussu vestro revisi et, si in aliquo ab edictis eorum exorbitavimus, explorari, quoniam grave quidem est, si ausim dicere, in tam brevi articulo tertia vice pauperes vestros ingredi, et ab eo, quod a tam multis claris viris iniunctum est, per virorum neophytorum aliquem abduci."

confounded." The father said: "Provided, however, they finally agree to have someone to help them, someone with expertise in the Rule who would live among them for some time!" When Kebo started to rise to make some reply to that, Henry stopped him with a shake of the head. He beckoned Kebo and whispered in his ear: "Do not say anything against it, because from what we have come to know about them, there is no monk in our kingdom today who could come into their midst and surpass them in living righteously. Whoever that might be, he will perhaps either extend his hands to such authoritative servants of God or eventually somehow yield place."

Ekkehard said: "Your Majesty, may we also be permitted 3
to say something on behalf of our abbot, by whom we have been sent here for this very purpose. Your son has spoken well, even excellently in saying that it behooves you to feel compassion for our poverty so that in the end, after the meager supplies we have collected for the community are consumed, your starving monks are not forced to live without any rule at all. As for the suggestion that your glorious Majesty has made that we be given someone with more expertise in the Rule to help us—having been initiated, so to speak, by your envoys, the abbots with the most expertise in the Rule, we now ask you, father and son, that one of them visit us again, by your order. And let him make investigations to find out if we have deviated from their prescriptions in any way. If I may presume to say this: it would be very hard for your beggars to be descended upon for a third time in such a short period and to be led by some neophyte off the course that so many eminent men had prescribed."

Et Henricus: "Clavum quidem tu," inquit, "legationi nostrae fixisti." Cui sic peroranti plures assenserant.

118. Et pater rem in crastinum distulit, hoc inter cetera
quasi de intimo cordis protestatus: prius se coronam suam
confracturum, quam monachos sancti Galli absque solaciis,
quibus regulam exsequi possint, dimissurum. In crastinum,
Ottone magno per noctem solito aliquo dolore tacto, cum
in publicum procedere non posset, Henricus et Kebo domos
ire dimittuntur, Wormatiae in octava pentecostes iussi ad-
2 esse. Ekkehardus vero interea, ut solebat, aulae immoratus
et rem sancti Galli, quaqua poterat, agens, *non modice consolatus est,* Hadawiga quidem regibus, patruo et patrueli, litteras
pro regiminis rebus aliis dirigente, sed et pro nobis, quod res
tantae se nescia agerentur, velut irascente et, ne tandem
quid de nobis severius decerneretur, rogante. Iubetur ipse
litterarum portitor Huozo presbyter, magni quidem apud
dominam vir momenti, diem exspectare et pro ipsa decretis
interesse.

3 Conveniunt die dato Wormatiam non solum Henrich et Gebo, sed et ceteri legatorum aliqui. Magis autem pro nobis sollicitus erat ipsius episcopus loci. Cum autem colloquio inito varie hinc inde res traherentur, malevolis nobis aliquem abbatem regularem praeponi suadentibus, regulariores abbatem et monachos hodie in regno non esse, si

Henry said: "You have hit the nail on the head for our mission!" This is how he concluded, and a great number of people agreed with him.

118. The father postponed the matter until the following
day, and among other things, he proclaimed the following,
as from the bottom of his heart: he would sooner break his
crown into pieces than let the monks of Saint Gall go without
the assistance that would allow them to observe the
Rule. On the next day, since Otto the Great had suffered
from some chronic illness during the night and could not
appear in public, Henry and Kebo were given leave to go
home and ordered to be present at Worms on the Sunday
after Pentecost. Meanwhile Ekkehard stayed at the court as 2
usual, handling the affairs of Saint Gall as best he could. He
found considerable comfort in the fact that Hadwig had sent a
letter to the kings, her uncle and her cousin, in which she
dealt with other government business but also appeared to
be burning with anger that matters of such importance concerning
us were being handled without her knowledge; and
she asked that no excessively harsh decision be made concerning
us. The bearer of the letter, the priest Huozo, who
had great influence with his mistress, was ordered to wait
until the appointed day and to participate in making the decisions
on her behalf.

On the appointed day it was not only Henry and Kebo 3
who met at Worms, but also some of the other members of
the delegation. The bishop of Worms was most anxious on
our behalf. When the council began, matters were discussed
back and forth in various ways; when those who wished us ill
argued that some Rule-abiding abbot should be put in
charge of us, Huozo responded that if they were only given

reliqua facultas sit, Huozo respondit. Cui cum legati ceteri
consentirent, Henricus surgens: “Nostris,” inquit, “domini
reges, qui legatione vestra, qua maxime potuimus, fide
4 functi sumus, credere habetis responsis. Quoniam quidem
alii, qui hic sua, prout libet, interserunt, quid nos apud sanctum Gallum invenerimus quidque reliquerimus, nesciunt,
quae autem nos vobis nuper, quam verissime noveramus,
narravimus, iterum, si vultis, ut et ipsi audiant, repetimus.
Viros nos virtutum magnarum patrum viam sanctissimam
gradientes ibi invenimus, a qua eos in regulae viam, quoniam
5 quidem eadem paene erat, convertimus. In ea quidem nullius doctrinae nunc egentes degunt; sed sumptus, quibus
eam perficiant, infecundae illius terrae penuria desunt. Quapropter neminis alio praeter sumptuum, qui desunt, egent
solacio. Abbatem autem eis imponi, cum optimum habeant,
vanissimum duco. Enimvero abbatem et monachos nemo
nostrum aliter credit quam Dei esse servos. Atque ideo vos,
domini, et nos rei quidem erimus, si non eos aut illam viam
tenere sinamus aut hanc idonee exsequi sinamus. Illorum
igitur ex parte cum nullus nodus relictus sit, si aliquis iam fuerit, nostrae partis erit.”

119. Tandem post multa consiliorum colloquia, Adalheida etiam per Ekkehardum adesse rogata, dantur Keboni abbati et sibi de scriniis regum sexaginta argenti librarum rata pondera abbati nostro et fratribus solacio in sancti Iohannis die ferenda; iusso etiam Kebone in loco ipso usque

the opportunity, no abbot and monks in the kingdom were
more Rule abiding. When the other members of the delegation agreed with him, Henry rose and said: "My lord kings,
you can trust our responses, for we faithfully accomplished
our mission as members of your delegation to the best of
our ability. Since other people, who jump in with their sug- 4
gestions at will, do not know what we found at Saint Gall
and what we left behind, we shall repeat again, if you wish,
what we recently related to you as accurately as we could, so
that they, too, may hear it. There we found men who walk
the most holy path of the great virtues of the fathers, from
which we have caused them to turn to the path of the Rule,
since it is almost the same. They now live according to it and 5
need no instruction, but they lack the resources with which
to bring this path to perfection because of the poverty of
their infertile land. For this reason they need no other assistance from anyone but the resources they lack. I consider
that setting an abbot over them would be entirely in vain because the one they have is excellent. None of us believes the
abbots and monks to be anything other than servants of
God. Accordingly, you, my lords, and we too will be at fault
if we do not allow them to keep on their former path or to
follow this other path in a suitable manner. Since there remains no obstacle on their part, if there is to be an obstacle,
it will be on our part."

119. Finally, after much advice and discussion, at which Ekkehard asked that Adelheid be present, too, Abbot Kebo and Ekkehard were given sixty pounds of silver from the royal treasury, precisely weighed, to be conveyed as assistance to our abbot and brothers on Saint John's Day. Also, Kebo was told to stay as a guest at the monastery until

dormitionem Mariae hospitari atque Benedicti viam discretione, qua nosset, coram Galli pullis ingredi moreque suo eos docere vivere.

2 Venit ille tandem carus ad carissimos; et quicquid instituit, omnes unanimes ad exsequendum invenit, abbate ei cum Ekkehardo seniore decano quidem ad omnia et de oblatis et de loci impensis copias suggerentibus, Ekkehardo etiam iuniore, quem multum ille prae oculis habuit, favente et cum eo, donec recessit, nocte dieque versante.

3 Operae autem pretium erat, si vacaret, multa, quae eum iucunde fecisse et eleganter audivimus locutumque esse, sermoni inserere. Ut in die sanctae Mariae, post quem iam dolore omnium discessurus erat, cruces foras sequendo cum antiphonae nocturnales cum capitibus psalmorum in via canerentur: "Nonne regulae nostrae, sed et canonum est," ait, "semel hodie matutinos agere? Enimvero si istos Kebo futu-
4 ros scisset, non strato surrexisset. Quam autem omnes mentiti sunt, qui in hoc loco regulam non esse dixerunt, cum in tanto vacationis die non simplex, sed duplex solita sit persolvi!" Cum autem abbas claudus quidem esset, sed et decanus pede nutasset: "*Melius,*" ait, "*claudicare reges quam regna.*" Et: "O utinam tales egomet claudos Lorisham haberem! Enimvero prae regibus," inquit, "diligerem." Et cum statuta Hartmuoti in victualibus ei optima visa sint, caritates in ieiuniis prae ceteris extulit et amore nostro easdem suis provisurum promisit.

Assumption, and to walk the path of Benedict as wisely as he could in the presence of Saint Gall's chickens, and to teach them to live according to his ways.

Finally he came as a dear friend to those dearest to him. 2
He found them all of one mind, ready to follow what he assigned, and the abbot and Ekkehard Senior, the dean, provided him with the means for everything, both from the silver that had been brought and by adding to the monastery's expenses. Also, Ekkehard Junior, of whom Kebo saw a great deal, was well-disposed toward him, and spent days and nights in his company until he departed.

It would be worth the effort, if we had the time, to in- 3
clude in our account the many things that I have heard Kebo pleasantly accomplished and gracefully said. For instance, on Saint Mary's Day, after which, to everyone's sorrow, he was to depart, when the monks' procession followed the crosses outside, singing the nocturnal antiphons along with the first verses of psalms on their way, he said, "Doesn't our Rule, and also canon law prescribe a single performance of Matins today? Had Kebo known they would be performed,
he would not have risen from his bed. What a lie all those 4
people have told who said that there was no Rule at this place, when on such a great day of rest the custom is to follow the Rule's prescription not once but twice!" Then, since the abbot was lame and even the dean was unsteady on his feet, Kebo said, "*It is better for kings to limp than kingdoms.*" He continued: "If only I had such lame men as these at Lorsch! I would prize them above kings." Since Hartmut's statutes regarding food seemed the best to him, he extolled love feasts during the time of fast above others and out of love for us he promised that he would provide those from his own means.

120. Rediit tandem lacrimis prosecutus ad reges; et inter optima, quae eis de edoctis a se regularibus hilariter dixit, nisi illis locum aliquem vinarium et alias frugiferum de suo dederint, deficientibus datis illis solaciis, quae inceperant, perficere non posse asseruit.

2 Dein regibus cum principibus crebro quidem collatis, cum operas trivissent consiliis, post aliquot dies Henrico episcopo monente Sahspach, Hadewigae beneficii villam, si ab ea rogatu regum avelli possit, sancto Gallo tradere conspirant. Quod illa, cum multotiens tum per reges tum per ipsos nuntios peteretur, sicut *varium et mutabile semper* est *femina,* nunc concedere se spem dedit, nunc facturam sancte
3 abiuravit. Postremo quidem abbate nostro in ipso monasterio et fratribus illi supplicantibus, facturam tandem pollicetur, si ei missa cottidiana in loco pro viva et defuncta in perpetuum promittatur agenda, sed et Ekkehardo eius loci, usque dum vivat, committatur cura. De quo cum aliquos ex fratribus nostris invidos homini haesitare audisset, irata exsiliit reque infecta conventum diremit. Seque post hanc horam numquam cuiquam pro hac re aurem iuravit adhibere. Sicque quorundam invida incautela Gallus villam illam, cum iam in manibus habere posset, amisit, Ekkehardo tandem carissime iurante numquam se causa sui in hac re illi verbum fecisse.

120. He went back to the kings eventually accompanied by tears. Among the best things that he lightheartedly told them about the Rule-abiding monks who had been thoroughly instructed by him, he declared that unless the kings granted them some land from their own estates that could produce wine and was fertile for other crops, the monks would not be able to accomplish what they had begun once the assistance given them ran out.

Then after the kings and the leading men had conferred 2
repeatedly and devoted much effort to discussions, a few days later at bishop Henry's urging, they agreed to hand over Sasbach, an estate from Hadwig's benefice, to Saint Gall, if it could be wrested from her at the kings' request. Although she was asked many times by the kings as well as by the envoys themselves, since *woman is always a fickle and changeable creature,* at times she gave them hope that she would concede, at other times she solemnly swore that she would not
do so. At last, when our abbot and the brothers entreated 3
her in the monastery itself, she finally promised to do it if they promised to conduct daily Masses in the monastery in perpetuity for her, living and dead, and also if the management of the monastery was entrusted to Ekkehard for as long as he lived. When she heard that some of our brothers, envious of the man, were hesitating, angrily storming out of the room she broke off the meeting with the business unfinished. She swore that from that moment on she would never bend her ear to anyone concerning this matter. So it was that due to envy and lack of foresight on the part of some monks, Gall lost this estate when he could now have it in his hands; all the time Ekkehard solemnly swore that in this situation he had never said a word to her to promote his cause.

4 Fratres autem, quamvis hac spe frustrati, instituta tamen Kebonis sollicite tenebant. Sicque communiter vivebant donariis regum, symbolis quoque, quae diximus, legatorum, quamvis anni penuriae fuerint, ut neminis invidorum in se ora patefacerent.

121. Chuonradus autem episcopus crebro eos visitans, ut diximus, annis aliquot iam elapsis cum diuturna eos penuria vidisset afflictos, senibus et invalidis pietate sibi solita consuluit et caminatas claustri abbatem aperire rogavit; Constantiaque et Arbona, in quantum copia erat, solacia privata talibus transmisit. Validiores vero haec considerantes amicis suis foris locum, qui sibi ab eis solacia petant, permisso abbatis mittunt. Allata autem mensae communi imponunt.

2 Factum est autem, ut quidam pauperum parum quid, quod ab amicis datum est, solus comederet. Intrantesque cum eum ob hoc increparent, ille quidem avide comedens: "Si calceus," inquit, "dividitur, nemo calciatur." Quod cum risum astantibus moveret, decanus tamen, ut audivit, ingemuit; nihilque fame improbius et sacrius esse respondit. Cumque palam factum sit multis elogium hoc monachi esurientis, Ruodmannus id in pharetra sua reposuit et, ut occasione data eo in fratres uteretur iaculo, ut postea fecit, reservavit.

122. Purchardus igitur abbas senio iam gravescens corylum illam antiquam, sub qua Gallus quondam vepribus

4 As for the brothers, although they had been frustrated in their hope, they meticulously carried out Kebo's instructions. As a result they lived as a community on donations from the kings and on the contributions from the envoys that I mentioned earlier, although there were years of scarcity so that none of the envious opened their mouths to speak against them.

121. As for Bishop Conrad, he visited them often, as I said, and when he saw that after several years had passed they were still afflicted by persistent poverty, with his habitual compassion he provided help for the old and weak and asked the abbot to open up the heated chambers of the cloister; he also sent them as much private assistance from Constance and Arbon as he could. Reflecting on this, with the abbot's permission the monks sent those who were stronger to their friends outside the monastery to ask for assistance from them. They laid what had been brought on the communal table.

2 It happened, however, that one of the poor monks was eating by himself a little something that his friends had given him. When the monks entered his cell and rebuked him for this, he said, still eating greedily: "If a shoe is divided, no one is shod." Although this remark made those standing around laugh, the dean sighed when he heard it and responded by saying that nothing was more monstrous and horrible than hunger. When this remark of the hungry monk came to be widely known, Ruodmann stored it away in his quiver and kept it to use as an arrow against the brothers when a suitable opportunity presented itself, as he later did.

122. Abbot Burchard, now burdened by old age, after consulting the bishop, cut down that ancient hazel tree beneath which Saint Gall had once sunk down on thorn bushes and

corruens: *Haec requies mea* cecinit, consulto episcopo succidit, capellaque aedificata aram in loco arboris statuit. Fenestellam quoque ad meridiem ei humilem imposuit. Ad quam septo deforis aptato semet includere et finem vitae
2 abbatia relicta devovit exspectare. Parata capella et in honore sanctae crucis, sed et sancti Galli per Chuonradum nostrum dedicata, vir ille sanctus septo iam illi tabulata per artifices praeparans, Notkerum pro se, Ekkehardo favente, Notkeri medici ex sorore nepotem, eligi rogavit et regibus eum pro se inthronizandum direxit. Ipse autem—episcopo Chuonrado, ne tantae teneritudinis senex includeretur, obstante—regum iussu loca abbatibus a Karolo decreta, multa reluctatus, Ekkehardo se procurante retinuit et caminatam antecessorum abbatum quietis gratia tandem invitus intro-
3 iit. Nisi enim quod penuriam timuerat, nil per se habere volebat. Supervixit autem suffecto tandem suo, et Immonem quoque fore edixit abbatem. Episcopus autem, semper intimus eius, defungi eum parantem oleo sancto adveniens unxit. Defunctum vero multorum lacrimis prosecutum, maxime pauperum, ante hostium capellae, quam ipse "*Haec requies mea*" vocabat, sollemniter sepelivit, Ekkehardo decano, qui, ut diximus, cor suum erat, ante annum quidem modo, quo iam dixisse meminimus, assumpto.

123. De Notkero vero doctore pictore et medico, cum

prophesied: "*This is my resting place.*" When a chapel had
been built on the site of the tree, Burchard set up an altar
there. He also put in a little window in the chapel, low down
and facing south. Adjoining it an enclosure was built outside, and he vowed after leaving the abbacy to enclose himself in the chapel and wait for his death. The chapel was 2
made ready and dedicated by our bishop Conrad to the Holy
Cross and to Saint Gall. After this the holy man, who by this
time had craftsmen prepare floorboards for the enclosure
for him, with Ekkehard's approval requested that Notker,
the nephew of Notker the Physician by his sister, be elected
abbot in his place and sent Notker to the kings to be installed as his successor. As for Burchard, though Bishop
Conrad objected to such a frail old man shutting himself
away, he retained, in the face of much resistance, in accordance with the kings' decree and with Ekkehard's help, the
estates assigned by Charles to the abbots. Eventually, for the
sake of peace and quiet, he unwillingly entered the heated
chamber used by the abbots who preceded him. Except for 3
the fact that he feared destitution, he wished to have no
personal possessions. In the end, he survived his successor,
and he also pronounced that Immo should be abbot. The
bishop, who was always a close friend, came to Burchard as
he was about to die and anointed him with holy oil. When
Burchard died amid the tears of many, especially of the poor,
the bishop buried him with due ceremony before the entrance to the chapel, which Burchard himself used to call
"*This, my resting place,*" and before a year had passed Ekkehard the dean, who as I said was his soul mate, now died in
the manner I have already indicated, as I recall.

123. Although I have enough material about Notker, who

materiam grandis voluminis habeamus, succincte quidem ad alia festinando dicemus. Picturas quidem post arsuram plures Gallo fecerat, ut videre est in ianuis et laqueari ecclesiae et libris quibusdam. Sed haec quid sunt ad mille alia, quae dictans et medens insigniverat? Fecit enim Otmaro decoras illas antiphonas. Et hymnum *Rector aeterni metuende saecli.* Et quaedam susceptacula regum. Et hymnum de una virgine non martyre, id est *Hymnum beatae virgini.* In quo cum de quodam uno verbo, quod metro congrueret, diutius haesitaret, Ekkehardo decano, ut id de suo adderet, inclinatus, ille autem continuo: "Ovis," inquiens, "ad capram lanam petitum venit," sed ut "labilem" poneret, emonet.

2 Haec pro exemplo humilitatis et caritatis patrum praeterire non potui. Medendo autem mira et stupenda frequenter fecerat opera, quoniam et in aphorismis medicinalibus, speciebus quoque et antidotis et prognosticis Hippocraticis singulariter erat instructus. Ut in urina Henrici ducis, versute se decipere temptantis, apparuit. Qui cum ei urinam mulierculae cuiusdam cameralis pro sua inspiciendam mitteret: "Miraculum," ait, "nunc et portentum Deus facturus
3 est, quod numquam est auditum, ut vir utero pareret. Nam dux iste circa trigesimum ab hodie diem filium ex utero suo editum ad ubera suspendet." Erubuit tandem deprehensus ille viroque Dei, ne se medicare renueret—nam ad hoc adductus erat—munera misit. Feminamque illam virginem

was a scholar, artist, and physician, to fill a large volume, I will talk about him briefly, to get to other matters promptly. After the fire he created many paintings for Saint Gall, which one can see on the doors and the ceiling of the church, and in certain books. But what are these objects compared to a thousand other remarkable achievements he made in poetry and healing? For instance, he composed the beautiful antiphons for Otmar, and the hymn *Dread Ruler of the World Everlasting* and some hymns welcoming rulers, and the hymn about a virgin who was not a martyr, that is, the *Hymn to the Blessed Virgin.* When he was composing the latter hymn, he hesitated for quite a long time over a word to fit the meter and turned to Dean Ekkehard to see what he would supply; Ekkehard said at once, "The sheep comes to the goat to ask for wool," but he nonetheless advised Notker to put in the word "faltering."

I could not omit this story in view of its value as an ex- 2
ample of the humility and love of our fathers. As a healer Notker also often achieved wonderful and astonishing results, because he was exceptionally well versed in medical aphorisms, drugs, antidotes, and Hippocrates's diagnostics. This became evident in the case of Duke Henry's urine, when the duke attempted to deceive him with a sly trick. He sent Notker the urine of a chambermaid instead of his own for examination: Notker said, "God is now about to perform a miracle and a prodigy, because it is unheard of for a man to
give birth from a womb. Around thirty days from now this 3
duke will give birth to a son and put him to his breast." Caught out and embarrassed, the duke sent gifts to the man of God so that Notker would not refuse to treat him, for it was for this reason that Notker had been brought there.

putatam medicus Sanctigallensis supplicem sibi reduxit in
gratiam. Nam ut prognosticus ille praedixerat, ipsa partum
4 dederat. Sed et episcopo nostro Kaminoldo cum fluorem
narium diuturnum adductus citissime sedaret, odorato cruore variolam morbum die ei tertia praedixit futurum. Sed pustulas ille die dicta sibi erumpentes cum eum restringere peteret: "Enimvero," ait, "facere potero; sed nolo, quia necis tuae reus carinas tot ferre non potero, quia, si restrinxero, morti te trado." Pustulasque tandem eruptas ita in brevi sanaverat, ut nec saltem de una fuerit signabilis. Haec pauca de plurimis, quae scriptor pictor medicus egit, quoniam iterum nobis narrandus occurret, hic libasse sufficiat.

124. De Keraldo autem, non minoris materiae viro, quoniam plura non vacat, item quaedam, ut, in quantis columnis locus Galli crebro steterit, pateat, interseram. Erat a subdiaconatus sui principio scholarum semper ille magister. Presbyter vero factus, praedicator altissime apertus, etiam episcopis aliquando praesentibus et iubendo cedentibus populo declamator et, ut apostolus tales vocat, propheta erat mellitissimus. Unde, ut antiquitus loci nostri mos statutus erat, publicus populo nostro etiam presbyter positus est, ut in ecclesia sancti Otmari omnibus, qui inter Coldaham

The woman, previously deemed a virgin, pleaded with Notker, and the Saint Gall physician restored her to favor. She gave birth, just as the diagnostician had predicted. Also, 4
when Notker was brought to our bishop Kaminold and very quickly alleviated the bishop's chronic case of runny nose, he predicted by smelling the bishop's blood that on the third day he would be sick with smallpox. When pustules broke out on the day Notker had predicted, and the bishop asked Notker to put a stop to them, Notker said: "I could certainly do that; but I do not want to because I would be guilty of murdering you and I would not be able to stand all the penances, because if I stop the pustules from coming, I would condemn you to death." When the pustules finally burst open, Notker quickly cured them so well that not a single pockmark remained. These few examples of his many achievements as a scribe, artist, and physician will suffice for now to give you an idea of his skills, because we will meet him again in our story.

124. Concerning Gerald, a man of no lesser substance, I will also add one story—because I do not have time for more—to make clear what great pillars constantly supported the monastery of Saint Gall. He always served as schoolmaster from the beginning of his subdiaconate. After becoming priest, he was a preacher of remarkable clarity, sometimes addressing the people even in the presence of the bishops and at their command, when they yielded this task to him, and, as the apostle called such men, he was a prophet of honeyed sweetness. As a result, in accordance with a long-established custom of our monastery, he was also appointed public priest for our people so that in the church of Saint Otmar serving all those who live between

et Sint-tria-unum fluvios degunt, synodica quaeque praeter
2 disiunctiones coniugum pro episcopo faceret. Cuius rei privilegia cum a Iohanne papa cum Salomone episcopo nec non Karolo astipulante habeamus, invidi monachis nunc temporis episcopi vix nobis et nostris halitum relinquentes, ut Salustii verbis utar, *nil* nobis *reliqui facere* moliuntur. Ministrosque odii et invidiae iniustaeque potentiae Holophernicos asciscunt sibi archipresbyteros, qui animas hominum carissime appretiatas vendant, feminas nudatas aquis immergi impudicis oculis curiosi perspiciant aut grandi se pretio redimere cogant. Hos tales quomodo faucibus strangulati vix evaserimus, Purchardum secundum dicturi, plenius scribere habebimus.

125. At Kerholdus—ut ad capacissimum sancti spiritus dolium revertamur—in his et aliis mille virtutibus animo et corpore diu attritus longoque senio fessus, sed non defessus, cum iam plebis sibi commissae fides in eum esset certissima, si quem corpore dolentem benedicens tangeret, alleviaret, confessione eis quadam die data et remissione petita, mox se in lectum colligere velle et in Christo emori flens pronuntiabat, et missionem ab ipsis sollicite postulans, *in die Domini* semet utrimque videndos spem se certam habere spon-
2 debat. Exutus vero alba et revestitus clamoreque familiae usque cancellos Galli prosecutus, domum infirmorum per se, nemine fultus multisque, quid facere vellet, mirantibus

the rivers Goldach and Sint-tria-unum, he would perform all
synodal duties as a bishop, except for the dissolution of mar-
riages. Although we received privileges concerning this mat- 2
ter from Pope John, with confirmation from Bishop Salomo
and also Charles, the bishops of our time, envious of monks,
barely allow us and our people to draw breath and, to use the
words of Sallust, they contrive to ensure that there is *nothing
left* for us *to do.* They attach to themselves archpriests, men
like Holofernes, servants filled with hatred, envy, and unjust
power, who set a high price on people's souls and sell them
accordingly, and with unchaste eyes pruriently gaze at naked
women immersed in water or force them to redeem themselves at a high price. How we were caught up in the jaws of
such men and barely escaped I will relate when I talk about
Burchard the second.

125. As for Gerald—to return to this most capacious vessel of the Holy Spirit—he was worn out, body and soul, by
his daily practice of these and a thousand other virtues. He
was also wearied by a prolonged old age but not to the point
of utter prostration, since the people entrusted to his care
had unshakable faith in him, believing that if he blessed and
touched someone suffering bodily pain, he could bring them
relief. One day, after making his confession to them and asking forgiveness, he tearfully announced a little later that he
wished to take to his bed and die in Christ, and anxiously
asked their permission to leave, declaring that he firmly expected to see them again *on the day of the Lord.* He took off 2
his alb and dressed again, and amid cries from all monastic
household he walked up to the altar screen of Saint Gall and
entered the house of the sick on his own, supported by no
one, while many wondered what he intended to do. There,

introiit. Ibi ergo parumper residens, substerni sibi faenum
terra nuda rogabat superque cilicium. In quo se quasi *nihil
mali passus* reponens, fratres omnes vocari rogabat. Quos
cum adesse videret, salutatis omnibus surrexit, et stans et
erumpens in lacrimas: “Video,” ait, “domini et fratres mei,
vocationem meam, quam semper reus ego timebam, adesse.
3 Ideoque, quia pium Deum nostrum confidens spero, confessione coram vobis data securus abibo.” Tandemque assensu
omnium confessus indulgentiam recepit. Osculatisque per
singula omnibus, a patribus, ubi doleret, requisitus, respondit: “In pectore et praecordiis.” Et: “Utinam,” inquit, “Notkerus meus adesset!”—erat enim ille tunc pro remediis in
4 aula regia—et residens requiescere se velle ait. At fratrum
singuli quietem illi aeternam precantes, praeter custodes illi
datos et quos ille rogabat psalmicanos, domo cesserant. Ipse
autem quasi nihil adhuc quidem passus: “Sancte Iohannes
evangelista,” ait, “dilecte Domini, recipe me!” Et capitium
capiti imponens brachialeque rocci subter caput revolvens,
super illud nobile stratum se recollegit. Et paulisper, ut
sperabant, dormiens, subito: “Mi domine, bene venias,” ait.
5 At illi disloqui eum, ut aegroti solent, putantes, unus tandem
ex illis: “Videamus, quid agat,” ait; “enimvero, quisquis fuerit, aliquem salutavit.” Accedentes vero quantocius ad illum,
oculis transversis labiisque albidulis vident praemortuum.
Signumque cursim pulsantes fratres advocant. Quibus quam
concite circa se astantibus, per semet ipsum manus pedes-

he sat down for a little while and then asked that some hay
be strewn for him on the bare ground, covered by a hair
shirt. He reclined on it, as if he had *suffered no harm,* and
asked that all the brothers be summoned. When he saw that
they were present, he greeted them all, got up, stood upright, and bursting into tears, said: "I see, my lords and
brothers, that my summons, which I, sinner that I am, always feared, has come. Since I am confident in my expec- 3
tation that our God will be merciful, I will make my confession before you and depart unafraid." At last, with
everybody's consent, he confessed and received absolution.
After he kissed them all, one by one, the fathers asked him
where it hurt, and he replied: "In my chest and my heart."
He also said: "If only my dear Notker were here!"—Notker
was then at the royal court providing treatment—and, sitting down again, he said he wanted to rest. Each of the 4
brothers prayed for his eternal rest and left the house, except those who were to look after him and the psalm singers
that he asked for. He said, apparently not yet suffering any
pain: "Saint John the Evangelist, beloved of God, receive
me!" And he covered his head with his hood, rolled up the
sleeves of his habit to his armpits, and lay back on that noble
bed. When he had slept a little, as they had expected, he
suddenly said: "Welcome, my Lord!" They thought he was 5
babbling, as often happens with the sick, until finally one of
them said: "Let us see what he is doing; he did greet someone, whoever it may have been." After they ran up to him as
quickly as they could, they saw that he was on the brink
of death, his eyes averted and lips white. They hastily rang
the bell and summoned the brothers. When the monks had
gathered around him as quickly as possible, he stretched out

qunue extendens, omnes apertis oculis arrisit tandemque quasi excusso risu cachinnulans exspiravit.

6 Tali exitu homine virtutum finito, erant qui dicerent: "Iohannes eum <vocavit>, cuius, dum viveret, assertor erat assiduus in virginitate et in omni integritate; atque ideo absque dolore sicut ille assumptus est, quia ipsi se obiens commisit et se visitantem in obitu salutavit." Sepultusque est non longe a Notkero Balbulo, magistro quondam suo sibique amicissimo.

126. De Waltone decano nec non et Chuniberto Altaha abbate grandia siquidem, quamvis non his similia, si vacaret, dicere poteramus. Quorum prior, quod eius officii quidem erat, memorabilem se posteris in secessus nostri structura difficillima fecerat. Non solum autem in hoc, sed et in aliis multis magnitudinem suam ostendit operibus. Nam Saracenos, quorum natura est in montibus multum valere, cum e parte australi nos et nostros adeo infestarent suis temporibus, ut alpes nostras et montes obtinentes, etiam fratribus crucem circa urbem sequentibus tela proximo iacerent militumque abbatis manu, ubi laterent, investigari non possent,
2 ipse quadam nocte cum familiae audacioribus sibi, ubi laterent, proditos invasit dormientesque nactos; lanceis et falcibus, securibus quoque quibusdam trucidatis, quibusdam quoque captis, ceteros fuga lapsos insequi inane duxit, cum

his arms and legs without assistance, smiled at them all with his eyes open, and finally, as if chuckling with forced laughter, breathed his last breath.

After the virtuous man died in this manner, there were 6
some who said: "John called him, because while he was alive he was John's constant champion thanks to his virginity and overall rectitude, and it was because he had committed himself to John as he was dying, and had greeted John who visited him on his deathbed that, like John, he was taken painlessly." He was buried not far away from Notker the Stammerer, his former teacher and his greatest friend.

126. If there were time, I could tell you great things about Waldo, the dean, and also about Cunibert, the abbot of Niederaltaich, great things indeed, though not similar to those just described. The former became memorable to posterity because he accomplished the difficult task, for which his office was responsible, of building our latrine. Yet it was not only in this that he showed his greatness, but in many other achievements also. For in his day the Saracens, whose nature it is to thrive in the mountains, attacked us and our people so persistently from the south that they came to occupy our hill pastures and mountains, even hurling missiles from close range at the procession of the brothers as they followed the cross around the fortress, while the abbot's
knights could not find where they were hiding. One night, 2
after their hiding place had been revealed to him, Waldo, together with the more daring among his knights, found the Saracens and attacked them as they slept. Some they slaughtered with lances, scythes, and axes, others they captured, while others slipped away in flight and Waldo thought it pointless to pursue them because they ran faster than goats

capris fugatiores montes percurrerint. Quos autem ceperat, vinctos in monasterium ante se egerat. Qui tamen ipsi manducare nec bibere volentes omnes perierant. Haec de tragoedia eius temporis et de Waltonis magnitudine tetigisse sufficiat. Nam si miseriam omnem, quam nostrates a Saracenis sunt passi, percurrerem, volumen efficerem.

127. At Chunibertus, si extrema illum infortunia sinerent, inter omnes esset spectaculo dignus. Ipse enim vir ille erat, cui generis nobilitatem plurima, quae in illum Deus congesserat, dona quam maxime nobilitabant, scriptor directissimus, doctor summe planus, pictor ita decorus, ut in laquearis exterioris sancti Galli ecclesiae circulo videre est. Hic ab Henrico duce Salzpurgis doctrinis studere ab Kraloo postulatus, post annos aliquot abbatiam Altaha promeruit. Ubi cum quot annos praeesset, taedio, quod sancti Galli claustro tam diu careret, corde tactus, abbatiam reliquit claustrum-
2 que suum aegre exspectatus revisit. Fit itaque in annum decanus noster. Et quia quot annis more Romano officia apud nos mutari solent, propter tutelam cognatorum suorum, qui ibi abundabant, coactus in Priscouve constituitur praepositus. Ubi cum multa erronea ad unguem corrigeret, monasterium aliquando cum reverti parasset, circa villam Wilaham cum Kerhardo, post abbate, ut psalterii, quod reliquum erat, iam pransus absolveret, praeivit. Ministri autem, morum eius non ignari, sibimet a longe in equis curracibus luserant,

through the mountains. Those he had captured he drove to the monastery in chains in front of his men. However, they refused to eat or drink and they all died. Let this brief account of the tragic events of that time and of Waldo's greatness suffice. If I were to mention all the suffering inflicted by the Saracens upon our people, I would fill a volume.

127. Among all the others Cunibert would merit very high
regard, if only the misfortunes of his last days allowed him
that. He was the sort of man in whom noble birth had been
enhanced to the highest possible degree by the many gifts
that God had lavished upon him: he was a very accurate
scribe, a teacher of the most remarkable clarity, and a beautiful painter, as one can see in the outer circular ceiling panel
in the church of Saint Gall. At Duke Henry's request Craloh
sent him to Salzburg to pursue teaching, and in a few years
he earned the abbacy of Niederaltaich. After ruling the abbey for several years, he felt weary in his heart because he
had been absent from the monastery of Saint Gall for so
long, and he left the abbacy and returned to his monastery,
where he was eagerly awaited. So he became our dean for a 2
year. Because offices at our monastery are usually changed
annually according to the Roman custom, he was forced to
become provost in Breisgau, to protect his numerous relatives who lived there. While he was correcting with fine pre-
cision many erroneous practices found there and had made
preparations to return to his monastery at some point, in
the vicinity of the estate called Wilaha, he rode ahead of his
company together with Gerhard, later the abbot, to finish
reciting what remained of the psalter right after breakfast.
Meanwhile, the attendants, well aware of his ways, kept
their distance as they frolicked around on their fast horses,

tandemque post illum accelerabant. Ambulator autem, cui ipse insederat, alacritatem equorum post se sentiens, caput concutiens exsultare cepit. Atque ille, cum eum urgueret, ne curreret, exsiliens gravem senio et corpore virum deiecerat.
3 Erat autem in ore eius versus ille, ut aiebant: *Venientes autem venient cum exsultatione.* Quod "exsultatione" clamose, timore casus perculsus, ultimum dixit. Corruens autem et quam cito resurgens, Gerhardus illum, cum iterum recideret, equo descendens retinuit et caput eius residens in sinum suum reclinavit. Sicque, viris pro aqua currentibus, spiritum ex alto resumens obiit. Hic finis Cuniberti, statura proceri et canitie venerandi et, ut plurimis visum est, hominis sanctissimi. Corpus vero eius allatum monasterio, plurimis lacrimis sepultus est in coemeterio.

4 Necesse est autem, ut ordine praepostera sint, quae dicimus, quia quae simul facta sunt, simul dici non possunt. Propterea, unde digressi sumus, redeamus.

128. Dirigitur Notkerus electus cum litteris Purchardi Ottonibus Spiram, comitibus novem de patribus plerisque canitie venerandis ipse decimus, sed regibus non adeo ut praecessor quondam eius erat acceptus. Affuit illis advenientibus cito Ekkehart, nihil rerum, priusquam aderant, praescius. Multumque anxius, quoniam Sandrat, quem prius diximus, tunc aderat et obloquia quaedam iterum in nos

eventually picking up speed behind him. The ambling horse that he was riding, sensing the speed of the horses behind him, began jumping around and tossing his head. When Cunibert reined him in to stop him from running away, the horse leaped up and threw off his rider, burdened with old
age and corpulence. They say that the following verse of the 3
Psalms was on his lips: *Those who come will come with joy.* That word, "joy," was his last word, which he said very loudly, shaken by fear of falling. But it was Gerhard who fell to the ground and got up as quickly as possible, then dismounted and caught Cunibert as he was collapsing again, and sat down and laid Cunibert's head in his lap. In this position, while his men ran to get water, Cunibert drew a deep breath and died. Such was the end of Cunibert, a man of tall stature and venerable old age, deemed by many to be a very holy man. His body was carried to the monastery and buried in the cemetery amid many tears.

Now it is necessary to talk about certain things out of 4
chronological order, because events that happen simultaneously cannot be simultaneously described. For this reason let me return to the point from which I have digressed.

128. Notker, the abbot-elect, was sent to Speyer with a letter from Burchard to the Ottos with nine companions chosen from among the fathers, mostly venerable gray-haired men, but he was not as warmly welcomed by the kings as his predecessor had once been. Ekkehard, who had known nothing about the state of affairs before they arrived, quickly joined them after their arrival. He was very anxious because Sandrat, whom I mentioned earlier, was present at the court at that time and, as Ekkehard had found out, was once again whispering disparaging things about us to the

susurrari regibus sciverat, animo fluctuabat. Consilio tamen in brevi habito litteras sumpsit ad se regibus hora apta praesentandas. At Otto iunior casu cum Ottone duce amplexu
2 mutuo non procul steterat. Et Otto dux regi Rupertum subdecanum, gravitatis monachum, videns: "Numquam," ait, "leporem ille curriculo capiet." At ipse id audiens, inclinatus gratias egit. Et Otto rex: "Vae tibi misero!" ait, "Ipse enim audivit." Et Ekkehardo approximanti Otto rex: "Qui sunt," inquit, "magister, patres illi?" "Sanctigallenses," ille ait, "domine mi, sunt et hodie auxilio tuo iuvandi." Cumque pedes amborum ipsi peterent, Ekkehardus causam eorum in brevi perorat. Et rex: "*Deus,*" ait, "*in cuius manu corda sunt regum, faciat vobis* leonem meum mitem et *placabilem!*" Sic enim patrem vocabat.

3 Et dimissis illis magistro in aurem, quis illorum electus sit, dicit. "Quem prae se ferebant, ipse est." Et ille: "Illum delicatum iuvenem?" ait. "Enimvero, ut pater meus ad hoc consentiat, ut ipse eum nosti, non puto. Talibus viris canitie venerandis sancto Gallo habundantibus, iuvenem puellae similem nobis quidem mittere! Convenite adhuc," ait, "et te, qui homines nosti, consiliante graviorem eligite! Aliter enim
4 vos, ut petitis, leoni meo sistere non audeo." "Privilegium," Ekkehardus ait, "patribus a Karolo datum et per vos solidatum nos paucos quemquam eligere non patitur. Praeterea de litteris abbatis nostri, fratris tui, quid fiet? Nam Nokeri medici, tibi et patri tuo semper bene meriti et dilecti, ex sorore

kings, and Ekkehard did not know what to do. Nevertheless, after they held a brief discussion Ekkehard took the letter into his own hands to present it to the kings at a suitable moment. It chanced that Otto the Younger stood close to
Ekkehard, sharing a warm embrace with Duke Otto. When 2
he saw Subdean Rupert, a monk of considerable weight, Duke Otto said to the king: "Never will that man catch a hare in a race." Hearing this, Rupert bowed and gave thanks. King Otto II said: "Woe to you, wretch—he heard it!" Otto the king said to Ekkehard as he approached: "Master, who are those fathers?" "They belong to Saint Gall, my lord," Ekkehard said, "and they need your help today." When they sank down at the feet of both men, Ekkehard briefly pleaded their case. The king said: "May *God who holds in his hand the hearts of kings make* my lion *be gentle to you* and treat you with mercy!" This was what he called his father.

After they were allowed to leave, the king whispered in 3
the ear of his teacher, asking which of the monks had been elected abbot, Ekkehard answered: "It is the man who knelt in front of the others." The king said: "That tender young man? I do not think my father will agree to this—you know him yourself. With so many men of venerable old age that Saint Gall has—to send us a youth who looks like a girl! Have another assembly," he said, "and on your advice, since you know the men, elect someone of more substance! Otherwise I do not dare to set you before my lion, as you ask."
Ekkehard said, "The privilege given to the fathers by Charles 4
and confirmed by you does not allow a few of us to elect anyone. Besides, what about the letter written by our abbot, your brother? The man is a nephew of Notker the Physician, that very worthy man who is dear to you and your father, the

nepos et ab Ekkehardo, avunculo meo, mecum nutritus et doctus, *virtutibus patriis* semper assueverat; et nisi virtutum virum nossent, numquam eum frater tuus et avunculus meus cum ceteris, ut ipse homines nosti, dominum eligerent."

129. Audito rex rationis tantae responso, maxime autem de Nokero, mitescere tandem cepit; litteras tamen neque ipsos postea patri sisti, priusquam ipse illum praestrueret et animo eius explorato ad alloquia eos leonis sui praepararet, placere sibi aiebat. Vocatis tandem ipsis, bonae spei esse monuit et nocte precibus invigilare, ut, quoniam invidos haberent, Deus eos iuvaret. Monet deinde Ekkehardum mensa cenae levata cum litteris sibi commode non deesse. Qua le-
2 vata patris et matris secretum postulat alloquium. Matre autem de mensa sua veniente, ad ostium occurrens, ut sancto Gallo faveret, Ekkehardus in aurem rogat. Audiverat enim a dicentibus Sandratum adventum monachorum sancti Galli magno Ottoni nec non et omnem causam eorum clam et sinistrorsum dixisse et sui memorem fore pedibus petitis rogasse. Quod Ottoni etiam suo silenter patre assidente paucis nudat.

3 Silentio tandem, omnibus aliis cenaculo eliminatis, facto Otto filius ait: "Sunt hic, domine mi, nuntii filii tui, quondam

son of his sister, and because he was raised and educated along with me by my uncle Ekkehard, he grew accustomed to *the virtues of the fathers;* if they had not known him to be a man of virtue, your brother and my uncle—you know the men yourself—would never have elected him along with the rest as their master."

129. After hearing such a reasonable response, especially the part concerning Notker, the king eventually began to soften; nevertheless, he said that he would not like to present either their letter or themselves to his father before he had personally laid the groundwork and tested the king's mood and then prepared them for an audience with his lion. When they were finally summoned, he told them to have hope and to spend the night in vigil and prayer so that God might help them because they had enemies who were envious of them. Then he advised Ekkehard to stay close to him with the letter once the evening meal had been cleared away. When dinner was cleared away, the king requested a secret
audience with his father and mother. When the mother was 2
walking from the table, Ekkehard ran to meet her at the door and, whispering in her ear, beseeched her to show favor to Saint Gall. He had heard people say that Sandrat had told Otto the Great, in secret and giving it a sinister significance, about the arrival of Saint Gall's monks, as well as about their entire case, and had fallen at the king's feet and beseeched the king to remember him. Ekkehard also quietly communicated this in a few words to his dear Otto while the father sat nearby in silence.

Finally, when all the others had been cleared from the 3
dining hall and it had become quiet, Otto the son said: "My lord, present here are the envoys from your son, the former

abbatis Purchardi, Dei iussu diu infirmi. Quid autem postulent, experiri habebis." "Scio," ait pater, "eos matutinos quidem affuisse; sed quare se a meo conspectu celaverint, nescio. Sunt meorum quidam, qui eos non simpliciter venisse asserant: quoniam *qui ambulat simpliciter, ambulat confidenter.*" Et ille: "Malo suo, pater," ait, "valeant odibiles illi, qui te acu-
4 tiis suis a bono avertere moliuntur." Et regina: "Vide," ait, "domine semper amande, ne talibus, quales filius tuus notat, inconsulte et nimium assenseris! Nam et prius Dei servos illos imperialiter quidem impetitos, sicut ab ipsis quibusdam, quos misimus, audivi, sine causa molestavimus." Et Otto: "Ecce, pater, ut ipse illos nosti, assunt ex eis viri venerandi a filio tuo paene praemortuo missi, quos, cum me quidem, ut eos tibi sisterem, praepeterent, paucis cum eis locutus in crastinum ipse viros distuli; et ideo mentiti sunt, qui tibi dixerant duplici illos animo quicquam machinari. Nam et litteras, quas tibi missas manu habebant, ego recepi, et ecce ipsas; quas cum audiveris, si clandestini assunt, videbis."

130. Et a patre sigillum recludere iussus, ipsi illud—nam sancti Galli semifacies erat—in manum dabat. Quod ille sollicite intuitus: "Filii mei, pauperis Domini, imaginem," ait, "esse putavi. Sed tu quidem, quid litterae velint, insinua!" Haec verba: "Summae post Deum maiestatis dominis meis regnum aeternum Purchardus abbas semivivus. Annis meis et senio finem mihi vitae in ianuis habentibus, ne pastor

abbot Burchard, who, by the will of God, has been ailing for
a long time. You can find out what they are asking." "I know,"
his father said, "that they were here in the morning; but I
don't know why they have stayed hidden from my sight.
There are some among my associates who claim that the
monks have not come without guile because *he who walks*
without guile walks with confidence." Otto the son said: "May
those hateful men, father, who strive by their intrigues to di-
vert you from what is good bring about their own destruction." The queen said: "See to it, my ever-beloved lord, that 4
you do not rashly pay too much attention to the men of the
sort your son describes! We also disturbed those servants of
God in the past without cause, accusing them on imperial
authority, as I have heard from the very same men whom we
sent." Otto said: "Here they are, father, you know them
yourself, venerable men from their number sent by your son,
who is now close to death. They asked me earlier to present
them to you, and after briefly talking with them I myself put
them off until the next day. So the people who told you that
these monks were plotting something with deceitful intent
lied. I also took the letter addressed to you that they had in
their hands, and here it is; once you have heard its content,
you will see if they are being underhanded."

130. Told by his father to break open the seal—it depicted Saint Gall in profile—Otto put it in his father's hand. The father carefully examined it and said: "I thought it was an image of my son, a poor man of God. But explain to us what is the purpose of the letter!" The letter included the following words: "To my lords, the highest in majesty after God, Abbot Burchard, half-alive, wishes the eternal kingdom. Since my advanced age holds the end of my life at the door

oves, pater filios improvisos relinquam, domini mei, privile-
2 gium gratiae vestrae me sollicitavit. Misi itaque vobis, fiduciam vestri habens, dilectum meum mihi adhuc vivo sufficiendum, a viris virtutum optimis moribus assuefactum, sancto Gallo, ut confido, vobisque placiturum. Misi autem vobis et testes meos ter tres idoneos, qui eum coram vobis, ferula mea reddita et indulgentia mihi petita, singuli eligant. Valeat regnum vestrum et imperium in Domino dominorum. Amen."

3 Perlecta epistola Otto eam patri et matri *fidus interpres* Saxonice reponens insinuavit et, ut petita facerent amore eius, quem posthac visuri non sint, sollicite rogavit. Et Ekkehardus: "Meminere vos, domini, Nokeri medici, eius, qui eligendus est, avunculi! Sed et Ekkehardi vestri, qui eum,
4 nisi idoneus esset, vobis dirigi numquam consentiret." Tandem post verba multa Otto pater: "Cras," ait, "diluculo appareant in conspectu meo, ut, illo cum ceteris viso, decernam, quid faciam." Et Otto filius: "*Homo,*" inquit, "*videt in facie, Deus in corde.* Neque enim ille ita," ait, "ut magister meus est aspectabilis neque, ut Sandratus vester se exhibet, despectibilis." Et ille: "Utinam, fili mi," ait, "omnes monachi nostri Sandrati animum gererent!" At ille monitu Ekkehardi, ne patrem commoveret, conticuit. Sicque pater colloquium diremit.

for me, the privilege of your grace has caused me concern, my lords, to ensure that as a shepherd I not leave my sheep, and as a father, I not leave my sons, unprovided for. Accord- 2
ingly, with full confidence in you, I have sent you my beloved son, to be appointed to stand in for me while I am still alive; the highest moral standards have been ingrained in him by men of virtue and I believe that he will be pleasing to Saint Gall and to you. I have also sent to you nine appropriate witnesses, each of whom will elect him in your presence after returning my staff and asking forgiveness on my behalf. May your kingdom and your empire thrive in the Lord of Lords. Amen."

After the letter had been read through, Otto, a *faithful* 3
translator, by rendering it into Saxon related its contents to his father and mother, and urgently beseeched them to do what he requested out of love for the man whom they would never see again. Ekkehard said: "Remember, my lords, Notker the Physician, the uncle of the man who is to be elected! Remember also your Ekkehard, who would never have agreed that he should be sent to you if he were not suitable." Finally, after much discussion, Otto the father said: "Tomor- 4
row at dawn let them appear in my sight, so that I can see him together with the others and decide what to do." Otto the son said: "*Man looks at the outward appearance, but God sees in the heart.* He is neither as pleasing to look at as my teacher nor as despicable as your Sandrat shows himself to be." The father said: "I wish, my son, that all our monks had Sandrat's heart!" Following Ekkehard's warning not to make his father angry, the son said nothing. On this note the father broke off the meeting.

131. Ekkehardus autem, notularum peritissimus, paene omnia haec eisdem notavit in tabula verbis. Quibus Otto suus postea, ut ipse nobis retulit, multum delectatus est sibi relectis, cum ipse praeter notulas nihil viderit in tabula.

2 At Ekkehardus suos, ubi hospitabantur, continuo petiit, optimaeque spei fore Ottonis sui eos verbis monuit. Cumque ab eo, si sui apud reges mentio aliqua fuerit, quaererent: "Magna," ait, "si mihi dicere liceat. *Sacramentum enim regis celare honorificum est.* Sed hoc tamen vobis pandere audeo, quia sollicitum apud patrem filium habuistis interpretem. Venturi enim estis in conspectum patris diluculo ipsius edicto. Sed eius horae et articuli fortunam committere habemus Deo."

3 Veniunt illi, precibus nocte muniti, in aulam matutini patre cum filio iam laudes, quarum Ekkehardus semper curam egerat, audientibus. At Palzone, loci episcopo, preces recitante Ekkehardus hostium pandit, ut videat, si adsint. Cumque eos conspiceret, restans paulisper Ottoni significavit. Pater autem eum egredi volentem chlamyde retinuit parumque subrisit. Et ille: "Numquam oculi perspicatiores,
4 leo mi, erant quam tui." "Enimvero ita et de leone legitur," Ekkehardus ait, "quia oculis apertis dormit." Et Palzo: "Unde sponsus," ait, "ecclesiae: *Ego dormio et cor meum vigilat.* Sed, domine pie, foris te exspectant, qui talia dormientes melius quam nos vigilantes sciant." "Unde tu illos," ait,

131. Ekkehard, who was very skilled at shorthand, recorded almost all of this, word for word, on a tablet. When he read these notes back to the king afterward, his dear friend Otto, as Ekkehard told me himself, was utterly delighted since he could see nothing on the tablet except squiggles.

Immediately thereafter Ekkehard went to find his broth- 2
ers at their lodgings and told them, in his dear Otto's words, to be of good cheer. When they asked him if there had been any mention of them in the conversation with the kings, Ekkehard said: "Yes, and an important one, if I may say so. *It is honorable to keep the secret of the king;* but nonetheless I venture to reveal this to you because you have acquired the son to act as your diligent mediator before the father. You are to appear in the father's presence, at his order, first thing tomorrow morning. But we must entrust the outcome of this hour and critical moment to God."

They arrived at the court in the morning, strengthened 3
with prayers during the night; the father and son were listening to the hymns of praise of which Ekkehard was always in charge. While Palzo, the local bishop, was reciting prayers, Ekkehard opened the door to see if the monks were there. When he saw them, he paused for a while and gave a signal to Otto, but when Otto sought to leave, his father held him back by his mantle and gave a little smile. The son said: "Never have there been eyes more penetrating than
yours, my lion." Ekkehard said: "Yes indeed, and this is what 4
is written about the lion, namely, that he sleeps with his eyes open." Palzo said: "This is why the bridegroom of the Church said: *I sleep but my heart stays awake.* However, my merciful lord, the men who know such things better asleep than we do awake are waiting for you outside." "How is it

"nosti? "Quare illos," ait, "non sciam, inter quos nutritus et, quae optima scio, sum doctus?" Et ille: "Scio," ait, "quia *pauper et mendicus* quondam circumiens terram, peram paupertatis tuae mendicando farciebas." "Non nego," ait; "sed quod illi dabant, in summis ponebam."

132. Tandem ille terribilis egressus cum Ottonem ducem
cum eis offendisset assistentem, arridens ei: "*Bôn mân*" habere Romanisce dixit. Dein et eos salvere ait. Ille etiam ac-
clinis cum ipsis gratias egit. Waninc vero primus ordine, si
loqui liceret, quaesiit. "Fidenter," Otto filius ait. "Abbas noster, domini, invalidus, multum in vobis, sed et in domina
nostra confisus, nos ad pietatem vestram transmisit et gra-
2 tiam, regnum vobis optans sempiternum et imperium. Causam autem adventus nostri quoniam litteris ab eo mandatam
attulimus, nos forsitan oportet, ut interim, dum legantur,
sileamus." "Litterarum," Otto pater ait, "molimina audivi;
sed eum, dum vivit, deponere nescio, si possit decere." Et
Cunibertus propius regibus accedens: "At nos, domini, modum forsitan optimum scimus, quo vos deceat efficere, quod
pater noster et nos eius iussu postulamus. Sit ille dominus
3 noster omni tempore, quo vivit. Quem subrogari sibi vult,
nihil capitale absque eius nutu faciat, tantummodo, quod
valde ille benivolentissimus formidat, *ne nos* moriens *orpha-
nos relinquat.* Est enim ille magnae spei vir, quem destinat."
Illoque conticente Otto pater: "Quem tamen mihi nepos
meus," inquit, "miserit, monstrate!" At pariter illi Nokerum

that you know them?" he asked. Palzo replied: "How can I not know the men among whom I was raised and taught the best things I know?" Otto said: "I know that you once roamed the earth as *a poor beggar* and filled your beggar's satchel by asking for alms." "I do not deny it," Palzo said, "but what they gave me I held dearest."

132. When that formidable man finally left and encountered Duke Otto standing near the monks, he smiled and
said to him "Good morning" in Romance. Then he also
greeted the monks. The duke bowed to give thanks, and so
did they. Waning, as the first in rank, asked if it would be
permitted for him to speak. "Speak with confidence," said
Otto the son. "My lords, our ailing abbot, who puts great
trust in both of you and also in our lady, has sent us to your
pious and gracious Majesties and wishes for your everlasting
royal and imperial reign. Since the reason for our coming 2
here was committed by him to the letter we brought, it is
perhaps appropriate that we keep silent until the letter is
read." "I have heard," Otto the father said, "the tenor of the
letter; but I do not know if it would be proper to depose him
while he still lives." Cunibert approached the kings and said:
"But perhaps, my lords, we know the best way for you fittingly to accomplish what our father and we, by his command, are requesting. Let him be our master for all the time
that he lives. Let the man he wants to succeed him do noth- 3
ing important without his approval—for the sole purpose of
preventing what that most benevolent man fears might happen, namely, that he would *leave us orphans* upon his death.
His intended successor is a man of great promise." When
the monk stopped talking, Otto the father said: "At least
show me the man my nephew has sent me!" At that moment

in ultimis, ut ordo eius erat, stantem produxerant. Et pater
in aurem filio: "Modo," ait, "quoniam viros disertos inter illos video, quid dicere velint, probare volo." Et Ekkehardus
audiens: "*Aliud,*" ait, "domine mi, *curato!* Absque responso
enim illos non invenies." Et ille: "Istene est, quem aetate
4 vobis quasi filium eligere mihi proponitis? O maturitatem
vestram et paene omnibus vobis sparsam canitiem, abbatem
vestrum inter tot canutos, qui sibi possit subrogari, invenire
non potuisse!" Et Rupertus, quem dixi, subdecanus: "Er-
rasti, domine mi rex," ait, "et oppido erras. Inter tot utique
Marias, *optimam partem* dudum *eligentes,* Martham nec unam
quidem, quae *sollicita sit* et *circa frequens ministerium satagere*
velit, nepos tuus invenire potuit. Ideoque talibus relictis ad
minorem aetatem descendit, et optimam, mihi crede, si eam
digneris, invenit." Ad haec pater: "Ut video, tu ipse dignior
illo."

133. Interea pater ad calceandum in caminatam ivit. Illis
autem, ut se exspectent, iussis ambo Ottones regem comi-
tantes, regina accita, ne tales viros diu detineret, rogant. At
ille in dubio se esse ait, quid faceret; neque illum adeo placere, quem attulerant. Regulam autem quoniam in loco illo
numquam stabilire potuerit, regularem eis aliquem ponere
velle, si suadeant, ait. Et continuo filius Sandratum eum
2 velle et Ekkehardus senserant. Ekkehardus autem ad pedes
procidens tacitus surrexit. Et pater: "Quid petis?" ait.

they brought forward Notker, who had been standing at the rear, as befitted his rank. Otto the father whispered in his son's ear: "Now that I see well-spoken men among them, I wish to put their intentions to the test." Hearing this, Ekkehard said: "*Don't you worry about it,* my lord! You will never find them at a loss for words." Then the father said: "Is this the man, young enough to be your son, whom you propose
to me for election? So much for your maturity and the gray 4
hair covering almost all of your heads, when your abbot could find no one to succeed him among so many gray-haired men!" Rupert the subdean, whom I mentioned, said: "You are mistaken, my lord king, completely mistaken. Among so many Marys, who surely *chose the best part* a while ago, your nephew could not find a single Martha who *would be eager and willing to perform assiduous service.* For this reason he passed them over and went a step down to those younger in age, and believe me, he has found the best Martha, if you deem her worthy." To this the father replied: "As I see it, you are worthier than he is."

133. Meanwhile the father went to his bedroom to put on his shoes. They were ordered to wait, and after sending for the queen, both Ottos who accompanied the king asked him not to keep these men waiting for long. The king said that he was not sure what he should do and that he did not much like the man they had brought. He also said that since he was never able to enforce the Rule at that monastery, he wished to put someone with expertise in the Rule over them, if they so recommended. Both Otto the son and Ekkehard immediately understood that he wanted Sandrat.
Ekkehard fell at the king's feet and rose without saying a 2
word. Otto the father said: "What are you asking for? To be

"Enimvero etiamsi tibimet abbatiam illam dari vis, absque
regulari aliquo comite ab Ottone non ibis." "Enimvero," ille
ait, "ea causa, summe Domini, pedes vestros hodie non petii
nec petam. Longe aliud est, quod vestra quidem omnium
trium vice, domini et domina, lacrimascere etiam potero,
quod cogitavi et cogito. Ubi est veritatis semper inconvulsa
3 firmitas etiam apud ethnicos regum? Dico enim privilegia a
Karolo sancto Gallo usque vos data, vestrum autem famulis
vestris prae omnibus semper potissimum; in quo nepos vester abbas, Ekkehardus vester et Nokerus cum ceteris spiritus sancti viris adeo confisi sunt et confidunt, ut neminem
alium, praeter quem vobis certissimi vestri miserant, exspectent abbatem." Ottones tandem rex et dux surgentes,
regina quoque supplice, privilegii memorem fore rogant. At
ille silens secumque deliberans tandemque quasi invitus, ac-
4 ciri homines iubet. Quibus coram stantibus: "Propter allatum," ait ille, "vestrum tunica, qualem Benedictus quidem
numquam induit, decorum, non statim vos, viri Dei, osculatus sum. Osculamini igitur!" Cumque eum praeire innu-
erent, ille vitato eo ceteros osculatus est: "Hora osculi eius
adhuc," inquit, "forte erit." Cumque plura de statu monasterii cum eis disceptasset et de moribus eorum et vita, quaesivit, si adesset, qui dixisse fertur: "Si calceus dividitur, nemo

sure, even if you wish that the abbey be given to you, you
will not go away from Otto without someone expert in the
Rule as a companion." "Truly, Lord's highest," Ekkehard
said, "this is not the reason why I fell down at your feet today or why I will do so in the future. What I have thought
about and am thinking about is something entirely different, something over which I could even weep, standing in
for the three of you, my lords and lady. Where is the forever
firm and unshaken compact of loyalty that exists even
among heathen kings? I mean the privileges granted to Saint 3
Gall, beginning with Charles and ending with yourselves,
especially your privilege granted to your servants, always
above all the others. Your nephew the abbot, your own
Ekkehard, and Notker, along with the other men of the
Holy Spirit, have trusted and trust in this privilege to such
an extent that they expect no one else to be their abbot but
the man whom your monks sent to you in full confidence."
Then both Ottos, the king and the duke, stood up and together with the queen they beseeched Otto the father to be
mindful of the privilege. He stayed silent, thinking to himself, and at last, as if unwillingly, he ordered the men to be
summoned. When they were standing before him, he said to 4
them: "Because of the man you have brought with you, who
is adorned with a tunic such as Benedict surely never wore, I
did not immediately kiss you, men of God. So kiss me!"
When they made a sign for Notker to go before them, Otto
avoided him and kissed the others. "The time for his kiss,"
he said, "will perhaps yet come." After discussing with them
at length the state of the monastery, their customs, and their
way of life, he asked if the man who, as rumor had it, said "If
you divide the shoe, no one will be shod," was among them.

5 calceatur." Risuque suis moto: "Ecce iterum Ruodmannum," Ekkehardus ait, "sentimus." Quo audito: "*Tu dixisti,*" rex ait. Tandemque ferula recepta, abbate coram se, ut moris est, electo, condicto quidem tali eam Nokero dedit, ut vivo abbate suo, sicut ipse vellet, illum curaret nihilque capitale absque eius nutu et Ekkehardi Nokerique consilio ageret. Et continuo: "Meus tandem eris," ait. Manibusque receptum osculatus est.

6 Moxque ille evangelio allato fidem iuravit. Dimissoque eo in ecclesiam ad *Te Deum laudamus,* milites Galli, qui aderant, reverso coram se accitos iurare iussit. Tandemque surgens in partem illum cum patribus sumpsit. Salutemque nepoti mandans et gratiam: regulaeque eos tenorem habere qui perspiciat eis in proximo missurum. Quem, quo gratantissime possent, edixit, ut receptum tractarent. Et re vera scirent, si sibi boni quid talis ille redicturus foret, in nullo se aerario suo parcere velle, quin eis, in quibuscumque possit, accommodaverit. Tandemque eis missione data, si quid ab oeconomis suis victualium exigere velint, abunde dari iussit.

134. Veniens domum Nokerus, gratanter ab omnibus susceptus Purchardique manu in sedem potentiae locatus, colloquium in capituli domo facere basilicam egreditur. Ibique

This elicited laughter from the brothers, and Ekkehard said: 5
"Here, once again we sense Ruodmann's influence." Hearing this, the king said: "*You have said it.*" At last, after the staff had been received and the abbot was elected in his presence, as is customary, the king gave the staff to Notker, on the condition that while the abbot was still alive, Notker would look after him according to his wishes and that he would do nothing important without Ekkehard's and the abbot's approval and without Notker's counsel. Right after that he said: "At last you will be mine." And taking him in his arms, he kissed him.

Next a Gospel book was brought in, and he swore an oath 6
of allegiance on it. Then he was sent off to the church to sing the hymn *We Praise You, God,* and when he returned Otto summoned the knights of Gall who were present there and ordered them to swear allegiance to Notker. Then he rose and took Notker aside, together with the fathers. He sent greetings and goodwill to his nephew, and he said that he intended soon to send someone to them to ensure that they were keeping to the tenor of the Rule. He decreed that this man should be welcomed by them and treated as graciously as possible. He also said that they should know this for a fact: if that man brought him a favorable report, he would spare no expense from his treasury to put whatever resources he could at their disposal. Finally, he gave them leave to go and ordered his stewards to give them ample provisions, should they ask for anything.

134. When Notker came home, he was joyfully welcomed by all and after being placed in the seat of power by Burchard's hand, he left the church to hold a meeting in the chapter house. There he was unanimously elected to the

in sancti Benedicti vicem ab omnibus electus, qualem se mox et semper, quoad vixit, exhibuerit, partim vix narrare, partim vix credere est. Hilaritas enim eius, quae ei quodam ingenita modo quasi naturalis inerat et, ut nunc temporis
2 est, deliciis ascribatur, partim dicenda non est. Propter quod invidi detrahere, desueti autem cum gemitu clamare nunc poterunt: *O tempora, O mores!* Enimvero cum ubertas, quae ultimos Purchardi annos nobilitabat, officinas omnes monasterii, Richero Ekkehardi monitis colligente, suppleverit, largifluo in omni hilaritate viro etiam suos Deus adeo frugibus oneraverat annos, ut regiminis sui meritis id quivis iure ascribere possit; ut cum Tullio meliori quidem ipse concinnare potuerit metro:

O fortunatam Galli me consule cellam!

3 Paucis utique ille post adventum suum diebus elapsis, decessore suo cum allectis *sanioris consilii* monente, Kebonis doctrinam paulisper quidem sopitam sollicite excitavit disciplinamque semper loco Galli inolitam recuperavit. In necessariis autem ubertate annua abundante fratres suos omnimodis procuravit. Vineas enim, postquam ab Hadewiga frustrati sunt, Richerus, homo sancto Gallo conquisitivus, decani sui monitis tum pretio, tum concambio tantas collegit, ut ubertate redundante, communi fratrum tum abbatis penu repletis, vasa vinaria non pauca in corte abbatis, deforis

role of Saint Benedict; the kind of man he showed himself to be shortly afterward and consistently throughout his life is, on the one hand, hard to relate and, on the other, hard to believe. For instance, the innate cheerfulness that was natural with him and that nowadays would be ascribed to a life of
self-indulgence can only be partly described. For this reason 2
the envious can disparage it and those who have not experienced it can groan and exclaim: "*Alas for the times, alas for the morals!*" In fact, when the abundance that distinguished Burchard's final years filled up all the utility rooms of the monastery with supplies that Richer collected following Ekkehard's advice, God so filled the years of this generous and joyful man with crops so rich that anyone could rightfully attribute this to the success of his rule, and he himself could have said in agreement with Tullius but in better meter:

O fortunate monastery of Gall, with me as a consul!

In any case, a few days after his arrival, on the advice of 3
his predecessor and select monks *of sounder judgment,* Notker carefully reinstated Kebo's precepts, which had been suspended for a little while, and restored the discipline that had always been deeply ingrained at Saint Gall. As for necessities, thanks to abundant annual harvests he fully provided for his brothers. After they had been frustrated in their hopes by Hadwig, Richer, a man who was good at acquiring property for Saint Gall, on his dean's advice accumulated so many vineyards, sometimes by purchase, sometimes by exchange, that, thanks to an overflowing abundance, the communal cellar of the brothers and that of the abbot were filled with provisions. Quite a few wine barrels were placed in the

quoque sub divo locarentur sub custodibus pluresque, qui alicuius momenti in loco erant, rubeum vinum, quamvis alias bonum, prae deliciis repudiarent.

4 Sed abbas, Cralohi de fratre quidem, Notkeri autem de sorore cum nepos esset, ingenita sibi ab utrisque severitate, partim quia sub Purchardo vacillante liberius vixerant, partim ut fama haec regum aures attingeret, fratres artius in claustro, qui eiusmodi erant, stringere curabat. Taliumque ille culpas palam saeculo factas foris claustrum interdum puniverat. Sed et plerumque in cortes longius sitas pane sordidiore aquaque alendos exsiliaverat. Neque sic quidem linguas detrahentium restrinxerat, cum et suimet patrui filium multa *scientia inflatum* Furintowam, alterum autem Nechirburc diu relegaverit. Pro quibus eum et aliis quidem similibus per nuntios et litteras cum reges regratiassent, non tamen apud eos secure tutus esse longo tempore poterat. Quod in loco suo post apparebit.

135. Talis ille cum in claustro fuisset, laicis quidem et militibus et famulis longe alius erat. Milites quidem, quando sibi absque fratribus esse vacabat, intus et foris mensae suae propositores et pincernas hebdomadarios habere solebat; disciplinanterque sibi ab eis ministrari volebat. Filios autem aliquorum, qui patrum beneficia habituri erant, ad se

abbot's court and also outside in open air under guard, and many of those who were of some importance at the monastery shunned red wine, despite its generally good quality, on the grounds that it was a delicacy.

But since the abbot was the nephew of both Craloh, on 4
his brother's side, and Notker, on his sister's side, he had a severity inherited from both sides. Partly because under the tottering Burchard the monks had lived with more freedom, and partly so that word might reach the kings' ears, he took measures to bind the brothers of that sort more closely to the monastery. Sometimes when the transgressions of these monks were committed publicly in the secular world he had them punished outside the monastery. However, he also commonly banished them to distant estates, to live on plain bread and water. But even so he could not restrain the tongues of detractors, even though he dispatched one of his own uncle's sons, who was *puffed up* with much *learning,* to Faurndau for a long time and another one to Neckarburg. Although the kings thanked him for these and other similar measures through messengers and in letters, he still could not be entirely free from worries regarding them for a long period of time. This will become evident later in its proper place.

135. While acting within the monastery in this way, he was very different with laypeople, knights, and dependents. So, when he spent leisure time without the brothers, he usually had fighting men as food servers and cupbearers serving at his table for a week at a time, inside and outside the monastery, and he liked to be attended by them in a disciplined fashion. As for some of the sons who were destined to inherit their fathers' land holdings, he took them in and gave

sumptos severe educaverat. Qui coram eo interdum nudi tabulis luserant. Sed et pro avibus captoriis et ceteris, quibus libertatis indoles exerceri decet, si deliquissent, a magistris exacti vapulabant. Quibus tamen missionis pro aetate temporibus armaturas ille et munera dabat. His similibusque, quae se frugi hominem vulgassent, operibus adeo se ille commendabat, ut ubique de eo *fama volaret,* sed et coram ipsis quoque regibus non aliter nisi "boni abbatis" praenomine memoraretur.

2 Hartmuoti vero constitutiones cum omnimodis servari sollicitus esset, loco plerumque cedebat, ut effusius fratres eo absente laetificarentur, dicens decano et symmystis suis: "Si eorum causa, quorum his temporibus in monachos sunt ora patula, inflexibilem rigorem semper tenuerimus, aut arcum regulae frangemus aut chordam eius, mihi," ait, "credite, rumpemus. Ideoque, quia id palam pati non audeo, clausis super se ostiis, ut aliquando remissius fratres mei agant, consulto carissimis loco cedere," ait, "volo. Videte tamen," ait, "obsecro vos, domini, in quibus reclinor, ne effuse effluant et ne laici hilaritati illorum omnino intersint, maxime autem servi, quorum nec iusiurandis credere saepius," ait, "didicimus."

136. Claustrum autem sancti Galli, quoniam locum hunc incidimus, ab antiqua patrum memoria tantae venerationi semper est habitum, ut nemini vel potentissimorum saeculi canonicorum seu laicorum introitus vel etiam introspectus

them a rigorous education. They sometimes played board games in his presence wearing only their undergarments. Also, when they failed at hunting with birds of prey and other pursuits that are fitting for freeborn youths to exercise, they were summoned and flogged by their teachers. However, when they came of age and it was time for them to leave, he gave them armor and gifts. By these and similar actions, which made him widely known as a prudent man, he earned so much praise that not only did *word* about him *fly* everywhere, but also in the kings' presence his name was accompanied by no other title than that of "the good abbot."

Since he took care to preserve Hartmut's statutes in ev- 2
ery way, the abbot very often left the monastery so that the brothers could enjoy themselves in a more relaxed manner in his absence, and he would say to the dean and to his confidants: "If we always stick to inflexible rules because of those who open their mouths wide these days to speak against the monks, believe me, we will either break the bow of the Rule or snap its string. Accordingly, since I do not venture to allow this openly, it is my intention to depart from the monastery so that my dear brothers can for a while act in a more relaxed manner once the doors close behind me. But I implore you, my lords, for I rely on you, see to it that they do not let themselves go too much and that laymen take absolutely no part in their merriment, especially not servants, whose oaths, as we often have learned, are not to be trusted."

136. The cloister of Saint Gall, ever since we happened on this place, has always, as far back as the fathers can remember, been held in such veneration that no one of even the most powerful people of the secular world, whether canons or laymen, has been allowed entry or even a glimpse inside.

eius licuerit. Unde et dicere habeo, quod ab religiosis huius temporis mihi quidem discredi scio. Vidi egomet ante tempora, quae a Gallis patimur, monachorum schismatis comites aliosque potentes, loci quoque milites, pro delectatione festis diebus crucem nobiscum per claustrum sequendi, iuvenes et senes, quosdam ad cingulum barbatos, monachicis indutos roccis, nobiscum, quaqua ivimus, ingredi. In refectorio quoque octo de illis, qui tamen emeriti videbantur, circa abbatem et decanos ad mensam monachico consedisse habitu in die paschae vidi.

2 Sed et ut risum de commessatorum ipsorum uno moveam: Bernhardus quidam, domi supra mensam silere non solitus, hic cum circa subdecanum Ruopertum mensuram purae potionis suae coram se habentem consedisset, ut domi solitus erat, statim bibere volens, eam manu sumpsit et impiger hausit. At ille sciens eum iucundum, silenter in aurem homini: "Regulariter nostrum est," ait. Et ille immemor, quo praestructus erat, silentii: "Si nostrum est, bibamus illud!" palam omnibus dixit. Continuoque sibi poculo oblato: "Ecce et istud nostrum est; bibamus igitur et ipsum!" Raucosus enim ludibundae vocis erat et morum, manu fortis quidem.

3 At Nokerus, annorum suorum ubertate quidem oppido abundus, plurima, quae nemo antecessorum eius umquam ausus sit, aggressus est et fecit. Muros enim ille super vallos ab Annone patruo coeptos cum interpositis turribus et

For this reason, I can tell you something that, I know, the religious of our time will not believe. Before the time of monastic schism that we endure because of the Gauls, I myself saw counts and other powerful men, as well as the monastery's fighting men, young and old, some with beards reaching down to their belts, dressed in monastic robes come into the monastery wherever we went; they did so for the enjoyment of following the cross on feast days along with us throughout the monastery. On Easter Day I also saw that eight of those men, apparently distinguished, had taken their seats at table in the refectory, dressed in monastic habits, next to the abbot and the deans.

Now, to make you laugh, here is a story about one of those 2
table companions. When a certain Bernhard, who was not used to keeping silent at the table at home, sat down near Rupert, the subdean who had his measure full of unmixed wine before him, Bernhard, who wanted to drink at once, as he habitually did at home, lifted the beaker with his hand and quickly drank it up. Rupert, who knew that Bernhard was a good-humored man, quietly whispered in his ear: "According to the Rule, this is ours." Bernhard, forgetting that he had been warned to keep silent, said for all to hear: "If it is ours, let us drink it!" A cup was immediately offered to him, and he said: "Here, this one is ours too; so let us drink it as well!" Coarse and good-natured in speech and manners, he was physically strong.

Notker, who had very rich resources thanks to his years 3
of plenty, undertook and accomplished a great many things that none of his predecessors had ever dared to do. He finished building the walls on the ramparts which his uncle Anno had begun with towers and gates at various points. In

portis perfecit. Ad has impensas ille plura profundens, universae familiae praebendariis, id est centum septuaginta viris, cum numquam ante se nisi avena pascerentur, pura de spelta dederat grana. Et quod amplius erat: spicarium ille novum, quia sic homo erat, solis feris et beluis avibusque domesticis et domesticatis iuxta fratrum condi fecit, quod et ipse iam fieri iussit magnificum.

4 Talibus bonis innatanti non tamen deerant interdum adversa inter prospera. Nam absque beneficiis multis, pro quibus artabatur a regibus, ut ea quasi dives opum et homo largissimus vocatus praestaret, quibus nollet, Ruodman eum iterum more solito apud aulicos accusat et, Ekkehardo nescio, spiritum eius *fetere fecerat* nihil minus sperantis.

137. Et ecce Ottonis, celato Ottone filio et Ekkehardo,
consilio Sandratus, litteras ferens, in ipsa sancti Galli vigilia
vespertina incepta templum deforis inter laicos est ingressus. Latere se posse, dum omnia perspiceret, quasi nemini
notus, credidit. Volebat enim, ut postea fassus est, diebus illis sanctis, hospitio sibimet qua posset petito, de mercato se
curare, ut, exploratis quae posset omnibus, astus suos tan-
2 dem acturus erumperet in medium liberius. Decanus autem
de Muorbac iuxta abbatem astans: "Ecce Sandrat," ait, "inter
illos, si umquam eum vidi, domine mi, vitabundus graditur.

addition to these expenses, he was extremely generous, giving grains of pure spelt to all the people fed by the monastic household, that is to 170 men, whereas before his time they had lived on nothing but oats. What was even more significant—because this is the kind of man he was—he had a new barn built next to that of the brethren, specifically for wild animals and livestock, as well as for domestic fowl and domesticated birds, and he ordered that it be a magnificent building.

Although swimming in such blessed waters, he did not 4
lack occasional bouts of adversity intermingled with his good fortune. Apart from the many benefices that he, as a rich and very generous man, was compelled by the kings to grant to people he did not want to give them to, Ruodmann in his usual manner accused him again in the presence of the courtiers and *made* his name *stink,* while Ekkehard was unaware of the situation and the abbot suspected nothing.

137. In keeping with Otto's plan that had been kept secret from Otto the son and Ekkehard, on the very eve of Saint Gall's feast day at the beginning of Vespers, there came Sandrat, bearing a letter and entering the church from the outside among the lay people. He thought that he could escape attention, unknown to anyone, while he observed everything. He wanted, as he admitted afterward, to find himself lodging for the feast days wherever he could and to get his food from the market in order to spy on everything that he
could and then come out into the open to put his cunning
plans into operation more readily. But the dean from Mur- 2
bach who was standing next to the abbot said: "Look, my lord, there's Sandrat, if ever I saw him, walking stealthily among those people. Yes—the one you are looking at, that is

Despectabilis ille enim, quem prospicis, ipse est." Et abbas: "Video illum. Sed si ipse est, mihi quidem despectabilis non est." Accitoque quodam fratrum, digito monstratum in chorum duci et locari iubet. Quem ille non sine rubore, vellet nollet, secutus, deprehensum se celare non potuit. *Oculi enim omnium intenti erant in illum.* Abbas autem post laudes egressus in auditorio eum salutat, mirarique inter cetera ait, quod tam palam promissus ita supervenerit occultus. Responsi ille dubius epistulam porrigit et: "Haec pro me loquatur," ait, "quam tibi magnus Otto quidem direxit." Acceptis ille litteris et osculo veneratis: "In turba hac festi nostri," ait, "legere domini litteras tutum non puto, ad quas otium ha-
3 bere volo. Sed pro hospitii tui commodis satagere portanarium volo, teque, quia forte lassus es, dies aliquot, ut post expeditior sis, in domo quietis pausare et quomodolibet per te curam tui gerere. Hospitibus vero et aliis in claustro et deforis me oportet providere. Quapropter et a refectorio," ait, "ne oculos tuos ibi quid laedat, hos dies, volo, ut abstineas." "Lecta epistula domini mei, quicquid libuerit, mihi," ait, "velim, loquamini, tantum ut in principio introitus nostri nihil regulae absonum inveniamur perpeti." His dictis discessum est; illeque in alta illa, quam Sindolfus sancto Nokero quondam clausit, locatur caminata.

138. Epistula, adventu regum et reginae Italiam vere proximo petentium intimato, Sandratum ad instituendam

that despicable man himself." The abbot said: "I see him. But if it is indeed him, he does not seem despicable to me." He summoned one of the brothers, pointed the man out to him, and gave orders for him to be brought to the choir and settled there. Sandrat, not without blushing, followed the brother willingly or not, unable to hide because he had been caught. *Everybody's eyes were fixed on him.* After the hymns of praise had been sung, the abbot went out and greeted him in the reception room, and he said among other things that he was surprised that someone so openly expected had arrived so secretly. Unsure how to respond, Sandrat offered him the letter and said: "Let this speak for me, the letter that Otto the Great has sent you." The abbot took the letter, showed his respect for it with a kiss, and said: "I do not think that it is safe to read my lord's letter now amid the commotion of
our festivities, since I want to have a quiet time for it. But I 3
will have the gatekeeper attend to your accommodation, and since you are perhaps tired, I want you to rest for a few days in our quiet house and to take care of yourself in any way you like so that you are more relaxed afterward. I have to attend to the guests and other business within the monastery and outside. Accordingly, during these days I want you to stay away from the refectory so that nothing there offends your eyes." Sandrat said: "After you have read my lord's letter, I would like you to tell me anything you wish so that at the beginning of our visitation we are not found to be enduring anything inconsistent with the Rule." With these words they parted, and Sandrat was put in the upper heated cell that Sindolf had once closed for the holy Notker.

138. The letter contained information about the arrival of the kings and queen the next spring when they would be making their way to Italy, and an order that Sandrat, who

regulam missum gratanter iubet recipi et, quoad ipsi in locum veniant, paterne tractari. At abbas accitis domno Purchardo decanoque cum patribus primo sancti Galli diei diluculo in colloquium, Sandratum bene mansionatum hospitaliter tractari decernunt usque post festum, eoque transacto integrius utrimque, *quid facto opus sit,* tractari quidem posse. Quod ubi per decanum Richerumque praepositum homini demandatum est, tanta asperitate accepit, ut, nisi quantocius sibi versari detur cum eis, quos docere venis-
2 set, mora omni postposita se minaretur abscedere. At Rikerus—decano, ne quicquam contra loqueretur, in aurem monente—proterviam tamen verborum eius ferre non valens: "Si *fidelis nuntius* es," ait, "responsum, pro quo missus es, exspectabis. Sin autem *in commisso fidelis* esse nolueris, *infidelis,*" inquit, "*si discedit,* ut ait apostolus, *discedat.*" Et decanus: "Nequaquam," ait; "enimvero litteris nobis regiis missum abire non patimur, sed et sub custodia, quoniam fugam minatur, volo, servetur." Moxque praepositus ministris accitis ait: "Omni honore et impensorum," inquit, "opulentia seniorem istum, domini regis nuntium, curate! Ipsum autem, ne abbate nostro inscio abeat, sollicite servate! Veniet dies tertius, et hominibus suis missionem quidem dabimus."

139. Talibus ille utriusque verbis adeo est consternatus, ut stupidus eis abeuntibus sedens diceret suis neminem

was sent to establish compliance with the Rule, was to be received graciously and treated like a father until the royals should arrive at the monastery. On Saint Gall's Day, first thing in the morning, the abbot summoned Lord Burchard and the dean together with the fathers for a meeting, and they decided to provide Sandrat with good lodgings and treat him hospitably until the end of the festivities and that after they were over both sides could more fully discuss *what needed to be done.* When Sandrat was informed of this decision by the dean and Provost Richer, he received the news with such acrimony that he threatened to depart on the spot unless he was allowed to engage immediately with those whom he had come to teach. Although the dean, whis- 2
pering in Richer's ear, urged him not to say anything in opposition to Sandrat, the provost, unable to stand Sandrat's impudent words, said: "If you are a *faithful envoy,* you will wait for the answer you have been sent to receive. But if you refuse to be *faithful to your mission,*" he said, "*if the one who lacks faith departs,* as the apostle said, *let him depart.*" The dean said: "No, we can certainly not allow someone sent to us with a royal letter to leave; rather, I want him kept under guard since he is threatening to flee." Soon after this the provost summoned the servants and said: "Take care of this senior monk, the envoy of our lord king, according him every honor and sparing no expense! At the same time watch him carefully so that he does not leave without our abbot's knowledge! Come the third day and we will give his men leave to go."

139. On hearing these words from the two men Sandrat was so dismayed that he sat there stunned as they walked away, and he said to his men that he would never have

cucullatum in regno se putasse fuisse, qui sibi contra votum suum tanta praesumeret respondere. Tandem, ut multa, quae audivi, praeteream, tertia die in consessum adducto abbas consulto est locutus: "Nobis, frater, quibus ad opus optimum, ut opto," ait, "directus es, prudentiorem te episcopis et abbatibus opus est fore, qui nos mira caritatis discretione nuperrime in regulam sancti Benedicti stabilitos,
2 ut volebant, reliquerant. A qua in aliquo nos cogere deviare, plerosque fratrum habeo, qui *immissionem per angelum malum, peccatis nostris* id *exigentibus,* planissime asserant. In quo uni tibi, quamvis sanctissimo homini, repentino motu obsequi, non excusse rationis, sed regalis esse scimus imperii." "Mihi," ait ille, "miror, si de immissione mea, si angelus malus sim, quisquam attribuat, cum sponte mea, credite mihi, non venerim neque ad vos neque ad ullos, quorum tamen, Deo laus, multos in regno correxeram. Apud quos, quoniam ab imperio missus sum, imperiose quidem egeram, neque deprecative quicquam, sicut et apud vos, ubi primo advenēram, facere, si permissus sim, volueram et, si adhuc hodie permittor, volo."

3 Et decanus abbati: "Age igitur, domine mi! Cedamus angelo imperii, et ordinem ei congruum dato, nobiscumque, ut, quomodo vivamus, videat, ubique versetur. Hebdomadae tamen indutias ante magistratum eius," inquit, "petere volumus, ut, regulae viam, qua gradimur, perspiciens, si nos

thought there was a single monk in the kingdom who would presume to give him a response that was so directly opposed to his wishes. Eventually—to pass over the many details I have heard—on the third day he was brought to the assembly and the abbot, choosing his words carefully, said to him: "Brother, you need to be more prudent in your behavior toward us—since you have been sent here, I hope, to do us excellent service—than the bishops and abbots who with wonderful and loving discretion recently strengthened us in our observance of the Rule of Saint Benedict as they saw fit
and then departed. I have a great many brothers who openly 2
maintain that forcing us to deviate from this course in any way is *the invasion of an evil angel, brought upon us by our sins.* Even though you are a very holy man, we know that making a sudden turn and following you alone in this would not result from careful consideration but from a royal command." "I am amazed," the other said, "that anyone would interpret my mission as that of an evil angel, since, believe me, I did not come of my own accord either to you or to any of those men, many of whom in this kingdom, glory be to God, I have corrected. Since I was sent by the emperor, I acted in an imperial manner in their midst and never asked permission for my actions, just as I also wished to deal with you, had I been allowed when I first arrived, and the way I still wish to do it today if I am allowed."

The dean said to the abbot: "Well then, my lord! Let us 3
submit to the emperor's angel and assign him a fitting rank and let him engage with us in every nook and cranny so that he can see how we live. However, we want to ask for a one-week grace period before his term of office begins to let him thoroughly examine the path of the Rule on which we walk

exorbitare regula lecta docuerit, reducentem secundum imperii iussum sequamur. Et quia regularis monachus absque abbate esse non poterit, qui sibimet abbas decanusque sit, hic invenisse inter doctrinas suas regulares viros patienter ferat." "Coloniae," ille ait, "abbatem meum carissimum reliqui." "*Eius* nobis," decanus ait, "etiamsi *litteras commendaticias* dederis, ea tamen te ipsum facere et pati renuere, quae docueris, etiam regi ipsi magno nos tibi perpeti nolle rescriberemus."

140. Talibus ille auditis secum fremens adeo, ut prae ira etiam lacrimasceret, commotus est. Sed abbas conventu dirempto surgens, bono animo esse illum per se monuit; neque semet ipsum quidem rationabilitati tanti viri ausum ait reniti, cum talium in loco sint plurimi, qui, ab episcopis et abbatibus nuperrime in regula Kebone commanente stabiliti, non possint in impetu ab ea revelli; se autem regis, quas attulit, litteris contraire nolle, si sub longis moris et examine regulae rationabilia suis ingerat et a tantorum virorum doctrinis tamdiu inolitis eos avertat. Iubet tandem ei ordinem dari post decanos, et hebdomadam illam omnia nostra perspiciendo quietius agere tandemque cum ratione, quaecumque non placuerint, regula teste mutare.

so that we may follow him as he leads us back in accordance with the emperor's order if, after reading the Rule, he informs us that we are straying. Since a Rule-abiding monk cannot remain without an abbot, let him patiently endure the fact that here he has found in the course of his teachings Rule-abiding men who can be abbot and dean for him." Sandrat said: "I left my dearest abbot at Cologne." To this the dean responded: "Even if you had brought us *his letter of recommendation,* we would still reply to the great king himself that we refuse to put up with your reluctance to practice and endure what you teach."

140. When Sandrat heard these words, he groaned to himself and became so agitated that he even began to shed tears of anger. However, after the meeting had been dissolved, the abbot rose from his seat and personally urged Sandrat to be in good spirits. He also said that he did not dare to oppose the rationality of so important a man on his own because there were very many brothers in the monastery who had recently been strengthened in their observance of the Rule by bishops and abbots under Kebo's supervision and could not be violently wrenched away from that. On the other hand, the abbot said, he did not wish to oppose the king's letter that Sandrat had brought if, after a long period of time and an examination of the Rule, Sandrat presented sensible suggestions to his monks and turned them away from the long-established doctrines of such great men. Finally the abbot ordered that Sandrat be given a rank following the deans, and told him to spend that week in quiet examining all our practices, and eventually to change whatever did not please him on reasonable grounds and in accordance with the guidance of the Rule.

2 Finitur hebdomada, et in capitulo considens plura sibi displicere ait, maxime autem in ecclesia exaltationes vocum gloriosas et nequaquam monachicas, et alia, quae post dicere vellet, plura, praeter quod dominicam in ea cottidie agi videret, feriam autem sextam in refectorio. Porcini autem liquaminis nidorem nares suas omnino ferre non posse, carnesque se omnibus et liquamen infirmis et sanis edicto regis interminare. Vinum autem, quoniam bibulus quidem erat, nimis nobis parce dari aiebat, calicemque nostrum *ad refocilandum potius quam ad potandum* sufficere. Cetera plura, quae docuit et fecit, praeter quaedam insignia, quoniam omnia exitum malum habent, ex quibus quidem volumen facere possem, omitto.

141. Monet abbas decem tandem nec non et omnes, quoniam parum firmitatis in eo quidem viderat, ut ei, sicut se diligerent, ad congrua et incongrua cuncta parerent, praedicens eis magistratus eius rigorem non diu duraturum. Iubet autem in summo dexterae refectorii mensae omnia ei, quae ipse diceret, sine mensura proponi et, si ipse desineret, bibere moneri. Iam enim illum, potando quis esset, exploraverat.

2 Decanus autem cum praeposito singulis fratrum, ut idoneis illum moribus frangerent, frequenter inculcabant. Erat autem ille fratribus semper post mensam in disciplinis propter potum quidem asperior. Accidit vero quadam die, ut

The week came to an end, and, sitting in at the chapter 2
meeting, Sandrat said that many things displeased him, but especially the monks' practice of raising their voices in church, in a manner that was ostentatious and not at all monastic, and many other things that he would talk about later—except that he saw Sunday being celebrated every day in the church, but Friday in the refectory. He said that his nose absolutely could not stand the smell of pork broth and that by the king's command he forbade meat and broth to everyone, sick and healthy alike. As for wine, being fond of a drink he said that we were given it too sparingly and that our goblet was suitable *for refreshment rather than for drinking to quench one's thirst.* I leave out a great many other suggestions he made and things he did, except some of the noteworthy, because they all came to a bad end. I could write a volume about them.

141. The abbot saw too little conviction in Sandrat, and so he advised ten brothers, and all the others as well, to obey all his orders, appropriate and inappropriate, just as they showed loyal devotion to himself; he predicted that the rigor of Sandrat's term in office would not last long. He also ordered that everything Sandrat required be set before him at the head of the refectory table to the right without measuring, and that he be reminded to drink if he should stop on his own. The abbot had already discovered how Sandrat behaved when drunk.

The dean, together with the provost, also repeatedly im- 2
pressed upon each of the brothers that they should soften Sandrat up by the propriety of their ways. Sandrat was always very harsh with the brothers in the matters of discipline after meals because of his drinking. It happened one

quidam iuvenum, cui iam plures dies ille infestior erat, cum
in illum severius, ut in omnes solebat, verbis inveheretur:
"Ecce iterum semimagister noster, *postquam mero incaluit!*"
diceret. Ille verbum clam, ut putabat, a iuvene dictum ab ore
eius ilico rapiens: "Semimagister tuus," inquit, "ego, si in-
3 sanio, tibi ostendere quantocius habebo!" Insiliensque in
hominem, bene quidem natum, sed et admodum litteratum,
grandem ei manu in maxillam dedit. Ille vero multum eo ro-
bustior, bracchio dicto citius extento, pugno illum in tempus validissime percussit seminecemque in terram cadere
fecit et, nisi quod eum ceteri retinebant, maiora ei adhuc
facere volebat. Superveniunt cum decano continuo fratres;
abbate accito signum pulsatur ad capitulum; ibi iussu abbatis iuvenis ille adhuc furens, ad columnam piralis ligatus,
4 acerrime virgis caeditur. Et inter dolores, quoniam litteratus
erat, mirum esse ait, quod Christus ad columnam technis
quondam passus est diaboli, se alterius satanae technis ad
columnam quidem pati; neque enim minus mirum quandoque evenire, si Sandrato per manus suas, quod equivoco eius
accidit, accidat. Talia eo inter verbera sibi praesagante, ipse
adhuc de ictu illo stupidus residens valde expavit. Humique
coram abbate stratus, ut eum absolveret, petiit, quidque sibimet post haec faciendum sit, pro regis amore se doceat.

142. Et decanus: "Nimis urgues," ait, "dominum nostrum,

day that Sandrat railed very severely against one of the young men whom he had been harassing for many days, as he was in the habit of doing to everyone, and the youth said: "Here he goes again, our half master, *warmed up by the wine!*" The young man said those words secretly, as he believed, but Sandrat caught them and retorted: "As your half master, I'll
show you right away if I have lost my wits!" He pounced on 3
the young man, who was not only wellborn but also very well educated, and slapped him on the cheek with his hand. Then the young man, who was much stronger, swung his arm faster than you can say a word, and with his fist dealt him a powerful blow to the temple, causing Sandrat to fall down on the ground half-dead; had the others not held him back, he was ready to inflict even more damage. The brothers immediately came over with the dean; they summoned the abbot, and the bell was sounded for the chapter. There, by the abbot's order, the youth, who was still furious, was tied to a pillar in the heated room and given a very severe
flogging. Since he was a learned man, he said as he suffered 4
the pain that it was amazing that Christ had once suffered at a pillar due to the wiles of the devil, and now *he* was suffering at a pillar due to the wiles of another Satan; he also said that it would be no less amazing if what had befallen his namesake eventually befell Sandrat, at his hands. While the young man made these prophecies about himself in the midst of the flogging, Sandrat sat there, still dazed by the blow, completely terrified. He prostrated himself before the abbot and begged him to pardon him and, for the love of the king, to teach him what he should do thereafter.

142. The dean said: "You put too much pressure on our

ut te, qui tot monachos, ut ais, docuisti nosque post tot episcopos et abbates docere venisti, doctor tuus esse praesumat." Et abbas: "Quia regi domino fide, O vir Dei," ait,
"iuravi, quicquid nobiscum feceris, ego habeo pati usque ad
id, quod nescio cuius regulae esse tu dicis, si fratres meos
quasi stolide audax manu cedendos insiliveris. Etenim in
fide assero: uterque nostrum contra regulam etiam nunc
operati sumus, tu filium meum absque iudicio cedendo ma-
2 nibus, ego, ut tibi satisfacerem, verberibus." Cumque omnes
eum, ut litteris gesta eius Ottoni filio mittendis tradi iuberet, <rogarent>, surgens ille quasi ceteris exemplum dando
roccum exuit et coram se expandit superque illum se ex-
tendit, utque puniretur pro tali excessu, gemens oravit.
Cumque plerique omnes, ut vapularet, optarent, abbas illum
induere, quoniam quidem nuntius regius honorandus sit,
iussit. Dein illum cum fratre laeso per potestatem pacifi-
cans, quomodolibet tamen agere vellet, arte sua non pro-
hibuit.

3 At ille cum eo minus vino non parceret transactisque ab
hoc articulo aliquot diebus in magistratu suo iterum insolesceret, quadam nocte *vino sepultus* stertendo et sternutando
fratres inquietaverat. Servum vero suum Hattonem, qui
olim post adventum suum loco discesserat, inclamans:
"*Serve nequam,*" ait, "ubi es?" Sicque insaniens tandem ad urinam surrexit sine rocco et nudipes; Ruomonisque patris,

master, in asking him to take up the role of your teacher, you who have taught so many monks, as you say, and who have come here after so many bishops and abbots to teach us." The abbot said: "O man of God, since I have sworn allegiance to my lord the king, I have to suffer whatever you do with us, even to the point—and I do not know in what Rule you say it is written—where you jump on my brothers like some rash brute to strike them with your hand. I dutifully declare: both of us acted just now contrary to the Rule, you, by striking my son with your hands without due process, I,
by striking him with rods to satisfy you." When they all 2
asked him to ensure that Sandrat's deeds be committed to a letter to be sent to Otto the son, Sandrat stood up and, as if setting an example for the others, took off his habit, spread it before him, stretched out on top of it, and, groaning, begged to be punished for such a transgression. Although most of the brothers wanted him to be flogged, the abbot told him to put on his clothes because as the king's envoy he had to be treated honorably. Then the abbot used his authority to restore peace between Sandrat and the offended brother, but astutely did not forbid Sandrat to behave in whatever manner he chose.

As for Sandrat, he was no more sparing of the wine than 3
before, and a few days after that incident he once again grew arrogant in administering his official duties. One night, *buried in wine,* he disturbed the brothers by his snoring and sneezing. He loudly called for his servant Hatto, who after his arrival had long since left the monastery: "Where are you, you *wicked servant?*" Ranting in this way, he eventually stood up, barefoot and without his robe, to pass water; he urinated all over the stool next to the bed of Father Ruomo,

propter inquietudinem eius tunc absentis, scamnum lecti
perminxerat. Crastina vero a decano querela ebrietatis et
turpitudinis capitulo incusatus, iterum, ut et prius, sponte
sua roccum exuit, et super expansum se extendens puniri
4 postulavit. At Ruomo surgens, decano quidem non iubente,
flagello fratrum, quod comminus pendebat, modeste
sumpto maximos illi infregit. Decanoque illum quidem,
quidnam faceret, inclamante: "Quod iussistis," ait, "et quod
ipse petiit, facio." Simulabat enim se nutum eius putasse.
Interimque maiores adhuc fortissime infregerat. Illoque vae
sibi, quod umquam in locum venerit, vociferante, decano
surgente vix ereptus est. Ruomo autem tantae auctoritatis
meritis suis erat, ut a nemine sit notatus, ab aliquibus etiam
idonee fecisse sit dictus.

143. Iubet tandem abbas consulto omnium lectum illi sterni in caminata, qua primo hospitatus est, vigilemque ei industrium de familia dari. Ibi ille aliquando de completorio veniens, videns vigilem sibi carnes paratas super mensulam habentem—nam illum nimis diligens, fidum esse confidebat—"Anime mi," ait, "de carnibus et mihi dato, et celatum habeto!" Quod cum libens fecisset, de carnibus saturato etiam vinum porrexit. At ille de sacculo, a nemine umquam in loco viso, denarios proferens, unanimi suo osculato, ut et

who was not there at the time because he had been disturbed by Sandrat. On the next day, when he was accused by
the dean in chapter following a complaint about his drunk-
enness and disgraceful behavior, Sandrat once again took off
his robe of his own free will, just as he had done earlier,
spread it out, stretched out on it, and demanded to be punished. At that point Ruomo stood up, and although the dean 4
had not ordered this, quietly took the brothers' whip that
hung nearby, and lashed him vigorously. When the dean
cried out to him, asking what on earth he was doing, Ruomo
said: "I am doing what you directed and what he himself
asked for." He pretended, you see, that he had thought the
dean had indicated this punishment with a nod. In the
meantime, he continued lashing even harder. When Sandrat
yelled that it was his misfortune ever to have come to this
place, the dean stood up and Sandrat was rescued—but only
just. Ruomo, however, was a man whose merits lent him
such authority that no one reproached him, and some even
said that what he did was right.

143. Finally, by a common decision, the abbot ordered a bed made for Sandrat in the heated cell where he was first lodged and a diligent guard given to him from the retinue of dependents. One day Sandrat came back there from Compline and saw that his guard had meat prepared for him on a small table. Sandrat said to him—he was very fond of this man and trusted in his loyalty—"My dear friend, give me some of that meat too and keep it secret!" The servant was happy to do it, and when Sandrat had had his fill of the meat, he even offered him wine. Sandrat produced some money from a pouch that no one in the monastery had ever seen, kissed his accomplice, and gave him the money so that he

2 aliis noctibus par faceret, dedit. Cumque hoc ille iam crebro, clausis super se intus hostiis, fecisset, quadam die Richero sciscitanti, quomodo se magister fratrum noctu haberet: "Enimvero optime," ait, "si ei carnes iam dare haberem; nam quas habere potui, consumpsimus." "Bene," ille ait, "mi sodes, narras; neque enim tibi per me deerunt. Sed quod tibi dico, ut de vita cures, facito! Ianuas nocte proxima serare te simulato, reseratasque sinito! Et a ministris nostris, quae abundent, carnibus sumptis opipare eas vobis parato!"

3 Venit ille nocte proxima de completorio; et ut solebat, mensam ei minister fidissimus apponens carnibus onerabat, laetamque noctem habituros promittebat. Et ecce praepositus, assumptis quibusdam de fratribus, avide illis supervenit comedentibus. *Et stans super illos:* "In bonis," inquit, "operibus te, magister sancte, invenimus. Enimvero," ait, "aegrotis
4 nostris, si tu velles, scutella haec magis liceret quam tibi!" Et allevans illam, in faciem eam minatus percutere, non tamen fecit. Vigilem autem, quasi et ipsi iratus, *servum nequissimum* vocans, numquam in conspectum suum venire iussum domo expulit. Soloque illo deceptore quidem regum et regni relicto abierunt, ianuis, ne ultra intus intraret, claustri post se sollicite clausis.

5 At ille malum sibi aliquot maximum cras futurum timens, de nocte fugam iniit latibulumque die illo inter frutecta

would do the same on other nights too. One day, after he 2
had repeatedly done this behind the door locked from the inside, Richer asked the servant how the brothers' instructor was behaving himself at night, and the servant said to him: "Very well, I assure you, up till now, if I had meat to give him; we have eaten what I was able to get." "I am glad to hear it, my friend," Richer said, "and for my part, I'll make sure that you are not short of meat. But to safeguard your life, do what I tell you! Tomorrow night pretend to lock the doors but leave them unlocked! Get some meat from our attendants, who have plenty of it, and prepare a lavish meal for the two of you!"

On the next night Sandrat came back from Compline; his 3
loyal attendant set the table for him as usual, loading it with meat, and promised that they would have a merry night. Suddenly, the provost, accompanied by some of the brothers, arrived, surprising them just as they were greedily eating their food. *Towering over them,* he said: "We find you engaged in your good works, holy master. Surely, this dish, if you so chose, would be more permissible for our ailing brothers
than for you!" He picked up the plate, threatening to throw 4
it in Sandrat's face, but did not do so. Then, pretending also to be angry with the guard, the provost called him a *very wicked servant* and expelled him from the house with orders never to appear before his eyes. The monks left that beguiler of kings and kingdom alone, went away, and carefully locked the door of the cloister behind them so that he could no longer enter.

Fearing that some great evil would befall him the follow- 5
ing day, Sandrat fled during the night and on the next day found a hiding place among the bushes of the nearest moun-

montis proximi habuit. Sed et abbas cum neminem illum persequi vellet, securus tandem suimet factus, deambulatoribus peregrinis, qui Romam ibant, iungitur. Sed quid postea fortunae habuerit, quia dubie affirmatum est, odio nominis eius libens ignoro. Et haec est tragoedia Sandrati hypocritae iussu Ottonis magni in nos moliminum.

144. Misit tandem abbas litteras Ottonibus et reginae in Saxoniam cum muneribus, sciscitans tempus adventus eorum, nec non et Ekkehardo quaternionem omnem seriem Sandrati tenentem. Quam ille Ottoni filio cum in secretis legere daret, in tantos ironiae cachinnos solutus est, ut mater eius superveniens, quid esset, quaereret. At ille scripturam illam ipsi dans, legere eam rogavit—nam litteratissima erat—quae fortuna se celato missum a patre sanctum Sandratum comitata sit et secuta. Quam cum et ipsa quidem studiose perlegeret risumque non contineret, filio ait:
2 "Enimvero, fili, tam indecens mihi videtur fuisse patrem tuum talibus viris, quales et nos nuper de illis vidimus, tale scelus immisisse *monstrumque hominis* tantae reverentiae viros post se trahere iussum fuisse. Eia," ait, "auricularis patris tui fuit ille hominum vilissimus et *Deo odibilis.* Sed et ego fallebar in illo, macilentum videns et pallidum habituque neglectum, magnumque aliquid nos in eo exspectare sperabam. Scio autem tibi et Ekkehardo quicquam de hac re patri tuo loqui minus," ait, "convenire; sed ego quidem, quando primum copia fuerit, scripturam istam *fida interpres* auribus eius aperiam."

tain. Since the abbot did not want anybody to pursue him, he eventually began to feel safe and joined up with pilgrims who were passing by on their way to Rome. Of what kind of fortune he met with afterward, supported as it is by dubious information, I happily disregard out of contempt for his name. Such is the tragic story of Sandrat the hypocrite's machinations against us, as he acted under the orders of Otto the Great.

144. Finally the abbot sent a letter, accompanied by gifts, to the Ottos and the queen, who were in Saxony, asking about the time of their arrival. He also sent Ekkehard a sixteen-page booklet that contained a detailed account of Sandrat's actions. When Ekkehard gave it to Otto the son to read in secret, Otto dissolved in such fits of ironic laughter that his mother came over and asked what was going on. He gave her the document and asked her—she was very well educated—to read about the misadventures that had embraced and dogged the holy Sandrat, who had been sent by his father without his knowledge. She carefully read it through and, unable to suppress her laughter, said to her
son: "Really, my son, it seems to me to have been quite im- 2
proper that your father let loose such a rascal against men whose mettle we recently observed, and ordered *a monster of a man* to drag men of such reverence in his train. Well, that most vile of men, *hateful to God,* was your father's confidant. But I was also deceived by him: when I saw him, haggard and pale and carelessly dressed, I thought that we could expect great deeds from him. I also know that it is not appropriate for you and Ekkehard to talk to your father about this matter, but as soon as opportunity presents itself, I will act as a *faithful interpreter* and uncover the sense of this account for him."

3 Miles quidam abbatis, nuntius datus, regi tandem regina astante litteras dans, munera offert. Continuoque grate acceptis, quomodo Sandrat se habeat, interroganti regina infert: “Mihi,” ait, “hoc, domine mi, iniunctum est epistula lecta tibi interpretari.”

145. Quam cum ipsa legisset, finis eius erat: “Moveatque
maiestatis tuae pietatem indiscreta varietas molestiarum,
quas per sedecim hebdomadarum spatia cum fratribus meis
perpessus sum.” Et illa: “Has, domine, in his cartis breviatas,
si me amas, clementer,” ait, “audi!” Cumque ei scripturam illam totam, quam citissime poterat, fidelis interpres absolveret: “Taedet me,” ait, “mi dilecta, et piget audisse vana homi-
2 nis totque indiscreta molimina. Sed et miseret me,” ait, “mei
timore talium et tantae humilitatis patientiaeque Dei virorum. O,” inquit, “in conspectum daretur deceptor ille levis-
simus, quam cunctis hypocritis in exemplum esset futurus!”
Accitoque reginae consilio Ekkehardo: “Scribe,” ait, “Nokero tuo cum suis non meam tantum illis, sed et illorum
mihi, quia commoti sunt, gratiam! Et si eos contristavi in-
scius, propter invictam illorum mei causa patientiam eos, si
vixero, sciens laetificabo. Adventumque nostrum in maio
Deo donante ad eos futurum et vulnera, quibus a perversis
seductus eos laesi, sanaturum.”

3 Ingreditur interea Otto filius. Pater illi scripturam illam

One of the abbot's knights who had been sent as a mes- 3
senger eventually gave the letter to the king in the queen's
presence and offered him gifts. The king gratefully accepted
them and when he promptly asked how Sandrat was doing,
the queen replied to him: "My lord, it is incumbent on me to
read the letter and explain this to you."

145. She read the letter, which ended as follows: "May the
wide range of troubles that my brothers and I endured for
sixteen weeks elicit Your Majesty's compassion." She said:
"My lord, *if you have any regard for me,* kindly hear about the
troubles, which are briefly described in these pages!" After
she had read the entire document to him as quickly as possible, translating it faithfully, he said: "My beloved, I am
grieved and disgusted to hear about the many pointless and
foolish machinations of this man. I also feel compassion for 2
these men of God who have shown so much humility and
patience because they feared me." "Oh," he said, "let that
utterly unreliable deceiver be brought before my eyes so he
can serve as an example to all hypocrites!" On the queen's
recommendation he summoned Ekkehard and said: "Write
to your dear Notker and to his monks to tell them not of the
favor I have done them but rather of the favor they have
done me, since they have been provoked! If I have unwit-
tingly caused them grief, I will, if I live, intentionally bring
them joy to reward their indomitable patience, as they suffered on my account. Also tell them that, God willing, we
will arrive at their monastery in May, and that this visit will
heal the wounds that I, led astray by depraved men, inflicted
upon them."

Meanwhile Otto the son came in. His father gave him 3
the document to read, thinking that he was unaware of its

quasi rerum inscio dat legendam. Ille autem inter legendum dum rideret: "Miror te," pater ait, "ridere, quod me libet flere." "Quod verax factus sis," ait, "hoc, pater, gaudeo. Crebro vobis cum eum insinuarem, et vos tamen me inconsulto illuc hominem misistis, quisquis esset, celare non potuit. Sed vel nunc quaeratur, pater, ubi sit, ut, cum nos in locum," ait, "venerimus, in conspectu discipulorum suorum, quos indigne tractaverat, ipse digne tractetur." Et regina: "Si patri tuo, fili," ait, "prius ille ad manus venerit, non meo consilio eum illuc reservabit."

146. Dimissus hilariter miles abbatis, boni nuntii gerulus, omnes sancti Galli viros laetificans regum eis verbis edixerat, ut, quoniam ipsi iam experti sunt, quod bene quidem vellent, posthac viverent, quocumque modo vellent. Neque enim iam ultra ullum eis hypocritam spondent immissuros.

2 Parantur in adventum illorum multimoda laudum recens dictatarum, ceterarum, ut solet, rerum copiosa impendia. Veniunt in locum in vigilia ascensionis, quae fuit in die sanctae Potentianae virginis. Suscipiuntur honore, quo decuit. Otto magnus, a fratre Prunone Coloniae archiepiscopo sinistra ductus, dextra baculo fultus, filio autem matrem ducente, longe ipse prae aliis quasi leo prae bestiis, fratre manu osculata decedente, solus in medio, fratribus hinc inde ad

contents. He laughed as he read, and his father said: "I am surprised that you laugh at what makes me want to weep." "I am delighted by this, father," Otto said, "because you have come to see the truth. Although I frequently warned you about him, you still sent him there without consulting me and he could not conceal what kind of man he was. But perhaps now, father, we should try to find out where he is so that when we come to the monastery he can be treated appropriately in full view of his students whom he treated inappropriately." The queen said: "My son, if he falls into your father's hands earlier, my advice will be against reserving his punishment until we get there."

146. The abbot's knight was amicably dispatched, and, being the bearer of good news, caused all the men of Saint Gall to rejoice when he announced to them in the words of the kings that, since they now realized that the monks wished to live virtuously, they should live hereafter in whatever manner they chose. They also promised that never again would they send them a hypocrite.

In preparation for the royal visit, there was a varied and 2
abundant expenditure of effort in the form of recently composed hymns of praise and, as usual, various other arrangements. They arrived at the monastery on the eve of the feast of the Ascension, which was the feast day of the holy virgin Potentiana. They were welcomed with fitting honors. Otto the Great was escorted, on his left side, by his brother Bruno, archbishop of Cologne, and was supported by a staff on his right side, and the son escorted his mother. His brother kissed his hand and drew back, and Otto the Great, far in front of the others like a lion ahead of other beasts, stood there alone like a statue in the middle of the church,

laudes in lateribus ecclesiae directim statutis, quasi statua
3 constitit. Oculisque grandibus in fratres hinc inde versatis, quam antea noverat, si adhuc sit, disciplinam probans, baculum sibi decidere sivit. Cuonone autem duce, genero eius, accurrente baculumque sibi timorate restituente, stare illum iubens ait: "Ecce, ego disciplinam horum, quam et tu forsitan audisti, temptans, baculum mihi decidere sivi, neminisque illorum caput aut oculos ad hoc motos vidi. Dic vero Adilheide meae et filio versutiam, quam feci!" Filius autem saepe facete loqui solitus, Cuononi referenti: "Miramur," ait, "cum tam firmiter imperium teneat, quod baculus deciderit. Enimvero quasi leo regna, quae adhuc cepit, firmissime tenuit. Neque mihi, quamvis filio, partem vel unam dedit."

147. Tandem post laudes finitas rex magnus neminem, nisi quem abbas velit, secum claustrum ingredi edixit. Decano et aliis primoribus ad oscula vocatis, Nokerus suus ubi esset, interrogat. Nam ille tunc senio caecus in sedili quodam sedens ei monstratus est. Iubet ergo filio, ut ipse sibi adduceret illum. Qui mox osculatum ad patrem manu duxerat illum. Qui et ipse osculatus virum sub clamyde astrictum, multum consolatus est illum, et manum ei dans duxit secum in claustrum. "O me," ille ait, "felicissimum caecum, qui tantos, quantos nullus umquam meruit, hodie habeo ductores!"

while the brethren were standing directly opposite him along the aisles on either side, ready to begin singing the
hymns. He looked around at the monks with eyes wide open 3
and his gaze shifting from one side to the other, and he let his staff fall to the floor, testing whether they still had the kind of discipline he had previously come to recognize. Duke Conrad, his son-in-law, ran up to return the staff reverently to his hands, but the emperor ordered him to stop and said: "Look, I let my staff fall in order to test their discipline, which you may have heard about also, and I did not see one of them move his head or eyes at this. So go and tell my wife Adelheid and my son about the trick I have played!" When Conrad told him about it, Otto, who was often witty, said in response: "I am amazed that his staff fell from his hand when he keeps such a firm grip on his empire. Like a lion, he has kept a very firm grip on the kingdoms he has conquered so far. He has not even given so much as a single bit of them to me, though I am his son."

147. Finally, after the hymns of praise were over, the great king decreed that no one was to enter the cloister with him unless the abbot chose to allow it. When the dean and other high-ranking brothers were summoned for a kiss, he asked them where his dear friend Notker was. They pointed out Notker, by that time blind in his old age, who was seated nearby. He told his son to bring the old man to him. Then his son kissed Notker and led him by the hand to his father. The father, in his turn, kissed the man, pulled him closer, embracing him under his mantle, and then, after many words of consolation, took him by the hand and led him into the cloister. "Ah!" Notker said, "I am the happiest among the blind, because today I have guides that no one has ever

In claustro autem residens iuxta se locaverat illum. Ibi illum episcopi et abbates laicique, quibus saepe profuit, salutabant.

2 Abbate interea assumpto Otto filius armarium sibi aperiri rogat. Quod ille renuere non ausus, condicto tamen risibili, ne tantus praedo locum et fratres spoliaret, aperiri iubet. Ille autem libris optimis illectus, plures abstulit, quorum tamen aliquos Ekhardo rogante postea reddidit.

deserved!" In the cloister, the emperor sat down and placed Notker at his side. There he was greeted by the bishops and abbots and laymen, whom he often helped.

Meanwhile, Otto the son got hold of the abbot and asked 2
that the library be opened for him. The abbot did not dare to refuse and ordered it to be opened on the condition, as he playfully suggested, that so great a thief not rob the monastery and the brothers. Nevertheless, Otto, enticed by the most valuable books, carried away a great many but later returned some of them at Ekkehard's request.

Abbreviations

AH = G. M. Dreves, C. Blume, and H. M. Bannister, eds., *Analecta Hymnica Medii Aevi,* 54 vols. (Leipzig, 1886–1922)

CESG = Codices electronici Sangallenses (www.cesg.unifr.ch)

Cronache = Gian Carlo Alessio, Peter Erhart, and Fabrizio Crivello, eds. and trans., *Cronache di San Gallo* (Turin, 2004)

CSEL = *Corpus Scriptorum Ecclesiasticorum Latinorum,* 105 vols. (Salzburg, 1866–2019)

DA = *Deutsches Archiv für Erforschung des Mittelalters*

Haefele, *Casus* = Hans F. Haefele, , ed. and trans., *St. Galler Klostergeschichten* (Darmstadt, 1980)

LCL = Loeb Classical Library, 542 vols. (Cambridge, Mass., 1912–2019)

MGH = *Monumenta Germaniae Historica,* 300 vols. (Munich, 1826–2020). http://www.dmgh.de/

AA = *Auctores antiquissimi*

Capit. = *Capitularia regum Francorum*

DD = *Diplomata*

Epist. = *Epistolae*

Fontes Iuris = *Fontes iuris Germanici antiqui in usum scholarum separatim editi*

Necr. = *Necrologia Germaniae*

Poetae = *Poetae Latini medii aevi*

SRG = *Scriptores rerum Germanicarum in usum scholarum separatism editi*

SRG NS = *Scriptores rerum Germanicarum, Nova series*

SRM = *Scriptores rerum Merovingicarum*

SS = *Scriptores*

PL = Jacques-Paul Migne, ed., *Patrologia Latina,* 217 vols. (Paris, 1841–1865)

RB = The Rule of Saint Benedict

Tremp, *Casus* = Hans F. Haefele, Ernst Tremp, and Franzisca Schnoor, eds., *St. Galler Klostergeschichten (Casus sancti Galli),* by Ekkehard IV, MGH SRG 82 (Wiesbaden, 2020)

UBSG = Hermann Wartmann, ed., *Urkundenbuch der Abtei Sanct Gallen,* 6 vols. (Frankfurt am Main, 1981)

Note on the Text

Ekkehard's *Casus sancti Galli* survives in six manuscripts, none of them an autograph. The earliest is Saint Gall, Stiftsbibliothek MS 615 *(B),* produced at Saint Gall around 1200. This codex includes Ratpert's *Casus,* Ekkehard's text, and continuations written by three anonymous authors. The other five manuscripts, dating from the fourteenth and fifteenth centuries, are all derived from *B,* either directly or indirectly.[1]

The Latin text printed here is based on the comprehensive MGH edition produced by Hans F. Haefele, Ernst Tremp, and Franzisca Schnoor. We thank Ernst Tremp who has generously made it available to us ahead of publication. According to the policy of Dumbarton Oaks Medieval Library, medieval spelling has been silently changed to conform with classical norms (for instance, *e* has been expanded into *ae* or *oe* where necessary). The notes record deviations from the MGH edition as well as some glosses and corrections in manuscripts that contribute to understanding Ekkehard's text. Glosses made by later hands in *B* and *C* often appear incorporated in the body of the text in *D.* For a comprehensive apparatus the reader should consult the MGH edition.

Sigla

B = Saint Gall, Stiftsbibliothek MS 615

C = Saint Gall, Stiftsbibliothek MS 612

C1 = Saint Gall, Stiftsbibliothek MS 611

D = Saint Gall, Kantonsbibliothek, Vadiana MS 70

D2 = Saint Gall, Kantonsbibliothek, Vadiana MS 69

H = Hans Haefele, ed. and trans., *Casus sancti Galli: St. Galler Klostergeschichten* (Darmstadt, 1980)

MvK = Gerold Meyer von Knonau, ed., *Ekkeharti (IV) Casus Sancti Galli,* Mitteilungen zur vaterlandischen Geschichte, N. F. 5–6 (Saint Gall, 1877)

T = Hans F. Haefele, Ernst Tremp, and Franzisca Schnoor, eds., *St. Galler Klostergeschichten (Casus sancti Galli),* by Ekkehard IV, MGH SRG 82 (Wiesbaden, 2020)

vA = Ildefons von Arx, ed., *Casus sancti Galli,* in *Scriptores rerum Sangallensium: Annales, chronica et historiae aevi Carolini,* ed. Georg Heinrich Pertz, MGH SS 2 (Hanover, 1829), 75–147

Notes

1 Haefele, "Untersuchungen," part 1; Haefele, *Casus,* 11; Ernst Tremp, "Zur Neuausgabe von Ekkeharts *Casus sancti Galli,*" in Kössinger, Krotz, and Müller, *Ekkehart IV,* 250; Tremp, *Casus,* 62–84.

Notes to the Text

2.1 allecto: *gloss* seducto vel electo *B*

3.1 Iram: *gloss* fluvius *B*

3.2 proclive: *gloss* gradatim *B*

lineus: *gloss* id est lineis vestibus *B*; cum lineis vestibus *instead of* lineus *D*

diatim: *gloss* cottidie *B C*

obloquia: *gloss* detractorum *B*

4.1 homo artificiosus: *glosses* Salemon *B*; Salomon *C*

5.1 senserat: *appears in the singular in all codices except* senserant *D2*. *Meant to emphasize the* "unitas" *of the three friends (T 127n4).*

6.2 praetexta: *gloss* pallium puerile sub disciplinae cultu habitum *B* *(Isidore, Etym. 19.24.16); included in the body of the text before* praetexta *C*

8.1 trutinat: *gloss* perpendit *B*

11.1 ut alias relatum est: *gloss* in alio libro *B*

Hattonem: *gloss* maguntinum *B*

16.3 unum periodum: *gloss* versum uno spiritu prolatum *B C*

20.1 Chuonrado: *gloss* rege *B*

veredarii: *gloss* cursores *B C*

24.1 Pater iuste: *supralinear neumes B C*

25.2 satulatior *T*: *corrected from* saturatior *B*; saturatior *other manuscripts and earlier editions*

26.2 in peius *D*: impeius *T B*

28.1 doxa: *supralinear gloss* gloria vana; *gloss in the margin* ceno *B*; zenodoxa *C*; ξενόδοξα *C1*; cenodoxa *D*; cenodoxia *vA, MvK*

29.1 lenoniae: *gloss* fornicationis *B*

procis: *gloss* petitoribus *B*

29.2 Chuonrado: *added in later hand* Sub isto Salomone fuerunt simul in monasterio nostro presbyteri XLII, diaconi XXIIII, subdiaconi XV, pueri XX *B (p. 99)*; *incorporated into the text C D. See T 212n13: "This note by a 13th-century hand is based on the long list of names preserved in the document of 895* [*UBSG vol. 2, no. 697*], *which was witnessed by the entire monastery; the* monachi *of the document are here erroneously called* pueri."

32.1 aegre: *gloss* vix *B C*

39.3 anaglyphas: *gloss* sculpturas *B*; id est sculpturas *C*

epigrammis: *gloss* superscriptionibus *B*

40.2 anaglipham: *gloss* sculpturam *B*

46.1 reposuit . . . aras: *an empty space of about twelve letters B*

sponte . . . velut: *an empty space of about four letters B*

47.4 alterum *H and codices*: <alter> alterum *T*

48.1 maiores: *gloss* nunc villici *B*; id est nunc villici *D*

51.3 Sint-tria-unum: *spaces between the words B*; *gloss* Sittern *C*

52.2 pergerent, ut et *H*: pergerent <et>, ut *T*

53.3 vibrata: *gloss* iactata *B*

54.1 Wiborada: *in majuscule; in the lower margin in later hand* Anno Domini DCCCCXXV *(sic)* passa est beata Wiborada *B*; *the same gloss in red D*

armos: *gloss* stapulas B

55.3 avehunt: *emendation follows vA's suggestion (vA 106n94; compare 67.4* evehunt*)*: aveunt *T, H, MvK, vA, following the manuscripts (for instance, B D)*

56.2 immunitionem *T (following B)*; in municionem *C D*

56.4 De sancta Wiborada: *in the upper margin in red* Nota de canonizacione sancte Wiborade *D*

57.3 strophio: *gloss* cingulo virginali *B*

58.1 suboleat: *gloss* displiceat *B*

59.3 Bozanarium: *gloss* vinum a loco sic dictum *B*

63.4 decessoris: *gloss* Hartmanni *B C*

64.3 Missilia: *gloss* sagittas *B*

65.1 Adelheidae: *gloss* imperatricis *B*

65.3 Parmis: *gloss* clipeis *B*

66.3 tragoediam: *gloss* luctuosam relationem *B*

67.4 evehunt: eveunt *B, changed to* evehunt *by later hand*; evehunt *C D*; *eveunt T. Compare 55.3* avehunt.

71.2 oeconomis: *gloss* procuratoribus *B*

71.3 fausta: *gloss* felicia *B*

frugi: *gloss* temperati *(?) B*

72.1 elegos: *gloss* versus miserabiles *B*

76.1 tragoediam: *gloss* luctuosam relationem *B*

76.4 facessere: *gloss* capere *B*

76.5 Laus . . . deus: *supralinear neumes B*

77.1 abbatem: *gloss* Fabarie *B*

80.4 Prompta . . . occasu: *supralinear neumes B*

martyr . . . patris: *supralinear neumes B*

Ambulans . . . gloriosissimum *supralinear neumes B*

82.1 Oudalrich: *heading in red* De Burkhardo ingenito et parentibus eius *D*

83.1 ligurrire: *gloss* summatim gustare *B*

83.2 martyrem: *gloss* Rachildam scilicet *B C*

magistra: Wiborada scilicet *B C*

84.4 opipare: *gloss* laute *B*; *gloss* habunde eleganter *C*

88.2 rustice: *gloss* Gallice *B*

91.2 Altaha: *gloss* nomen loci *B C*; *incorporated into the text* Altaha id est nomen loci *D*

94.3 Thalassi . . . alleluia *supralinear neumes B*; *written in Greek letters by Aegidius Tschudi in the lower margin C, p. 184*; *in Greek letters in text, then in Latin* Latine sic: Maria et flumina benedicite domino, hymnum dicite fontes domino. Alleluia *C1*

99.1 clinicus: *gloss* paraliticus *B C*

102.2 Lorisham: *gloss* Lauressensis *B*

103.1 Wirziburgensis: *gloss* Erbipolensis *B*; *incorporated into the text* Herbipolensis id est Wirtzinburgensis *D*

archiepiscopus: *gloss Treverensis B*

105.1 Elewangensis: *gloss* abbas *B*

105.2 Henricus: *gloss* Treverensis *B*

Thietricus: *gloss* Metensis *B*

106.1 Henricus: *gloss* Treverensis *B*

106.2 Kebo: *gloss* Lauressensis abbas *B*

108.1 Henricus: *gloss* Treverensis *B*

108.2 Poppo: *gloss* Erbipolensis episcopus *B*

109.1 Chuonradus: *gloss* Constantiensis episcopus *B*

Palzo: *gloss* Spirensis episcopus *B*

110.2 Milo: *gloss* Elewangensis *B*

113.3 Henricus: *gloss* Treverensis *B*

Thietericus: *supralinear gloss in a later hand* Metensis *B*; *incorporated into the text* Dietricus Metensis *D*

117.1 Kebo: *gloss Lauressensis B*

123.1 Rector aeterni: *supralinear neumes in a later hand B*

140.1 Kebone: *gloss* abbate Lauressense *B*

147.1 Nokerus: *gloss* balbulus, *in the margin* <sequenti>as compo<suit> *B*

Notes to the Translation

Pref.1 *such are the ways of our times*: An allusion to the exclamation that often occurs in Cicero's speeches (see, for instance, *In Catilinam* 1.2 and *In Verrem* 2.4.56). Later, in chapter 134, Ekkehard quotes Cicero's words directly.

discipline: Ekkehard means monastic discipline, that is, following the Rule of Benedict.

who walk in levity: Tobit 3:17.

other people: Ekkehard refers to the Lives of Saint Gall and Saint Otmar, Ratpert's *Casus sancti Galli,* and other texts, some of them now lost. He also draws heavily on an oral tradition.

Pref.2 *Salomo*: Salomo III, bishop of Constance and abbot of Saint Gall (890–919).

Hartmann: Ekkehard discusses most of the abbots listed here in his later chapters; see notes to corresponding sections.

Gerhard: Abbot from 990 to 1001.

Norbert: Abbot from 1034 to 1072.

not as he and we, as they say, wish, but as we can: See Terence, *Andria* 805.

Ratpert: A monk of Saint Gall (ca. 855–ca. 911), he wrote the first installment of the house chronicle, *Casus sancti Galli.* Ekkehard writes about him in chapters 34–36 and 44.

Constance: Episcopal city at the western end of Lake Constance, about nineteen miles from Saint Gall. In the first half of the ninth century the abbey gradually gained independence from the bishopric of Constance, but its relations with individual bishops remained complicated.

the second had demanded a tribute: Ratpert, *Casus* 21. However, in this chapter Ratpert talks about Salomo I (839–871), who wanted to reinforce the payment of tribute that the bishopric of Constance had been receiving from the monastery. He was succeeded as bishop by his brother's son, Salomo II (d. 889).

1.1 *Iso*: Ekkehard writes about him in chapters 30–32.

initiated into the clerical life: This refers to the first steps in a cleric's career, his tonsuring and perhaps the first grade of ordination; see Julia Barrow, *Clergy in the Medieval World* (Cambridge, 2015), 27–70.

Notker, Tuotilo, Ratpert, and Hartmann: According to other sources from Saint Gall, these monks were roughly of the same age, and Hartmann (abbot of Saint Gall from 922 to 925) may have been the youngest.

like a canon: A member of a community of clergy but not a monk. Salomo seems to have received a special training in preparation for his career as a cleric, but it is not clear what exactly that comprised; see Grotans, *Reading*, 62–63, and the bibliography there. For the education of clerics at monasteries, including Saint Gall, see Barrow, *Clergy*, especially 182–83.

1.2 *King Louis*: Ekkehard probably thought of Louis the German (king of East Francia, 843–876) by analogy with Grimald, who served that king, but other sources do not support this. In a diploma of October 5, 889, Salomo is named as a member of the chapel under King Arnulf (MGH DD Arn nos. 61, 103, pp. 88–89, 149–52), and then, in 884–886, as a notary and chaplain under King Charles III the Fat (notary: MGH DD Karl III nos. 98, 120, 131, pp. 158–60, 189–91, 209–10; chaplain: MGH DD Karl III nos. 122, 132, pp. 193–95, 210–12).

Grimald: Abbot of Weissenburg (833–839 and 847–872) and abbot of Saint Gall (841–872). He served Emperor Louis the Pious (814–840) and King Louis the German (he appears in documents as an archchaplain to Louis the German; see, for instance, MGH DD Ludwig der Deutsche nos. 69, 79, pp. 96–99, 115–16). See also Eric Goldberg, *Struggle for Empire: King-*

ship and Conflict under Louis the German, 817–876 (Ithaca, N.Y., 2006), especially 71–72 and 169–71.

obtained Ellwangen . . . Kempten: No other source confirms this for the abbeys of Ellwangen, located in Baden-Württemberg and Kempten in the Allgäu region.

Hatto: Archbishop of Mainz from 891 to 913.

friendly: This word had a wide range of meanings in the Middle Ages, from "personal friendships" or "political alliances" to "patronage"; for the social context, see Gerd Althoff, *Family, Friends and Followers: Political and Social Bonds in Medieval Europe* (Cambridge, 2004).

bishop of Constance: See chapter 11.

2.1 *Hartmut*: Grimald was abbot from 841 to 872. Hartmut served as dean from 849 to 872, and later abbot from 872 to 883.

Marcus, a bishop of Irish stock: The grave of Gall, a saint of Irish origin, was located at the abbey and attracted Irish pilgrims who traveled to the continent in the ninth and tenth centuries. Marcus arrived at Saint Gall around 850. See Clark, *The Abbey of St. Gall in Literature and Art,* 34–35; Johannes Duft, "Irish Monks and Irish Manuscripts in St. Gall," in King and Vogler, *Culture,* 119–32, at 120; Sven Meeder, *The Irish Scholarly Presence at St. Gall: Networks of Knowledge in the Early Middle Ages* (London, 2012), 46–47.

Moengal: The Saint Gall necrology (MGH Necr. vol. 1, p. 481) records the death of Moengal, named Marcellus, on September 30; he appears in Saint Gall sources between 853 and 865.

divine and human disciplines: The study of scripture and the liberal arts, two subject areas that formed the traditional medieval curriculum. The terms used by Ekkehard go back to Cassiodorus's *Insitutiones divinarum et saecularum litterarum (Institutions of Divine and Secular Learning),* a text preserved in the library of Saint Gall in a ninth-century manuscript (Saint Gall, Stiftsbibliothek MS 855). All the cited manuscripts are available online at CESG.

out of fear . . . entourage: Acts 23:10, slightly paraphrased.

In fact, they were railing at him: A paraphrase of Mark 14:5.

books: The library of Saint Gall owned manuscripts written in Irish script, some of which may go back to this time; see Duft, "Irish Monks," 120, and Meeder, *Irish*, 53–62.

precious cloths: *Pallia* can also mean "altar cloths" or "monks' cloaks."

stole: A liturgical vestment, a long band of cloth worn around the back of the neck; priests who administered the sacrament of confession wore stoles as a symbol of their authority.

2.2 *claustral school . . . external school*: The former, often termed "internal school," appears to have been designated for educating future monks, while the latter was intended for canons. The Synod of Aachen (817) prohibited monasteries from holding a school for any students except those "destined to become monks." The evidence for such schools in the Carolingian period comes from just three sources: the *Casus;* the *Life of Saint Notker* likely written by a thirteenth-century monk of Saint Gall and with information on the schools based on material gleaned from the *Casus;* and the Plan of Saint Gall. Produced at Reichenau for Gozbert (abbot of Saint Gall, 816–837) and preserved in Saint Gall, Stiftsbibliothek MS 1092, available online at http://www.stgallplan.org, the Plan provides an ideal representation of a monastic complex. For a full discussion of the issue, see M. M. Hildebrandt, *The External School in Carolingian Society* (New York, 1992); see also Grotans, *Reading*, 53–67.

3.1 *an enrolled brother*: A monk, cleric, or lay person enrolled as a member of a monastic community, whose name was entered into a confraternity book; for discussion of the term and the institution, see Karl Schmid, "Von den *fratres conscripti* in Ekkeharts St. Galler Klostergeschichten," *Frühmittelalterliche Studien* 25 (1991): 109–22.

Goldach: Located in canton of Sankt Gallen to the south of Lake Constance, not far from the monastery.

the Ira: A small stream that flows through the city of Sankt Gallen, which began as a settlement around the monastery, became urban in the ninth century, and grew into a large town in modern times.

a dwelling place had been prepared: A strong echo of John 14:2. Ekkehard may also have been thinking of the hymn to Saint Magnus, *Carmina nunc festis;* see Tremp, *Casus,* 123n6.

the monastic household: The word Ekkehard uses, *familia,* encompassed all persons related to the monastery of Saint Gall and its properties, from monks to servants to dependents.

3.2 *playing a game with Fortune*: Ekkehard is most likely thinking of Boethius, *Consolatio Philosophiae (The Consolation of Philosophy),* and he develops this theme in chapter 21 by alluding to *Consolatio* 2.

King Louis: Ekkehard probably means Louis the German; see, however, note to 1.2.

the abbeys mentioned above: Ellwangen and Kempten; it is unclear whether they were ever under his control.

dressed in linen . . . considerable embarrassment: Linen per se was not prohibited in a monastic environment: monks' tunics and liturgical garments could be made of linen; see, for instance, Hildemar, *Commentary on the Rule of Benedict* 55 (*The Hildemar Project,* http://hildemar.org). Here and below, however, Ekkehard uses this word to describe nonmonastic dress worn by Salomo and Grimald as canons; see Tremp, *Casus,* 123n12, 125n19.

two cowls: In accordance with RB 55.10, which prescribes two cowls and two tunics for a monk.

put these words in your mouth: A paraphrase of Isaiah 51:16.

your abbot: Grimald, who was a canon.

4.1 *as I have said . . . transaction*: See chapter 3.

Füssen: A monastery under the jurisdiction of the bishop of Augsburg, founded in Allgäu at the place where Saint Magnus died.

Adalbero: Bishop of Augsburg from 887 to 910. Ekkehard talks about him in chapter 7.

our special patron: The *Life* of Magnus presented him as an associate of Saint Gall's.

Degenau, Bernhardzell, Sitterdorf: Located on the river Sitter; in 898, King Arnulf confirmed the foundation of the church of Saint Magnus and Salomo's endowments (MGH DD Arn no. 165, pp. 251–53). For the locations, see UBSG vol. 2, no. 716, pp. 317–19.

was still abbot at that time: See note to 2.1.

wanted to be buried there: In chapter 27, however, Ekkehard reports that Salomo was buried in Constance.

5.1 *thief in the night*: 1 Thessalonians 5:2.

cowl: The word Ekkehard uses, *cappa,* had a range of meanings, including a monastic cowl and an ecclesiastical cloak that could be worn by monks and priests; see Maureen C. Miller, *Clothing the Clergy: Virtue and Power in Medieval Europe, c. 800–1200* (Ithaca, N.Y., 2014), especially 46–48.

who alone were allowed to speak: The Rule of Benedict prescribes silence at all times, especially at night (RB 42.1).

after canon-abbots: According to Ratpert, *Casus,* chapters 13, 17, and 18, Grimald's immediate predecessors were monks.

much beloved: *Amantissimus* is here understood in the passive sense; see *Dictionary of Medieval Latin from British Sources* (Turnhout, 2015), under "amare," 4.

5.2 *went in again as yesterday and the day before*: A possibly ironic paraphrase of Daniel 13:15, the verse describing the innocent Susanna who enters the garden without suspecting that the elders are about to assault her.

father Ruodker: He cannot be identified; the name often occurs in Saint Gall sources. Ermenrich of Ellwangen, for instance, mentions "master Ratger, a very simple man" *(domnus Ratger, vir simplicissimus),* who may have served as Ekkehard's inspiration for this character; see Rupert Schaab, *Mönch in St. Gallen: Zur inneren Geschichte eines frühmittelalterlichen Klosters* (Ostfildern, 2003), 64n80.

he who rises before dawn: An allusion to Psalms 119(118):147.

6.1 *the senate of our republic*: Ekkehard is consciously drawing on vocabulary from the Roman republic to describe his community. He appears to have been the first medieval writer to do so, although Roman terminology was often appropriated for describing medieval political institutions; for discussion, see Wolfgang Wehlen, *Geschichtsschreibung und Staatsauffassung im Zeitalter Ludwigs des Frommen* (Lübeck and Hamburg, 1970).

Hartmann, great in counsel: Probably the Hartmann who later became abbot; see note to 2.1. Many monks at Saint Gall had similar names, which suggests that they were related even when Ekkehard reports no family connections. Ekkehard quotes Jeremiah 32:19.

With a Humble Prayer: For the text, see AH vol. 50, no. 191, pp. 253–56. The author of this composition is probably not the Hartmann Ekkehard has in mind; see Wolfram von den Steinen, *Notker der Dichter und seine geistige Welt* (Bern, 1948), vol. 1, pp. 526–57. For other Saint Gall compositions, see Johannes Duft, "The Contribution of the Abbey of St. Gall to Sacred Music," in King and Vogler, *Culture,* 57–68.

Notker, the author of sequences: Compare below, chapter 47. The sequence is a hymn sung on festivals during the celebration of the Mass, before the Gospel. For the edition of Notker's sequences, see von den Steinen, *Notker der Dichter,* vol. 2.

The Lofty Hope of the World: For edition and discussion, see Peter Stotz, *Ardua spes mundi: Studien zu lateinischen Gedichten aus Sankt Gallen,* Geist und Werk der Zeiten 32 (Bern, 1972), 36–72.

Today We Must Sing: AH vol. 49, no. 1, pp. 7–8.

as I said: See chapter 1.

6.2 *boy's toga*: A supralinear gloss in the earliest surviving copy, Saint Gall, Stiftsbibliothek MS 615 *(B),* borrows a misleading explanation from Isidore, *Etymologiae* 19.24.16: "a boy's robe, worn while the boy was being educated" *(pallium puerile sub disciplinae cultu habitum)*. Ekkehard, however, most likely refers to the custom of ancient Rome, where freeborn boys wore the *toga praetexta,* a purple-bordered garment that they put aside when they assumed the *toga virilis* upon reaching the age of manhood. Ekkehard develops this allusion further in chapter 7.

Either this device . . . hidden here: Virgil, *Aeneid* 2.46 and 2.48.

to dress a wolf in a sheep's clothing: An allusion to Matthew 7:15.

6.3 *abbey*: The word used by Ekkehard could include not only the abbey of Saint Gall but also all its estates; see Jan Frederik

Niermeyer, ed., *Mediae Latinitatis lexicon minus,* 2nd rev. ed. (Leiden, 2002), under "abbatia," especially 4 and 5.

received a privilege for the third time: Ratpert reports the details of how the privileges of immunity (freedom from public taxation and jurisdiction) and free election were granted and confirmed under Gozbert, Grimald, and Hartmut. For Gozbert, see Ratpert, *Casus* 15 (MGH SRG vol. 75, p. 180); for Grimald, see *Casus* 19 (p. 190); for Hartmut, see *Casus* 29, 31, 33 (pp. 218, 230, 236). See also the two charters given by Charles III the Fat in 877 and 873 that confirm the privilege of free election (MGH DD Karl III nos. 5, 67, pp. 7–8, 113–14). For other charters, see note to 16.1 below.

6.4 *the nighttime lectern*: The Saint Gall Plan shows "two lecterns for reading at night" *(analogia duo ad legendum in nocte)* within the church, on both sides of the entrance to the choir for the psalmodists; see "Plan Notations," Carolingian Culture at Reichenau and St. Gall, copyright 2012, http://www.stgallplan.org/StGallDB/plan_components/public_list_berschin_english. Although the Plan of Saint Gall is an ideal representation, not based on any existing structure, it helps us understand various aspects of early medieval monasticism, from architecture to reform policies.

7.1 *our would-be monk*: Literally, "our boy wearing the *toga praetexta*" (see note to 6.2). Ekkehard's clever wordplay suggests that Salomo will wear a proper monk's habit when he grows up. The expression also carries the sense of both pretense and disguise.

King Charles . . . week of Saint Otmar: Ratpert, *Casus* 33 (MGH SRG vol. 75, pp. 234–236) described a visit by Charles III the Fat (emperor, 881–888), which has been dated to December 4–6, 883, but the feast day of Saint Otmar was celebrated on November 16. Either Ekkehard writes about a different visit here or his dates are confused. The title provides no indication because Ekkehard often used royal and imperial titles interchangeably (for instance, see below, 9.1).

from the village of Stammheim: Using the income from the royal estate at Stammheim (canton of Zurich) to commemorate

Saint Otmar, one of the two patrons of Saint Gall. Charles the Fat later gave this property to Saint Gall; see chapter 16 and Ratpert, *Casus* 32 (MGH SRG vol. 75, p. 232).

he had us eat fowl: Ekkehard emphasizes the special circumstances here because RB 39 prohibits monks from eating fowl.

Adalbero: Compare chapter 4; his visit is recorded under the year 908 in *Annales Sangallenses maiores* (MGH SS vol. 1, p. 77) and in Saint Gall, Stiftsbibliothek MS 915, pp. 6–7 (MGH Necr. Suppl., 137–38). *Annales Sangallenses maiores* (MGH SS vol. 1, p. 77) report his death under 910, and the Saint Gall necrology (MGH Necr. vol. 1, p. 472) mentions him under April 28.

signs and miracles: Acts 8:13.

surpasses the report I have heard: A paraphrase of 1 Kings (3 Kings) 10:7.

7.2 *A chapter . . . Rule*: The entry is found in Saint Gall, Stiftsbibliothek MS 915, pp. 6–8 (MGH Necr. Suppl., 137–38). The manuscript is available online at CESG.

8.1 *Peter*: There is no other evidence of this bishop of Verona.

welcoming . . . Gospel: Reception with the Gospel, not mentioned specifically in RB 53, which concerns the reception of guests, was part of the ceremony of welcoming distinguished visitors to the monastery. Compare the episode in chapter 74.

8.2 *thumb . . . like this*: This may be part of a sign language that developed in medieval monasteries because of the need to observe silence prescribed by monastic rules; see Scott G. Bruce, *Silence and Sign Language in Medieval Monasticism* (Cambridge, 2007).

as I said earlier: See chapter 3.

then also our fellow monk, and finally our abbot: See chapters 10–11.

9.1 *as Ratpert also writes*: Ratpert, *Casus* 26–33.

he handed over his abbacy: Ratpert, *Casus* 34–35.

Bernhard: Abbot from 883 to 890.

King Charles . . . imperial authority of Charles: Charles the Fat. Ekkehard often uses the titles “king” and “emperor” interchangeably.

Herisau . . . Waldkirch . . . Minderbüren: Herisau is in modern canton Appenzell-Ausserrhoden (see also chapters 79 and 81); Waldkirch and Minderbüren are in canton Sankt Gallen.

when he was dying: The Saint Gall necrology records his death on January 23 (MGH Necr. vol. 1, p. 465); he died sometime after 895.

Landaloh: According to the Saint Gall necrology, which records his death under September 10, he was bishop of Treviso (MGH Necr. vol. 1, p. 480); see Tremp, *Casus,* 142–43n14.

9.2 *the mountain of Jupiter*: The Great Saint Bernard Pass, one of the routes through the Alps that, along with the Septimer Pass, was used in the Roman times and in the Middle Ages.

Lolingen: Nollingen in modern Baden-Würtemberg was donated to Saint Gall by a charter in 752 (UBSG vol. 1, no. 15, pp. 17–19).

Count Ulrich . . . Aadorf: A charter records Count Ulrich's donation of the monastery in Aadorf (canton Thurgau) to Saint Gall in 894 (UBSG vol. 2, no. 691, pp. 292–93). This is probably the *Uodalrih iunior* (junior Ulrich) whose death the Saint Gall necrology records under May 26 (MGH Necr. vol. 1, p. 276).

Rorschach: A town on Lake Constance, not far from Saint Gall, which provided a convenient landing for approaching the monastery by the lake.

on the seventh day after his death: The dead were commemorated by Masses on the third, seventh, and thirtieth days after death. Ekkehard appears to place particular importance on the seventh day; compare chapter 44.2.

10.1 *the point from which we digressed*: See chapter 6.

before God and men: Luke 2:52.

for the father's kiss: This is part of the ceremony of the reception of guests according to RB 53.

as will later become clear: See chapter 13.

Charles: Most likely Charles the Fat (see Tremp, *Casus,* 146–47n10).

10.2 *the angel of great counsel*: Ekkehard refers to Ruodker, borrowing the words from the introit to the Christmas Mass; he uses the same quotation again in chapter 99.

the monk's tunic and cowl: That is, monastic dress prescribed by the Rule of Benedict (see RB 55.4).

became a monk of Saint Gall: Different dates have been suggested for this event, from soon after 885 to between 887 and 895. Apart from this passage, Salomo is not attested as a monk; see *Cronache,* 460n84, and Tremp, *Casus,* 147n14.

served under him: For the military language, compare RB 1.2.

10.3 *eventually increasing them*: See note to 1.2.

Reichenau: Other sources report that it was Hatto of Mainz who received the abbacy in 888.

twelve abbeys: Compare the same statement that Ekkehard makes about Hatto in 11.1.

11.1 *Abbot Bernhard was deposed, as related elsewhere*: He was deposed in 890 by King Arnulf for participating in a revolt. The sources Ekkehard refers to seem to have been lost.

made God's prelate in Constance: In 890.

presided over twelve abbeys: Compare the same statement about Salomo in 10.3. Only four abbeys are known: Reichenau, Ellwangen, Lorsch, and Weissenburg.

a monk and abbot of Fulda: According to other sources, he was a monk of Reichenau.

He ordered Mainz to be moved: This enterprise is not mentioned in other sources. Ekkehard's statement may be based on what he heard or read about the construction of new city walls and other work, which archeologists date to the late ninth century: see L. Falck, "Geschichte von Mainz," *Führer zu vor- und frühgeschichtlichen Denkmälern* 11 (1969): 58–100, at 94; Karl Heinz Esser, "Grabungsergebnisse zur rheinseitigen Stadtmauer," *Führer zu vor- und frühgeschichtlichen Denkmälern* 11 (1969): 132–40; Mechthild Schulze-Dörrlamm, "Mainz im 9. und frühen 10. Jahrhundert," in *Hatto I. Erzbischof von Mainz (891–913): Glanz der späten Karolinger von der Reichenau in den Mäuseturm,* ed. Winfried Wilhelmy (Regensburg, 2013), 88–107, at 103–5.

11.2 *royal fisc*: The properties that belonged to the king and comprised important sources of his revenue.

agents of the treasury: Ekkehard is the only source for this title.

Adalbert with Werinher in Franconia: This account is not supported by other sources and appears to link two men who were not active in the same time period. Adalbert (d. 906) belonged to the Franconian branch of the noble Babenberger family. Werinher has been identified as Werner, count in the Lobdengau from 836 to 877.

Berthold and Erchinger: Prominent counts in Alemannia who belonged to the noble Alaholfinger family. Their rise to power led to conflicts with King Conrad I (911–918) and Bishop Salomo, especially when Erchinger was proclaimed duke of Swabia in 915; see Michael Borgolte, *Die Grafen Alemanniens in merowingischer und karolingischer Zeit: Eine Prosopographie* (Sigmaringen, 1986), 110–11.

Adalbert . . . beheaded: Adalbert's execution took place on September 9, 906, and according to Regino of Prüm (*Cronicon,* entry for the year 906, MGH SRG vol. 50, p. 152), it followed the surrender of Theres rather than Babenberg. The conflict is also described in Widukind, *Res gesta Saxonicae* 1.22, and Liudprand, *Antapodosis* 2.6.

12.1 *Bodman*: A royal palace and town at the northwest end of the Überlinger Lake. Salomo received some of the Bodman properties for Saint Gall in the reign of King Louis the Child in 902 and 905 (see MGH DD Ludwig das Kind nos. 14, 37, pp. 116–17, 153–54).

Werinher and Ruodhart: Werinher (or Warin, d. 774), count of Thurgau in the Bertoldsbaar region and Linzgau (see Borgolte, *Grafen,* 282–87). Ruodhart (or Ruthard, d. ca. 790), count of Argengau (Borgolte, *Grafen,* 229–36). The persecutions are described in Walahfrid, *Vita sancti Galli* 2.14 (MGH SRM vol. 4, pp. 322–23); Walahfrid, *Vita sancti Otmari* 4–6 (MGH SS vol. 2, pp. 43–44); and Ratpert, *Casus* 6.

12.2 *Turbental*: Numerous charters record donations of properties located in Turbental (canton Zurich) to Saint Gall.

12.3 *king . . . Arnulf*: The *Annales Alemannici* report that this occurred later, in the year 913, that is, during the reign of King Conrad I (MGH SS vol. 1, p. 56).

Ingelheim: The palace, built in the 780s in the Rhine valley, was an important center of governance for Carolingian and Ottonian kings and emperors.

power: The word used by Ekkehard went back to Roman antiquity and indicated the fullness of legal, political, and magisterial power.

13.1 *The bishop invited the two men*: Apparently aiming at a reconciliation; for discussion of the following episode, see Philippe Buc, "Ritual and Interpretation: The Early Medieval Case," *Early Medieval Europe* 9 (2000): 192–96, and Gerd Althoff, "The Variability of Rituals in the Middle Ages," in *Medieval Concepts of the Past: Ritual, Memory, Historiography,* ed. Gerd Althoff, Johannes Fried, and Patrick J. Geary (Cambridge, 2002), 71–87, at 82–84.

as I have said: See chapter 10.

13.2 *four hundred pecks*: Equals eight hundred gallons; a German dry measure *(maltra),* used by Ekkehard, equals four pecks. See Loth, *Study,* 13.

guests . . . bishop's tall tales: *Fraudulenti* (deceitful) is ambivalently placed, so that it can modify either the bishop (as above) or the guests, or even both.

13.3 *Glass friends*: probably an allusion to the proverb *anulus ex vitro vitreo debetur amico* (a ring of glass befits a glass friend), attested in the Middle Ages and going back to antiquity; compare the first century BCE writer Publilius Syrus, *Sententiae* F24 (*Fortuna vitrea est: tum, cum splendet, frangitur,* "Fortune is made of glass: just when it shines, it breaks").

14.1 *Conrad*: Conrad I (911–918).

said the king: The speaker is not explicitly identified in the text, but context suggests that the idea of visiting Saint Gall came from the king; Hans Haefele, "Untersuchungen," part 2, pp. 141–42.

new hymns of praise: The hymns were likely composed for the occasion and sung in honor of the special guests during the official welcome ceremony *(adventus)*. For discussion, see Walther Bulst, "*Susceptacula regum:* Zur Kunde deutscher Reichsaltertümer," in *Lateinisches Mittelalter: Gesammelte Beiträge,* ed. Walther Berschin (Heidelberg, 1984), 130–68; Ernst H. Kantorowicz, *Laudes regiae: A Study in Liturgical Acclamations and Mediaeval Ruler Worship* (Berkeley, 1946). This visit has been dated to December 26–29, 911. *Annales Alemannici* (MGH SS vol. 1, p. 55) and *Annales Sangallenses maiores* (MGH SS vol. 1, p. 77) record the king's visit under 912.

Arbon: A town on Lake Constance, in canton Thurgau.

14.2 *The Feast of the Innocents*: A commemoration of the massacre of children by King Herod (Matthew 2:16–18). It is celebrated on December 28 in Western European Christendom.

14.3 *This one . . . lives*: A close paraphrase of Paulinus, *Vita Ambrosii* 3.4, also used by Notker, *Gesta Karoli* 2.10 (MGH SRG NS vol. 12, p. 66).

15.1 *men of the woods*: Learned readers might have recognized this phrase from a widely used school text, Horace's *Ars poetica* (line 391).

silently: Ekkehard is referring to sign language used by monks who observe the prescription of RB 6 to keep silence (see Bruce, *Silence and Sign Language*).

15.2 *what had been said earlier*: See chapter 13.

16.1 *but not yet confirmed*: Ekkehard does not seem to have consulted the documents that contradict this statement. A charter dated June 3, 818, records the grant of immunity made by Louis the Pious, which placed the abbey, and its possessions, under the defense of the emperor and freed it from public taxation and jurisdiction. See MGH DD Ludwig der Fromme vol. 1, no. 139, pp. 353–55. Louis the German confirmed it in a charter dated July 22, 854 (MGH DD Ludwig der Deutsche no. 70, pp. 99–100). Conrad I once again confirmed immunity on March 14, 912 (MGH DD Konrad I no. 5, pp. 5–6). Ekkehard may have misinterpreted Ratpert's account of the monastery's dispute with Bishop Salomo I of Constance concerning dues (Ratpert, *Casus* 21–24.)

16.2 *by the authority of Rome*: This was probably done by Bishop Salomo I in 864 (compare Iso, *De miraculis sancti Otmari* 2.2, MGH SS vol. 2, p. 53). Rome did not begin to canonize until the twelfth century.

the king's ancestors: Ekkehard thought that Conrad was descended from Werinher and Ruodhard, the persecutors of Saint Otmar; see also chapter 21 and Ratpert, *Casus* 6.

the village of Stammheim: Ratpert describes this and other donations in *Casus* 32.

advocate: An advocate was a layman who represented the interests of the monastery. In particular, advocates were responsible for secular jurisdiction over the lay tenants of a major church with an immunity. By the period when Ekkehard was writing, advocates had developed positions of power over the estates of major churches in the Empire (this tended not to happen further west) and were quite exploitative. But this development had not yet occurred by the turn of the ninth and tenth centuries. See Wolfgang Dohrmann, *Die Vögte des Klosters St Gallen in der Karolingerzeit* (Bochum, 1985); Charles West, "The Significance of the Carolingian Advocate," *Early Medieval Europe* 17 (2009): 186–206.

the week celebrating this lord of mine: The week following November 16, Saint Otmar's feast day. Ekkehard implies that Charles the Fat instituted this celebration during his visit of 883 (compare Ratpert, *Casus* 32, and above, chapter 7).

enrolled brother: For the king's name in the confraternity book, see the reconstructed version in Karl Schmid, "Versuch einer Rekonstruktion der St. Galler Verbrüderungsbücher des 9. Jahrhunderts," in *Subsidia Sangallensia 1: Materialien und Untersuchungen zu den Verbrüderungsbüchern und zu den älteren Urkunden des Stiftsarchivs St. Gallen,* ed. Michael Borgolte, Dieter Geuenich, and Karl Schmid (Saint Gall, 1986), 81–283, at 192.

16.3 *Love that does no wrong*: Compare 1 Corinthians 13:4.

monks: Ekkehard uses the genitive rather than the nominative, probably to fit in with the rhymed prose of the passage.

Actors: The word *satirici* used by Ekkehard here means "performers," "actors," or "players" (see Loth, *Study,* 49).

unaccustomed nature: The word *insolentia* can also mean "presumption, arrogance, insolence." For this intepretation, see Nelson, "Feasts," 269–76, at 272; Ludger Koerntgen, "*Regularissimi* and *Sancti huis temporis*: Reformers as Seen by Their Opponents," in *Rethinking Reform: Concepts and Narratives of Change in the Medieval Church 800–1150,* ed. Julia Barrow and Catherine Cubitt (forthcoming). We thank Professor Koerntgen for letting us read his paper ahead of publication.

16.4 *The oft-mentioned brothers*: Berthold and Erchinger.

17.1 *the brothers*: Berthold and Erchinger.

that episode: Described in chapter 12. By reminding the brothers of their debt to him and of their public humiliation, Salomo insults them and causes the escalation of the conflict (see discussion in Althoff, "Variability").

17.2 *Liutfrid*: Mentioned in other sources as an ally of Berthold and Erchinger; Ekkehard is the only source for this information about his family, as well as for most of the details of Salomo's capture and release.

you are letting him live: Exodus 22:18, paraphrased.

seized him: The *Annales Alamannici* and *Annales Sangallenses maiores* record Salomo's capture in the year 914 (MGH SS vol. 1, pp. 56 and 77).

18.1 *more reasonable group*: Compare RB 64.1 and 81.1.

to act with any further madness against: Acts 26:11, paraphrased.

Thietpoldsburg: Its identification and exact location are uncertain; suggested possibilities include the Hegau region not far from Hohentwiel, and Diepoldsburg near Lenningen, Baden-Würtemberg; see Meyer von Knonau, *Ekkeharti Casus,* 70n243, and Tremp, *Casus,* 170–71n5.

Bertha: Ekkehard is the only source that mentions this woman.

18.2 *lick their feet*: The brothers inflict public humiliation on Salomo, thus reversing the roles they had to play in the past (see Althoff, "Variability," 84).

chamber: The word Ekkehard uses refers to a living space, furnished with a fireplace, that is the most comfortable quarters in a castle or a monastery.

18.3 *blasts of trumpets*: Compare Virgil, *Aeneid* 2.313 and 8.526, and Lucan, *Pharsalia* 1.237.

19.1 *The men*: Berthold, Erchinger, and Liutfrid.

Mount Hohentwiel: Located in the Hegau region, Baden-Württemberg, about twenty miles west from Lake Constance.

According to the entry for 915 in the *Annales Alamannici* (MGH SS vol. 1, p. 56), the fortress atop the mountain was held by the enemies of King Conrad I.

Siegfried: He is mentioned only by Ekkehard.

fighting men: The word Ekkehard uses can mean "soldiers" or "garrison" or "household troops"; see David Stewart Bachrach, "*Milites* and Warfare in Pre-Crusade Germany," *War in History* 22 (2015): 298–343.

on short notice: 2 Maccabees 8:26, slightly paraphrased.

captured them alive: 2 Kings (4 Kings) 10:14, slightly paraphrased.

led them away: Ekkehard offers a much-simplified version of these events. According to the *Annales Alamannici,* after he had captured Salomo, Erchinger was himself captured by the king and exiled. In 915, he returned from exile and together with Burchard, Berthold, and others rebelled against the king. In 916, Erchinger, Berthold, and Liutfrid were executed.

19.2 *weeping and wailing*: Mark 5:38, slightly paraphrased.

19.3 *change of fortune*: Boethius, *Consolatio philosophiae* 2, prosa 1.6.

19.4 *A second Peter rescued from his Herods*: An allusion to Acts 12:11.

a third Cato . . . fallen from the sky: Ekkehard alludes to Juvenal, *Satires* 2.40, a passage that contains a rather crude satire of Roman depravity and is dripping with sarcasm.

20.1 *to be held there for an official hearing*: An allusion to Acts 25:21.

News of the affair reached: 1 Maccabees 7:3.

Couriers . . . racing: Esther 8:14.

having regained his composure: Luke 15:17.

wept . . . held back: Compare Genesis 43:30, and Walahfrid, *Vita sancti Galli* 1.5 (MGH SRM vol. 4, p. 288).

20.2 *public assembly . . . synod*: No other source mentions an assembly at Mainz. The synod (church council) that Ekkehard probably means convened at Hohenaltheim, district Donau-Ries in Bavaria, on September 20, 916. Erchinger and Berthold appeared there when summoned. They were accused of rebelling against the king and seizing Bishop Salomo and were sentenced to the life of penance in a monastery; see Horst Fuhrmann, "Die Synode von Hohenaltheim (916)—quellenkundlich betrachtet," *DA* 43 (1987): 440–68.

Burchard: The son of Count Burchard, who had attempted to establish a duchy in Alemannia and was killed in 911. According to other sources, Burchard II's elevation followed his long struggle against royal power. In 915 he was allied with Erchinger and in 916 was also summoned to the synod at Hohenaltheim but did not appear. After the death of Erchinger (proclaimed duke in 915), Burchard became duke in 917 or 918. His death is recorded on the first page of the codex that contains the confraternity book of Saint Gall (Saint Gall, Stiftsbibliothek MS 915, online at CESG; MGH Necr. Suppl., p. 136).

benefice: An estate granted by an owner to another person to use during his lifetime, typically in return for some form of service.

executed: Erchinger, Berthold, and Liutfrid were put to death on January 21, 917. This is reported, with varying details, by other sources, such as the *Annales Alamannici* (MGH SS vol. 1, p. 56), the *Annales Sangallenses* (MGH SS vol. 1, p. 78), and Hermann of Reichenau, *Chronicon*, MGH SS vol. 5, p. 112).

21.1 *hateful castle*: The castle built on the Stammheim property, mentioned in chapters 16 and 17.

the cause of such great misery: Virgil, *Aeneid* 6.93 and 11.480.

murderers: Werinher and Ruodhard; see note to 16.2.

tribute in wax: Wax was used for lighting in churches, especially to the north of the Alps, where olive oil was rare and expensive. From the mid-eighth century on, charters increasingly record provisions for lighting; see Paul Fouracre, "Eternal Light and Earthly Needs: Practical Aspects of the Development of Frankish Immunities," in *Property and Power in the Early Middle Ages,* ed. Wendy Davis and Paul Fouracre (Cambridge, 1995), 53–81; Paul Fouracre, "'Framing' and Lighting: Another Angle on Transition," in *Italy and Early Medieval Europe: Papers for Chris Wickham,* ed. Ross Balzaretti, Julia Barrow, and Patricia Skinner (Oxford, 2018), 305–14.

Rudolf . . . Welfhard . . . that stock: Counts Rudolf and Welfhard belonged to the Welf noble family, which rose to prominence in Swabia and Bavaria in the early Middle Ages. Their rise was assured when Louis the Pious married Duke Welf's daughter

Judith. Ekkehard believed that Werinher and Ruodhard belonged to that family.

the eve of Saint Otmar's Day: November 16.

was killed: This account suggests that Henry died not long before 1000. For his death, compare *Historia Welforum* 7 (Ernst König, ed., *Historia Welforum* [Stuttgart, 1938], p. 12).

21.2 *Fortune ... wheel around*: Compare chapter 3 and Boethius, *Consolatio Philosophiae* 2, metrum 1 and prosa 2.9. The image of the Wheel of Fortune, famously depicted in the thirteenth-century *Carmina Burana* manuscript (Codex Buranus, now in the Bavarian State Library in Munich), was widely used in medieval literature and art; see for instance poems 14, 16, and 17 in David Traill, ed. and trans., *Carmina Burana,* 2 vols., Dumbarton Oaks Medieval Library 48 and 49 (Cambridge, Mass., 2018). For the image, see Christopher de Hamel, *Meetings with Remarkable Manuscripts* (New York, 2017), 330.

God was demonstrating his might to him: Terence, *Eunuchus* 1032–33, paraphrased.

accuser of himself: Proverbs 18:17.

went to Rome: The only journey of Salomo to Rome that other sources confirm took place earlier, in 904.

I have deserved ... against heaven: Salomo's laments draw on Genesis 42:21, as well as on Luke 15:18 and 15:21.

relics as gifts: Relics received from the pope bestowed a special prestige and created ties of patronage that connected the recipients to the pope. While the bishops of Rome were initially very reluctant to distribute corporeal relics, from the mid-eighth century on various popes used such gifts to establish and strengthen connections to the Church north of the Alps. See John McCulloch, "From Antiquity to the Middle Ages: Continuity and Change in Papal Relic Policy from the 6th to the 8th Century," in *Pietas: Festschrift für Bernhard Kötting,* ed. Ernst Dassmann and K. Suso Frank (Münster, 1980), 313–24; Patrick Geary, *Living with the Dead in the Middle Ages* (Ithaca, N.Y., 1994), especially 208–10; Julia Smith, "Old Saints, New Cults: Roman Relics in Carolingian Francia," in *Early Medi-*

eval Rome and the Christian West: Essays in Honour of Donald A. Bullough, ed. Julia Smith (Leiden, 2000), 317–39.

Pelagius: A child believed to have been martyred in the third century, one of the patron saints of Constance. The translation of his relics may have taken place under Salomo I; see Helmut Maurer, *Die Bistümer der Kirchenprovinz Mainz,* vol. 2, *Die Konstanzer Bischöfe vom Ende des 6. Jahrhunderts bis 1206,* Germania Sacra, Neue Folge 42, part 1 (Berlin, 2003), 74–75, 106.

on whose day: August 28.

22.2 *set . . . off*: The word *dyptivit* occurs only in Ekkehard's text; it was probably his own neologism modeled on the Greek *dyptein,* "to dip" (Tremp, *Casus,* 188n20; Loth, *Study,* 10).

22.3 *two ivory tablets*: Since Ekkehard says below that these tablets served to make two sets of book covers, it has been suggested that here he means two pairs of tablets; see Johannes Duft and Rudolf Schnyder, *Die Elfenbein-Einbände der Stiftsbibliothek St. Gallen* (Beuron, 1984), 23–26.

Charles . . . when he went to sleep: Charlemagne; Ekkehard draws on Einhard, *Vita Karoli Magni* 25.

One of the tablets: Identified as the covers of the Gospel of John, Saint Gall, Stiftsbibliothek MS 60.

Sintram: The Saint Gall necrology records his death on December 18 (MGH Necr. vol. 1, p. 486; he also appears in Saint Gall documents as deacon and scribe; see Anton von Euw, "Wer war Sintram? Zu Ekkeharts IV, *Casus sancti Galli,* c[h]. 22," in *Scripturus vitam: Lateinische Biographie von der Antike bis in die Gegenwart,* ed. Dorothea Waltz (Heidelberg, 2002), 423–34.

This Gospel book: This manuscript, the so-called *Evangelium longum* (Long Gospel), is still preserved, together with its ivory covers, as Saint Gall, Stiftsbibliothek MS 53. See also note to 28.1 below.

23.1 *Como*: An episcopal city in northern Italy, lying on the way to Alemannia over the Septimer Pass; compare chapters 9 and 47 for this main route between Como and Chur (modern canton Graubünden), a city at the crossroads of several major routes across the Alps and an important ecclesiastical and trade center.

the craftiest of men: Proverbs 12:23, paraphrased.

worked up a spirited rage: John 11:33, paraphrased.

Chur: An episcopal city in canton Graubünden, Switzerland.

with this dice and gaming board: Idelfons von Arx (MGH SS vol. 2, p. 89n15) has suggested that the word *tabula,* transmitted by the surviving manuscripts, was not present in the autograph, which is no longer extant. Other editors choose to treat it as part of the text, explaining that Ekkehard may have been referring to a combined dice and board game similar to backgammon (Tremp, *Casus,* 192n6).

drinking bowl: The word Ekkehard uses, *cantharus,* could hold different meanings, from a drinking cup or pitcher to a vessel for holy water. This is the same ornate vessel that Salomo used for drinking water in chapter 22 and that Hatto had carried away using one of his tricks.

23.2 *rock crystal*: Pliny the Elder (*Natural History* 37.10.2) reported that in his day workmen suspended from ropes quarried precious rock crystal in the Alps.

abandoned the claim you have raised: Virgil, *Aeneid* 1.37, paraphrased.

contracted Italian fever and died: Hatto died on May 15, 913; see the Reichenau necrology (MGH Necr. vol. 1, p. 276). For the Italian fever, compare chapter 9.

he never benefitted from them: Ekkehard reminds his audience of Proverbs 11:4, which states that riches do not help one at the Last Judgment.

our Solomon redeemed: A reference to Proverbs 13:8.

24.1 *for the honor of Saint Mary*: For the cathedral in Constance dedicated to Mary.

Hagia Maria: Saint Mary in Greek.

Just Father: According to extant Saint Gall antiphoners, this Gospel antiphon was sung at the monastery at Vespers on the eve of Holy Week; see Lori Kruckenberg, "Ekkehard's Use of Musical Detail in the *Casus sancti Galli,*" in *Medieval Music in*

Practice: Studies in Honor of Richard Crocker, ed. Judith Peraino (Middleton, Wis., 2013), 31–32.

ambling mare: Ekkehard uses a term, *ambulatrix* (also *ambulator* in later chapters), that refers to a horse with a gentle gait.

24.2 *necessary provisions*: Genesis 42:7.

church of the Holy Cross: The church of Saint Magnus.

from wooden steps, like Esdras: See Nehemiah (2 Esdras) 8:4. Ekkehard's audience would remember that Esdras restored the Law after the exile.

guest . . . invited: Ekkehard alludes to Matthew 25:35.

25.1 *the following Easter*: April 5, 918.

charters and seals: According to a charter of March 14, 912, Conrad confirmed Salomo's donations to Saint Gall as well as the monastery's privileges of immunity, jurisdiction, and election (MGH DD Konrad I no. 5, pp. 5–6).

Pfäfers Abbey: Located in canton Sankt Gallen, founded in the first half of the eighth century, it was given to Salomo by Louis the Child in 905. In 909, Salomo handed it over to Saint Gall. For its history, see Sebastian Grüninger, "Das bewegte Schicksal des Klosters Pfäfers im 10. Jahrhundert: Zum Quellenwert von Schilderungen Ekkeharts IV. von St. Gallen," *Schriften des Vereins für Geschichte des Bodensees und seiner Umgebung* 127 (2009): 25–46.

Pfäfers was taken away: See chapter 73.

provided for his beloved Saint Gall: Compare chapters 2 and 10.

exchange: Twenty-two charters recording exchanges survive from the period between 892 and 914.

25.2 *which of the two abbeys, Reichenau or Saint Gall*: Salomo did not have the abbacy of Reichenau (see note to 10.3).

more spacious . . . more . . . pleasant: In the word *saturatior* in the oldest surviving manuscript *B*, *r* is corrected to *l*, probably to make the pun *latior/satu(r/l)atior* more obvious; see Haefele, "Untersuchungen," part 2, pp. 164–65; compare Tremp, *Casus,* 201n15.

I have sought it out . . . beauty: Salomo expresses his fondness for the abbey of Saint Gall by quoting Wisdom 8:2, the passage that uses erotic language to express the desire for Wisdom.

beloved by him and men: A slight paraphrase of Sirach 45:1, where this refers to Moses; Notker used the same quotation to describe Gall in his hymn to this saint (von den Steinen, *Notker der Dichter,* vol. 2, p. 72; Tremp, *Casus,* 201–2n17).

26.1 *in the morning after the Feast of the Innocents*: On December 29, 918 or 919.

It was Students' Day at Saint Gall: For discussion of this episode, see Nelson, "Feasts."

new guest: The student quotes Virgil, *Aeneid* 4.10, and uses metric verse with double rhymes.

26.2 *the three days of play established by imperial rule*: By Conrad I; see chapter 16.

in its proper place: See chapters 51–55.

27.1 *On the eighth day after the Nativity of the Lord*: January 1, 919 or 920.

sacristy: A room in a church for keeping vestments and sacred vessels used in services.

canons: Here Ekkehard probably means cathedral canons (see Loth, *Study,* 26).

On the eighth day after the feast of Saint John: January 3.

Saint Mary and Pelagius: Patron saints of Constance and its cathedral.

Köllikon: See chapter 25.

the church . . . he had built: See chapter 4.

special royal privileges: A charter given by King Arnulf in 898 confirms this (MGH DD Arn no. 165, pp. 251–53); see also 4.1.

on the day before Epiphany: January 5, 919 or 920.

28.1 *he was a learned and extremely well-disciplined man*: Regino of Prüm (*Cronicon,* entry for 890, MGH SRG vol. 50, p. 136) also notes Salomo's nobility, prudence, and wisdom.

he was skilled at drawing: Ekkehard is the only source that mentions Salomo's artistic achievements.

L and C of the Long Gospel: For these decorated initials *L* (*Liber generationis,* "The Book of the genealogy," Matthew 1:1) and *C* (*Cum esset desponsata mater Ihesu,* "When the mother of Jesus had been betrothed," Matthew 1:18), see Saint Gall, Stiftsbibliothek MS 53, pp. 7 and 11, available online at CESG.

composing metrical verse: For two poems attributed to Salomo, see MGH Poetae vol. 4, part 1, pp. 296–310.

At the level where the apostle puts prophets: Ekkehard refers to 1 Corinthians 12:28, according to which God has placed prophets second only to apostles in the Church, and 14:1–5, which praises the gift of prophecy.

puffs up our ears: An allusion to Boethius, *Consolatio* 3, prosa 6.1, a passage freely translating a quote from Euripides, *Andromache* 319–20. These lines were well known to and commented upon by Carolingian scholars. Notker Labeo, or Notker the German, Ekkehard's teacher, included them in his German translation of Boethius; for discussion, see Hans Haefele, "Untersuchungen," part 1, pp. 177–78.

29.1 *she became abbess there*: There is no direct evidence of her identity, but Notker's poem addressed to Salomo (MGH Poetae vol. 4, part 1, p. 345, no. 6, lines 5–6) mentions an unnamed nun who was dear to the addressee.

daughter . . . ripe for a husband: Virgil, *Aeneid* 7.53.

our mountains derive their names: The hills Waltramsberg (now Rosenberg) and Notkersberg (now Freudenberg), located, respectively, to the north and the southeast of Saint Gall (Meyer von Knonau, *Ekkeharti Casus,* 113–15n393).

approached to become king Arnulf's mistress: Ekkehard's choice of Latin words may point to Ovid, *Heroides* 16.268.

29.2 *Louis, Charles, Arnulf, another Louis, and Conrad*: Louis the German (843–876), Charles III the Fat (881–887), Arnulf (887–899), Louis the Child (900–911), and Conrad I (911–918).

30.2 *parents*: A charter recorded by Iso in 868 gives his parents' names, Erimbert and Waltrada, and describes a donation made by his brother Luto of his possessions in the Weinfelden region in northern Thurgau (UBSG vol. 2, no. 539, pp. 152–53).

30.3 *they . . . fell at his feet*: The ritual described by Ekkehard mostly corresponds to instructions for public penance, a practice well established in Carolingian society by that time. The story also reflects ritual innovations introduced into the traditional context; see Mayke de Jong, "Pollution, Penance, and Sanctity: Ekkehard's 'Life of Iso of St. Gall,'" in *The Community, the Family, and the Saint: Patterns of Power in Early Medieval Europe: Selected Proceedings of the International Medieval Congress, University of Leeds, 4–7 July 1994, 10–13 July 1995*, ed. Joyce Hill and Mary Swan (Brepols, 1998), 145–58. For a recent exploration of penance, see Rob Meens, *Penance in Medieval Europe, 600–1200* (Cambridge, 2014), with this episode discussed at 152–54.

30.4 *Kyrie Eleison*: "Lord, have mercy," a Greek invocation that formed an important element of Western Latin liturgy.

pyx: Small container holding the Communion bread.

at a synod: No record of this survives.

31.1 *she dreamed*: Dreams and visions seen during pregnancy were a frequent motif in classical and medieval literature, especially in hagiography (for instance, Cicero discussed such dreams in *De divinatione* 1.39, 1.42, and 1.46, and Jonas described the dream of Columban's mother in *Vita Columbani* 1.2, MGH SRG vol. 37, p. 154). The specific details of Iso's mother's dream, however, seem to have no exact analogies in other dream descriptions.

the anchorite Eusebius: An anchorite is a person who has withdrawn into religious seclusion, enclosed in a sealed cell with only a window for food and pious contact. Eusebius was a monk who came to Saint Gall from Ireland and died in 884 as an anchorite at Victorsberg (Vorarlberg, Austria). Ekkehard mentioned his name in a poem about the most venerable monks of Saint Gall and added this gloss: "An Irishman who was enclosed there for fifty years and made prophecies to Charles (III) and others" (*Liber benedictionum* no. 44, line 10; Johannes Egli, ed., *Der "Liber benedictionum" Ekkeharts IV: Nebst den kleinern Dichtungen aus dem Codex Sangallensis 393* [Saint Gall, 1909], 223).

Your wife will bear a son: A paraphrase of Luke 1:13.

whom you will dedicate to Saint Gall: The child was to become an oblate, a person dedicated to monastic life by his parents, according to a practice widespread in early medieval Europe. The Rule of Benedict (RB 59) recommends the procedure to be followed in such cases. For discussion, see Mayke de Jong, *In Samuel's Image: Child Oblation in the Early Medieval West* (Leiden, 1996).

31.2 *fellow countryman*: *Compatrianus* is Ekkehard's neologism; compare his *Ad picturas claustri sancti Galli*, line 101 (Egli, *Liber*, 377); see Tremp, *Casus*, 219n8.

Charles: Charles the Fat.

as Ratpert also writes: Ratpert, *Casus* 31 (MGH SRG vol. 75, p. 230). The donation that Ratpert mentioned took place in 882.

The boy was born: A line from the introit to the Christmas Mass, going back to Isaiah 9:6.

As we have already mentioned: See chapters 1–3.

King Rudolf of Burgundy: Ekkehard is the only source for the information here provided, and he seems confused: Rudolf became king in 888, seventeen years after Iso's death. Ekkehard may have meant Rudolf's father, Count Conrad II of Auxerre.

Grandval: Moutier-Grandval Abbey (in today's canton Bern), founded in the seventh century, at the time described controlled by the counts of Auxerre, later kings of Burgundy.

31.3 *the power*: Ekkehard plays on the double meaning of *virtus* as "power" and "miracle."

32.1 *prolific in such miracles*: *Vita sancti Aridii* 17 (MGH SRM vol. 3, p. 588). This life, ascribed to Gregory of Tours, may have been available to Ekkehard in a collection of saints' lives, Saint Gall, Stiftsbibliothek MS 551, p. 372 (online at CESG).

money to be deposited in the bank: An allusion to Luke 19:23–25.

32.2 *set the limits that cannot be passed*: A paraphrase of Job 14:5.

died: *Annales Sangallenses maiores* record Iso's death on May 14, 871 (MGH SS vol. 1, p. 76).

33.1 *they were of one heart and soul*: A paraphrase of Acts 4:32.

as I have already said: See chapters 1 and 2.

divine and secular learning: See note to 2.1.

seven liberal arts: Grammar, rhetoric, dialectic, arithmetic, geometry, astronomy, and music. On the instruction in these arts at Saint Gall, see Grotans, *Reading*, 76–79.

I have already touched upon this earlier: See chapter 6.

33.2 *stumbling in speech*: Notker also described himself as a stutterer in several of his surviving writings; see von den Steinen, *Notker der Dichter*, vol. 1, pp. 519–20.

when demons attacked: See chapters 41–42.

34.1 *just as Fabius instructs . . . athletes*: Marcus Fabius Quintilian points out that athletes' well-formed muscles look beautiful and demonstrate their fitness for competitions (*Institutio oratoria* 8.3.10).

both languages: Latin and German. Ekkehard mentions Tuotilo's compositions in chapters 6 and 46.

our Charles: Charles the Fat, who was particularly associated with Alemannia, having received it in 876, along with Rhaetia, after the death of his father, Louis the German.

34.2 *clear . . . as a teacher*: Compare Quintilian, *Institutio oratoria* 8.2.22, and Cassiodorus, *Institutiones* 1.1.3. Ekkehard uses the same expression in chapter 127.

conducting the business of the chapter and administering punishment: At daily meetings of the chapter, monks' behavior was sometimes judged and punishment administered.

35.1 *senators of our republic*: Here and elsewhere Ekkehard turns to Roman republican vocabulary to describe the life of his monastery (see Introduction).

backbiting: *Dorsiloquia*, Ekkehard's neologism (Loth, *Study*, 10; Tremp, *Casus*, 229n3).

walking in levity: Tobit 3:17. Ekkehard uses the same quotation in the preface.

35.2 *so that from the one you may learn the extent*: Virgil, *Aeneid* 2.65–66, slightly paraphrased. Ekkehard also used this quotation as a gloss in the manuscript containing the Latin translation of Josephus Flavius's *History of the Jewish War* (Saint Gall, Stiftsbibliothek MS 627, p. 197, col. B, available at CESG).

Sindolf: The name of "priest Sindolf" appears among the monks' signatures in a charter issued by Salomo III in 895 (UBSG vol.

2, no. 697, p. 299). Sindolf's death is recorded in the Saint Gall necrology under January 10 (MGH Necr. vol. 1, p. 464).

the source . . . of the . . . hatred: Compare Gregory the Great, *Regula pastoralis* 3.14 and *Moralia* 7.17. Both works, available to Ekkehard, are still preserved at the Stiftsbibliothek Sankt Gallen (MS 219 and MS 207, available at CESG).

believed the story: John 4:50.

could not get out of: Compare Terence, *Eunuchus* 712–13.

36.1 *between the services . . . most suitable for such an hour*: The Rule of Benedict (RB 8) recommends studying the psalter and reading biblical texts after Vigils, during longer nights at wintertime.

confident in his strength: A paraphrase of Juvenal, *Satires* 10.10–11, a passage describing Milo of Croton, a sixth-century BCE athlete famous for his physical strength.

the brothers' whip: Corporal punishments were prescribed in cases specified in RB 23.5, 28.1, and 30, but they were to be administered only on the abbot's authority (RB 70).

warm room: One of the few heated rooms in a medieval monastery where monks could gather in the colder months after services or work.

be strong and courageous: Tuotilo uses an exhortation that occurs several times in the Old Testament. See Deuteronomy 31:7 and 31:23; Joshua 1:6, 1:7, and 1:9; and Daniel 10:19.

36.2 *flogged*: More literally, "unleashed a hailstorm." *Ingrandinat* is Ekkehard's neologism derived from *grando,* "hail" (Loth, *Study,* 12; Tremp, *Casus,* 234n11).

with his hands and feet: Terence, *Andria* 161.

After this severe punishment: Phaedrus, *Fabulae Aesopiae* 1.3.9; Terence, *Eunuchus* 774, slightly paraphrased.

I need to shout: Terence, *Phormio* 985.

36.3 *stalks in the darkness*: Psalms 91(90):6, slightly paraphrased.

36.4 *tattletale*: *Famidicus* is Ekkehard's neologism (Loth, *Study,* 11).

as I mentioned earlier: See chapter 35.

37.1 *before God are not forgotten*: Luke 12:6, slightly paraphrased.

Hartmann: Abbot from 922 to 925; see chapters 47–48.

Waltram: Waltram's autograph appears among the professions of Saint Gall monks, and he also acted as a scribe of various legal documents from 885/6 on. He was a librarian from 905 to 909 and also wrote a number of poems (for instance MGH Poetae vol. 4, part 1, pp. 310–14); for more references, see Schaab, *Mönch,* 94). Ekkehard also writes about him in 46.3.

Ruodker whom I mentioned above: See chapter 5.

saints with the saints, elect with the elect: Psalms 18(17):26–27, paraphrased; also used in 57.2.

37.2 *always the same*: Cicero, *Tusculanae disputationes* 3.31, thus describes Socrates, who always faced the world with equanimity as befit a wise man.

I have already described: See chapter 33.

lay in ambush: Terence, *Phormio* 229, slightly paraphrased.

because of the tenor of the Rule: The Rule of Benedict prescribes the observance of silence at all times (see especially RB 6).

38.1 *When King Charles came to the monastery*: See chapter 7.

as Ratpert also wrote: Ratpert, *Casus* 32.

With the new abbot installed: In 883, Hartmut resigned and was succeeded by Bernhard.

38.2 *he exalts the humble and humbles the haughty*: Notker refers to the idea often expressed in the Bible; see especially Matthew 23:12 and Luke 1:52 and 14:11.

devilish mocker: The word *temptator* used by Ekkehard often served as a code for the devil; see, for instance, Matthew 4:3.

city gate: This contradicts the later account in chapters 71 and 136, according to which the walls and gates of the city were constructed at a later time.

38.3 *to heal*: *Conbullire* is Ekkehard's neologism (Loth, *Study,* 39).

39.1 *servers for the week*: The Rule of Benedict (RB 35) requires that all monks serve each other in turn.

measure of drink: According to RB 40, which prescribes the daily amount of wine.

39.2 *Hartmann*: It is uncertain to which Hartmann Ekkehard refers. The name appears three times in the Saint Gall necrology; for discussion see Schaab, *Mönch,* 169–72, and Tremp, *Casus,* 243n9.

Waltram, who was then dean: Probably different from the Waltram mentioned in chapter 37, whom no other source identifies as dean. Another dean named Waltram, a possible relation, appears at a later time, on a charter issued in 959/60; compare Schaab, *Mönch,* 94n448 and 98n486; Tremp, *Casus,* 244n10.

meted out his punishment in accordance with the Rule: This is RB 67.6, slightly paraphrased.

39.3 *in a chapter about him*: Chapter 34.

traveled far and wide: Ezekiel 39:15, slightly paraphrased; also compare Zechariah 6:7.

abbots under whom he served: Compare RB 1.2 and chapter 10.3.

allowed, and often ordered: The Rule of Benedict (RB 67.7) forbids the monks to leave the monastery without the abbot's order.

relief work: Ekkehard develops this theme in chapter 45.

40.1 *serge*: The word can mean both the material (here, wool) and a garment. Wool was used for monks' clothes, especially those worn in winter (see RB 55.5).

the monastery of Saint Alban: Located to the south of the city and dedicated to the patron saint of Mainz, it was founded in the late eighth century.

roundsman: A monastic official whose responsibilities included supervising the monks. See Hugh Feiss, "*Circatores:* From Benedict of Nursia to Humbert of Romans," *American Benedictine Review* 40 (1989): 346–79, this episode at 351; and Scott G. Bruce, "'Lurking with Spiritual Intent': A Note on the Origin and Functions of the Monastic Roundsman *(Circator),*" *Revue Bénédictine* 109 (1999): 75–89. See also below, chapter 67.

sitting on a donkey out of reverence for God: Ekkehard's audience would think about the accounts of the Gospels describing Christ's entry into Jerusalem on a donkey (see, for instance, Matthew 21:2–7.) Closer to home, the *Life of Otmar* reported that the saint used a donkey whenever he needed to go outside on monastery business (Walahfrid, *Vita sancti Otmari* 2, MGH SS vol. 2, p. 42). Compare also Numbers 22:22.

40.2 *special friend*: Ekkehard uses the word of his own invention, *commatrina,* literally, "co-godmother" (Loth, *Study,* 4; Tremp, *Casus,* 247n11).

He eagerly drank it up: A paraphrase of Virgil, *Aeneid* 1.738. Ekkehard used an exact quotation in his *Liber benedictionum,* no. 8, line 30 (Egli, *Liber,* p. 51).

don't add sin to sin: Isaiah 30:1 and Sirach 5:5.

40.3 *the service of Martha*: An allusion to Luke 10:38–42, which describes the sisters Mary and Martha, who came to personify the spiritual and the practical service, respectively.

I have the sky . . . footstool: A paraphrase of Isaiah 66:1. Compare Ekkehard, *Liber benedictionum* no. 54, line 64 (Egli, *Liber,* p. 265).

40.4 *forgiveness on his and my behalf*: The monk should have been punished for his lack of discipline, but only by the abbot's order (see RB 2.25 and 70).

40.5 *a likely place for robbers*: Compare *Waltharius* 496 (MGH Poetae vol. 6, part 1, p. 44).

a valiant-looking man: Compare *Waltharius* 454 (MGH Poetae vol. 6, part 1, p. 43).

utterly unafraid: Virgil, *Aeneid* 10.770, slightly paraphrased. Ekkehard also uses this expression in 52.2 and 63.1.

41.1 *as I mentioned*: See chapter 33.

rose before dawn . . . chanting out: A paraphrase of Psalms 119(118):147, the verse used by Ekkehard in chapters 5 and 44.

tears . . . eyes: A paraphrase of Jeremiah 9:18.

from behind the altar: Compare the Plan of Saint Gall, which shows this altar and the crypt. See Carolingian Culture at Reichenau and Saint Gall, especially "Plan Notations."

fittingly it has turned out for you: Gregory the Great, *Dialogues* 3.4.

41.2 *service*: Ekkehard uses the word *servitium,* which can mean both "performing a task" or "duty," possibly as a slave or servant, and "divine service" or "liturgy." The latter meaning would imply a sarcastic reference to the devil's nasty growling as "infernal service," contrasted with the fallen angel's formerly angelic sounds (for ironic meaning, see Loth, *Study,* 115).

the staff . . . had belonged to the saint and his teacher: As reported in the *vitae* (lives) of Saint Gall, this staff was sent by Columban to Gall as a sign of forgiveness (see *Vita sancti Galli vetustissima* 1, MGH SRM vol. 4, pp. 251–52, and Wetti, *Vita sancti Galli* 26, MGH SRM vol. 4, p. 271).

sphere of the Holy Cross: Likely a *globus cruciger* (cross-bearing orb), a symbol of Christian dominion over the cosmos. Rooted in antiquity, this image was widely used throughout the Middle

Ages, from representations of Christ and the saints to imperial regalia. For discussion and illustrations, see Percy Ernst Schramm, *Sphaira, Globus, Reichsapfel: Wanderung und Wandlung eines Herrschaftszeichens von Caesar bis zu Elisabeth II* (Stuttgart, 1958), and Emily Albu, *The Medieval Peutinger Map: Imperial Roman Revival in a German Empire* (New York, 2014).

41.3 *sacristan*: A person who was in charge of the sacred vestments and vessels.

41.4 *wondering to himself*: Luke 24:12.

a man who was guided by the Rule: That is, a man observing silence (see RB 6).

41.5 *to occupy myself . . . for me*: A paraphrase of Psalms 131(130):1.

42.1 *it had thirteen seats*: Compare the Saint Gall Plan, which shows a space for the choir for the psalmodists *(chorus psallentium)* within the church. See "Plan Notations," Carolingian Culture at Reichenau and St. Gall.

the church of Saint Gall has more chapels than other churches: Compare the Saint Gall Plan, showing chapels in the side aisles.

None: The service performed at the ninth hour of the day.

Compline: The last service of the day before dark.

while it was still clear daylight: 2 Samuel (2 Kings) 3:35.

42.2 *I am writing down . . . today*: The devil mockingly chides Notker for failing to observe the Rule; for discussion, see Hellgardt, "*Casus sancti Galli* Ekkeharts IV," 45.

O God, come to my assistance: This verse from Psalms 70:1(69:2) is recited in the beginning of the Divine Office, a continuous cycle of monastic liturgy celebrated in eight prayer services according to the Rule of Benedict (see RB 16). Ekkehard quotes this verse again in 57.4.

42.3 *the time was still inappropriate*: The expression used by Ekkehard, *horis competentibus,* reminds his audience of RB 47.1 and especially 48.21, which prohibits the brothers from associating with one another at inappropriate times. Compare also RB 31.18 and 50.1.

to explain to me in detail: Virgil, *Aeneid* 6.723, paraphrased.

43.1 *son of a count and called Wolo*: His name appears in the sources with different spellings (see Schaab, *Mönch,* 18 and 86n352); the thirteenth-century *Life of Notker* specifies that he was the son of a count of Kyburg (in the modern canton of Zurich) and Notker's nephew.

restless and given to wandering: Compare RB 1.11, the critique of wandering monks.

disciplined with reprimands and rods: As RB 30.3 prescribes.

43.2 *Old men . . . dream*: A paraphrase of Joel 2:28.

For he was at the point of death: John 4:47.

where now: Virgil, *Aeneid* 5.670.

43.3 *he fell . . . and broke his neck*: An entry for the year 876 in *Annales Sangallenses maiores* contains an entry, "Wolo fell" (*Volo cecidit,* MGH SS vol. 1, p. 77). The Saint Gall necrology (MGH Necr. vol. 1, p. 486) records his death on December 12.

viaticum: The Eucharist given to a dying person.

44.1 *May we pass the night in joy, just as we spent the day in joy*: This prayer is found in an eleventh-century Saint Gall breviary (Saint Gall, Stiftsbibliothek MS 387, p. 693).

Let the day's own trouble be sufficient for the day: A paraphrase of Matthew 6:34.

44.2 *On the seventh day after the man's death*: Compare 9.2.

Many sins are forgiven him, because he has loved much: This paraphrased verse from Luke 7:47, which refers to the sinful woman, is here applied to Wolo.

44.3 *rise . . . prayers*: A paraphrase of Psalms 119(118):147. Ekkehard turns to the same psalm verse earlier, in chapters 5 and 41.

God, we praise you: The beginning of a hymn that had a prominent place in the Christian tradition from late antiquity on.

44.4 *he became shining bread*: Probably bread to be offered up in sacrifice. Ekkehard uses the same image when he talks about the death of Saint Gall; see *Liber benedictionum* no. 38, line 75 (Egli, *Liber,* p. 198); *Ad picturas claustri sancti Galli,* line 122 (Egli, *Liber,* p. 379).

passed: The Saint Gall necrology (MGH Necr. vol. 1, p. 483) records his death on October 25 (see also Schaab, *Mönch,* 89n386).

45.1 *in a moment, in the twinkling of an eye*: A paraphrase of 1 Corinthians 15:52.

45.2 *reprimanded . . . anyone*: A paraphrase of Luke 9:21.

45.3 *by invoking Saint Gall he cast out a demon*: This motif, well known to Ekkehard's audience from the Bible and saints' lives, would especially remind them of a similar miracle performed by Saint Gall himself (Wetti, *Vita sancti Galli* 15, MGH SRM vol. 4, pp. 264–65; Walahfrid, *Vita sancti Galli* 1.15, MGH SRM vol. 4, pp. 295–96; Ratpert, *Casus* 3).

our age is such: Ekkehard repeats the critique he has expressed in his preface. For discussion, see Introduction.

he passed away to joy: Tuotilo's death is recorded in the Saint Gall necrology under April 27 (MGH Necr. vol. 1, p. 472).

46.1 *chosen vessel*: A paraphrase of Acts 9:15.

bereft of his brothers: It is likely, however, that Notker died before Tuotilo; for dates, see Schaab, *Mönch,* 84n331 and 89nn385–86.

stricken with grief to his heart's core: Genesis 6:6, slightly paraphrased.

he had copied Greek canonical Epistles: Seven New Testament letters not written by Paul. Scholars disagree as to the extent of Notker's knowledge of the Greek but note that he showed an active interest in the language. See Bernice M. Kaczynski, *Greek in the Carolingian Age: The St. Gall Manuscripts* (Cambridge, Mass., 1988), especially 18–19; Walther Berschin, *Greek Letters and the Latin Middle Ages: From Jerome to Nicholas of Cusa,* trans. Jerold C. Frakes (Washington, D.C., 1988).

Liutward, the bishop of Vercelli: Very influential at the court of Charles the Fat as archchancellor starting around 878 and archchaplain between approximately 880 and 887, he was bishop from 880 on; see Simon MacLean, *Kingship and Politics in the Late Ninth Century: Charles the Fat and the End of the Carolingian Empire* (Cambridge, 2003), especially 178–85.

as I said: See chapters 35–36.

exquisitely written codex: This codex has not survived, but other Saint Gall manuscripts preserve evidence of Notker's work as scribe; for discussion, see Susan Rankin, "*Ego itaque Notker scripsi,*" *Revue Bénédictine* 101 (1991): 268–98.

he had stolen it from: In the earliest surviving witness *B* (Saint Gall, Stiftsbibliothek MS 615, p. 138, online at CESG), the passage that follows has lacunae, which probably result from a corrupted or missing text in the exemplar. Haefele's reconstruction of this fragment may be translated as follows: "... <Sindolf spoke of it> as if it had been caused by a miracle to avoid ever lending his assent to a prank of the advanced years of the great man"; see Haefele, *Casus,* 104n42. An abrupt transition to the next section may indicate that more of the text was lost, such as the description of Notker's death (Tremp, *Casus,* 270n13).

46.2 *a psaltery or a rotta*: String instruments, probably similar to the lyre.

Today We Must Sing and Adorned . . . Virtues: For the texts, see AH vol. 49, no. 1, pp. 7–8 and p. 283; for discussion, see Susan Rankin, "*Ut a patribus audiuimus:* Tuotilo, as Framed by Ekkehart IV," in Ganz and Dora, *Tuotilo,* 195–211. See also chapter 6, where Ekkehard mentions other Saint Gall compositions.

tropes: Additions to preexisting chants sung during the Mass.

Charles: Charles III the Fat.

offertory: Or *offerenda,* the antiphon sung during the oblation ceremony in the Eucharistic service.

Men of Galilee: Transmitted in Saint Gall, Stiftsbibliothek MS 381, p. 258, and MS 484, p. 123.

they say he prevailed upon Tuotilo: This may have taken place during Charles III's visit to Saint Gall in 883.

Since our Lord Jesus Christ: Here and below Ekkehard refers to various tropes; for the text see AH vol. 49, p. 19; for discussion of Saint Gall tropes and Tuotilo's compositions, see Susan Rankin, "From Tuotilo to the First Manuscripts: The Shaping of a Trope Repertory at Saint Gall," *Recherches nouvelles sur les tropes liturgiques* (1993): 395–413, reprinted in *Embellishing the Liturgy: Tropes and Polyphony* (Aldershot, 2009), 365–86.

Father Almighty, the Fount and Source: AH vol. 47, no.4, p. 50.

46.3 *I mentioned earlier*: In chapter 37.

Hartmann, who became our abbot: See chapter 47.

their names appear in the hymn books: Hartmann's name is found in the codex that contains the repertoire of Saint Gall chants, Saint Gall, Stiftsbibliothek MS 381, p. 22, with the texts of his compositions on pp. 23–35. The manuscript can be consulted online at CESG and in the facsimile edition, Wulf Arlt and Susan Rankin, eds., *Stiftsbibliothek Sankt Gallen Codices 484 and 381* (Winterthur, 1996), vol. 3.

Waltram's sequence: Edited in AH, vol. 50, no. 184, pp. 244–45, with other compositions by Waltram on pp. 245–49.

ambiguity in their names: The name Hartmann often occurs in Saint Gall sources (see discussion in von den Steinen, *Notker der Dichter,* vol. 1, 525–26, and Schaab, *Mönch,* 169–70).

in their own place: Ekkehard may refer to his account of Ekkehard I in chapter 80 and Notker the Physician in chapter 123.

47.1 *chose Hartmann as abbot*: In 922, three years after the death of Salomo, the period during which Dean Alberich ruled the monastery.

a short book about his time: This book, no longer extant, appears to have been available to the twelfth-century writer who continued the *Casus* from where Ekkehard had left off; see *Continuatio anonyma* (*Cronache,* p. 314).

subordinates: Literally, "almost equals."

Hartmut's statutes: See Ratpert, *Casus* 27.

antiphonary: A book containing antiphons, short chants based on the Psalms, sung responsively during the Divine Office.

47.2 *chanting*: Other accounts of how the Roman chant was introduced into the Frankish Church (written by Walahfrid Strabo, John the Deacon, and Notker the Stammerer) differ from Ekkehard's story and disagree in important points; see Susan Rankin, "Ways of Telling Stories," 371–94.

as John also wrote: John the Deacon (also known as John Hymmonides, ca. 824–ca. 882), the author of the *Life of Gregory the Great.* His account, far less favorable to the Franks, describes their chanting as barbaric (*Vita Gregorii Magni* 2.7–10, PL vol. 75, cols. 90–93, at col. 91A). In the Saint Gall copy of this work, Saint Gall, Stiftsbibliothek MS 578, p. 54 (online at CESG), Ekkehard complemented John's story by adding a gloss about Peter and Romanus.

Adrian: Adrian I (772–795).

47.3 *you have secured a fourfold reward*: Ekkehard alludes to Matthew 10:41.

He was a stranger . . . to drink: A reference to Matthew 25:35–40.

47.4 *the news spread*: Virgil, *Aeneid* 3.121, 7.392, and 11.139. Ekkehard also uses a variant of this expression later, in 63.1, 84.4, and 135.1.

Romana and *Amoena*: The melodies for these sequences, as well as for the *Frigdora* and *Occidentana,* are found in Saint Gall, Stiftsbibliothek MS 484, a collection of the Saint Gall chant repertory (facsimile in Arlt and Rankin, *Stiftsbibliothek,* vol. 2).

47.5 *as if in a mirror*: Just as one looks in a mirror to check that everything is in order.

significative letters of the alphabet: The significative letters were added to clarify neumatic notation for performance and to add information not found in the neumes, mainly concerning rhythm or pitch.

Notker the Stammerer elucidated the significance: In the *Epistola ad Landbertum,* preserved in Saint Gall, Stiftsbibliothek MS 381, pp. 6–9, edited in Ernst Dümmler, *St. Gallische Denkmale aus der karolingischen Zeit* (Zurich, 1859), 223–24, and Jacques Froger, "L'épitre de Notker sur les 'lettres significatives,'" *Études grégoriennes* 5 (1962): 23–71.

Martianus: Martianus Capella, the fifth-century author of the treatise *On the Marriage of Philology and Mercury (De nuptiis Philologiae et Mercurii),* one of the main texts for studying the liberal arts in the Middle Ages. Ekkehard may be referring to the text entitled *De sono singularum litterarum* (an excerpt from Martianus Capella, *De nuptiis* 3.261), which follows Notker's letter to Landbert in Saint Gall, Stiftsbibliothek MS 381, pp. 10–12.

48.1 *Hartmann died*: The Saint Gall necrology records his death on September 21 (MGH Necr. vol. 1, p. 481).

sound: *Clanctus* is Ekkehard's neologism (Loth, *Study,* 8).

Tuscan boars, as someone said: The Tuscan boar is often mentioned in classical literature; see, for instance, Juvenal, *Satires* 1.22–23.

cellarers: According to RB 31, the officials who looked after the property of the monastery.

farms: Ekkehard's use of this term, in contrast with "benefices," suggests that he is thinking here about lands managed by cellarers.

49.1 *Engilbert*: Abbot from 925 to 933; see Schaab, *Mönch,* 91n407.

sent to Conrad: Conrad I was king of East Francia earlier, from 911 to 918. In chapter 51 Ekkehard reports that Engilbert went to King Henry (919–936), which agrees with the entry for the year 925 in *Annales Sangallenses maiores* (MGH SS vol. 1, p. 78).

vicar of Saint Gall: Gerold Meyer von Knonau suggests that the saint was perceived as the actual abbot, and the current abbot as his deputy (*Ekkeharti Casus,* 180n627).

stewards I have mentioned: See chapter 48.

49.2 *Eberhard*: Duke of Franconia (918–939).

at the point of death: A paraphrase of John 4:47, a verse also quoted in 43.2.

I did not wish to make you sad: Ekkehard may have meant this as an allusion to Leviticus 25:14.

49.3 *Count Henry, ennobled by his wife Mathilda*: The future King Henry I the Fowler, who was born in 876, became duke of Saxony in 912 and ruled as king from 919 to 936. He married Mathilda, the daughter of a Saxon count, in 909. Mathilda was venerated as a saint after her death in 968, her religious devotion celebrated in her two Lives and medieval chronicles.

a long story: Virgil, *Aeneid* 1.341–42, slightly paraphrased.

raised to the kingship: Henry was elected king at Fritzlar in 919. Ekkehard's account of these events generally agrees with other sources, such as Widukind, *Res gestae Saxonicae* 1.26.

50.1 *Giselbert, the duke of Lotharingia*: Giselbert (928–939). Lotharingia was initially a successor kingdom of the Carolingian Empire that comprised parts of present-day Germany and Lorraine; it became a duchy in 900.

Both rose up in arms: Ekkehard's story of the dukes' rebellion appears to refer to the conflict that took place later, in 936, after the death of Henry I and the accession of Henry's son Otto I.

Breisach: Although this castle on the Upper Rhine, held by Eberhard's army, was one of the places where the war between Otto I and the rebellious dukes played out, the events described here happened elsewhere, in the vicinity of Andernach, on October 2, 939.

Chuono, a man of royal descent: Chuono (Conrad), count in the Niederlahngau (d. 948), was a relative of King Conrad I.

50.2 *narrow chested*: Virgil, *Georgics* 4.83.

women and apples: An allusion to the story of Eve; see Genesis 3.

like a new David: Ekkehard refers to the famous battle between David and Goliath in 1 Samuel (1 Kings) 17.

50.3 *Burchard, the duke of Swabia*: Burchard II of Swabia (917–926), also mentioned in chapter 20.

Saint Wiborada: A Benedictine nun and anchoress at Saint Gall, killed in 926 during the Hungarian invasion. She was venerated as a martyr and formally canonized in 1047. Ekkehard records several stories about her in chapters 57 and 82.

these events are described elsewhere: Compare *Vita sanctae Wiboradae* 25–28; see MGH SS vol. 4, pp. 453–54, and Walther Berschin, *Vitae sancta Wiboradae: Die ältesten Lebensbeschreibungen der heiligen Wiborada* (Saint Gall, 1983), 68–74.

51.1 *King Henry*: Henry I the Fowler. Compare chapter 49, where Conrad is erroneously named as the king who confirmed Engilbert as abbot.

Hungarians: An ethnic group that migrated from the steppes of eastern Europe to the Carpathian Basin in the late ninth century and began incursions into Bavaria, Alsace, Burgundy, and Saxony. The Hungarians were pagans until 1001.

ferociously invaded: Ekkehard may be borrowing the turn of phrase from Silius Italicus, *Punica* 10.126.

besieging Augsburg: Scholars disagree as to the date of the siege of Augsburg that Ekkehard had in mind, arguing for 926 or 955. See Meyer von Knonau, *Ekkeharti Casus,* 194n662; *Cronache,*

469n241; Tremp, *Casus,* 291n5. Ekkehard describes it in chapter 60.

Ulrich: Bishop of Augsburg (923–973). Ekkehard talks about him at length in chapters 57–60.

meeting no opposition: Duke Burchard was in Italy with his army and died there, as Ekkehard reports in chapter 50.

51.2 *like a giant of the Lord, put on a breastplate*: A paraphrase of 1 Maccabees 3:3.

51.3 *Sint-tria-unum*: "Let-Three-Be-One," the Sitter river. The fort was probably located in the Waldburg near Bernhardzell (for discussion, see Meyer von Knonau, *Ekkeharti Casus,* pp. 472–73).

the life of Saint Wiborada: The story of the Hungarian invasion as told by *Vita Wiboradae* 31–33 is largely similar to that of the *Casus* but differs in details; see MGH SS vol. 4, pp. 454–56; Berschin, *Vitae,* pp. 78–84. Later on, in chapter 57, Ekkehard follows this *vita* when relating the story of Ulrich.

library books: The expression suggests books kept on stands, that is, in a library, distinct from those used in the church services (Meyer von Knonau, *Ekkeharti Casus,* 197n675; Loth, *Study,* 48).

number was right: Possibly an allusion to Terence, *Phormio* 53.

Wasserburg: At that time it was an island on Lake Constance, not yet linked to the mainland.

52.2 *Heribald*: Ekkehard's description fits none of the monks by this name who appear in the Saint Gall necrology; see Schaab, *Mönch,* 72n181, 86n346, and 87n357. Ekkehard may have invented this character to show the Hungarians' behavior from his unsophisticated point of view; see Ernst Tremp, "Eine Randfigur im Rampenlicht: Heribald von St. Gallen und die Ungern," in Waltz, *Scripturus vitam,* 440. Ekkehard writes more about Heribald in chapter 61.

chamberlain: A monastic official whose duties included taking care of the monks' clothing (compare chapter 87). However, the simple monk may be confusing *camerarius* with *coriarius* (leatherworker), in which case Ekkehard would have meant this passage to be humorous (we thank David Traill for this insight).

without a trace of fear: Virgil, *Aeneid* 10.770. Ekkehard also uses this quotation in chapters 40.5 and 63.1.

53.1 *armed with quivers*: This recalls Virgil's epithet for the female warrior Camilla (*Aeneid* 11.649).

no mercy shown: Lucan, *Pharsalia* 1.147.

53.2 *in their haste to flee*: A paraphrase of Virgil, *Aeneid* 4.575.

weathercock: Ekkehard's wordplay is based on the double meaning of the saint's name: *gallus* can also mean "rooster" or "weathercock."

the fire: No other evidence exists of a fire at Saint Gall during the Hungarian invasion. See István Fodor, "Sankt Gallen und die Streifzüge der Ungarn," in *Die Ungarn und die Abtei Sankt Gallen,* ed. György J. Csihák and Werner Vogler (Saint Gall and Budapest, 1999), 41–42.

54.1 *Wiborada suffered martyrdom*: On May 2, 926.

54.2 *upon the green grass*: Mark 6:39. By quoting this passage, Ekkehard cleverly alludes to the feeding of the five thousand by Jesus.

54.3 *Warmed up by the wine*: A paraphrase of Esther 1:10, the verse also used in 141.2.

shouted loudly: Daniel 3:4.

Bless Us: This antiphon is found in Saint Gall, Stiftsbibliothek MS 391, p. 65.

on the following day: On May 3.

54.4 *clashed weapons with others*: This appears to be the first known description of the Hungarian sword dance (see Tremp, "Randfigur").

picchin: Middle High German for "to stab, pierce."

55.2 *god . . . ignipotent*: A common classical epithet for Vulcan, the god of fire. Virgil uses it six times in the *Aeneid,* for instance, in 12.90.

56.1 *the Feast of the Holy Cross*: May 3.

because their lives were at stake: A paraphrase of 1 Maccabees 12:51.

56.2 *learned . . . about the . . . ways of the enemy*: A paraphrase of *Waltharius* 568–69 (MGH Poetae vol. 6, part 1, p. 47). Ekkehard paraphrases it again in 64.3.

56.4 *a book specially devoted to her*: See note to 50.3.

this was finally accomplished under Norbert: In January 1047, when Clement II was pope.

57.1 *Saint Ulrich*: See chapter 51. Ekkehard shows high regard for Ulrich in the following chapters and also in his verse account of the famous Saint Gall monks, where Ulrich is named first; *Liber benedictionum* no. 44 (Egli, *Liber,* p. 222).

three times: Gerhard, who knew Ulrich personally, wrote the first version between 983 and 993. Gebhard, bishop of Augsburg (996–1001), revised Gerhard's *Vita.* The third version was written by Berno, while he was abbot of Reichenau (1008–1048). Excerpts from Gerhard's version are edited in MGH SS vol. 4, pp. 377–425; for a complete edition, see Walter Berschin and Angelika Häse, eds., *Vita sancti Uodalrici: Die älteste Lebensbeschreibung des heiligen Ulrich* (Heidelberg, 1993). For Berno, see Dieter Blume, *Bern von Reichenau (1008–1048), Abt, Gelehrter, Biograph: Ein Lebensbild mit Werkverzeichnis sowie Edition und Übersetzung von Berns "Vita sancti Uodalrici"* (Ostfildern, 2008). Ekkehard's critical comments on Berno's *Vita* are preserved in Saint Gall, Stiftsbibliothek MS 565.

57.2 *the holiest . . . the elect*: A paraphrase of Psalms 18(17):26–27, the verses also used in 37.1.

Hartmann the Younger: Hartmann who later became abbot of Saint Gall (see chapters 47–49).

lector: Usually a monk who read aloud from scripture or other edifying texts for the monks at meals. The Rule of Benedict (RB 45.1–3) prescribes punishment for errors in such cases.

57.3 *he usually visited the recluse Wiborada*: He could not have done so as a student because he left Saint Gall sometime before 910, while according to *Annales Sangallenses maiores,* Wiborada was enclosed as an anchoress in 916 (MGH SS vol. 1, p. 78).

57.4 *silly women*: Possibly a reference to 2 Timothy 3:6.

O God, come to my assistance . . . help me: A verse from Psalms 70:1(69:2), recited in the beginning of the Divine Office. Ekkehard also quotes it in 42.2.

58.1 *his nurse*: Or more literally, "wet nurse." The term could also mean "teacher" or "foster mother." The same expression, "his one-time wet nurse/teacher," is used in *Vita Wiboradae* 45 (MGH SS vol. 4, p. 456; Berschin and Häse, *Vita sancti Uodalrici,* p. 102) to describe Ulrich's visit to Wiborada's tomb. *Nutrix* is a term sometimes used to refer to Mother Church or an abbess, and also to Mary or Saint Paul.

58.2 *Nocturns*: A night office.

58.3 *people of higher understanding*: A possibly ironic comment at the expense of people too sophisticated to believe the miracle of the pilfered stylus—the "hard-hearted people" mentioned at the beginning of this paragraph.

58.4 *speech . . . meaningless*: Ephesians 5:6.

provoked laughter: Compare RB 6.8, condemning words that provoke laughter.

shield strap: An ironic allusion to a deacon's stole.

59.3 *Kyrie Eleison*: See note to 30.4.

Benedict and Maurus: This episode is modeled on a similar story from the *Life of Saint Benedict* (Gregory the Great, *Dialogues* 2.7).

59.4 *the Feast of Saint Magnus*: September 6.

eagle-bearing cape: A ceremonial cloak worn by a priest or a bishop. An eagle motif was used in the Middle Ages in decorating ecclesiastical vestments; for an eagle chasuble (ca. 975–1006), see Miller, *Clothing the Clergy,* 126, figure 29. The usage of the word *aquilifer* as an adjective occurs only in the *Casus* (Loth, *Study,* 38). As a noun, it is the classical term for a standard-bearer of the Roman legion. Ekkehard may have coined the adjective as a tribute to his fascination with ancient Rome.

60.1 *monastic community*: Although the Latin word refers to all religious by profession, or to clergy in general, Ekkehard appears to use it in a narrower sense here, to contrast with the secular canons of Augsburg where Ulrich spent much of his life.

60.2 *abbot Immo*: In fact, Immo became abbot in 976, three years after Ulrich's death.

Lech: A tributary of the Danube that passes the city of Augsburg.

called out to come to him: A turn of phrase echoing Mark 3:13.

as I have already recounted: See chapter 51 and note to 51.1. Compare the description of the siege of 955 in Gerhard's *Vita Uodalrici* 1.12 (MGH SS vol. 4, p. 401; Berschin and Häse, *Vita sancti Uodalrici*, pp. 192–94).

60.3 *like a second Ezechias*: An allusion to 2 Kings (4 Kings) 19.

61.1 *Hugo*: No other sources mention him.

sister: Gerhard's *Vita Uodalrici* 1.3 (MGH SS vol. 4, p. 389; Berschin and Häse, *Vita sancti Uodalrici*, p. 110) has an oblique reference to a sister of Ulrich.

cart rider: Hugo's mockery evokes the humiliation and low status associated with riding in a cart in the Middle Ages. Compare Einhard's critique of the last Merovingian king who traveled about in a cart (*Vita Karoli Magni* 1) and Chrétien de Troyes, *Lancelot, the Knight of the Cart*, where Lancelot, determined to rescue Guinevere no matter the personal cost, agrees to ride in a cart.

61.3 *Buchau*: A monastery founded in the eighth century on an island in Lake Federsee (modern Swabia) and dedicated to Saints Cornelius and Cyprian; it was included in the Saint Gall confraternity of prayer (MGH Necr. Suppl., p. 144).

Lord of compassion and mercy: A paraphrase of Sirach 2:13.

62.3 *In truth, I tell you*: Luke 4:25.

63.1 *undaunted*: Virgil, *Aeneid* 10.770. Ekkehard also uses this expression in chapters 40.5 and 52.2.

rumor, flying: Virgil, *Aeneid* 3.121, 7.392, and 11.139. Ekkehard also uses a variant of this expression in 47.4, 84.4, and 135.1.

Wasserburg: See 51.3.

63.2 *entered the monastery*: Probably on May 8; according to *Vita Wiboradae* 35, eight days after the Hungarians' attack.

Noting: Bishop of Constance (919/20–934).

63.3 *carried the scattered sheep . . . shoulders*: A close paraphrase of RB 27.9, the section that describes the duties of the abbot and draws on Luke 15:5 and John 10. Ekkehard uses the same reference in 73.1.

63.4 *improved it beyond the cloister*: Ekkehard describes the problems that the monastery experienced with its estates in chapters 48 and 49.

yielded his governance to Thieto: Engilbert resigned in 933 and died sometime soon after August 13, 934. Thieto became abbot on October 28, 933 (*Annales Sangallenses maiores,* MGH SS vol. 1, p. 78).

abbots' estates that I have mentioned: See chapter 9.

64.1 *Frickgau*: An administrative district between the Aar and Rhine rivers, created in the late ninth century.

he was the father of six Maccabees: An allusion to 1 Maccabees 2, where there were only five sons.

64.2 *the monastery of the Holy Cross in Säckingen*: Founded in the sixth or seventh century on an island in the Rhine, not far from modern Basel, by Fridolin, believed to have been an Irish missionary. The monastery belonged to the Saint Gall confraternity of prayer (MGH Necr. Suppl., p. 144).

buried in sleep and wine: A paraphrase of Virgil, *Aeneid* 2.265.

64.3 *he was now familiar with the enemy's ways of fighting*: A paraphrase of *Waltharius* 568–69 (MGH Poetae vol. 6, part 1, p. 47). Ekkehard paraphrases it earlier in 56.2.

64.4 *Black Forest*: A region of forests and mountains in southwestern Germany stretching from the Rhine almost to Lake Constance.

Liutfrid: Belonged to the noble Etichonid family that held power in Alsace in the ninth and tenth centuries. He has been identified as Liutfrid III, count of Sundgau (Tremp, *Casus,* 329n13).

Besançon: A city in present-day eastern France, located around 160 miles from Lake Constance across the Vosges. First mentioned in Caesar's *Gallic Wars,* at the period described here the city belonged to the kingdom of Burgundy.

65.1 *Conrad*: King of Burgundy (937–993).

Adelheid: The daughter of Rudolf II, king of Burgundy, she lived from 931 to 999. Her first husband was Lothar II, king of Italy; in 951, she married Otto I and was crowned empress during Otto's imperial coronation in 962.

Saracens: A term used by medieval Christian writers to refer to Muslim Arabs. See also chapter 126.

settled down in the valley of Fraxinetum: A Muslim military settlement in Fraxinetum (present-day La Garde-Freinet in Provence) was established in the late ninth century and existed until 973; see Scott G. Bruce, *Cluny and the Muslims of La Garde-Freinet* (Ithaca, N.Y., 2015), 21–30. Ekkehard's story about its beginnings and about Conrad's routing of the Saracens and Hungarians is not found in other sources. It may draw in part on accounts about the relations of Hugh, king of Italy (942–947), with those peoples and on stories about the wars of Otto I.

65.4 *whose sword and lance*: Saint Maurice, a fourth-century martyr, was especially revered by the royal house of Burgundy and by the Saxon royal dynasty. The sword and lance of Saint Maurice (sometimes identified as the Holy Lance that pierced Christ's side) were among the regalia used at coronations of Holy Roman Emperors from the tenth century on. The lance was carried by Saxon kings on military expeditions: Widukind reports that Otto I carried it in the battle of Lechfeld (955), where he defeated the Hungarians (*Res gesta Saxonicae* 3.46). The lance is now displayed in the Imperial Treasury in Vienna.

66.1 *Thieto*: Abbot (933–942); see chapter 63.

the monastery burned down: The fire is described in chapter 67.

66.2 *The Greater Litany fell on a Sunday*: In 937, however, this date, April 25, fell on a Tuesday. The *Annales Sangallenses maiores* report that the fire happened on Wednesday, April 26 (MGH SS vol. 1, entry for 937, p. 78).

66.3 *Conrad was spending Easter at Ingelheim*: Other sources confirm that Conrad II, emperor (1027–1039), was indeed present at Ingelheim on March 29, 1030.

a monk of Saint Gall: Ekkehard likely refers to himself; he spent the years between 1022 and around 1031 in Mainz.

tonsured monk: The word *coronatus* used by Ekkehard can also refer to the crowned emperor.

66.4 *the empress*: Gisela (989/90–1043), the daughter of Duke Hermann II of Swabia.

Mathilda: Mathilda of Swabia (988/9–1032).

66.5 *in order to boast*: For the expression used by Ekkehard, *aurium inflatio,* see note to 28.1.

67.1 *the feast day of Saint Mark*: Coincides with the day of the Greater Litany, April 25.

On the Tuesday: Compare 66.2.

roundsmen: See note to 40.1.

67.3 *Hartmut*: Abbot from 872 to 883.

a passageway: Virgil, *Aeneid* 2.453, slightly paraphrased.

apse: Semicircular recess at the east end of a church, where the altar stood.

68.1 *golden talents*: Ekkehard's audience would have recognized this as an expression occurring in the Bible, see, for instance, 1 Kings (3 Kings) 9:14. Here it refers to the artwork created in the church at Saint Gall during Hartmut's abbacy and described by Ratpert, *Casus* 26, 27, 29 (MGH SRG vol. 75, pp. 204, 216, 220).

68.3 *cast off the yoke*: A paraphrase of RB 58.16.

69.1 *Victor*: Ekkehard is the only source for this character, but the name often occurred in documents from early medieval Rhaetia, where the Victorides were a powerful family who held both secular and ecclesiastical power for over two hundred years (see Schaab, *Mönch,* 173).

Craloh, the abbot's brother: His name is found in the profession book (MGH Necr. Suppl., p. 125), and the *Annales Sangallenses maiores* in an entry for 942 mention that he was Thieto's brother (MGH SS vol. 1, p. 78). See Schaab, *Mönch,* 98n493.

Anno: Later abbot (953–954); see chapter 71. No other sources mention his relationship to Thieto.

69.2 *to elect Craloh abbot in his stead*: According to *Annales Sangallenses maiores,* this happened on May 31, 942 (MGH SS vol. 1, p. 78).

Otto: Otto I (912–973) was king from 936 and emperor from 962 on.

the last day of his life: The Saint Gall necrology records the day of his death as April 6 (MGH Necr. vol. 1, p. 471); his name does not occur in sources after 942.

mentioned above: See chapters 9 and 63.

70.1 *Pfäfers*: See chapter 25.

70.2 *wandering*: *Errovagari* is Ekkehard's neologism; compare his *Liber benedictionum* no. 37, line 35 (Egli, *Liber,* p. 191); see Loth, *Study,* 10, and Tremp, *Casus,* 342n2.

to draw and release the bow: An image going back to antiquity; see Phaedrus, *Fabulae Aesopiae* 3.14, in which Aesop suggests that letting students rest and play improves their studies. Ekkehard uses the same image in chapter 135.

harbored deep within his heart: Virgil, *Aeneid* 1.26, slightly paraphrased.

70.3 *Enzelinus*: No other source mentions him.

in its proper place: See chapters 72–73.

71.1 *stormy dispute*: The rebellion of Liudolf, duke of Swabia (950–954) against Otto I, which took place from 953 to 954.

he came to the monastery of Saint Gall: According to Ekkehard's chronology, this does not appear to be the visit mentioned by the *Annales Sangallenses maiores* under 948 (MGH SS vol. 1, p. 78).

Waning: He has not been identified; see Tremp, *Casus,* 364–65n5. Ekkehard also mentions him in chapters 77 and 132.

came . . . to seek refuge: Virgil, *Aeneid* 1.2.

71.3 *Liudolf made him their abbot*: *Annales Sangallenses maiores* (MGH SS vol. 1, p. 79) report, without mentioning Liudolf's role, that Anno's rule as abbot began in 953 and lasted one year, two months, and one week.

laid the groundwork for the walls: In chapter 136, Ekkehard reports that Abbot Notker brought this work to completion in 975.

72.1 *whom I have mentioned*: See chapter 70.

72.2 *What is your business here*: Terence, *Andria* 849 and *Adelphi* 638.

as a Rhaetian rather than a German: Enzelinus, whose native tongue is Rhaetian, a Romance language, speaks German with an accent, dropping the initial *h*'s in *hilf* and *herro,* which, in Ekkehard's account, makes German speakers laugh (Grotans, *Reading,* 122–23). German speakers may also have perceived a different meaning of the word *Cot,* hearing instead of *Gott* (God) the word *Kot,* namely "shit" or "dung." We thank Julia Barrow for pointing this out to us.

Liudolf had died in Italy: On September 6, 957. See *Annales Sangallenses maiores* (MGH SS vol. 1, p. 79).

Anno, too, had passed away: On December 1, 954. See *Annales Sangallenses maiores* (MGH SS vol. 1, p. 79).

73.1 *Hartpert*: Bishop of Chur from 951 to approximately 970.

to the fold, I am going to place a sheep on your shoulders: The king reminds Craloh of the abbot's duties described in RB 27.9. Ekkehard refers to the same sources in 63.3.

73.2 *Salomo's machinations*: The abbey of Pfäfers initially belonged to the king, as the stewards state in the next sentence. Salomo received it in 905 and gave it to Saint Gall Abbey in 909. In 920 it was given to Waldo, the bishop of Chur, and it became an imperial abbey in 950; see Grüninger, "Das bewegte Schicksal." See chapters 25 and 70.

73.3 *You who bring assistance . . . trouble*: Psalms 9:9(9:10).

staff: The pastoral staff carried by an abbot or a bishop as a symbol of their authority. See also chapter 86.

73.4 *Craloh returned home with Ulrich*: *Vita Wiboradae* 45 (MGH SS vol. 4, p. 456; Berschin, *Vitae,* pp. 102–6) mentions Ulrich's visit to Saint Gall during Craloh's abbacy but does not report the events described by Ekkehard.

74.1 *to welcome him with the Gospel*: For reception with the Gospel, see also chapter 8 and the note at 8.1.

even though he was not an enrolled brother: Compare chapters 58, 59, and 75, where Ekkehard mentions that Ulrich was an enrolled brother.

74.2 *God, You Who Sit*: This responsory, based on Psalm 9, calls out to God for assistance in trouble; in 73.3, Craloh asked Ulrich for help using verse 9(10) of the same psalm. This episode sets the stage for a developing dispute between the monks and Craloh, which is described in later chapters (Kruckenberg, "Ekkehard's Use of Musical Detail," especially 45–48).

between Prime and Terce: Between the two parts of the Divine Office, the prayer said at the first daylight hour and the next prayer, at the third daylight hour.

74.3 *Ekkehard*: Ekkehard I, whose activity as a scribe is reflected in documents between 956/7 and 968/9. The *Annales Sangallenses maiores* report his death in 973 (MGH SS vol. 1, p. 80). Ekkehard IV wrote his epitaph (MGH Poetae vol. 5, parts 1–2, p. 550). See chapter 80 and also Schaab, *Mönch,* 99n509 and 172–73.

Notker: Notker II "Peppercorn," or "the Physician," died on November 12, 975 (*Annales Sangalenses maiores,* MGH SS vol. 1, p. 80; see also the Saint Gall necrology, where he is identified as *medicus,* MGH Necr. vol. 1, p. 484). For more on him, see chapters 125 and 147. See also Johannes Duft, "Notker Pfefferkorn in den Sankt-Galler Quellen," in *Die Abtei St. Gallen: Ausgewählte Aufsätze in überarbeiteter Fassung,* ed. Peter Ochsenbein and Ernst Zielger (Sigmaringen, 1991), vol. 2, pp. 149–64.

Gerald: According to the Saint Gall necrology (MGH Necr. vol. 1, p. 473), he died on May 10, probably sometime before 975. Ekkehard mentions him in chapters 79, 89, 91, and 103 and writes about him at length in chapters 124–25.

74.4 *Burchard*: Abbot (958–971). Ekkehard writes about him at length in chapters 85–87.

Amalungus: He may be the "layman Amalungus" *(Amalungus laicus)* mentioned in the Saint Gall necrology under February 17 (MGH Necr. vol. 1, p. 467).

75.1 *turned them from children into slaves*: Ekkehard plays with the different meanings of *liberi* as "children" and "free persons," at the same time alluding to Saint Paul's letters, which frequently mention slaves and free persons (see especially 1 Corinthians 7:22 and 9:19, Galatians 3:28, and Ephesians 6:8).

to be obedient unto death: Philippians 2:8.

a shepherd . . . not swallow them: By substituting *glutire* (to swallow, gulp down) for *deglubere* (to skin), Ekkehard modifies the image of a good shepherd who ought to shear rather than to skin his sheep, which goes back to Suetonius, *Tiberius* 32.5. Ekkehard's immediate source may have been Orosius, *Histories* 7.4. In the copy of Orosius annotated by Ekkehard (Saint Gall, Stiftsbibliothek MS 621, p. 276) there is a gloss, now illegible, above this passage; see Heidi Eisenhut, *Die Glossen Ekkeharts IV. von St. Gallen im Codex Sangallensis 621,* Monasterium Sancti Galli

4 (Saint Gall, 2009), available online at http://orosius.monumenta.ch, gloss at p. 276, col. B, line 15, and note 28. Ekkehard uses the same image in chapter 91.

75.2 *when the wolf came in the night, had fled*: An allusion to John 10:12.

left them to the wolves: Neglecting the responsibilities of the abbot, described in RB 27, modeled on John 10:11–12. Compare chapter 63.

losing . . . abbey: This may refer to Saint Gall, as in this translation, or, as in Tremp, *Casus,* 355n6, to the abbey of Pfäfers, which was given by Otto to Enzelinus and thus lost to Saint Gall (compare chapter 73).

as if he has done a good job: Terence, *Adelphi* 775.

75.3 *Dean Waldo*: He cannot be identified with certainty; the name occurs in the Saint Gall necrology five times.

our nest: This characteristic of the monastery also appears in a letter of Ermenrich of Ellwangen to Abbot Grimald (MGH Epist. vol. 5, p. 565.) In the context of this chapter, the expression may specifically refer to the cloister, the inner enclosure within the monastery, called "our inner space" *(intima nostra)* in 5.1; see Mayke de Jong, "Internal Cloisters," 211. Ekkehard uses the same expression in 102.2.

tyrant: Compare RB 27.6, which describes the abbot's duty as care for souls, not tyranny over them.

75.4 *add this grievance to previous grievances*: 2 Corinthians 2:3.

76.1 *the situation would be worse than before*: A paraphrase of Matthew 12:45.

76.2 *more valued for their counsel*: An allusion to Jeremiah 32:19.

76.3 *The first contact is the fiercest*: A paraphrase of Terence, *Phormio* 346.

be patient, and strengthen your hearts: James 5:8.

As the wood fills with sound . . . so the echo responds: A proverb still circulating in German. This passage is recorded as the earliest instance of its use in Latin; Hans Walther, *Proverbia sententiaeque latinitatis medii aevi: Lateinische Sprichwörter und Sentenzen des Mittelalters in alphabetischer Anordnung,* 9 vols. (Göttingen, 1963–1969), no. 29606.

76.4 *the abbot . . . "Bless me!"*: The formula goes back to Daniel 3:57–90, where it appears a number of times, but as Amalungus points out in the next sentence, the order of greeting prescribed by RB 63.15 is here reversed.

hastened . . . to exchange kisses: A paraphrase of Genesis 29:13, a verse also used in 111.2.

76.5 *offered*: The word used by Ekkehard, *oblatum,* can also mean "oblate," at that time usually a child given to the monastery.

Praise Be to You, O True God: For the text of this sequence, written by Notker the Stammerer, see von den Steinen, *Notker der Dichter,* vol. 2, p. 46. The themes of reconciliation and peace present in this sequence had a special significance in the context of this scene (Kruckenberg, "Ekkehard's Use of Musical Detail," 49).

The day was spent in joy: A paraphrase of 1 Maccabees 7:48.

maddened in his heart, could not bear this sight: A paraphrase of Virgil, *Aeneid* 2.407.

77.1 *permission from the dean*: In accordance with RB 67.7, which prohibits the monks to leave the monastery without permission. While the abbot was absent, the dean took up his responsibilities (compare RB 21).

newly made abbot: That is, of Pfäfers; see chapter 73.

77.4 *whose blindness the abbot himself had caused*: The acts of the Frankfurt Synod of 794 contain an explicit admonition to the abbots not to blind disobedient monks (MGH Capit. vol. 1, no. 28.18, p. 76).

Waning: See also chapters 71 and 132.

78.1 *Notker the Physician*: Or Notker Peppercorn; compare 74.3 and note.

Erchinbald: Bishop of Strasbourg (965–991).

recluse: Ekkehard uses the word *solitarius,* which is not specific and does not make it clear whether he is talking about a hermit (more mobile) or an *inclusus* (walled up).

Long Lake: located near Lake of Longuemer, department of Vosges, France.

79.1 *fighting the Danes in Schleswig*: Ekkehard probably refers to Henry I's campaign of 934.

79.3 *Gerhilda*: *Annales Sangallenses maiores* (MGH SS vol. 1, pp. 78–79 and 81) report that she became a recluse in 952 and died in 1008.

79.4 *Rachilda*: She became a recluse in 920 and died on November 23, 946 (*Annales Sangallenses maiores,* MGH SS vol. 1, p. 78; the Saint Gall necrology, MGH Necr. vol. 1, p. 485). See chapter 83.

Bertrada: Recluse from 959 on, died in 980 (*Annales Sangallenses maiores,* MGH SS vol. 1, pp. 79 and 80).

in Salomo's cell . . . Saint George: That is, in the cell that Wiborada occupied until 916; compare chapter 56.

79.5 *Burchard*: Probably Burchard I, who later ruled as abbot, from 958 to 971. See Schaab, *Mönch,* 98n499.

Ekkehard: Ekkehard I; see note to 74.3.

as if elected by popular vote: Ekkehard uses the term *comitiis,* which refers to the people's assemblies in republican Rome. Compare chapter 127, where Ekkehard refers to Roman customs to explain the election process.

Herisau: One of the estates reserved for abbots in their retirement; see chapters 9 and 63.

80.1 *Jonswil*: Now a municipality in the canton Sankt Gallen.

as I said: The surviving text of Ekkehard's *Casus* has no information about this.

with plenty of bread: This may exceed the amount of bread specified by RB 39.4.

every fifth of these measures (the Nones, so to speak): The drink taken after None (prayer service at the ninth hour of the day); see also chapter 112.

80.2 *bad air*: Ekkehard also mentions pernicious Italian air in 9.2.

beautiful church for the relics: The church of Saint John the Baptist at Saint Gall, mentioned by the thirteenth-century continuator (Conrad of Fabaria, *Casus* 5; *Cronache,* p. 374).

80.3 *Let Us Sing . . . Setting of the Sun*: These sequences are edited in AH vol. 50, nos. 204, 207, 205, 206, pp. 272–76.

a sequence about Saint Afra: On chronological grounds, this sequence has been attributed to Ekkehard II. For discussion of Ekkehard's sequences, see von den Steinen, *Notker der Dichter,* vol. 1, pp. 439–57, and Walter Berschin, "Sanktgallische Offiziendichtung aus ottonischer Zeit," in *Lateinische Dichtungen des X. und XI. Jahrhunderts: Festgabe für Walther Bulst zum 80. Geburtstag,* ed. Walter Berschin and Reinhard Düchting (Heidelberg, 1981), 13–48. For the text, see von den Steinen, *Notker der Dichter,* vol. 2, pp. 116–17. Saint Afra, an early fourth century martyr, was especially venerated in Augsburg.

Liutold: Bishop of Augsburg from 988/9 to 996, that is, after the death of Ekkehard I.

O Martyr of the Eternal Father: See the edition in AH vol. 50, no. 209, p. 278, and von den Steinen, *Notker der Dichter,* vol. 1, pp. 441–42, with discussion.

antiphons: See Berschin, "Sanktgallische Offiziendichtung," 13–23.

80.4 *Life of Waltharius*: The Latin epic poem *Waltharius,* composed in the ninth or tenth century; its authorship has been a subject of much discussion. See Dieter Schaller, "Von St. Gallen nach Mainz? Zum Verfasserproblem des *Waltarius,*" in *Lateinische Kultur im X. Jahrhundert: Akten des I. Internationalen Mittellateinerkongresses, Heidelberg, 12.–15. IX. 1988,* ed. Walter Berschin (Stuttgart, 1991), 423–37; and a recent survey in Rachel Stone, "*Waltharius* and Carolingian Morality: Satire and Lay Values," *Early Medieval Europe* 21 (2013): 50–70.

Aribo's: Aribo was archbishop of Mainz (1021–1031).

song of Carloman: The Latin word used by Ekkehard may refer to a hymn in the Lydian mode or be derived from the German word *Lied* (song). In the latter case, Ekkehard may have meant a composition about a king by the name of Carloman, the melody of which was based on the sequence for Saint Paul; see Loth, *Study,* 31; Dieter Schaller, "Die Paulus-Sequenz Ekkeharts I von St. Gallen," in Berschin and Düchting, *Lateinische Dichtungen,* reprinted in Dieter Schaller, *Studien zur lateinischen Dichtung des Frühmittelalters* (Stuttgart, 1995), 224–25n15.

He too died from the massive weight of victory: The line comes from stanza 10b of the sequence for Saint Paul, *Concurrite huc populi.*

80.5 *his namesakes*: Ekkehard II and Ekkehard III.

Burchard: Burchard II (1001–1022).

Notker, who was my own master: Notker III "the German" or "Labeo" (d. 1022), described in the Saint Gall necrology as "the most learned and benevolent teacher" (MGH Necr. vol. 1, p. 476), a poet, translator, and commentator of philosophical texts; for bibliography see Evelyn Scherabon-Firchow, *Notker der Deutsche von St. Gallen (950–1022): Ausführliche Bibliographie* (Göttingen, 2000).

in an appropriate place: Ekkehard writes about Ekkehard II in chapters 89–103 but not about the others in the surviving text.

this vine produced these branches: Compare John 15:2–5.

harvested on the day of Saint Felix in Pincis: Ekkehard I died on January 14, 973. Ekkehard IV composed his epitaph; see MGH Poetae vol. 5, parts 1–2, p. 550.

Saint Michael's: The chapel on the territory of the monastery, also mentioned in Iso, *De miraculis sancti Otmari* 2.2 (MGH SS vol. 2, p. 53).

Behold, O Lord, and consider what vine you have so harvested: Lamentations 2:20.

81.1 *to tell you about his remarkable deeds*: See chapters 86–88.

Herisau: See chapters 9 and 63.

wiser: Literally, "of sounder judgment," an expression used in RB 64.1, the section that deals with electing an abbot.

set his house in order: A paraphrase of Isaiah 38:1.

went the way we all go: Craloh died on February 26, 958; see *Annales Sangallenses maiores* (MGH SS vol. 1, p. 79) and the Saint Gall necrology (MGH Necr. vol. 1, p. 468).

81.2 *Otto*: Otto I. Ekkehard seems to be confusing the chronology of characters and events here.

Adaltag: This may refer to King Aethelstan, a half brother of Edith (Otigeba; see note 86.3), Otto I's first wife; however, he died in 939, before the time Ekkehard describes.

Cnut, king of the Danes: Ekkehard may have been thinking of King Chnuba, defeated by Henry I during his Danish campaign in 934, and of his own contemporary, King Cnut of Denmark (1019–1035).

approval of all the brothers: In accordance with RB 64.1.

Burchard . . . mentioned above: See chapters 74 and 79.

82.1 *Ulrich*: Tentatively identified as the sixth Alemannian count of that name (see Borgolte, *Grafen*, 267–70), who participated in the alliance that defeated the Hungarians near the river Inn in 913; see *Annales Sangallenses maiores,* entry for 913 (MGH SS vol. 1, p. 77).

Wendilgart, a granddaughter . . . daughter: This is not supported by other sources and by the known chronology: Wendilgart, who probably died around 926, could hardly have been a granddaughter of King Henry I (d. 936).

Buchhorn: Now Friedrichshafen on Lake Constance, Baden-Württemberg, Germany.

Hagarenes: A term used by medieval Christian writers to describe Arabs or Muslims. The Muslims were considered the descendants of Hagar, the Egyptian slave who bore Abraham a son, Ishmael (Genesis 16).

far off the mark: The criticism is aimed at the compilers of the *Annales Sangallenses maiores,* entries for 888 and 913 (MGH SS vol. 1, p. 77). Ekkehard also added a similar but more pointed comment to the Orosius manuscript (Saint Gall, Stiftsbibliothek MS 621, p. 315A, available online at CESG, glosses edited in Eisenhut, *Glossen,* available online at http://orosius.monumenta.ch). The expression may be an allusion to Terence, *Eunuchus* 2.2.245.

82.3 *very sour wild apples*: Throughout this passage, Wiborada is punning on different meanings of *malum* (apple/evil), referring to the story of Eve in Genesis 3.

83.1 *aforementioned bishop*: Salomo; see chapter 82.

Rachilda: See note to 79.4.

83.2 *brains to be splattered*: A paraphrase of Terence, *Adelphi* 782. Wiborada was killed during the Hungarian invasion in 926; see note to 50.3.

pus with a potsherd: Job 2:8.

Ekkehard . . . mentioned earlier: Ekkehard I; see chapters 74, 79–80.

Satan tormented . . . keeping vigil: No other source mentions this poem.

83.3 *trust one who has experienced it*: Virgil, *Aeneid* 11.283. Ekkehard uses the same expression in 103.1 and borrows the turn of phrase from the next line in the *Aeneid* in 87.2.

84.1 *distributed freely and gave to the poor*: Psalms 112(111):9. Ekkehard also uses this verse in 87.3.

84.3 *as if awaking from sleep*: Genesis 45:26.

84.4 *Word spread quickly*: Virgil, *Aeneid* 3.121, 7.392, and 11.139. Ekkehard also uses a variant of this expression in 47.4, 63.1, and 135.1.

85.2 *The woman conceived*: 2 Kings (4 Kings) 4:17.

placed his son on the altar: As prescribed by RB 59, on offering children to monasteries. The language in this passage is influenced by 1 Samuel (1 Kings) 1:24–28, the main source of inspiration for dedication of children (see de Jong, *In Samuel's Image*).

Höchst: Located in the Rhine valley in district Bregenz, Vorarlberg, Austria; mentioned as a property of Saint Gall in documents dating from 808 on (see UBSG vol. 1, no. 198, pp. 188–89).

86.1 *defeating King Cnut at Schleswig*: See chapter 79 and notes to 79.1 and 81.2. Ekkehard may be confusing this with the 934 campaign of Henry I or the 974 campaign of Otto II.

my little nephew: *Nepotulus* could refer to a nephew or a grandson; it could also mean "favorite"; see Charlton T. Lewis and Charles Short, *A Latin Dictionary* (Oxford, 1879), under "nepos," 1.A.1, 1.B.3; Loth, *Study,* 78. No other source mentions such kinship, but according to Ekkehard, Burhard's mother (Wendilgart) was the granddaughter of Henry I, Otto's father (see 82.1, with note).

man who blinds his monks: See chapter 77.

86.3 *took . . . by the chin*: 2 Samuel (2 Kings) 20:9.

Queen Otigeba: Otigeba (Edith), one of the daughters of Edward the Elder of Wessex, died in 946; at the time described here, in 958, Otto I was married to his second wife, Adelheid.

God, We Praise You: See 44.3 and note.

86.4 *emperor*: Otto I did not actually become emperor until 962.

Ekkehard sometimes seems strategic in choosing where he uses the terms "emperor" and "king."

87.1 *he used to eat meat thanks to an edict of Conrad*: The Rule of Benedict (RB 39.11) prescribes that all monks, except the gravely ill, abstain from the meat of quadrupeds. However, the Rule leaves the matters of food at the discretion of an abbot rather than a bishop. Conrad, bishop of Constance from 934 to 975, had strong connections to Saint Gall and was enrolled in its confraternity (see MGH Necr. Suppl., p. 138). Ekkehard writes about him in chapters 113 and 121.

novel behavior of monks: Ekkehard refers to the proponents of the Lotharingian reform (see Introduction).

provoke God to anger . . . so that more and more disasters befall them: A paraphrase of Psalms 106(105):29.

87.2 *rich variety of vestments at church . . . woven into the fabric*: Some scholars have interpreted this passage as an allusion to the different color and style of monastic dress worn by the reformers; see Kassius Hallinger, *Gorze-Kluny: Studien zu den monastischen Lebensformen und Gegensätzen im Hochmittelalter,* Studia Anselmiana philosophica theologica 22, 23 (Graz, 1971), vol. 1, pp. 496, 609–10. Others have seen it as an allegorical reference to virtues, which implied a veiled critique of the reformers; Albert Hauck, "Zur Erklärung von Ekkeh. cas. s. Galli c. 87," in *Kleinere Beiträge zur Geschichte: Festschrift zum Deutschen Historikertage in Leipzig Ostern 1894* (Leipzig, 1894), 107–13, at 111–12. The imagery goes back to Psalms 45:8–9(44:9–10) and 45:13(44:14); for other possible sources, see Meyer von Knonau, *Ekkeharti Casus,* 311–12n1041.

rise up . . . more accurately: Ekkehard borrows the imagery from Virgil, *Aeneid* 11.282–84 and 11.574–78, adding the wordplay in *acrius/aciem/acutius* and the punning in *acutius* (more expertly/more pointedly).

87.3 *distributed them freely and gave . . . to the poor*: A paraphrase of Psalms 112(111):9; also used in 84.1.

Richer, his brother's son: Probably the son of the Adalhard mentioned in 82.1.

87.4 *the dean*: Ekkehard I.

88.1 *almoner*: A monastic official who distributed alms.

a house designated for this purpose: A "house for pilgrims and paupers" *(domus peregrinorum et pauperum)* is shown on the Plan of Saint Gall.

Gaul: The word used by Ekkehard could refer to any person of Romance origins, here most likely a Rhaetian; see Iso Müller, "Ekkehart IV. und die Rätoromanen," *Studien und Mitteilungen zur Geschichte des Benediktiner-Ordens und seiner Zweige* 82 (1971): 271–88, at 279–84; Grotans, *Reading*, especially 123–36.

88.2 *big and fat*: *Grossum* and *crassum* can also mean "thick" and "dense."

Hot . . . cold: Ekkehard plays on different meanings of the word *cald*: "cold" in German and "hot" in Rhaetian.

88.3 *as I live . . . right away*: A paraphrase of Terence, *Andria* 866.

88.4 *hurt a hair of this man's head*: Literally, "break off his little horn," an image that occurs in the Bible; compare, for instance, Psalms 75:10(74:11) and Jeremiah 48:25.

you gallows rogue of a servant: Terence, *Andria* 618.

Don't I have the right to do what I want: Matthew 20:15. The verse continues, "Or are you envious because I am generous?"

89.1 *Ekkehard II*: The older of the two nephews of Ekkehard I mentioned in 80.5. Ekkehard II Palatinus ("the Courtier") died on April 23, 990; see *Annales Sangallenses maiores* (MGH SS vol. 1, p. 81) and the Saint Gall necrology (MGH Necr. vol. 1, p. 472). Ekkehard writes about him at length in the following chapters.

Gerald: He was mentioned in 74.3; see note.

attractiveness made people stop and stare: Josephus, *Antiquitates Judaicae* 2.9.6.

Otto the Red: Otto II. Ekkehard is the earliest source for this nickname.

Because I cannot bear the lightning flash of your eyes: Pseudo-Aurelius Victor, *Epitome de Caesaribus* 1.20.

89.2 *both schools*: The internal school, for those children who were to become monks, and the external school, for the future canons; see note to 2.2.

studying letters: *Litterae* can refer to the letters of the alphabet, handwriting, the liberal arts, literature, and learning. Ekkehard plays with different meanings here and below.

Gozpert erected for kindly Saint Gall: Ratpert also writes about this in *Casus* 16 (MGH SRG vol. 75, p. 182).

Abbot Immo adorned with pictures and gold: This verse is also quoted in the *Continuatio anonyma* 3 (*Cronache,* p. 320).

89.3 *Willigis*: Archbishop of Mainz (975–1011).

90.1 *Hadwig, Duke Henry's daughter*: Henry, duke of Bavaria (948–955), was a younger brother of King Otto I. Hadwig was born around 939 and died on August 28, 994.

duchess of Swabia: Ekkehard uses the male title, *dux,* and depicts Hadwig as possessing the full ducal power, without mentioning that after the death of her husband Swabia had male dukes, Otto I (973–982) and Conrad (982–997). Diplomas from the time of Otto III also refer to her as *dux;* see, for instance, MGH DD Otto III no. 63, p. 469. For a recent discussion, see Jürgen Dendorfer, "Herzogin Hadwig auf dem Hohentwiel—Landesgeschichtliche Perspektiven für das Früh- und Hochmittelalter," *Zeitschrift für die Geschichte des Oberrheins* 161 (2013): 11–42, available online at https://freidok.uni-freiburg.de/fedora/objects/freidok:10225/datastreams/FILE1/content.

Burchard: Burchard III, duke of Swabia (954–973).

Hohentwiel: See chapters 19 and 20 and note to 19.1.

Constantine: This cannot be Constantine VII, who ruled from 913 to 959; it could have been his son, Romanos II (938–963).

Greek letters: For Hadwig's knowledge of Greek, see also chapter 94.

90.2 *very soon after the wedding*: The wedding took place in 954 or 955, so they were actually married for eighteen years but had no children.

90.3 *Burchard*: According to other records, by 973, when Hadwig became a widow, Notker (abbot 971–975) had already succeeded Burchard. This visit may have taken place earlier, in 965.

his uncle: Ekkehard I the dean died in 973, one more argument for Hadwig's earlier visit.

90.4 *hair shorn off*: Ekkehard uses a rare word that can refer to a removal of hair but also to a more violent assault.

90.5 *Steinach*: The harbor on the southwest shore of Lake Constance that served Saint Gall. Ekkehard also mentions it in chapter 92.

chasubles, copes, and stoles . . . alb . . . dalmatic and a subdeacon's liturgical garment: Liturgical vestments, mainly worn for Mass.

Marriage of Philology: A reference to Martianus Capella, *On the Marriage of Philology and Mercury;* see also chapter 47 and note to 47.5.

91.1 *the mouths of the envious opened up to accuse*: This passage may have been inspired by Psalms 50(49):19.

Ruodmann: Abbot from 972 to 985, a champion of the Lotharingian reform movement, appointed by Otto I.

not knowing how to shear his sheep's fleece, he shredded it: Ekkehard uses the same image in chapter 75 (see note to 75.1).

91.2 *Ekkehard the very capable dean*: Ekkehard I; see note to 74.3.

Gerald: He is also mentioned in chapter 74; see note to 74.3.

Notker: Notker II "Peppercorn," or "the Physician"; see note to 74.3 and chapter 123.

Cunibert, later the abbot of Niederaltaich: Ekkehard writes about him later, in chapter 127. Sources mention him as dean of Saint Gall in 962/3. He probably was the abbot of Niederaltaich, located on the Danube in Bavaria, earlier, during the period from around 943 to 963.

Waldo the Second: Not the Waldo mentioned in chapter 75; he cannot be identified.

moderate his tongue: Wisdom 1:11.

91.3 *mountain*: That is, the Hohentwiel.

91.4 *secretly entering the cloister*: Ruodmann's intrusion is recorded by Ekkehard's own hand in *Annales Sangallenses maiores* (see Saint Gall, Stiftsbibliothek MS 915, p. 214, online at CESG; MGH SS vol. 1, p. 79).

cautiously: Ekkehard uses the same rare word, *pedetemptivus,* that he had employed describing Salomo's furtive visit in 5.2.

91.5 *man on his own*: Monks had to go in groups when they went to the latrine at night.

91.6 *made signs*: Obeying the rule of silence, Ekkehard uses a sign language employed by monks; see notes to 8.2 and 15.1.

informed his uncle the dean: Ekkehard I, who took up the responsibilities of the absent abbot, as prescribed by RB 21 (compare chapter 77).

92.2 *a lion seeking someone to devour*: A slight paraphrase of 1 Peter 5:8.

93.1 *bishop*: Bishop Conrad of Constance, also mentioned in chapter 87.

Ekkehard the deacon, later dean: Ekkehard III, whose death is recorded in the Saint Gall necrology under March 21 (MGH Necr. vol. 1, p. 469).

Burchard, later abbot: Burchard II, abbot from 1001 to 1022.

93.2 *Kotelinda*: Possibly the recluse Kotelinda mentioned in the Saint Gall necrology under September 15 (MGH Necr. vol. 1, p. 480) and in the *Annales Sangallenses maiores,* entry for 1015 (MGH SS vol. 1, p. 82).

your beloved dialectics: This translation follows the interpretation of Haefele, who has argued that according to the rhetorical balance of this sentence, *caram* modifies *dialecticam* ("Untersuchungen," part 2, p. 140). According to earlier translators, *caram* modifies *discipulam:* "Taught dialectics to the nun Kotelinda, your beautiful and beloved female student." Dialectics was one of the seven liberal arts and focused on logical argumentation.

Otker: He has not been identified. He is also mentioned in chapter 115.

93.3 *the two brothers I mentioned*: Ekkehard's cousins, mentioned in 93.1.

Vespers: An evening prayer sevice, at the time of sunset.

wolf that got into the sheepfold by another way: A paraphrase of John 10:1.

94.1 *silence according to the Rule*: The prescription is in RB 42.

monastery on the mountain: The monastery of Saint George, founded by Hadwig and her husband between 968 or 970 and 973; see *Casus monasterii Petrishusensis* 1.43 (MGH SS vol. 20, p. 637).

little boy: Burchard, Ekkehard II's cousin; see 93.1.

lovely to look at: 1 Samuel (1 Kings) 16:12, 17:42.

94.2 *eager for new things*: Sallust, *Bellum Catilinum* 28.4. Or "eager for change," *res nova* most commonly meaning revolution.

94.3 *Seas and rivers . . . alleluia*: A Latin antiphon based on Daniel 3:77–78, here in corrupted Greek.

95.1 *younger Ekkehard*: See chapter 93.

I fear the Greeks even when they bear gifts: Virgil, *Aeneid* 2.49.

95.2 *to hear from the beginning the whole*: Terence, *Andria* 48, paraphrased.

95.3 *played a great part*: A paraphrase of Virgil, *Aeneid* 2.6.

my uncle: Ekkehard I.

village Walewis: Located in southern Germany, district of Constance, Baden-Württemberg.

96.1 *Kaminold*: Or Gaminolf, bishop of Constance (975–979); he is mentioned in the Saint Gall necrology under May 22 (MGH Necr. vol. 1, p. 474).

96.2 *imperial liberty*: The privileges of immunity granted and confirmed earlier were once again confirmed by Otto I in 940 (MGH DD Otto I, no. 25, pp, 111–12; see also notes to 6.3, 16.1, 25.1). This status also protected the abbey against violations by secular or ecclesiastical magnates, such as Ruodmann's incursion.

96.3 *Ekkehard*: Ekkehard II "the Courtier."

97.1 *Rickenbach*: In the modern district of Münchwilen, canton Thurgau.

Notker: Notker II "Peppercorn," or "the Physician." See also chapter 123.

97.2 *aforementioned Richer*: See chapter 87.

98.1 *member of the court chapel*: Under Ottonian kings, royal chaplains *(capellani)* played an important role in administration; see Josef Fleckenstein, *Die Hofkapelle der deutschen Könige,* 2 vols. (Stuttgart, 1959–1966); Karl J. Leyser, "Ottonian Government," *English Historical Review* 96 (1981): 721–53, at 725–27; Wolfgang Huschner, *Transalpine Kommunikation im Mittelalter: Diplomatische, kulturelle und politische Wechselbewirkungen zwischen Italien und dem nordalpinen Reich (9.–11. Jahrhundert)* (Hanover, 2003).

Adelheid: See note to 65.1.

98.2 *Sandrat*: A monk of Saint Maximin at Trier, then of Saint Pantaleon at Cologne, later abbot of Gladbach, Ellwangen, and Weissenburg and a prominent champion of the Lotharingian reform; he died in 985/6. For analysis of the Sandrat episodes, see Wojtek Jezierski, "Paranoia Sangallensis: A Microstudy in the Etiquette of Monastic Persecution," in *Frühmittelalterliche Studien* 42 (2008): 109–46, reprinted in Jezierski, *Total St Gall,* article 3.

99.1 *my nephew*: See note to 86.1.

99.2 *they . . . sent*: Ekkehard made an entry about the visit in *Annales Sangallenses maiores* under 966, which immediately follows his report of Ruodmann's incursion (Saint Gall, Stiftsbibliothek MS 915, p. 214; MGH SS vol. 1, p. 79; see above, note 91.4). Ekkehard's date and his list of the visitors sometimes contradict the information provided by other sources, and scholars have argued for an earlier date of 964 (see note 102.1 and Tremp, *Casus,* 424–25n3).

most recent error worse than the original one: A paraphrase of Matthew 27:64.

angels of great counsel: A slightly paraphrased line from the introit to the Christmas Mass; Ekkehard also uses this expression in 10.2.

knowledge . . . puffs up: 1 Corinthians 8:1.

100.1 *Arnolf, the bishop of Toul*: Bishop Arnolf of Toul, a city in the Meurthe-et-Moselle department in northeastern France, ruled from 847 to 871, much earlier than Ekkehard's chronology suggests.

to embark on a difficult task: Ekkehard uses the same turn of phrase in Pref.1 and 30.1.

100.2 *the kingdom of God . . . is within us*: Luke 17:21.

mansions . . . in the Father's kingdom: A paraphrase of John 14:2.

100.3 *Hildebald*: He was bishop of Chur between approximately 972 and 988, later than the time of the visit described by Ekkehard.

have personal property and consume meat dishes: Against the prescriptions of RB 33, 36.9, and 39.11.

permission of their abbots: The Rule of Benedict (RB 39.6) allows the abbot to increase the food portions of the monks in case of expediency.

100.4 *the just man is a law to himself*: An allusion to 1 Timothy 1:9 and Romans 2:14.

100.5 *The king*: Otto II.

101.2 *of sounder judgment*: From RB 64.1, also quoted in 81.1 and 134.3.

power . . . without end: Imperial rhetoric recalling Jupiter's promise of Roman dominion unlimited by time or space (Virgil, *Aeneid* 1.278–79).

101.4 *Conrad*: Bishop of Constance; see chapters 87, 113.

You alone . . . must eat it: A paraphrase of Terence, *Phormio* 318.

burst into laughter: Compare RB 6.8.

an accuser of brethren: In Revelation 12:10, this epithet refers to Satan.

102.1 *the day to honor Desiderius*: May 8, 966, would correspond to that Tuesday, but Saint Desiderius's feast day is usually celebrated on May 23.

Saint Gall himself . . . monastery: This is also mentioned in the lives of Saint Gall: Wetti, *Vita sancti Galli* 11, and Walahfrid, *Vita sancti Galli* 11 (MGH SRM vol. 4, pp. 263 and 293).

Fellow Citizens of the Apostles: This responsory was sung as part of the reception of church dignitaries (see Meyer von Knonau, *Ekkeharti Casus*, 362n1242).

section from Scripture . . . Discretion: This reading probably came from 1 Corinthians 12:10 and 1 Corinthians 13.

was read to them: The Rule (RB 53.4–9) prescribes reading from scripture when receiving guests and praying before exchanging the kiss of peace.

May you be blessed by the Lord . . . Who made heaven and earth: Psalms 115:15(113:23).

102.2 *Henry*: Archbishop of Trier from 956 till his death in 964, that is, several years before the events described here. His death was recorded in the Saint Gall necrology under July 3 (MGH Necr. vol. 1, p. 476).

to whom leadership . . . had been entrusted: A paraphrase of 2 Maccabees 9:24.

nest: See note to 75.3.

Kebo: Gerbod, abbot of Lorsch (951–972); see chapters 110 and 118.

102.3 *Kerho*: Gerricus I, abbot of Weissenburg (960–964).

103.1 *Poppo*: Bishop of Würzburg (961–983).

Abundance . . . with her full horn: Horace, *Epistles* 1.12.29.

Palzo: Balther, bishop of Speyer (970–986/7).

trust one who knows: Virgil, *Aeneid* 11.283. Ekkehard uses the same quotation in 83.3.

to whom . . . trusted: A paraphrase of 2 Maccabees 9:24; Ekkehard's cross-reference ("as I said") is to 102.2, where he uses the same verse.

103.2 *Dietrich*: Bishop of Metz (965–984).

Gerald: See note to 74.3.

104.1 *the archbishop I mentioned*: Henry of Trier.

masters of the realm: Otto I and Otto II.

so many men dear to them . . . so many excellent men: In Latin, Ekkehard uses similar-sounding rhyming words as a rhetorical device.

Erpho: He was bishop of Worms for three days in 999, according to *Vita Burchardi episcopi* 4 (MGH SS vol. 4, p. 834). At the time described here, however, the bishop of Worms was Anno (950–978).

104.2 *from Prime to Prime*: That is, in the twenty-four hours between prayers said at the first hour of the day, at dawn.

105.1 *Milo*: No other source mentions this abbot of Ellwangen.

a monk should eat and drink . . . prescribes: The Rule of Benedict (RB 41.5) specifically requires that the abbot regulate the matters of food.

105.2 *nor is it very abundant in fish*: Nevertheless, Ekkehard lists various kinds of fish as foods to be blessed in his *Benedictiones ad mensas* (Egli, *Liber,* pp. 285–89, verses 39–73).

nobleman: The word Ekkehard uses allows for a range of meanings, including "free man," "a man who has military prowess," "a righteous man," or simply "a good man."

fowl: Allowed because birds belong to the same class of creature as fish, both created on the fifth day (Genesis 1:21).

meat of four-legged animals: The Rule (RB 39:11) states that all monks, except the gravely ill, must abstain from eating the meat of quadrupeds.

106.2 *everyone . . . together*: Reinforcing the prescriptions of RB 39 and 43.13–19, which were emphasized by the reformers; RB 36.9 and 39.11, however, make exception for the gravely ill.

buying time, because these were evil days: A paraphrase of Ephesians 5:16. Compare also Colossians 4:5.

107.1 *Holy Spirit . . . knows no delay*: An allusion to Ambrose, *Expositio evangelii secundum Lucam* 2.19 (CSEL vol. 32, part 4, p. 52). Compare also 2 Peter 3:9. The Saint Gall library preserves a copy of Ambrose's commentary with Ekkehard's annotations (Saint Gall, Stiftsbibliothek MS 96).

it is my fault: According to RB 2, the abbot is fully responsible for his monks' spiritual and physical well-being.

resources needed for building the tower of the Gospel: An allusion to Luke 14:28.

Ekkehard, the courtier: Ekkehard II; see chapter 98 for his career at the court.

107.2 *like beasts of burden before God*: A paraphrase of Psalms 73:22(72:23).

to be burdened with a double load: An allusion to Psalms 38:4(37:5).

108.1 *feast-day*: Saint Desiderius's Day; see note to 102.1.

108.2 *With the Greatest Effort*: A sequence in honor of Saint Desiderius (for discussion and text, see von den Steinen, *Notker der Dichter,* vol. 1, pp. 458–60, and vol. 2, pp. 113–14).

108.3 *would I have believed . . . renowned for wisdom . . . works*: A paraphrase of 1 Kings (3 Kings) 10:7. Ekkehard refers to this place earlier, in 7.1.

109.1 *sequentiary*: A book containing sequences.

Conrad: The bishop of Constance.

his uncle: Ekkehard I; see also chapter 103.

110.1 *Book of Life*: The confraternity book.

110.2 *Milo*: See note to 105.1.

110.3 *one of the servers*: The monk who was performing kitchen duty on that week, according to RB 35.

sank down to the ground asking forgiveness: The Rule (RB 71) requires monks' obedience to their seniors and to one another and prescribes lying prostrate on the ground seeking forgiveness for a transgression.

110.4 *Kebo*: Abbot of Lorsch; see chapter 102.

not one of the brothers . . . was tempted to laugh: The Rule of Benedict contains numerous prohibitions against loud laughter (for instance RB 6.8 and 7.59), especially during reading at meals when complete silence is required (RB 38.5).

111.2 *to embrace and kiss*: A paraphrase of Genesis 29:13, the verse also used in 76.4.

inappropriate time: See note to 42.3.

111.3 *joyfully rejoicing*: John 3:29, slightly paraphrased.

112.1 *Gather the fragrant honey of the Ambrosian nectar*: This line is found on the flyleaf (p. 2) of Saint Gall, Stiftsbibliothek MS 96, which contains Ambrose's commentary on Luke with glosses by Ekkehard's hand. It is edited in MGH Poetae vol. 5, parts 1–2, p. 530, no. 6. Ekkehard quotes Ambrose's commentary in chapter 107; see note to 107.1.

after-None drinks: See chapter 80 and note to 80.1.

113.1 *stole wearers*: See note to 2.1.

113.2 *in a royal fashion*: Compare 7.1, where Ekkehard describes King Charles III serving the monks.

The same . . . of you: Literally, "but you," the first two words of the verse from Psalms 41:10(40:11), *Tu autem, Domine, miserere nobis* (But you, O Lord, have mercy on me), which is said at the end of the biblical readings in church services and in the refectory.

113.3 *Henry and Dietrich*: Archbishop of Trier and bishop of Metz.

114.1 *Ekkehard*: Ekkehard II.

Bless me: See 76.4.

Lies always have short legs: The earliest Latin attestation of this proverb (see Walther, *Proverbia,* vol. 1, no. 14641); it is still used in its German version.

115.1 *Otker, whom I mentioned above*: See 93.2 and note.

the abbot: Burchard, the abbot of Saint Gall.

115.2 *privy to their plans*: A paraphrase of Terence, *Andria* 576.

115.3 *entrusted to you*: A reminder that according to RB 27.5 the abbot's duty is to care for the sheep entrusted to him. Compare chapter 73.

116.1 *Bavaria*: The name of the Roman province Noricum was used in the Middle Ages to refer to Bavaria, although the territory of the latter only partially overlapped with the former. In the Saint Gall copy of Orosius, which Ekkehard read and commented on, an earlier glossator explained that the Norici were now called Bavarians (Saint Gall, Stiftsbibliothek MS 621, pp. 41B and 267A, glosses to Orosius, *Historiae adversus paganos libri septem* 1.2.60 and 6.21.14; the glosses are edited in Eisenhut, *Glossen;* compare notes to 75.1 and 82.1).

Rottweil: Located on the river Neckar, in what is now Baden-Württemberg.

Thietingen: Dietingen in the municipality of Rottweil, Baden-Württemberg, where Saint Gall had possessions from the eighth century on.

116.2 *restraining . . . remember*: *Reservare* can mean both "restrain/refrain from" and "preserve, keep." Kebo's response plays on this double meaning.

Rogation Days: Three days before Ascension during the sixth week after Easter.

117.1 *other small expenses*: This translation follows the emendation made by Haefele, Tremp, and Schnoor; according to the reading of the manuscripts, *regulae,* this passage translates as "other expenses prescribed by the Rule."

117.3 *for a third time*: After Ruodmann's break-in and the first visit of the delegation.

118.2 *found considerable comfort*: A paraphrase of Acts 20:12.

priest Huozo: He cannot be identified with certainty.

118.3 *The bishop of Worms*: See note to 104.1.

119.1 *Saint John's Day*: June 24.

Assumption: August 15.

Saint Gall's chickens: Wordplay on *Gallus/gallus;* compare 53.2.

119.2 *Ekkehard Junior*: Ekkehard II.

119.3 *Saint Mary's Day*: The Feast of the Assumption, August 15.

Matins: The night service, which RB 8 prescribes for the eighth hour of the night in wintertime and for dawn during the summer.

119.4 *abbot was lame . . . dean was unsteady on his feet*: See chapter 97 for Burchard and 81 for Ekkehard I.

It is better for kings to limp than kingdoms: A paraphrase of a passage that goes back to Justin, *Epitoma historiarum Philippicarum* 6.2, and was also used in Orosius, *Historiae* 3.1.9.

Hartmut's statutes: See note to 47.1.

120.2 *Sasbach*: Located in modern Baden-Württemberg.

woman is always a fickle and changeable creature: Virgil, *Aeneid* 4.569–70.

120.4 *the envoys that I mentioned earlier*: See chapter 108.

none of the envious . . . against them: Ekkehard uses a similar turn of phrase in chapter 91; see note to 91.1.

121.1 *as I said*: See chapter 113.

with the abbot's permission the monks sent: The Rule (RB 33 and 54) forbids the monks to send or receive anything, including letters, without the abbot's permission.

121.2 *made those standing around laugh*: Ekkehard's choice of words echoes RB 6.8, which prohibits wisecracks.

122.1 *after consulting the bishop*: Conrad of Constance.

This is my resting place: Psalms 132(131):14. The lives of Saint Gall report this incident; see Wetti, *Vita Sancti Galli* 11, and Walahfrid, *Vita Sancti Galli* 1.11 (MGH SRM vol. 4, pp. 263 and 293).

enclosure: An anchorite's cell.

122.2 *Ekkehard's*: Ekkehard I the dean.

Notker . . . elected abbot in his place: *Annales Sangallenses maiores* record Notker's election on May 18, 971, and his death in 975 (MGH SS vol. 1, pp. 79 and 80); the Saint Gall necrology lists him under December 15 (MGH Necr. vol. 1, p. 486).

estates assigned by Charles to the abbots: See chapter 9.

heated cell used by the abbots who preceded him: Probably the same cell to which Thieto retired; see chapter 69.

122.3 *he survived his successor*: According to the Saint Gall necrology, Burchard died earlier than Notker, on August 9, 975 (MGH Necr. vol. 1, p. 478).

Immo: Abbot (976–984), elected in January 976, after Burchard died.

This, my resting place: Psalms 132(131):14. Compare 121.1.

I have already indicated: See chapter 80.

123.1 *Notker*: Notker II "Peppercorn," or "the Physician"; see note to 74.3.

Dread Ruler of the World Everlasting: Hymn in honor of Saint Otmar; for the text see AH vol. 51, no. 186, pp. 213–14.

hymns welcoming rulers: For this genre, compare chapter 14.

Hymn to the Blessed Virgin: Edited in Johannes Duft, *Notker der Arzt: Klostermedizin und Mönchsarzt im frühmittelalterlichen St. Gallen* (Saint Gall, 1972), 45.

The sheep comes to the goat asking for wool: A saying that may ultimately go back to Horace, *Epistles* 1.18.15.

faltering: The third verse of the hymn does include this word, *labilem* (see Duft, *Notker der Arzt,* 45).

123.2 *medical aphorisms, drugs, antidotes, and Hippocrates's diagnostics*: The Saint Gall library had numerous texts on medicine; for the list of manuscripts dating from the ninth to the eleventh century, see Duft, *Notker der Arzt,* 31–32.

Duke Henry's: This may be Henry of Bavaria, Hadwig's father (see note to 90.1).

123.4 *bishop Kaminold*: See note to 96.1. Other documents suggest, however, that he was consecrated as bishop about one month after Notker died; see Maurer, *Konstanzer Bischöfe,* 146; Tremp, *Casus,* 480n11.

we will meet him again in our story: See chapters 125 and 147.

124.1 *Gerald*: See note to 74.3.

from the beginning of his subdiaconate: That is, when he was relatively young, probably in his early twenties.

as the apostle called such men: See 1 Corinthians 14.

public priest: That is, one performing pastoral care outside the monastery for the local lay people, which also involved control over local ecclesiastical jurisdiction and tithes. These practices were subject to debate throughout the early Middle Ages and especially strongly contested by bishops during the eleventh and twelfth centuries; see Giles Constable, "Monasteries, Rural Churches and the *Cura animarum* in the Early Middle Ages," in *Settimane di studio del centro Italiano di studi sull'alto medioevo* (Spoleto, 1982), vol. 1, pp. 349–89, reprinted in *Monks, Hermits and Crusaders in Medieval Europe,* Variorum Collected Series 273 (Aldershot, 2002); Susan Wood, *The Proprietory Church in the Medieval West* (Oxford, 2006); Thomas F. X. Noble, "The

Christian Church as an Institution," in *The Cambridge History of Christianity*, ed. Thomas F. X. Noble and Julia M. H. Smith (Cambridge, 2008), 247–74; John Eldevik, *Episcopal Power and Ecclesiastical Reform in the German Empire: Tithes, Lordship, and Community, 950–1150* (Cambridge, 2012).

Goldach and Sint-tria-unum: Two rivers to the east and the west of the monastery of Saint Gall. For the latter, now called the Sitter, compare chapter 51.

124.2 *privileges . . . Charles*: No such document survives from the period of Pope John VIII (872–882), Salomo II (875–890), and Charles III (876–887).

bishops of our time: Probably a reference to the bishops of Constance and their conflicts with Saint Gall, which may have involved rural pastoral care and ecclesiastical jurisdiction; see Meyer von Knonau, *Ekkeharti Casus,* 404–5n1445; Paul Oberholzer, *Leutkirchen des Klosters St. Gallen im Früh- und Hochmittelalter* (Saint Gall, 2002), 120–21; see also note to 124.1 above.

nothing left for us to do: A paraphrase of Sallust, *Bellum Catilinae* 11.7.

Holofernes: An allusion to Judith 12.

I will relate: There is no such account in surviving manuscripts.

125.1 *on the day of the Lord*: 1 Corinthians 5:5 (cited in RB 25.4) refers to the day of the Last Judgment.

125.2 *alb*: A long, white liturgical vestment.

suffered no harm: Acts 28:5.

125.3 *Notker*: Notker II.

125.5 *chuckling*: The word *cachinnulans,* diminutive from *cachinnare* (to laugh uproariously) is only attested in Ekkehard (Loth, *Study,* 7).

125.6 *like John, he was taken painlessly*: Ekkehard appears to be referring to an alternative version of the death of the apostle John. According to this tradition going back to the apocryphal *Acts of John* and known to some Latin writers in the West (see Tertullian, *De praescriptione haereticorum* 36.3), John was cast into a cauldron of boiling oil, which caused him no harm. Ekkehard also described John's martyrdom as painless in *Liber benedictionum* no. 4, lines 31–34 (Egli, *Liber,* p. 34).

126.1 *Waldo, the dean*: He is mentioned in chapter 75; see note to 75.3.

Cunibert, the abbot of Niederaltaich: See note to 91.2.

Saracens: Compare chapter 65. Other sources also mention their incursions into Swabia and Alemannia; see Liudprand, *Antapodosis* 5.17 (MGH SRG vol. 41, p. 139), and Flodoard, *Annales,* entry for 936 (MGH SS vol. 3, p. 383).

127.1 *Duke Henry's*: He has been identified as Henry I, duke of Bavaria from 948 to 955 (Tremp, *Casus,* 489–90n3), or Henry II the Wrangler, duke of Bavaria from 955 to 976 and from 985 to 995 (*Cronache,* 478n454).

earned the abbacy of Niederaltaich: See 91.2, with note.

127.2 *Wilaha*: Now the city of Wil, canton Sankt Gallen.

Gerhard: See note to Pref.2.

127.3 *Those who come will come with joy*: Psalms 126:6(125:7).

died: This happened sometime after 976; see Schaab, *Mönch,* 99n511.

128.1 *to Speyer . . . to the Ottos*: In 971, the year of the election, Otto I and Otto II were in Italy.

Sandrat, whom I mentioned earlier: See chapter 98.

Duke Otto: Otto I, duke of Swabia (973–982) and Bavaria (976–982), was Emperor Otto I's grandson. Saint Gall necrology commemorates his death on October 31 (MGH Necr. vol. 1, p. 483).

128.2 *Subdean Rupert*: Ekkehard appears to be the only source for this character.

God who holds . . . kings: Proverbs 21:1, paraphrased. This verse begins the first prayer in the ceremony of imperial coronation; see for instance MGH Fontes Iuris, vol. 9, p. 10.

make . . . be gentle to you: Genesis 43:14.

128.3 *his teacher*: Ekkehard II.

128.4 *The privilege given to the fathers by Charles and confirmed by you*: Ekkehard may mean Charlemagne, who granted the privilege according to Ratpert, *Casus* 3 (MGH SRG vol. 75, pp. 160–62), or Charles III (see note to 6.3). For confirming the privileges, see also the diplomas of Otto I from April 7, 940 (MGH DD Otto I, no. 25, pp. 111–12) and Otto II from August 18, 972 (MGH DD Otto II, no. 26, pp. 35–36). Compare note to 96.2.

my uncle Ekkehard: Ekkehard I.

the virtues of the fathers: Virgil, *Eclogues* 4.17.

129.3 *he who walks without guile walks with confidence*: Proverbs 10:9.

129.4 *your son*: Abbot Burchard.

with deceitful intent: An allusion to James 1:8.

130.3 *faithful translator*: Horace, *Ars poetica* 133–34. Compare 144.2.

the man whom they would never see again: Burchard.

your Ekkehard: Ekkehard I.

130.4 *Man looks at . . . heart*: This verse from 1 Samuel (1 Kings) 16:7 in the Vetus Latina translation forms part of a responsory, which is found in Saint Gall, Stiftsbibliothek MS 391, p. 206. See also John 7:24.

131.1 *shorthand*: A version of Tironian notes, a system invented in the first century BCE and used throughout the Middle Ages.

131.2 *It is honorable to keep the secret of the king*: A paraphrase of Tobit 12:7.

131.3 *Palzo*: See note to 103.1.

131.4 *lion . . . awake*: This information, together with the quotation from Song of Songs 5:2, comes from the *Physiologus,* which Ekkehard may have read in Latin or German. Compare the edition of the so-called Old High German *Physiologus,* accompanied by a closely related Latin text, in Elias von Steinmeyer, ed., *Die kleineren althochdeutschen Sprachdenkmäler* (Berlin, 1916), 124. Note that while Ekkehard here attributes the quotation to "the bridegroom of the Church," in Song of Songs 5:2 these words are actually spoken by the bride.

a poor beggar: a paraphrase of Psalms 40:17(39:18).

132.1 *Romance*: Probably a local Latin-derived dialect.

Waning: See note to 71.1.

the first in rank: According to RB 63, which addresses monastic ranking.

132.3 *leave us orphans*: A paraphrase of John 14:18.

Don't you worry about it: Terence, *Phormio* 235.

132.4 *whom I mentioned*: See chapter 128.

chose the best part . . . assiduous service: A paraphrase of Luke 10:40–42, the story of Martha and Mary. Ekkehard also alludes to it in chapter 40.

133.1 *both Ottos*: Otto II and Duke Otto.

Sandrat: See note to 98.2.

133.3 *privileges granted to Saint Gall*: See notes to 6.3 and 128.4.

Your nephew the abbot: Burchard; see note to 86.1.

Ekkehard . . . Notker: Ekkehard I and Notker II.

133.4 *If you divide the shoe, no one will be shod*: See chapter 121.

133.5 *You have said it*: Matthew 26:25.

134.2 *Alas, for the times, alas for the morals*: Cicero, *In Catilinam* 1.2; compare Pref.1.

Richer: See note to 87.3.

Tullius: Cicero. Paraphrasing the verse, Ekkehard follows Quintilian, who quoted and criticized the original line (*Institutio oratoria* 9.4.41 and 11.1.24). Juvenal also ridiculed it in *Satires* 10.122–24.

134.3 *of sounder judgment*: From RB 64.1. Ekkehard makes the same reference in 81.1 and 101.2.

Kebo's precepts: See chapter 119.

frustrated in their hopes by Hadwig: See chapter 120.

134.4 *puffed up . . . learning*: 1 Corinthians 8:1, paraphrased.

Faurndau: Located in modern Baden-Württemberg, this monastery was confirmed by King Arnulf as Saint Gall's possession in 895 (MGH DD Arn no. 133, p. 199).

Neckarburg: Located in modern Baden-Württemberg, it was mentioned as a donation in a Saint Gall charter of 793 (UBSG vol. 1, no. 135, pp. 126–27).

later in its proper place: See chapter 137.

135.1 *word about him fly*: A paraphrase of Virgil, *Aeneid* 3.121, also used in 47.4, 63.1, and 84.4.

135.2 *Hartmut's statutes*: See note to 47.1.

break the bow of the Rule or snap its string: See note to 70.2.

136.1 *monastic schism that we endure because of the Gauls*: An allusion to the Lotharingian reform movement; see Introduction.

counts and other powerful men . . . fighting men: This story and the one that immediately follows emphasize Ekkehard's critique of the reformers and their strict rules. In these stories of a remembered past, it was the monks, not the reformers, who negotiated the boundaries with the world outside. For an analysis of this episode, see de Jong, "Internal Cloisters," 211–12.

136.3 *years of plenty*: Compare Genesis 41:53.

which his uncle Anno had begun: See chapter 71.

136.4 *made his name stink*: A paraphrase of Exodus 5:21.

137.1 *on the very eve of Saint Gall's feast day*: October 15, 972.

137.2 *Murbach*: The monastery of Murbach in the Vosges, modern department Haut-Rhin, belonged to the Saint Gall confraternity of prayer (MGH Necr. Suppl., pp. 136, 144).

Everybody's eyes were fixed on him: A paraphrase of Luke 4:20.

137.3 *I have to attend to the guests*: For the abbot's responsibility for the reception of guests and monks from other monasteries, see RB 53 and 61.

that Sindolf had once closed for the holy Notker: This episode is missing in the extant text of the *Casus;* Haefele suggests that it could belong with the stories about Sindolf in chapter 46 (Haefele, *Casus,* 268n95).

138.1 *making their way to Italy*: In August 972, Otto I, Otto II, and Adelheid were returning from Italy, and they arrived in Saint Gall on August 14; see chapter 146.

Saint Gall's Day: October 16.

Lord Burchard and the dean: The former abbot Burchard I and Ekkehard I.

what needed to be done: Terence, *Phormio* 762.

Richer: See chapter 87.

138.2 *faithful envoy*: Proverbs 13:17, paraphrased.

faithful to your mission: A slightly paraphrased line from a responsory in honor of Saint Sebastian, found in Saint Gall, Stiftsbibliothek MS 390, pp. 106–7 (this line at p. 107). See *Corpus antiphonalium officii,* 6 vols. (Rome, 1963–1979), no. 6663.

if the one who lacks faith departs . . . let him depart: 1 Corinthians 7:15.

139.1 *on the third day*: Probably October 17.

139.2 *the invasion of an evil angel*: Psalms 78(77):49.

brought upon us by our sins: Gregory the Great, *Moralia* 14.37.

139.3 *at Cologne*: See note to 98.2.

letter of recommendation: The Rule (RB 61.13) states that a traveling monk should not be permanently received without his abbot's consent or a letter of commendation.

140.1 *under Kebo's supervision*: See chapter 119.

140.2 *forbade meat and broth to everyone*: The Rule (RB 36.9 and 39.11), however, allows the consumption of meat to the gravely ill. Compare chapter 106.

for refreshment . . . thirst: Judith 7:7.

141.1 *as they showed loyal devotion to himself*: A reminder of RB 72.10, which instructs the monks to love their abbot.

141.2 *warmed up by the wine*: Esther 1:10, paraphrased, also used in 54.3.

141.4 *Christ had once suffered at a pillar*: See Matthew 27:26, Mark 15:15, John 19:1.

another Satan: Ekkehard plays on the similarity of names Sandrat and Satan.

what had befallen his namesake eventually befell Sandrat: An allusion to the fate of Judas Iscariot, also playing on the similarity: Sandrat/Scarioth.

142.1 *The dean*: Ekkehard I.

both of us . . . contrary to the Rule: Sandrat violated RB 70, which prohibits striking anyone without the abbot's authority, and the abbot acted contrary to RB 23, which requires that prior to administering corporal punishment, the culprit has to be reprimanded twice, in private and in public.

142.2 *restore peace*: Following the prescription of RB 4.73.

142.3 *buried in wine*: Virgil, *Aeneid* 3.630.

wicked servant: Matthew 18:32, Luke 19:22. The same quotation is used in 143.4.

without his robe: Contrary to RB 22, which states that the monks should sleep in their clothes.

Ruomo: This name occurs several times in Saint Gall documents; see Schaab, *Mönch*, 98n491 and 98n500.

143.1 *give me some of that meat . . . produced some money*: In violation of RB 36.9 and 39.11 (no meat except for the gravely ill) and RB 33 (no property for monks).

143.2 *Richer*: See chapter 87.

143.3 *Towering over them*: Luke 4:39, slightly paraphrased.

good works: An ironic allusion to RB 2.21.

143.4 *very wicked servant*: Matthew 18:32, Luke 19:22, paraphrased. The same quotation is used in 142.3.

144.1 *in Saxony*: According to other sources, Otto I and Otto II were in Italy at that time. See note to 138.1.

Ekkehard: Ekkehard II.

a sixteen-page booklet: Literally, "quire," a set of four sheets of parchment folded to form eight leaves.

144.2 *a monster of a man*: Terence, *Eunuchus* 696.

hateful to God: A paraphrase of Romans 1:30.

I thought that we could expect great deeds from him: The chronicle of Gladbach also reports that Adelheid was favorably disposed toward Sandrat, who was her confessor; see *Chronicon Gladbacense* 14 (MGH SS vol. 4, p. 76).

faithful interpreter: Ekkehard uses the same reference to Horace, *Ars poetica* 133–34 in 130.3.

145.1 *if you have any regard for me*: Terence, *Heauton Timorumenos* 1031.

145.2 *Ekkehard*: Ekkehard II.

Notker: The abbot.

146.2 *feast of the Ascension . . . Potentiana*: Potentiana's feast is celebrated on May 19. According to other sources, however, the royal visit took place in August. Ekkehard may have confused the feast of the Ascension, celebrated in May, with the feast of the Assumption of Mary, celebrated in August.

Bruno, archbishop of Cologne: In fact, he died earlier, in 965.

146.3 *let his staff fall to the floor*: A similar story about Walter of Aquitaine is found in the chronicle of Novalesa; see *Chronicon Novaliciense* 2.7 (MGH SS vol. 7, p. 86).

Conrad: Conrad, duke of Lotharingia, died earlier, in 955.

147.1 *dean*: Ekkehard I.

Notker: Notker II "Peppercorn," or "the Physician."

147.2 *Ekkehard's*: Ekkehard II.

Bibliography

Editions and Translations

Alessio, Gian Carlo, Peter Erhart, and Fabrizio Crivello, ed. and trans. *Casus sancti Galli.* In *Cronache di San Gallo,* 51–311, 455–80. Turin, 2004.

Arx, Ildefons von, ed. *Ekkehardi IV "Casus sancti Galli."* MGH SS vol. 2, pp. 75–147. Hanover, 1829.

Coulton, G. G., trans. *Life in the Middle Ages.* Excerpts, vol. 4, pp. 50–84. Cambridge, Mass., 1967.

Goldast, Melchior, ed. "Ekkehardi Iunioris coenobitae S. Galli liber *De Casibus monasterii S. Galli in Alamannia.*" In *Alamannicorum rerum Scriptores,* vol. 1, pp. 35–109. Frankfurt, 1606.

Haefele, Hans F., ed. and trans. *St. Galler Klostergeschichten.* Darmstadt, 1980. Reprinted, with "Nachtrag" by Steffen Patzold (from 2002), Darmstadt, 2003.

Haefele, Hans F., Ernst Tremp, and Franzisca Schnoor, eds. *St. Galler Klostergeschichten (Casus sancti Galli),* by Ekkehard IV. MGH SRG 82. Wiesbaden, 2020.

Helbling, Hanno, trans. *Die Geschichten des Klosters St. Gallen,* by Ekkehard IV. Cologne, 1958.

Meyer von Knonau, Gerold, ed. *Ekkeharti (IV) Casus Sancti Galli.* Mitteilungen zur vaterlandischen Geschichte, N. F. 5–6. Saint Gall, 1877.

———, trans. *Ekkeharts Casus sancti Galli.* Leipzig, 1891.

Tomaszek, Michał, trans. *Przypadki klasztoru świętego Galla.* Kraków, 2010.

Further Reading

Clark, James M. *The Abbey of St. Gall as a Centre of Literature and Art.* Cambridge, 1926.

De Jong, Mayke. "Internal Cloisters: The Case of Ekkehard's Casus Sancti

Galli." In *Grenze und Differenz im frühen Mittelalter,* edited by Walter Pohl and Helmut Reimitz, 209–21. Vienna, 2000.

Dümmler, Ernst. "Ekkehart IV. von St. Gallen." *Zeitschrift für deutsches Altertum und Literatur* 14 (1869): 1–73, 562.

Ganz, David, and Cornel Dora, eds. *Tuotilo: Archäologie eines frühmittelalterlichen Künstlers.* Basel, 2017.

Grotans, Anna A. *Reading in Medieval St. Gall.* Cambridge, 2006.

Haefele, Hans F. "Untersuchungen zu Ekkehards IV. Casus sancti Galli." Parts 1 and 2. *DA* 17 (1961): 145–90; 18 (1962): 120–70.

Hellgardt, Ernst. "Die Casus sancti Galli Ekkeharts IV. und die Benediktsregel." In *Literarische Kommunikation und soziale Interaktion: Studien zur Institutionalität mittelalterlicher Literatur,* edited by Beate Kellner, Ludger Lieb, and Peter Strohschneider, 27–50. Frankfurt am Main, 2001.

Jezierski, Wojtek. *Total St. Gall: Medieval Monastery as Disciplinary Institution*. Stockholm, 2010.

King, James C., and Werner Vogler, eds. *The Culture of the Abbey of St. Gall.* Stuttgart, 1991.

Kössinger, Norbert, Elke Krotz, and Stephan Müller, eds. *Ekkehart IV von St. Gallen.* Berlin, 2015.

Loth, Helen Edna. *A Study of the Lexicography of the* Casus Sancti Galli *of Ekkehardus IV.* Chicago, 1936.

Nelson, Janet. "Feasts, Games, and Inversions: Reflections on *The Ups and Downs of St-Gall.*" In *The Man of Many Devices, Who Wandered Full Many Ways: Festschrift in Honor of János M. Bak,* edited by Balázs Nagy and Marcell Sebök, 269–76. Budapest, 1999.

Rankin, Susan. "Ways of Telling Stories." In *Essays on Medieval Music in Honor of David G. Hughes,* edited by Graeme M. Boone, 371–94. Cambridge, Mass., 1995. Reprinted in *Oral and Written Transmission in Chant,* edited by Thomas Forrest Kelly, 385–408. Farnham, 2009.

Tremp, Ernst. "Ekkehart IV von St. Gallen († um 1060) und die monastische Reform." *Studien und Mitteilungen zur Geschichte des Benediktinerordens* 116 (2005): 67–88.

Venarde, Bruce L., ed. and trans. *The Rule of Saint Benedict.* Dumbarton Oaks Medieval Library 6. Cambridge, Mass., 2011.

Index of Names and Places

Subject Index